# Crossing Borders

This book explores the circulation of ideas in and around the spatial planning field. Ideas about planning and development, though often formed in response to very particular problems in specific contexts, have always spread beyond national borders.

Many involved in the planning field are actively involved in promoting the flow of knowledge and techniques across national and continental boundaries. This book takes a critical look at these flows. It explores how planning ideas and practices get to travel from one context to another and what happens when an exogenous idea gets to 'land' in a different context. It highlights the wider challenge of 'situating' planning ideas and practices in their particular contexts and the 'work' such ideas and practices get to do in different places. It underlines the need for critical attention to the political-economic, institutional, ethical and methodological issues of international exchange in the planning field.

The chapters cover a wide range of experiences and bring together different intellectual traditions which co-exist in the planning field, including the history of planning ideas, international development studies, the globalisation and postcolonial literatures, 'historical' institutionalist analysis and the policy transfer and social learning fields. Examples are drawn from Africa, Asia, Europe and North America. They cover large scales and small. Some authors draw on their research knowledge, while others contribute from their practical experiences.

**Patsy Healey** is Professor Emeritus at the School of Architecture, Planning and Landscape at the University of Newcastle, UK.

**Robert Upton** was formerly Secretary General of the Royal Town Planning Institute and is now Deputy Chair of the Infrastructure Planning Commission in England.

**The RTPI Library Series**

**Editors: Robert Upton, RTPI, London, UK, and Patsy Healey, University of Newcastle, UK**

Published by Routledge in conjunction with the Royal Town Planning Institute, this series of leading-edge texts looks at all aspects of spatial planning theory and practice from a comparative and international perspective.

**Planning in Postmodern Times**
Philip Allmendinger

**The Making of the European Spatial Development Perspective**
Andreas Faludi and Bas Waterhout

**Planning for Crime Prevention**
Richard Schneider and Ted Kitchen

**The Planning Polity**
Mark Tewdwr-Jones

**Shadows of Power**
**An Allegory of Prudence in Land-Use Planning**
Jean Hillier

**Urban Planning and Cultural Identity**
William JV Neill

**Place Identity, Participation and Planning**
Edited by Cliff Hague and Paul Jenkins

**Planning for Diversity**
Dory Reeves

**Planning the Good Community**
**New Urbanism in Theory and Practice**
Jill Grant

**Planning, Law and Economics**
Barrie Needham

**Indicators for Urban and Regional Planning**
Cecilia Wong

**Planning at the Landscape Scale**
Paul Selman

**Urban Structure Matters**
Petter Naess

**Urban Complexity and Spatial Strategies**
**Towards a Relational Planning for Our Times**
Patsy Healey

**The Visual Language of Spatial Planning**
**Exploring Cartographic Representations for Spatial Planning in Europe**
Stefanie Dühr

**Planning and Transformation**
**Learning from the Post-Apartheid Experience**
Philip Harrison, Alison Todes and Vanessa Watson

**Conceptions of Space and Place in Strategic Spatial Planning**
Edited by Simin Davoudi and Ian Strange

**Regional Planning for Open Space**
Edited by Terry van Dijk and Arnold van der Valk

**Crossing Borders**
**International Exchange and Planning Practices**
Edited by Patsy Healey and Robert Upton

# CROSSING BORDERS

## INTERNATIONAL EXCHANGE AND PLANNING PRACTICES

EDITED BY PATSY HEALEY AND ROBERT UPTON

Routledge
Taylor & Francis Group

LONDON AND NEW YORK

First published 2010
by Routledge
2 Park Square, Milton Park, Abingdon, Oxon, OX14 4RN

Simultaneously published in the USA and Canada
by Routledge
270 Madison Avenue, New York, NY 10016

*Routledge is an imprint of the Taylor & Francis Group, an informa business*

© 2010 selection and editorial material, Patsy Healey and Robert Upton;
individual chapters, the contributors

Typeset in Akzidenz Grotesk by Prepress Projects Ltd, UK
Printed and bound in Great Britain by TJ International Ltd, Padstow, Cornwall

*British Library Cataloguing in Publication Data*
A catalogue record for this book is available from the British Library

*Library of Congress Cataloging in Publication Data*
Crossing borders: international exchange and planning practices/edited by Patsy
Healey and Robert Upton.
p. cm. – (The RTPI library series ; 19)
Includes bibliographical references and index.
1. City planning. 2. City planning–Cross-cultural studies. 3. Land use–Planning.
4. Urban policy. I. Healey, Patsy. II. Upton, Robert, 1951–
HT166.C765 2010
307.1'216–dc22
2009034678

ISBN10: 0–415–55846–8 (hbk)
ISBN10: 0–415–55847–6 (pbk)
ISBN10: 0–203–85708–9 (ebk)

ISBN13: 978–0–415–55846–4 (hbk)
ISBN13: 978–0–415–55847–1 (pbk)
ISBN13: 978–0–203–85708–3 (ebk)

# CONTENTS

List of figures                                                                vii
List of tables                                                                  ix
Illustration credits                                                            xi
List of contributors                                                           xiii
Preface                                                                        xix
Acknowledgements                                                              xxiii

1   Introduction: the transnational flow of knowledge and expertise
    in the planning field                                                       1
    PATSY HEALEY

2   Poverty truths: the politics of knowledge in the new global
    order of development                                                        27
    ANANYA ROY

3   Transnational planners in a postcolonial world                             47
    STEPHEN V. WARD

4   Reimagining the American neighborhood unit for India                       73
    SANJEEV VIDYARTHI

5   Cities in transition: episodes of spatial planning in modern China         95
    BING WANG

6   Urban sustainability and compact cities ideas in Japan: the diffusion,
    transformation and deployment of planning concepts                        117
    ANDRÉ SORENSEN

7   When planning ideas land: Mahaweli's people-centered approach             141
    NIHAL PERERA

8   West–East policy transfer in Europe: the case of
    urban transport policy                                              173
    DOMINIC STEAD, MARTIN DE JONG AND IVETA REINHOLDE

9   Subaltern speak in a postcolonial setting: diffusing and contesting
    donor-engendered knowledge in the water sector in Zambia           191
    BARBARA MWILA KAZIMBAYA-SENKWE AND PETER LUBAMBO

10  Women's Safety Audits and Walking School Buses: the diffusion/
    de-fusion of two radical planning ideas                            219
    CAROLYN WHITZMAN AND JANA PERKOVIC

11  Institutional biases in the international diffusion of planning concepts   237
    SUKUMAR GANAPATI AND NIRAJ VERMA

12  Developmental planning for sustainable urbanization in Asia         265
    JIEMING ZHU

13  A trans-Pacific planning education in reverse: reflections of an
    American with a Chinese doctorate in urban planning and design     289
    DANIEL BENJAMIN ABRAMSON

14  Crossing borders: do planning ideas travel?                        313
    JOHN FRIEDMANN

15  Similarity or differences?: what to emphasize now for effective
    planning practice                                                  329
    BISHWAPRIYA SANYAL

Index                                                                  351

# FIGURES

| | | |
|---|---|---|
| 4.1 | Clarence Perry's neighborhood unit concept | 77 |
| 5.1 | The master plan of Greater Shanghai, 1931 | 104 |
| 5.2 | The new civic center of Shanghai, 1933 | 104 |
| 5.3 | The master plan of the central administrative area of Nanjing (Nanking), 1929 | 106 |
| 7.1 | Mahaweli area and towns | 142 |
| 7.2 | The hierarchical organization of service centres | 154 |
| 7.3 | Urban services provided from the outset: Teldeniya town | 162 |
| 7.4 | Action planning: Dehiattakandiya town | 165 |
| 7.5 | Each town has a unique character | 166 |
| 9.1 | Location map of Zambia and the Copperbelt | 197 |
| 9.2 | Water supply in the Copperbelt from colonial times to 2000 | 199 |
| 9.3 | Water supply in the Copperbelt, 2007–9 | 202 |
| 11.1 | Master plan of Rome | 244 |
| 11.2 | Spatial distribution of residential buildings by period of construction in Rome, 2001 | 245 |
| 11.3 | Quality of residential buildings by period of construction in Rome, 2001 | 246 |
| 11.4 | Rome's population growth, 1951–2001 | 248 |
| 11.5 | Population distribution in Rome, 2001 | 251 |
| 11.6 | Housing units in Rome, 1971–2001 | 256 |
| 12.1 | (a) Pecenongan, Jakarta, in the 1860s (b) Pecenongan, Jakarta, in 2006 | 276 |
| 12.2 | Development of private housing estates in Jabotabek | 277 |
| 12.3 | Fragmented land holdings in Niucheshui | 280 |
| 12.4 | Niucheshui, 2000 | 281 |
| 12.5 | Land redevelopment projects in Jing'an District, Shanghai, 1992–2000 | 282 |
| 13.1 | Haidian, 1985 studio vision and actual development | 296 |
| 13.2 | De-Wai project, 1992 studio vision and actual development | 297 |

# TABLES

 9.1 The Copperbelt districts with respective water utilities                           199
11.1 Median value of housing units in Rome, 1988–94                                    247
11.2 Household formation and housing units in Rome, 1951–2001                          249
12.1 Urbanization levels in Asia                                                        271
12.2 Estimated urbanization level in China, East Asia and West
     Europe (1950–2000), and in England and Wales (1650–1951)                          271
12.3 Urbanization and increase of urban population, China                              272
12.4 Population density in the world and in South-East Asian
     countries                                                                         273
12.5 Rising population density in Dhaka, Bangladesh                                     273
12.6 Land development in compliance and non-compliance with
     zoning in Botabek                                                                  275

# ILLUSTRATION CREDITS

The chapter authors have made considerable efforts to trace copyright holders where appropriate. On their behalf, we would like to thank Shalini Mariyathas for drawing Figure 7.2, and the following for granting permission to reproduce the Figures in the text: Taylor & Francis, for permission to reproduce Figure 11.1, Istituto Nazionale di Statistica (ISTAT), Rome for Figure 11.5, Archipelago Press, for Figure 12.1(a), Elsevier for Figure 12.2, Dennis Frenchman and Gary Hack at the Massachusetts Institute of Technology for providing access to the MIT-Tsinghua Studio reports and permission to use the studio sketches in Figures 13.1 and 13.2.

**Daniel Benjamin Abramson** is Associate Professor of Urban Design and Planning, and a member of the China Studies faculty at the University of Washington, Seattle. He organises demonstrations of participatory planning and design work in urban, peri-urban and rural communities in China and in immigrant neighbourhoods in the United States and Canada, and is currently researching informal Chinese urban development and property rights. He received his doctorate in urban planning from Tsinghua University in Beijing, and Masters in Architecture and City Planning from the Massachusetts Institute of Technology.

**John Friedmann**, retired after 27 years with UCLA's planning school, is currently Honorary Professor in the School of Community and Regional Planning at the University of British Columbia in Vancouver, Canada. He has taught at MIT, the Pontifical Catholic University of Chile, UCLA the University of Melbourne and the National University of Taiwan. Throughout his long life, he has been an advisor to governments in Brazil, Venezuela, Chile, Mozambique and China, where he was recently appointed Honorary Foreign Advisor to the China Academy of Planning and Urban Design. He is a prolific author on a wide range of topics, including regional planning, urbanisation, social development and planning theory, and his work has been translated into Spanish, Portuguese, Italian, Japanese, Chinese and Farsi. He was the first person to receive the prestigious Distinguished Planning Educator Award from the Association of Collegiate Schools of Planning and in 2006 received the first UN-Habitat Lecture Award for lifetime achievement in the service of human settlements.

**Sukumar Ganapati** is Assistant Professor in the Public Administration Department at Florida International University (FIU). He has a PhD in Planning from the University of Southern California, where he was also the Assistant Director of the Center for International Policy, Planning and Development. His research focuses on the role of institutions in the urban context, particularly with respect to housing, community development and information technology. Besides the United States, his research spans Asian and European countries.

**Patsy Healey** is Professor Emeritus of Planning at the School of Architecture, Planning and Landscape at Newcastle University. She retired as founder Senior Editor of the journal *Planning Theory and Practice* at the end of 2008. Her research interests have focused on the relation between planning theories and ideas and the practices associated with the planning field throughout her career. She has undertaken empirical work on spatial planning ideas, systems and practices in Latin America, mainland Europe and the UK.

**Martin de Jong** is Associate Professor of Public Policy in the Faculty of Technology, Policy and Management at Delft University of Technology and part-time Professor at Harbin Institute of Technology (China). His research interests include international policy transfer, cross-national institutional comparison and transport infrastructure planning. He is currently involved in research on the development of new infrastructure in emerging economies.

**Barbara Mwila Kazimbaya-Senkwe** is a Water and Sanitation Specialist with the Water and Sanitation Programme of the World Bank in Lusaka, Zambia. She works as technical advisor to the governments of Zambia, Malawi and Tanzania on urban and rural water supply and sanitation services, especially services for the poor. Her research interests are in the social construction and evolution of water supply and sanitation networks and policy, and infrastructure in general, in postcolonial countries.

**Peter Lubambo** is Director for the Department of Housing and Infrastructure Development in the Ministry of Local Government and Housing in Lusaka, Zambia. He is responsible for resource mobilisation, policy development, supervision of infrastructure development (including water supply and sanitation) and donor coordination for the water sector.

**Nihal Perera** is Professor of Urban Planning at Ball State University, Indiana, and Director of the CapAsia field-study programme in South Asia. His honours include a Fulbright Scholar award (Hong Kong, 2006–7). His research focuses on how subject peoples create spaces for their daily activities and cultural practices. His publications include 'People's Spaces: Familiarization, Subject Formation, and Emergent Spaces in Colombo' (*Planning Theory*, 2009), 'Contesting Visions: Hybridity, Liminality, and Authorship of the Chandigarh Plan' (*Planning Perspectives*, 2004), and 'Feminizing the City: Gender and Space in Colonial Colombo'

(*Trans-Status Subjects: Genders in the Globalization of South and Southeast Asia*, 2002).

**Jana Perkovic** is an undergraduate student in geography at the University of Melbourne and the recipient of the 2008 Women's Planning Network Rising Star Scholarship. She has worked as a research assistant on projects related to children's independent mobility, the history of women planners in Victoria, Australia, and planning for creative cities.

**Iveta Reinholde** is Assistant Professor of Public Policy and Administration in the Faculty of Social Sciences, University of Latvia. Her research interests include administrative reform, public management and policy transfer. She is currently involved in research on administrative accountability.

**Ananya Roy** is Professor in the Department of City and Regional Planning at the University of California, Berkeley. She also serves as Education Director of the Blum Center for Developing Economies, a centre focused on issues of global poverty and inequality. Her work lies in the field of comparative urban studies and is concerned with how processes of urbanisation in the global South demand new conceptual frameworks in urban studies and planning. She also does research in the field of international development. Her current book project, titled *Poverty Capital: Microfinance and the Frontiers of Milllennial Development*, examines how poverty is conceptualised and managed by experts.

**Bishwapriya Sanyal** is Ford International Professor of Urban Planning and the Director of the Special Program for mid-career professionals in Urban and Regional Studies at MIT. He writes on planning theory and education for an increasingly interconnected world. Recently, he brought together a collection of papers by authors from different parts of the world, published in 2005, as *Planning Cultures* (Routledge). He is currently working on a book about the flow of key planning ideas around the world.

**André Sorensen** is Associate Professor of Urban Geography in the Department of Geography and Programme in Planning, at the University of Toronto. He has published widely on Japanese urbanisation, land development, and planning history, and is currently engaged in comparative research on megacities, institutional change, and citizen engagement in planning processes. His book *The Making of Urban Japan: Cities and Planning from Edo to the 21st Century* (Routledge 2002) won the book prize of the International Planning History Association in 2004. In 2007 he was elected a Fellow of the University of Tokyo School of Engineering in recognition of his research on Japanese urbanism and urban planning. He is the editor, with P. J. Marcotullio and J. Grant, of *Towards Sustainable Cities: East Asian, North American and European Perspectives* (Ashgate, 2004) and, with C. Funck, of *Living Cities in Japan: Citizens' Movements, Machizukuri and Local Environments* (Routledge, 2007).

**Dominic Stead** is Senior Researcher at Delft University of Technology within its interfaculty Research Institute for Housing, Urban and Mobility Studies (OTB) and in the Faculty of Architecture. He is also honorary fellow at University College London. His research interests include spatial governance, comparative planning and transport policy in Europe. He is currently involved in European research on the role of planning in managing resource use in urban areas.

**Robert Upton** was, until mid-2009, Secretary General of the Royal Town Planning Institute, London, a post he took after a career as a planner in the UK and Hong Kong. As Secretary General, he helped to initiate the journal *Planning Theory and Practice* and to establish the RTPI-sponsored book series in which the present book is published. He has also vigorously promoted involving a wider community of those interested in the planning field in the work of the RTPI, and international exchange within the planning field, among professional planners and academics. In September 2009, he took up the challenging job of deputy-chair of the newly established English Infrastructure Planning Commission.

**Niraj Verma** is Professor and Chair in the Department of Urban and Regional Planning at the University at Buffalo (the State University of New York). His work focuses on the role of rationality in planning and particularly on how sentiments and reasons can be integrated. This has taken him to American pragmatism and the philosophy of William James and led to concepts such as 'pragmatic rationality' and 'similarity' as ingredients of planning and management. Verma is the author of *Similarities, Connections, Systems* (Lexington, 1998) and editor of *Institutions and Planning* (Elsevier, 2007).

**Sanjeev Vidyarthi** is Assistant Professor in the Department of Urban Planning and Policy at the University of Illinois at Chicago. His doctoral dissertation investigates the travel and travails of the American neighbourhood unit in India and explains how different urban actors appropriated the concept over time. Apart from international exchanges of planning ideas, his research interests include city-building processes, urban theory and design, and globalisation and development studies.

**Bing Wang** is Lecturer in Design and Real Estate at Harvard University Graduate School of Design. She also holds appointments as Visiting Professor at the

University of Ulster and Visiting Lecturer at the University of Cambridge in the UK. She is a founding partner of a real estate investment company in Shanghai and a design company in Cambridge, MA. Her academic research focuses on the interplay between the formal representation of a society and its underlying economic driving forces and social structure. As an author, her writings have appeared in the *Journal of Real Estate Portfolio Management* and in the books *Nexus: Field Studies in Real Estate, Planning, and Design* (Harvard Graduate School of Design, 2005), *Urbanization in China* (Lincoln Institute of Land Policy, 2007), *Regenerating Older Suburbs* (Urban Land Institute, 2007) and *The Professions in China* (Routledge, 2010).

**Stephen V. Ward** is Professor of Planning History at Oxford Brookes University. He is a former President of the International Planning History Society and editor of the international refereed journal *Planning Perspectives*. Many of his own writings focus on international flows of planning knowledge, most notably his major book *Planning the Twentieth-Century City: The Advanced Capitalist World* (Wiley, 2002).

**Carolyn Whitzman** is Associate Professor in Urban Planning at the University of Melbourne. She is the author of *The Handbook of Community Safety, Gender, and Violence Prevention: Practical Planning Tools* (Earthscan, 2008) and *Suburb, Slum, Urban Village: Transformations in a Toronto Neighbourhood 1875–2002* (University of British Columbia Press, 2009). Her research focuses on planning for safe and healthy communities, including current projects on planning for violence prevention at the local governance level and children's independent mobility.

**Jieming Zhu** is at the National University of Singapore. He is interested in institutional analysis of urban development in the transitional economy, and urban planning in high-density, low-income Asian cities. He has served as consultant to the East–West Center; International Senior Fellow at Johns Hopkins University (1999/2000); advisor to the China Academy of Urban Planning and Design (2000/1); Urban Studies Fellow at the Glasgow University (2006); Fellow at the Ronald Coase Institute (2007); Visiting Professor to Tongji University (2002–present); and Adjunct Professor to Xiamen University (2008–present). He is corresponding editor of the *International Journal of Urban and Regional Research*, editorial board member of the *Journal of Planning Theory and Practice* and guest editor for *Habitat International*.

## PREFACE

As the scale and depth of global interconnectivity has accelerated, so too has the circulation of knowledge and expertise. Yet, although some circulation channels remain dominant, and some borders between regions and nations of the world continue to act as significant boundaries to this flow, the twentieth-century geography of nation-states and empires, of cold war hegemonies and dependent spheres, is being broken up and re-composed. New and quite widely accessible technologies have also created different and fast ways of circulating information and knowledge about situations across the globe. The resultant patterns of relations that are emerging are often described as diffuse and fragmenting, although new patterns can also be discerned. In this context, ideas, concepts, images and techniques can circulate rapidly. It is often not clear where they have come from, and yet they get to be used in particular contexts that remain unique in their specific configurations.

This book explores the circulation of ideas in and around a specific area of policy practice and professional endeavour. Ideas about planning and development, although often formed in response to very particular problems in specific contexts, have always spread beyond national borders, through networks created by planning activists and by political and economic relationships. The context of such diffusion in the nineteenth and early twentieth centuries was that of imperial expansion and colonisation. In the mid-twentieth century, 'modernisation' in the context of cold war politics, industrial economic expansion and Keynesian ideas about economic policy shaped the nature and flows of planning ideas. Today, in the contemporary global context, with the rise of new economic and political power centres in Asia and Latin America, there is a strong challenge to the dominance of the hegemony of Western traditions in planning thought and practice, along with some appreciation of what has been achieved in enhancing the quality of life in places.

Many of those involved in the planning field are actively involved in promoting the flow of knowledge and techniques transnationally. The field has a strengthening infrastructure of international practitioner organisations, scholarly associations, municipal exchange programmes and other special initiatives. In their planning studies and practice careers, people are moving between countries and regions much more than in the past. These arenas and flows bring enormous potential benefits in increasing the knowledgeability of those involved in planning activity worldwide. But there are also many hazards as theories, methods and practices developed in one context are not necessarily transferable to another.

This book takes a critical look at these flows. It explores how planning ideas and practices get to travel from one context to another and what happens when an exogenous idea gets to 'land' in a different context. It highlights the wider challenge of 'situating' planning ideas and practices in their particular contexts and the 'work' that such ideas and practices get to do in different places. It underlines the need for critical attention to the ethical and methodological issues of international exchange in the planning field.

The project for the book originated as a way of celebrating the tenth anniversary of the journal *Planning Theory and Practice* in 2009.[1] Implicitly, the role of the journal has been to contribute to strengthening an international community of scholarship around the practices of spatial planning. As journal editors, we wanted to consider more explicitly the issue of the transfer of concepts and institutions from one context to another, especially when this involved crossing the national borders within which planning systems, professional associations and practices are often so deeply embedded. Armed with the agenda outlined above, and in consultation with members of the journal's editorial board, we invited contributions from people involved in the international exchange of planning ideas and practices in different ways. We sought out contributors who were critical academics, and also those actively involved in specific practices. We asked for contributions from senior academics, and from those relatively new in their academic careers. The resultant range is by no means comprehensive,[2] but it serves to provide a good overview about what is at stake as the planning 'community' internationalises more vigorously. Several of the papers were presented in draft at the ACSP/AESOP Joint Congress in Chicago in July 2008, and the discussion there helped to focus both the individual chapters and our own work as editors. Since then there has been considerable discussion between authors and editors and between us as editors about the overall shape of the book.

The chapters, all original, cover a wide range of experiences. They bring together different intellectual traditions that coexist in the planning field. Authors have used concepts from work in the history of planning ideas; from international development studies; from the globalisation and postcolonial literatures; from 'historical' institutionalist analysis; and from the policy transfer and social learning fields. Chapter 1 illustrates this variety and provides an overview of the issues raised by the chapters, centred around the themes raised above. In

Chapter 2, Ananya Roy then introduces the agenda of globalisation and shows how ideas about relieving poverty have been appropriated and used by dominant international agencies such as the World Bank, but are also being challenged. The next three chapters are from scholars working in the field of planning history. Stephen Ward looks at the 'experts' who took their ideas and technologies from one location to another in the second part of the twentieth century, in the wider context of the geo-politics of the cold war period. Sanjeev Vidyarthi takes up this story from a different angle and shows how the 'neighbourhood unit' concept was interpreted and used in newly independent India. Bing Wang goes further back in time to examine how ideas about urban planning were introduced into China in the first half of the twentieth century.

In Chapter 6, André Sorensen focuses on why ideas about urban sustainability and compact cities, largely derived from Western European discourses, have been slow to 'arrive' in Japan and how they have then been used. Nihal Perera draws on his own experiences in Sri Lanka to show how modernising concepts of how to organise and design settlements in a major regional development project were challenged by local planners, who evolved a different kind of design idea and practice. In Chapter 8, Dominic Stead, Martin de Jong and Iveta Reinholde examine how German experience was used in Poland and Latvia, in the context of a German federal aid programme, at a time when Western European countries were being encouraged to give more attention to post-Communist Eastern Europe. Barbara Kazimbaya-Senkwe and Peter Lubambo speak from their own experiences as intermediaries between World Bank funders, national government and municipalities to describe the struggle over the organisation of the water sector in Zambia's Copperbelt.

Carolyn Whitzman has also been actively involved in the cases she describes. In her chapter with Jane Perkovic, she shows how an idea that arose from feminist activism in Toronto got taken up internationally, but was shorn of its initial radical intent. Using another similar example, these authors highlight the role of a vigorous network of project champions. In Chapter 11, the focus shifts from the transfer of ideas about the spatial organisation and design of cities to the transferability of specific analytical techniques. Sukumar Ganapati and Niraj Verma explore what it might take to make a technique that has been seen as an inappropriate 'traveller' more adaptable to a quite different context. The technique they examine is that of 'housing' filtering as developed in the analysis of US housing markets. How, they ask, could it be adapted to the very different institutional dimensions of Italian housing markets, and that of Rome in particular.

The next three chapters highlight experiences in South and East Asia. Jieming Zhu argues that more attention should be given to the experiences of China and Singapore in facing up to the huge challenge of massively expanding urban complexes, and to creating the governance capacities available in these two countries. But Western planners are also very evident in China these days. Dan Abramson provides an unusual perspective for exploring the challenges involved in such flows, as he went as a graduate student from MIT in the United States to carry out his doctoral studies and engage in planning practice in China. In Chapter 13, he provides a reflective account of what he learned from this experience. John Friedmann has himself had a very substantial international impact on the ideas about regional development in his role as a writer and academic. In Chapter 14, he reflects back on his own experiences of acting as a transcultural advisor, both in Chile in the late 1960s and in China in the late 2000s. He urges the planning community to be cautious about the relevance of planning ideas developed in one context to the political, institutional and cultural conditions in another. Finally, in Chapter 15, Bishwapriya Sanyal provides an overview of the international development approaches that evolved in the second part of the twentieth century. Appreciating the importance of recognising the diversity of contexts and practices, he argues that, across the globe, we also share some common experiences and live in a world we 'share' in common. He thus underlines the positive value of engaging in international exchange and learning in the planning field.

This book thus provides an 'encounter' between different experiences and perspectives around the agenda we set out. On the way, the different authors have encountered each other, and our own understanding has been challenged and re-cast, opening up new avenues for development and critical reflection. We hope that readers will have a similar experience as they probe the richness of the collection, and that this book will act as encouragement for more vigorous engagement and critical examination of planning ideas as they flow from place to place and get used and abused in all kinds of ways.

## NOTES

1  Published in conjunction with the Royal Town Planning Institute, London, the journal offers an arena for international debate and more effective communication and sharing of ideas between practitioners and academics. Along with Heather Campbell, we were the founding editors of *Planning Theory and Practice*.
2  The chapters were selected from a larger number of initial propositions. We are very conscious that we lack contributions from Latin America and the Middle East.

## ACKNOWLEDGEMENTS

We would like to acknowledge the help of the editorial board and editorial team members of the journal *Planning Theory and Practice* in advising on this project generally and suggesting authors to approach. Very special thanks are also given to all of the chapter authors, who not only created original chapters but also tolerated the many questions we asked them as editors and textual sub-editors. The project of the book, and several papers in the book, were discussed at a special track of the AESOP/ACSP Congress in Chicago in July 2008, which provided further ideas to all of us about how best to shape the book. Our thanks to everyone who contributed to the vigorous discussion we had there. We also give a special appreciation to Francesca Raphaely, who provided invaluable astute and interested editorial assistance as we prepared the text to send to the publishers.

Our thanks to Alex Hollingsworth and Georgina Johnson-Cook of the publishers, Routledge, for believing in the project, and to Leah Gourley and Deborah Bennett of Prepress Projects for preparing the text for publication.

CHAPTER 1

## INTRODUCTION

### THE TRANSNATIONAL FLOW OF KNOWLEDGE AND EXPERTISE IN THE PLANNING FIELD[1]

**PATSY HEALEY**

## TRANSNATIONAL INTERACTION IN THE PLANNING FIELD

This book is about the flow of planning ideas and techniques across national boundaries, and their interaction with practices. Although exhibiting new forms and flows in the present period, such interaction is by no means a new phenomenon. Wherever and whenever elites and activists have been concerned about the qualities of their cities and territories, they have looked about for ideas to help inspire their development programmes. And people have always travelled from place to place, offering suggestions about ways of solving problems or improving conditions in one place based on their experiences in other places.[2] It is, therefore, important to consider what is distinctive about such interactions in the planning field at the start of the twenty-first century, and what challenges these present for both the development of planning expertise and the moral and intellectual responsibilities of those involved in such interactions.

A first task, however, is to identify the planning field. It is an 'open field'[3] of ideas and practices, but defining its character and qualities has always presented problems. The term 'planning', although much used, is not very helpful in indicating its range and scope. The English word 'planning' does not translate easily into other languages, and even in English terms used include not only 'planning' but also 'city planning', 'town planning', 'urban and regional planning', 'environmental planning' and 'spatial planning'.[4] 'Planning' in English has a meaning in everyday language that can simply indicate an intention to do something, but also points towards some kind of policy intention and an imagined practice to follow this into action. As an area of public policy, 'planning' takes on a more specific focus, ranging from national economic development planning to the physical organisation of neighbourhoods, cities and regions. From such a perspective, the substantive focus of the planning field is the management and development of the relations between people and places.

An alternative way to arrive at a sense of the scope of the planning field is to focus on 'what planners do' and on the concerns expressed in the 'cultures of practice' within which ideas and practices about planning arise.[5] I use the concept of cultures of practice to refer to communities of experts, advocates, officials and lobbyists who promote or work in distinct fields.[6] Such communities, however, vary in relation to national government priorities and governance cultures,[7] and in relation to disciplinary backgrounds. In some countries, such as China and the Netherlands, urban and regional planning has long been an important field of public policy. In the United States, the UK and Japan, national political interest has been much more ambiguous. However, in all these countries, there are communities of experts, officials and activists that focus on improving place qualities, on the development of territories, and on paying attention to spatial connections. The chapters in this book share this focus, but reflect also the diversity of 'planning cultures' to be found globally (Sanyal 2005).

The planning field has another important characteristic. It cannot be neatly tied to a particular academic discipline. It is a field of substantive concerns and practical activity, rather than a 'discipline' centred primarily on a specific body of academic scholarship and research. As with fields such as medicine, management and engineering, it is infused by a continual interaction between practical experiences, research inquiries and scholarly analyses.[8] Most planning work involves drawing on a range of bodies of substantive systematised knowledge – the formal academic disciplines – along with all kinds of experiential knowledge, in order both to develop an understanding of places and their development potentials and to propose and carry out specific interventions. Through this 'drawing together', the planning field has created its own distinctive, interacting traditions of practical activity and intellectual inquiry.

Just as other fields of practice share certain moral attitudes, so too does this broad field of 'spatial', 'urban' and 'territorial' planning. These attitudes are full of ambiguity and contestation, marked as much by debates and struggles between different ideas as by any common programme. Yet there have been some important shifts in the focus of planning during the twentieth century. In the early 1900s, when a vigorous advocacy movement for city/town/urban planning was gathering momentum, an emphasis on convenience, beauty and development efficiency often clashed with a social reformist concern with improving the living conditions of the working masses (Ward 2002; Sutcliffe 1981). In the 1930s, both the modernist CIAM[9] movement and the US regional development initiatives linked to the national 'New Deal' programme were underpinned by a strong strand of social reformist values (Ward 2002; Birch and Silver 2009). At the start of the twenty-first century, social radicalism had remained an important strand, with its consequent emphasis on the social justice of planning strategies, projects and practice enlarged by much more attention to the diversity of people's lifestyles, identities and aspirations (Fainstein 2005; Friedmann 2000). Roy, in Chapter 2 of this book, calls urgently for a reconsideration of this tradition, to inform struggles in global arenas over how the situation of the poorest in the world is understood.

The social reform agenda within the planning field has been challenged in the later twentieth century by a wider political emphasis on the 'economic competitiveness' of regions, nations and supranational groups such as the European Union, in a world of increasingly transnational or global economic relations. Accommodating economic growth strategies is a major concern in China today, as is reflected in the chapters in this book by Zhu and Abramson. This economic emphasis has, however, been moderated by anxiety about the environmental conditions of cities and about the global impacts of unrestrained economic exploitation of planetary resources, rather than by the more egalitarian concerns that influenced some post-independence nation-building in the mid-twentieth century (see Vidyarthi's discussion of the role of urban planning ideas in India's post-independence modernisation strategy in Chapter 4). Concern with environmental quality is linked to wider agendas centred on more ecologically sensitive and environmentally sustainable development strategies, which have become an important policy focus in many countries in the later twentieth century, although with a range of interpretations (see Sorensen in Chapter 6). Within Europe, the economic and environmental emphases are combined with a continuing concern for social welfare. 'Balancing' concern with social justice, environmental sustainability and economic well-being is a well-established principle in European Union policy initiatives, and has been expressed in influential initiatives to convey a continent-wide planning perspective (CSD 1999; Faludi and Waterhout 2002).

The chapters in this book illustrate a variety of 'probes' into this open field, presenting examples of the transnational flow of planning ideas and practices from the early twentieth century to the present. They range from examples of physical design in relation to nation-building (Vidyarthi, Perera), to competing notions of how to increase the access of poorer people to financial credit (Roy), the transfer of specific techniques (Stead, Whitzman and Perkovic, Ganapati and Verma), and overview discussions about development philosophy (Zhu, Sanyal). They include critical analyses by academic observers (Sorensen, Ward, Wang) and commentaries by practitioners reflecting on their experiences (Kazimbaya-Senkwe and Lubambo, Perera, Abramson, Friedmann). In their diversity, they mirror the various ways of thinking about the planning field to be found in the wider planning literature. Some books about planning with a transnational reach focus on designs for locales, cities and regions (see, for example, Wannop 1995). Others discuss the administrative and legal structure of 'planning systems', or look at different ways of analysing planning ideas and practices, or focus on particular technologies.[10]

The contributors to this book are themselves located within different schools of thought and trajectories of research inquiry. As a result, this book acts as an encounter between different academic communities within the planning field. Planning historians, those drawing on the international development and globalisation debates and institutionally minded policy analysts are all to be found here, complemented by contributions using critical insights from postcolonial analyses of development processes and the methods associated with 'actor-network theory'.

Such multiple contributions all overlap, yet reflect different emphases and traditions within the field. Those who contribute to the planning literature do not always make clear the trajectory of knowledge development within which their work is positioned. This creates difficulties for others who are trying to assess the meaning and relevance of an idea, an analysis or a practical example for their own concerns. It requires probing behind what is said or written to draw out the meanings and contextual assumptions out of which a planning idea or practice experience has been generated. As several of the chapters in this book emphasise, this effort may lead to new interpretations and the selective use of ideas as they are taken up in these different contexts. Sometimes, this leads to a loss of radical edge, as Sorensen finds in Chapter 6 in his analysis of how the 'compact city' idea was slow to arrive in Japan, and was then used to address particular Japanese policy concerns. Whitzman and Perkovic in Chapter 10 describe how ideas designed to improve the safety of women and children in local environments lost their original emphasis on a gendered understanding of the spatial arrangement of urban areas. Yet in Chapter 8, in contrast, Stead and colleagues show that those making use of international experience may be shrewdly aware of the institutional assumptions embedded within experiences promoted from elsewhere. In another example of this aspect of planning, Hein (2003) shows that, although many European urban planners in the late nineteenth century emphasised the design of the built form, Japanese planners were more interested in the administrative and legal tools used in Europe to manage the land development process.[11] Kazimbaya-Senkwe and Lubambo in Chapter 9 illustrate a context in which external ideas promoted by a global aid agency were shrewdly resisted by local actors, mobilising the language of resistance to Western colonialism.

If diffusion is selective in this way then it is helpful to consider the planning ideas and experiences that get to travel around the world as 'assemblages'[12] – of images of urban form and place qualities, of analytical approaches and specific techniques, of administrative and legal arrangements (such as 'planning systems'), and of ideas about ways of doing things associated with doing planning work. Items in these assemblages get into the academic literature, the practice manuals and the minds of those who 'carry' planning ideas from one place to another.

Academic authors, manual writers and travelling experts are themselves selective in putting together the specific 'bundles' they take from the wider assemblage of ideas and experiences to which they are exposed. The bundles they travel with reflect their interests and also the culture they have come from, though we are often unaware of the mental baggage we carry with us. Those who adopt ideas from such 'carriers' may be skilful at probing into the bundle, to pull out the less obvious aspects for implementation in new contexts. But many problems have occurred because carriers and adaptors have been insufficiently aware of the implicit assumptions shaping the ideas and suggestions encompassed in any given expert's bundle. In other words, diffusion processes are not simply about how an idea or technique moves from place to place. They involve complex processes of translation, interpretation and adaptation.[13]

The imagery used above about carriers and adaptors may suggest that planning ideas and practices are transported by particular individuals, 'travelling planners' perhaps, and are honed to local conditions either by the 'exogenous' expert or by a local client agency or planning expert. Studies in planning history and the chapters in this book provide examples of such apparently linear processes, but they also show that the diffusion paths of planning ideas and practices are, in reality, much more complex. Individual experts are located in networks and communities of practice through which their ideas have been developed. In Chapter 5, Wang discusses the Western and Russian ideas that influenced various eras of the development of planning ideas in twentieth-century China. Abramson, in Chapter 13, describes his own struggles as he tried to relate his approach to planning to that of his Chinese co-workers. Such encounters and struggles, in themselves, generate productive learning, as Banerjee (2009) underlines.

These networks and communities of practice are part of what Roy in Chapter 2 refers to as 'circuits of knowledge', to which planning experts contribute and which shape their thinking. These, in turn, are situated in wider contexts, which give momentum to the development of such networks and communities, and promote the circulation of ideas and experiences – such as the trade and administrative relations of imperial states at the start of the twentieth century, or the networks of aid agencies, of global multinational companies and of city administrations a century later. Interaction may be initiated not only by countries, regions and cities which feel that they have expertise to offer, but also from places that are seeking to 'aggrandise', 'develop' or 'modernise' themselves. Civic leaders may then explore available networks and circuits of knowledge to find places and experts that have gained a reputation for planning capacity. In Chapter 3, Ward describes the client relations that employed some of the most significant international planning experts of the mid-twentieth century. Vidyarthi, in Chapter 4, provides more detail about the work of some of these in postcolonial India, an experience which is discussed more generally in Banerjee (2009). Today, planners from places such as Vancouver and Milan have been invited to provide planning expertise to Dubai's energetic urban development project in the early twenty-first century,[14] just as French planners were asked to 'embellish' cities like Buenos Aires and Beirut a century before (Nasr and Volait 2003).

As Ward (2002) argues, the diffusion and adaptation of planning ideas and practices involve complex interactions of structural forces, individual agency and institutional cultures.[15] In particular instances and in the broader critical analysis, it is important to unravel how interactions that produce creative learning experiences – which both enhance the relevance of what is exchanged to a particular situation and contribute more widely to the 'pool' of knowledge, experience and institutional capacity available to those engaged in place development – differ from those that crudely impose or emulate an idea or practice promoted as some kind of 'universal' solution, often leaving a legacy of failed capacity or cynicism behind them. Vidyarthi, in Chapter 4, and Perera, in Chapter 7, describe how the celebration of modernist, universalist planning and engineering projects in the 1950s and 1960s tended towards the latter outcome. Cooke and Kothari (2001) take a critical look at the contemporary planning idea that 'beneficiaries' of aid projects should 'participate' in defining and implementing a project, and criticise the more 'universalist' interpretations of this practice in the context of international aid relations.

Planning history shows that there have been many such crude impositions and emulations, but, as noted above, there have always been situations in which the 'adaptors' have been sophisticated and selective in their approach to exogenous planning expertise. The chapters in this book illustrate the complexity of the processes of learning, challenging, adapting and inventing that take place in specific instances, and how these are tied into locally specific social, political and economic dynamics. Yet studies in the international development field, as well as within individual countries, show all too clearly that the crude emulation or borrowing of 'best practice' mantras remains common in the planning field today. So what, if anything, may be distinctive about the present period as regards the transnational flow of planning ideas and their interaction with planning practices?

A major difference today relates to the scale of urbanisation across the globe, the pervasive impact of global economic relations, and the geo-political shift from a polarised 'cold war' world to a more diffuse dynamic, in which newly emerging societies are challenging Western hegemony. The 'global many' now increasingly live in urban and urbanising contexts. Cities and urban areas are no longer just centres of trade, administration and culture, but agglomerations where we 'many' live our lives. Attention to the livability and sustainability of urban areas is, therefore, not brought to the political forefront only by the interests of elites.

It is demanded by those living in urban areas. Meanwhile, planning ideas and practices are not just diffusing from the 'West to the rest', or from the 'developed' to the 'developing' world, or the 'global North' to the 'South'. There are all kinds of cross-movements. This is encouraged by the expansion of regional, transnational and global networks of planners and planning academics working in many different situations. It is also promoted by the work of international aid agencies, by the massive expansion of planning education (see UN-Habitat 2009), and by the increasing production of academic work on planning experiences throughout the world, to which this book and academic journals such as *Planning Theory and Practice* contribute. This globalising of planning ideas and practices underlines the importance of understanding the diversity of contexts in which planning work is carried out (see Watson 2008). At the same time, it highlights common dynamics and commitments that inform the planning enterprise overall (see Sanyal's argument in Chapter 15). This does not mean that all those doing planning work around the world are aware of this circulation of ideas. But they cannot avoid being influenced indirectly, as influences permeate the planning cultures and communities of practice to which they belong.

In the rest of this introductory chapter, I develop the issues outlined above in relation to the three themes that informed the production of the book as a whole. I first expand on the diffusion and translation processes through which planning ideas spread out from one context to another, especially when this involves moving across national boundaries, each with their institutional and cultural specificities. I then consider what is involved in adapting exogenous ideas to specific situations, as an example of the general challenge of 'situating' planning practices. Third, I give some attention to the role of key actors and agencies in diffusion and adaptation processes.

## PROCESSES OF DIFFUSION

I referred earlier to planning ideas as existing in an accumulation or assemblage of loosely associated concepts and ways of doing things, some explicit and others existing as implicit assumptions. Each of the authors in the present book 'carries' his or her own bundle from this accumulation. For some, the spotlight is on the imagery of urban form. In Chapter 4, Vidyarthi discusses the appeal of the 'neighbourhood unit' concept as carrying an image of 'modern life' as lived in mid-twentieth-century America. Such a tradition dominated among planning experts a century ago. The 'new urbanism' movement in our own day provides a good example of the promotion and marketing of such design concepts (Grant 2006), alongside more ecologically informed images of idealised settlement patterns.[16] In Chapter 6, Sorensen focuses on ideas about sustainable urban development in Japan, and in particular the imagery of the 'compact city'. Perera, in Chapter 7, reports on the way in which engineers in the 1980s imagined the organisation of settlements in a regional development project in Sri Lanka, drawing on a body of ideas developed in nineteenth-century Germany, which spread widely in Western Europe and North America.[17] Other studies have emphasised the importance of planning processes and ways of doing planning work. Many planners will be familiar with the narrative of how the so-called 'rational scientific' method of expert analysis and policy formation displaced an earlier tradition that emphasised the history and geography of a place. This tradition informed much planning work in the early twentieth century,[18] and was then, in turn, displaced by a critical analysis of the political–economic dynamics driving planning projects. These days, there is more likely to be an emphasis on participative and collaborative ways of accumulating knowledge about what is at stake and what might be ways forward, and on grasping the political–administrative context of particular situations.[19] These last ideas have a prominent place in the 'bundle' I carry with me.

There are also studies of diffusion processes that focus on the appropriation and transfer of a particular policy measure, or intervention instrument – that is, a technique or 'technology'. Roy (Chapter 2) uses the example of the provision of 'microfinance' to those too poor to access the formal banking system. Whitzman and Perkovic (Chapter 10) look at the production of urban safety audits and the introduction of 'walking buses', and the struggles by certain networks to appropriate these to serve particular sets of interests and power relations. In Chapter 8, Stead *et al.* focus on organisation and management questions in their analysis of the diffusion of transport management arrangements. Ganapati and Verma, in Chapter 11, focus on a particular analytical technique, that of 'filtering' processes in local housing markets. Their starting point is the claim made by many analysts that this technique is so firmly rooted in the specificities of US housing markets that it is 'untranslatable' into other contexts. They explore how it could be adapted by careful attention to institutional specificities, using the case of housing markets in Rome, Italy.

Whichever aspect of the collection of ideas in the 'bundle' is explicitly emphasised, these concepts carry with them other assumptions and attitudes – about how the politics of practice works, about how people relate their individual concerns to wider social expectations, about the way the law works and how it is regarded, and about how 'doing planning work' should actually be performed not just as an organisational task, but as a real-life drama, with a staging and setting.[20] It is these assumptions that are often the most difficult to bring out into the open and question as planning ideas 'travel' and get translated into new contexts (Tait and Jensen 2007; Callon 1986). Such assumptions are partly linked to particular cultures and traditions, which affect how people in different countries (with particular constitutions, histories and geographies) come to think about development and governance. But they are also shaped by disciplinary cultures. Architectural training emphasises the workplace of the studio, the presentation of images, the model and the design sketch. Engineers will focus on structures and layouts, and on the costs of different structures and patterns. Social scientists focus on arguments and evidence, but with different emphases reflecting different disciplines. Economists tend to focus on models of relations, through which costs and benefits of alternatives can be calculated and compared. Sociologists question the models and both they and political scientists focus on power dynamics and the ways that excluded groups may get to challenge what is being proposed by more dominant groups. Activist advocates of technologies and designs 'walk the talk', engaging in persuasive work in all kinds of arenas. Those concerned with legal and administrative aspects look into organisational arrangements, bureaucratic capacity, enforcement potential and the role of law and legal practices. Clashes between these different 'cultures of practice' are well known from planning encounters within national contexts. But they can be exaggerated and very confusing when different practices from different countries 'collide' in a specific instance. Abramson, in Chapter 13, and John Friedmann, in Chapter 14, illustrate what it is like to experience such 'collisions' in China today.

Many planning ideas energetically promoted and 'carried' by strong advocates fail to make much progress when they arrive in a new context. This can be because, locally, key people were looking for something different, or because of tensions and struggles over whether to adopt a particular approach, or because the arena in which the exogenous planning idea was promoted was not connected to stakeholders whose backing was essential for an idea to work. Vidyarthi (Chapter 4) notes how the 'neighbourhood unit' concept was attractive to both long-established and modernising elites in postcolonial India, but for different reasons. He underlines the importance of the mental models or 'imaginations' within which a particular planning idea gets to be situated and interpreted. Politicians are often attracted by planning 'imagery', but fail to see the administrative and legal work needed to introduce a new style of building or layout, or to assemble sites. Powerful business groups, bureaucrats and politicians may see new ideas as threats to their established activities, positions and networks. Nasr and Volait (2003) provide rich examples of such experiences in their narratives of how exogenous planning ideas were used in many parts of the world in the early and mid-twentieth century.[21] Shrewd politicians and their advisers, who these days often include planning staff, are able to sort through what is being offered to them, selectively taking up ideas they can work with and rejecting those that seem less relevant or merely promotional hype. Sorensen (Chapter 6) and Wang (Chapter 5) note how vigorously Western (and Russian) planning texts have been translated in Japan and China. Stead *et al.*, in Chapter 8, show how knowledgeable local politicians and experts in Central and Eastern Europe made use of Western European experience of public transport management. But innovation inspired by exogenous initiatives does not always work out well. In Europe, studies of the introduction of Local Agenda 21 ideas into local governments show how persuasive advocates could sometimes get energetic programmes off the ground, but their activities were often corralled into sections of a municipality while the rest of the local government went on with 'business as usual'.[22] Kazimbaya-Senkwe and Lubambo (Chapter 9) show how World Bank conceptions of how to improve water management in the Zambian Copperbelt were positioned within struggles between municipal and private sector conceptions of appropriate organisational arrangements. Canny local politicians managed to get the benefit of external funding while effectively turning on its head the implied World Bank critique of them as 'others' resistant to change, politically 'othering' the World Bank technocrats as external colonisers to be resisted.

What gets diffused, and how the diffused ideas get translated and adapted, are thus highly variable processes. The tensions and contestations that arise in these interactions are often very productive in themselves, leading to new experiences which may then themselves diffuse. In Chapter 7, Perera is, in effect, actively diffusing lessons from his own experience of challenging an imported engineering model of settlement organisation in Sri Lanka. Whitzman comments on her own work as an advocate diffuser in her account (in Chapter 10 with Jane Perkovic) of women's safety audits. Kazimbaya-Senkwe and Lubambo were caught in the position of intermediaries between the World Bank and national and local politicians over how the water sector should be organised. These experiences underline the non-linear way that planning ideas diffuse. Planning ideas get re-shaped as they 'travel', losing some dimensions and accumulating others. This re-shaping may be the result of what Wang (in Chapter 5) refers to as 'passive' transfusion. But the chapters also show the importance of both active, shrewd 'learning' and adaptation, and intense struggle. As Roy argues, it is therefore important for planning researchers and scholars to maintain critical attention to these bundles of planning ideas as they flow around, as well as to the 'circuits of knowledge' through which ideas flow, and who gets to 'capture' the way a planning idea is translated within these flows. This is especially important today because of the multiple channels through which planning ideas are diffused, and the different groups who may 'capture' them. It is all too easy for the powerful 'aid and trade' networks to create a hegemonic monopoly over planning ideas 'in good currency', although, as Kazimbaya-Senkwe and Lubambo show, such pressure may be cleverly resisted.

This raises the question of what provides the momentum and channels through which planning ideas diffuse. The chapter authors have addressed this question in different ways, depending on their perspectives. Ward's grouping of possible explanations for the way planning ideas diffuse into those that focus on structural dynamics, those that emphasise the role of specific agents and those that emphasise cultural milieux (Ward 2002) has influenced many of those writing in the 'planning history' tradition, such as in Chapters 4 and 5 of the present book. Most of the other analyses in this book also underline the complex interplay of all these forces in determining which ideas 'travel' and what happens when they arrive in particular places, but they do so through different conceptual lenses. Sorensen, for example, makes use of Kingdon's conception of how policy agendas are formed. Kingdon argues that problems and solutions may often circulate in a governance context, but in disconnected 'streams'. A solution comes to prominence when it attaches to a problem for which there is increasing salience in a particular context (Kingdon 2003). Meanwhile, those involved in planning work in all kinds of situations across the world may be quite unaware of this flow of ideas, except as a part of slow shifts in the mental models available in their communities of practice and wider planning cultures.

Several structural explanations for the way that planning ideas circulate are drawn upon in the chapters in this book, emphasising changing and interrelated political and economic dynamics. Some emphasise the continuing relevance of the old imperial relations, as they live on in postcolonial networks of the exchange of professional expertise and training (see the chapters by Vidyarthi, Perera, and Kazimbaya-Senkwe and Lubambo). These include the relations not only of empires grounded in capitalist economies, but also of those of the socialist world (see Wang, in Chapter 5). Others look more directly at economic explanations, in terms of the promotion by wealthy countries of ideas and of consultancy expertise, which may open up new markets and sources of supply (Roy, Kazimbaya-Senkwe and Lubambo). Another force is the pressure on local elites to respond to the demands of fellow residents of urban areas by improving the livability and sustainability of urban conditions, and by sharing the benefits of development with the rest of the population – a pressure felt in non-democracies as well as in democracies (as Wang shows in her account of the development of planning ideas in twentieth-century China). This kind of force is expressed at a supranational scale in the work of aid agencies through bilateral, multilateral and supranational programmes. Many wealthy countries have aid programmes, while Russia and China have also actively provided aid to developing countries, dating from the period of 'cold war' politics, but now more linked to economic opportunities. In the European Union, a 'structural fund' creates resources for development in poorer EU countries, to help them cope with the pressures of economic integration and to reduce the gaps between the wealthier and poorer nations of the Union. The EU also provides aid to other parts of the world, adding to the increasingly complex array of multinational aid agencies involved in urban development and urban planning work, including the World Bank and UN-Habitat. There are also several international non-governmental agencies working in the planning and environmental field, which exchange experiences, advocate particular approaches and offer financial aid.[23]

These forces, however, and the programmes that result from them, are realised through flows of actual people and resources, and it is the networks generated by these flows, as well as the individual 'carriers', which transmit specific planning ideas and practices. Roy discusses how a 'Washington consensus' on poverty appropriated the microcredit concept. She argues instead that an alternative 'Bangladesh' consensus should be constructed, closer to the way that the original innovation was produced. The vigorous efforts of some coalitions of actors, maybe local politicians and experts, may create networks that then come to influence the priorities of 'aid and trade' structures. Briggs (2008) gives an example of how local protest leaders in Mumbai's slums were able to link to networks at the national and international level to promote a different approach to the treatment of slum dwellers. EU regional development programmes have deliberately encouraged such network building, providing funds for local governments across Europe to exchange experiences with each other. Local governments may individually seek out relations internationally. The municipality of Barcelona in Spain has been particularly active in this respect, helping to create networks of city politicians and officials within Europe, Latin America and globally, to lobby for more attention to urban issues (Marshall 2004). Professional associations may also engage vigorously in international networking, which is now an important objective of the British Royal Town Planning Institute. In addition to these are the networks of consultancies and academic institutions, which help to create a professional job market and a critical discussion of planning ideas and practices that is increasingly international in scope. Abramson describes the active efforts of the planning programme at the Massachusetts Institute of Technology to expose students to international practice experiences as part of their training, a model also used in some other planning programmes. Over the past 20 years, academics in the planning field have built up overlapping regional associations that increasingly link educators and researchers across the world. Although many of these networks are still divided according to language and 'discipline', there is a developing mutual awareness between different networks as people come across them in congresses, in exhibitions, through the internet and the literature, and in 'on-the-job' experiences where international consultants or aid workers meet up. This process is helped by the increasing use of international English as a medium of professional and academic exchange.[24]

However, none of this stitching together of disparate networks and structuring dynamics reduces the diverse particularities of the individual contexts in which planning work is done. It just adds to the complexity of the exogenous forces and flows of ideas and expertise that are available to, and get taken up in, specific instances. The challenge for critical planning action, committed to the moral attitudes that I suggested earlier are wrapped up in a loose accumulation of ideas associated with the planning field, is to work out how to create greater momentum for improving urban conditions through this complex interplay of exogenous and endogenous forces. Harnessing the potential of this interplay requires continual attention to the specific dynamics of structural influences, local agency, and cultures and institutions.

## SITUATING PLANNING PRACTICES

As Nasr and Volait (2003) note, students from different parts of the world who come to America or Europe to study planning often struggle to grasp what kind of practice their teachers are referring to and what contexts are assumed in the literature they are invited to read. Travellers themselves, they are forced to develop skills for comparing the different ways in which planning is thought about and practised. Many academics and practitioners are unaware of the distinctiveness of the contextual assumptions implicit in the accounts and arguments about the planning field they provide about their own countries.[25] Lecturers may live, as Sanyal suggests in Chapter 15, quite cloistered lives. Many 'home' students are also unaware of the specificities of their context, absorbing what is, in effect, a particular understanding as if it were a universal and 'natural' dimension of planning knowledge.[26] Students from very different backgrounds have to work hard to draw this 'implicit' baggage out from the fields of knowledge being opened to them. The great value of this 'reflexive' experience is as a resource, which returning students often use to scrutinise what is offered by 'travelling experts' encountered later in their academic and practice lives. In the present book, both Abramson and Friedmann underline the importance to their own intellectual development of their struggles to grasp the specificities of different contexts. But, locally, it may be hard to raise awareness of the need to be cautious about what outside experts can offer. Powerful elites in a specific situation – local political leaders, or business groups with major interests in land and property, perhaps – may prefer the prestige and international reputation of the outside expert over the critical, reflexive local 'returner'. And many involved in specific practices are not interested in changing how they do things, and resist suggested innovations. So there are many grounds for a critique of exogenous experience and expertise.

External expertise can crowd out attention to local specificities in all kinds of ways. This is a strong theme in the Latin American and African literature on planning ideas and practices, which are often grounded in arguments about the need to 'escape' from colonial impositions and postcolonial deference to expertise available from former colonising countries (see Kazimbaya-Senkwe and Lubambo in Chapter 9 and also UN-Habitat 2009). Yet the tension between a specific planning task and experience drawn from elsewhere is not confined to transnational situations. It is part of the wider challenge in planning work of recognising the specifics of a particular practice context, while applying 'expert' knowledge and judgement in advising how to respond appropriately to a local set of concerns. Every situation in which planning work is carried out needs some understanding of context, some grasp of who key actors are and of what networks are in play, and how this relates to local social, economic and political dynamics. People involved in specific planning practices for a long while know a lot about all of these, but they, too, may find it difficult to draw out what underpins their cares, concerns and aspirations, in order to make explicit what they take for granted.

The challenge of grasping what really is at stake is present in all situations in which an outside 'expert' is asked to deal with a local 'problem'. A British consultant, Kenneth Watts, referred to in Ward's chapter, once recounted a story of being asked to design a new bridge across a large river in South Asia, because every time the monsoon came there were major floods at the base of the bridge. He explored the situation and soon concluded that the flooding was not due to the design of the existing bridge. Instead it resulted from the way that the monsoon rains flowed off the surface directly down towards the river because the soakaways to the roadside drains got blocked up in the dry season. So he suggested a programme of clearing out the drains before the rains fell. Much cheaper than building a bridge, this would also create small-scale employment opportunities for the many poorer people in the area. This advice perhaps upset local engineers and politicians interested in visible projects, but it made a lot of difference to many people's living conditions when the monsoon came. It is possible that people living in the area could have arrived at a similar conclusion, and maybe already had. But they might not have been listened to.[27] And it is often the case that politicians with resources may prefer visible, big-capital projects over careful attention to effective ongoing maintenance programmes.

In cases such as the above, the initial 'problem' is clear. What is needed is a careful investigation of whether assumptions about causes are justifiable, followed by the re-framing of problems in relation to such investigations, and alternative suggestions about solutions that are worth exploring. However, urban problems are rarely this clear-cut and contained. The challenges of inadequate housing, a lack of employment, congested transport, limited access to credit for poorer people, ill-health due to poor water supply and drainage, air and water pollution, etc. are typically part of very complex sets of relations. Addressing them may involve confronting powerful, entrenched local groups and wider power dynamics far removed from the locale in question. In these situations there may be no clear-cut answers to what is at stake, what is a 'problem', and what is causing a problem. This makes it difficult to 'match' solutions to problems, and demands richly informed and attentive 'probing' of the assumptions and knowledge that lie behind the identification of problems and solutions. Yet there is often insufficient time or resources to do this. Such situations place considerable ethical demands on 'travelling experts' (see the next section). They raise questions about the concepts and theories we use to 'scope' a particular situation, as well as what actions might address what people see as 'problems' and they might consider relevant 'solutions'.

Sometimes, local actors in situations in which outside aid and expertise have been provided argue that external advisers have failed to understand local specificities, or that international exemplars are being used far too crudely. This suggests that local communities (and their 'local experts') should be left alone to develop their own approaches to the challenges they face. Local politicians in the Copperbelt water management conflicts (see Kazimbaya-Senkwe and Lubambo's account in Chapter 9) certainly held to this view, although they welcomed external funding. But such arguments are not just about the struggles of local actors against powerful exogenous forces. There may also be real differences of perspective within a local context that need to be explored. In Chapter 7, Perera shows how an engineering perspective on regional settlement patterns, provided by outside experts, was eventually displaced by a locally developed perspective that emphasised working with local institutions and agents to organise the design and location of settlements. This action-oriented perspective has been widely promoted, as Perera acknowledges, by the international consultant and educator, Otto Koenigsberger, who figures in the chapters of both Vidyarthi and Ward. Other studies of the conflict between outside and local experts also highlight the way that local actors may seek to protect their own business and land interests when faced with suggestions of taking a more regional view of a city, or of paying attention to popular housing rather than the embellishment of a city centre (see, for example, Verdeil 2003, and, from the rural development field, Mosse 2004). In such cases, outside experts 'disturb' local perspectives and encourage wider debate about urban futures, which may add strength to previously marginalised perspectives. Zhu, in Chapter 12, argues that South-East Asian countries urgently need to give more attention to the experiences of Singapore and China in managing burgeoning urban growth if many urban millions are to achieve more liveable and sustainable living environments.

It is not, therefore, the interplay of endogenous and exogenous planning ideas and practices that needs to be challenged as such, but crude transfer and limited adaptation. Following Roy's argument in Chapter 2, the appropriation of potentially useful ideas and technologies by powerful global aid agencies needs to be scrutinised critically,[28] as does the tendency for some powerful local groups to appropriate planning ideas and denude them of their original moral compass and intellectual justification. The exchange of planning ideas and practices in specific situations is thus best understood as a site of struggle – struggle to probe sufficiently deeply to learn enough, struggle to capture how ideas are developed and used, and struggle between competing groups for control of future place qualities.

It is here that academics working in the planning field, who read books such as this one and contribute to journals such as *Planning Theory and Practice,* have an important role to play. One contribution is to use theories and concepts as critical lenses through which to probe the claims about causes and consequences used to support planning ideas. Another is to provide critical analyses of specific experiences. These help to identify different ways of exploring the relation between ideas, practices and outcomes. Such analyses may suggest different concepts that may help in this probing work, or provide clues as to what to look out for when someone asks for advice about a problem. Academic work may also help in consolidating experience in critical, carefully analysed ways.[29] This places a strong moral obligation on academics, just as much as on those working on a specific assignment as an expert adviser. It is easy to be critical. What is more difficult is to be critically constructive, sensitive to the nuances of local particulars while keeping an eye open for the possibilities of creating new chances and new understandings to enrich the resources available in a specific situation.

## ACTORS, EXPERTISE AND ETHICS

Exploring the complex interchange of planning ideas and practices transnationally makes it difficult to avoid developing a sensitivity to institutional and cultural differences in the way that planning work is done in different parts of the world. It also encourages a search for structural explanations of both apparently common patterns and what seem to be major differences. But the planning field, with its concern for practices as well as ideas, is also always interested in planners as actors, that is, in the work of agency. As analysts, planning researchers who study transnational exchange experiences may focus on both 'carriers' of ideas about planning from one situation to another and those who get involved in adapting exogenous ideas to local circumstances. Ward's chapter looks at the former, as do those by Whitzman and Perkovic and by Vidyarthi, whereas Perera discusses the struggles of local experts to develop and find political space for their own approaches. The field of planning history and biography is rich in such studies. Abramson (Chapter 13) and Friedmann (Chapter 14) provide examples from their own biographies. These studies and comments illustrate the diverse roles, motivations, forms of expertise and moral commitments that carriers and adaptors display. They show the finegrain tensions that arise as 'outsider' perspectives and practices confront 'insider' ways of thinking and acting, and underline the importance of the resultant learning, which erodes simple dualistic distinctions between 'outsiders' and 'insiders'.

But there is another way of looking at outsiders and insiders that has been given prominence in the planning field by researchers such as John Forester and Charles Hoch.[30] This contrasts the perspective of the 'outside observer', who comments on what practitioners do, with that of the 'insider practitioner', the actual agent doing planning work. Academics, in their scholarly writing, make reference to trajectories of ideas and debates within and around their 'disciplines'. Those actively engaged in planning practices need always to keep in mind the specific institutional context in which those who employ their services are situated and which contribute to setting the parameters of the tasks they engage in. In the present book, Kazimbaya-Senkwe and Lubambo, Whitzman and Perkovic, Perera, Abramson and Friedmann draw on their experiences of this latter position, recasting them into a scholarly form, drawing out the contextual factors that helped to shape what they did and reflecting on the difference these factors made. But as 'insiders', that is, those involved in the flow of 'practising' – working out what to pay attention to, what to suggest and how to act, and making continual judgements with potential troubling consequences – their position at the time of their practice was not the same as that of observing academics, who draw on 'cases' to illustrate more general phenomena. Although many academics act both as practitioners and as academics, in our practice roles we hone what we know and grasp to the precise particulars of a situation in order to work out what to suggest, to whom to suggest it, what to do and how to act. In our academic work, or in any writing *about* practices, we draw out the particulars of cases and experiences to contribute to some wider understanding, making connections to referents within academic discussions about the relative merits of different interpretations and concepts. As academics or practitioners, we have moral commitments too, which orient our thinking about what should be valued and what criticised about particular instances of practice. But practitioners cannot spend their time debating and clarifying these issues before they 'go into the field', although most will have done some scoping and probing work before they embark on a task. They have to set their moral compass and do their intellectual probing in the flow of their work, as they work out what to notice, what to say and how to say it. They learn 'on the job', through practising.

One answer to the challenge of the practice experience, advocated some time ago by Argyris and Schon (1974), was to become a 'reflective practitioner' (Schon 1983), continually reviewing one's own performance and re-adjusting it in the light of experience, thus doing 'theory in practice'. This is never an easy task, even for the practitioner who works for many years in the same position and place. In such situations, the 'bundle of expertise' that a practitioner works with may become well honed to local particularities without needing to be probed for implicit assumptions and values. Yet this very honing process may make it difficult to understand sudden challenges that bring those assumptions into question. Experts who move from place to place soon realise that many of their initial assumptions need revision, as Ward shows in his account of planning consultants operating internationally, and as is evident in Abramson and Friedmann's accounts of their own experiences. But it may be very difficult to understand the depth of re-assessment that may be needed. This can affect at a very broad level how planning practitioners and academics come to understand the issues they deal with when working in contexts very different from their own. Those trained in Western cultural contexts, for example, may have great difficulty in recognising the distinctive shape that the traditions of Greek philosophy, as re-worked into Christian principles and re-worked again in the Enlightenment period, have given to the ways they make arguments, express values and reach agreements – all important dimensions of doing planning work. More specifically, unexplored assumptions may affect very detailed issues in planning work, such as how an expert thinks about land rights or a regulatory instrument. What may seem 'universal' about rights and regulations often turns out to be culture specific, or grounded in one of the several legal traditions to be found in the world (Glenn 2007). In other words, although 'travelling experts' soon learn to be reflective practitioners, they may find it hard to probe deeply enough into their bundle of assumptions to see how these affect what they notice and the judgements they make. For this reason alone, a critical examination of the internationalisation of the academic and practitioner 'community of planners' is worth promoting, to help probe more deeply and perceptively into the bundle of 'expertise' about the planning field that we all carry around with us. As Sanyal argues (Chapter 15), we all, academics and practitioners alike, need to look beyond our own accustomed practices not only to perceive our differences better, but also to recognise the commonalities we share through our interest in the planning field.

## BUILDING A CRITICAL, REFLECTIVE GLOBAL
## PLANNING COMMUNITY

This book, like the journal *Planning Theory and Practice*, is a contribution to expanding and deepening the horizons and imaginations of those engaged in the international flow of planning ideas and experiences of practice. This project is not about creating a global hegemonic discourse in the planning field. Instead, the ambition is to enrich the resources available to the overlapping knowledge circuits in which planners participate, and to cultivate critical exchange and debate through which crude hegemonies can be challenged (as Roy in the next chapter demands). Not only will this help to unravel the constraints that the hegemony of Western ideas has placed on our thinking about the nature, purpose and method of planning, it should also contribute to an internal renewal of planning debate in the 'old heartlands' of planning ideas in North America and Europe. What has been striking to me in editing the journal, in the enterprise of this book, and in other arenas in which planning academics from different parts of the world meet up is the intellectual energy that is being released through these encounters.[31] This energy is not only providing rich insights into the diversity of experiences, and enlarging our understanding of the range of dimensions that need to be taken into account to enable us to grasp the uniqueness of specific instances of planning work. It is also sharpening and directing more shrewdly our probing into the 'taken-for-granted' material that is hidden in the depths of our bundles of understanding about planning activity, what it is for and how it is done. 'Learning from other countries', as advocated by Masser and Williams (1986) a quarter of a century ago, if done with a critical imagination, is good for all of us.

Such work in the academic corners of the planning field is especially important at the present time, which has seen renewed energy in establishing global arenas for the interchange of planning ideas.[32] Public policy has been turning more strongly to the planning field for its emphasis on the livability and sustainability of places and territories. Such a trend is likely to continue despite and perhaps because of the economic crises of the late 2000s, because it is closely linked to the experience of an urbanised existence. This political and practical attention needs a vigorous and critical academic contribution to accompany it. Without this, there is always a danger that crudely crafted general ideas will gain hegemonic prominence. Instead, what is needed is encouragement to cultivate the challenging and probing work that enhances the overall 'intelligence' of the planning community.[33]

In this book, we have only been able to open a window on the issues that a critical academic contribution can raise in probing the transnational flow of planning ideas and their appropriation and translation into specific practices. As editors, Robert Upton and I hope that the encounter with the various authors will encourage others to expand such work. However, taken as a whole, the chapters offer suggestions about some of the qualities of the 'intelligence' that it would be helpful to develop in the planning community in the present period. One is a positive attitude towards the plurality of ways of understanding people–place relations, which I have suggested is at the core of the field. This means continuing the present openness to developing knowledge from other academic fields, as far as this is relevant to the challenge of understanding and acting to improve people's lives in sustainable ways and in particular places. A second goal is to recognise the complex ways in which the specific, the unique and the 'local' are intertwined with broader processes, general forces and 'globalising' tendencies. This suggests that it is important to move beyond the opposition between the 'structural' and 'agency' perspectives that dominated much planning debate in the 1970s and 1980s. Instead, what is needed to understand the diversity of practices encompassed in the planning field is an appreciation of the dynamic interaction between active agency and the development of systemic (structural) forces that come to shape how agents act. There are many theoretical contributions to choose from in this 'in-between' area, and energetic debate goes on about their relative merits.

Such attention to plurality and to structure–agency interaction should help in enhancing the intellectual sharpness and robustness of the planning field. But what about its moral compass? Many accounts of the diffusion of planning ideas note the way that values associated with a concept may get shorn off as they travel, and get re-interpreted and adapted in new contexts, particularly the more radical dimensions (see the chapters by Sorensen, and Whitzman and Perkovic). This is sometimes a positive action, aiding the domestication of exogenous ideas. Yet, as I argued at the start of this chapter, the planning field has always been motivated by certain values centred on improving the place-based conditions in which we humans live in the world. So maybe, and to accompany the recognition of the diversity of philosophies, cultures, politico-institutional dynamics and configurations of instances of practice, we also need to cultivate debates about the values that the planning field should promote, and how these might be manifest in the circulation of planning ideas and knowledge of diverse practices. As Sanyal argues, in our diversity we do, nevertheless, inhabit one world, and we need to care about its future, both in its unities and in its diversities. We know so much more now than a century ago about our interconnectedness. So maybe, as a planning community, we should have the courage to promote more shared debate on what it means, in our particular 'heres' and 'theres', to encourage a development that enhances the chances of the flourishing of the many, not just the few, and which reduces the stresses and strains that twentieth-century development has created for our planet and our relations with the rest of nature.

## NOTES

1   My thanks to Robert Upton, chapter authors, Zann Gunn, Gareth Relphs and Francesca Raphaely for helpful comments on earlier drafts of this chapter.
2   Accounts of urban development in Syria in Roman times, and of mediaeval travellers in the Muslim world, bring this out very clearly (see Butcher 2003; Mackintosh-Smith 2002).
3   I imply by this metaphor that it includes many phenomena and relations, and that it has only vaguely delimited and porous borders.
4   Ward (2002) lists terms used in the more developed world a century ago: 'city planning' (US), 'town planning' (UK), '*stadtebau*' (Germany), '*urbanisme*' (France) and '*Toshi Keikatu*' (Japan). See Williams (1996) for an account of the difficulties of translating 'planning' within the European Union.
5   See Faludi (1973) for such arguments.
6   Reflecting an increasing awareness in the field of public policy analysis of the significance of the institutional context of policy formation and practices, a number of terms have come into use to describe the various networks of relations that build up in and around a policy field. The term 'policy community' (Rhodes 1997) refers to a range of actors who cluster around formation and implementation processes in a particular area of public policy. 'Epistemic communities' is used by Haas (1992) to describe those who share a common knowledge base, as in an academic discipline. Wenger (1998) introduced the term 'communities of practice' to refer to the practices of work groups. All such groups have 'cultures', in terms of assumptions and ways of doing things, which are often taken for granted. The concept of a 'planning culture' may perhaps best be understood as evolving through infusions from all three forms of 'community' noted above.
7   The term 'governance' is a contested one in contemporary political science. Here I use it to refer to the broad area of expectations and practices of collective action, following Le Galès (2002).
8   Although the relation between these activities in the planning field is often 'sticky', with academics and practitioners commenting on the distance between them.
9   CIAM stands for Congrès Internationale pour Architecture et Urbanisme, but is usually known by its acronym.
10  See, for example, Alterman (1988, 2001), Booth (1996) and Davies *et al.* (1989).
11  Germany was a particularly influential source of ideas for Japanese planners (Sorensen 2002; Hein 2003). In contrast to this experience, a planning consultant working in North Africa, reading this chapter in draft, noted that northern European approaches to 'master planning' were being used there, without any attention to the administrative and legal underpinnings that would lend such plans any practical influence. Master planning is also used as a description of practice by many post-structural analysts (Hillier 2010).
12  The term 'assemblage' is leaking into the planning field from the anthropological and archaeological analysis of material cultures. It refers to what can be found together, although the linkages between what is found may not necessarily be clear.
13  See Tait and Jensen (2007), and for concepts of translation as developed in actor-network theory more generally see Callon (1986).

14  Namely Larry Beasley, formerly city planner for Vancouver City Council, and Alessandro Balducci, of the Politecnico di Milano, who has experience of strategic planning in the Milan area.

15  Ward (2002) uses the term 'milieux'. I use the English term 'culture' more or less as a synonym.

16  See Jenks *et al.* (1996), and for a recent review essay of the literature on 'green cities', etc. see Daniels (2008).

17  The German geographer, Walter Christaller, was the pioneer of this analysis of the urban and rural settlement system, known as 'central place theory'.

18  See in particular the work of Patrick Geddes (1915/1968).

19  A great deal of the 'planning theory' discussion that has built up since the mid-twentieth century has been about such questions of method. See Hillier and Healey (2008). It would be valuable to have more studies of the diffusion of such ideas.

20  The metaphor of planning activity as a drama is taken from the related fields of political science and policy analysis, through work such as Majone (1987) and Hajer (2005).

21  See also Ward (2002).

22  See Nilsson (2007) and Young (2000).

23  See, for example, the International Council for Local Environmental Initiatives (ICLEI), the World Urban Forum, the International Federation of Housing and Planning (IFHP), the International Society of City and Regional Planners (ISOCARP), and recent initiatives linked to the World Planning Forum, serviced by the British Royal Town Planning Institute (RTPI).

24  Ward (2002) reminds his readers that, a century ago, French was as influential a language of international exchange in the planning field as English, and remains an official language of the UN. The competitors for English today are Spanish and Chinese, although increasing amounts of Chinese planning material are now being provided in English and vice versa. The Spanish-speaking world provides links to the much wider world of languages rooted in Latin.

25  This has often struck me as I read papers submitted to academic journals. My own understanding of both planning ideas and planning practices has been greatly influenced by researching and teaching in Latin America, Western Europe, West Africa and the United States.

26  My thanks to Zann Gunn for pointing this out to me.

27  Watts recounted this story in a Masters Programme presentation at Oxford Polytechnic/ Oxford Brookes University some time in the early 1980s, where I was then located, but I regret I cannot remember the precise occasion.

28  See also Cooke and Kothari (2001) for a critique of the way that 'participation' was taken up in the rural development field.

29  Rather than through the currently fashionable 'mantras' of 'best practice manuals', which tend to ignore contextual assumptions and specificities.

30  See Forester (1999) and Hoch (1994).

31  See, for example, Roy's article in the recent special issue of the journal *Planning Theory*, which she edited (Roy 2009).

32  See the World Urban Forum, the recent UN-Habitat Global Report on Urban Planning (UN-Habitat 2009), the World Planning Schools Association and the new Global Planners Network.

33  This is a reference to pragmatist John Dewey's conception of cultivating democratic practices (Dewey 1927/1991).

## REFERENCES

Alterman, R. (Ed.) (1988) *Private supply of public services: evaluation of real estate exactions, linkage, and alternative land policies*, New York University Press, New York.

Alterman, R. (Ed.) (2001) *National level planning in democratic countries: an international comparison of city and regional policy-making*, Liverpool University Press, Liverpool.

Argyris, C. and Schon, D. (1974) *Theory in practice*, Jossey-Bass, San Francisco.

Banerjee, T. (2009) 'U.S. planning expeditions to postcolonial India: from ideology to innovation in technical assistance'. *Journal of the American Planning Association*, **75**, 193–208.

Birch, E. L. and Silver, C. (2009) 'One hundred years of city planning's enduring and evolving connections'. *Journal of the American Planning Association*, **75**, 113–22 and special issue.

Booth, P. (1996) *Controlling development: certainty and discretion in Europe, the USA and Hong Kong*, UCL Press, London.

Briggs, X. da S. (2008) *Democracy as problem-solving*, MIT Press, Boston.

Butcher, K. (2003) *Roman Syria and the Near East*, British Museum Press, London.

Callon, M. (1986) 'Some elements of a sociology of translation: domestication of scallops and fisherman in St. Brieuc Bay'. In *Power, action and belief* (Ed. Law, J.), Routledge and Kegan Paul, London, pp. 196–233.

Committee for Spatial Development (CSD) (1999) *The European Spatial Development Perspective*, Luxembourg, European Commission.

Cooke, B. and Kothari, U. (Eds.) (2001) *Participation: the new tyranny*, Zed Books, London.

Daniels, T. (2008) 'Review essay: works on green cities: from potential to imperative'. *Journal of the American Planning Association*, **74**, 521–2.

Davies, H. W. E., Edwards, D., Hooper, A. and Punter, J. (1989) *Development control in Western Europe*, HMSO, London.

Dewey, J. (1927/1991) *The public and its problems*, Swallow Press/Ohio University Press, Athens, OH.

Fainstein, S. (2005) 'Cities and diversity: should we plan for it? Can we plan for it?' *Urban Affairs Review*, **41**, 3–19.

Faludi, A. (1973) *Planning theory*, Pergamon Press, Oxford.

Faludi, A. and Waterhout, B. (Eds.) (2002) *The making of the European Spatial Development Perspective*, Routledge, London.

Forester, J. (1999) *The deliberative practitioner: encouraging participatory planning processes*, MIT Press, London.

Friedmann, J. (2000) 'The good city: in defense of utopian thinking'. *International Journal of Urban and Regional Research*, **24**, 473–89.

Geddes, P. (1915/1968) *Cities in evolution*, Ernest Benn Ltd, London.

Glenn, H. P. (2000/2007) *Legal traditions of the world*, Oxford University Press, Oxford.

Grant, J. (2006) *Planning the good community: new urbanism in theory and practice*, Routledge, London.

Haas, P. M. (1992) 'Introduction: epistemic communities and international policy co-ordination'. *International Organization*, **46**, 1–35.

Hajer, M. (2005) 'Setting the stage: a dramaturgy of policy deliberation'. *Administration and Society*, **36**, 624–47.

Hein, C. (2003) 'The transformation of planning ideas in Japan and its colonies'. In *Urbanism: imported or exported: native aspirations and foreign plans* (Eds. Nasr, J. and Volait, M.), Wiley-Academy, Chichester, pp. 51–82.

Hillier, J. (2010) *Conceptual challenges in planning theory: introduction to Part 11*, Ashgate, Aldershot.

Hillier, J. and Healey, P. (Eds.) (2008) *Critical readings in planning theory* (three volumes), Ashgate, Aldershot, Hants.

Hoch, C. (1994) *What planners do*, Planners Press, Chicago.

Jenks, M., Burton, E. and Williams, K. (Eds.) (1996) *The compact city: a sustainable urban form?*, E and FN Spon, London.

Kingdon, J. W. (2003) *Agendas, alternatives, and public policies*, Longman, New York.

Le Galès, P. (2002) *European cities: social conflicts and governance*, Oxford University Press, Oxford.

Mackintosh-Smith, T. (2002) *The travels of Ibn Battutah*, Picador, London.

Majone, G. (1987) *Evidence, argument and persuasion in the policy process*, Yale University Press, New Haven, CT.

Marshall, T. (Ed.) (2004) *Transforming Barcelona*, Routledge, London.

Masser, I. and Williams, R. (Eds.) (1986) *Learning from other countries*, Geo Books, Norwich.

Mosse, D. (2004) 'Is good policy unimplementable? Reflections on the ethnography of aid policy and practice'. *Development and Change*, **35**, 639–71.

Nasr, J. and Volait, M. (Eds.) (2003) *Urbanism: imported or exported? Native aspirations and foreign plans*, Wiley-Academy, Chichester.

Nilsson, K. L. (2007) 'Managing complex spatial processes'. *Planning Theory and Practice*, **8**, 431–47.

Rhodes, R. A. W. (1997) *Understanding governance: policy networks, governance, reflexivity and accountability*, Open University Press, Milton Keynes.

Roy, A. (2009) 'Strangely familiar: planning and the worlds of insurgence and informality'. *Planning Theory*, **8** (1), 7–11.

Sanyal, B. (Ed.) (2005) *Comparative planning cultures*, Routledge, London.

Schon, D. (1983) *The reflective practitioner*, Basic Books, New York.

Sorensen, A. (2002) *The making of urban Japan*, Routledge, New York.

Sutcliffe, A. (1981) *Towards the planned city: Germany, Britain, the United States and France, 1780–1914*, Blackwell, Oxford.

Tait, M. and Jensen, O. (2007) 'Travelling Ideas, power and place: the cases of urban villages and business improvement districts'. *International Planning Studies*, **12**, 107–28.

UN-Habitat (2009) *Planning sustainable cities: global report on human settlements 2009*, Earthscan, London.

Verdeil, E. (2003) 'Politics, ideology and professional interests: foreign versus local planners in Lebanon under President Chehab'. In *Urbanism: imported or exported? Native aspirations and foreign plans* (Eds Nasr, J. and Volait, M.), Wiley-Academic, Chichester, pp. 290–315.

Wannop, U. (1995) *The regional imperative: regional planning and governance in Britain, Europe and the United States*, Jessica Kingsley, London.

Ward, S. (2002) *Planning in the twentieth century: the advanced capitalist world*, Wiley, London.

Watson, V. (2008) 'Down to earth: linking planning theory and practice to the "metropole" and beyond'. *International Planning Studies*, **13**, 223–37.

Wenger, E. (1998) *Communities of practice: learning, meaning and identity*, Cambridge University Press, Cambridge.

Williams, R. H. W. (1996) *European Union spatial policy and planning*, Paul Chapman Publishing, London.

Young, S. C. (2000) 'Participation strategies and local environmental politics: Local Agenda 21'. In *The new politics of British local governance* (Ed. Stoker, G.), Macmillan, Basingstoke, pp. 181–97.

CHAPTER 2

# POVERTY TRUTHS

## The Politics of Knowledge in the New Global Order of Development

### Ananya Roy

## Prologue: ideas are also weapons

This chapter is premised on the provocation that planning, as a field and discipline, runs the risk of being irrelevant to the key issues and debates of the twenty-first century. The most urgent of these twenty-first-century issues are climate change and poverty. This essay focuses on poverty, with particular attention to how, in the new millennium, a global conscience and mandate to alleviate poverty has emerged. But this global consensus is also an articulation of power, including the power to determine the key ideas and practices of development, to shape and disseminate "poverty truths." In this essay, I chart the formation of a new hegemony on poverty, paying attention to how some poverty interventions, such as microfinance, are promoted as a panacea. I argue that the diffusion of poverty truths is inextricably linked to the diffusion of capital. Such circuits of knowledge, power and capital point to how "ideas are also weapons" (Marcos 2000, unpaginated). This stunning statement, sent to the world from the struggles in Chiapas, indicates that the hegemony of certain world views and knowledge paradigms has crucial implications for the organization of space, resources, opportunity, and justice – in short, what we may call planning. Yet neither the millennial issue of global poverty nor the struggle over "poverty truths" has entered current planning discourses. There is a persistent disjuncture between the concerns of planning, including its articulation of social justice, and the fierce battle of ideas that is raging about the new millennium and poverty. This chapter seeks to remedy this disjuncture by foregrounding the articulation and contestation of "poverty truths." In doing so, it not only makes the case for planning's role in the twenty-first century but also highlights how a study of circuits of truth and capital must serve as the prelude to planning action.

## Millennial development

There is nothing new about a concern for poverty. At various historical moments, poverty has become visible, served as a lightning rod for social action and change, and assumed prominence as a public issue. But at such moments poverty has usually been understood as a local issue – as in the anxieties about urban poverty in the late nineteenth century that led Anglo-American planners to regulate and reform spaces of poverty: the tenement, the slum, the immigrant settlement. Urban planning, as we know it today, was forged in the crucible of such encounters with poverty. Or, at other times, poverty has been interpreted as a national concern – as in the modernization theorems that underpinned the institutional framework of international development which was established at the close of World War II. At rare moments, poverty has become visible as a global issue, stirring a collective conscience and setting into motion global campaigns that seek to alleviate poverty. This turn of the century is such a moment, when, with great drama, poverty has become one of the most pressing public issues of global sweep (matched only, perhaps, by climate change).

This new concern about poverty lies at the heart of a new global order of development, which emerged from the confluence of various forces. In the 1990s, the World Bank, under James Wolfensohn, made the alleviation of poverty its top priority (Mallaby 2004), thereby echoing a previous era of development: the World Bank that was headed by Robert McNamara in the 1970s and which emphasized basic needs and "redistribution with growth" (Finnemore 1997).[1] In 2000, the member states of the United Nations adopted the Millennium Development Goals, with their explicit emphasis on human development and poverty reduction. Further, 2008 was the United Nations' year of the "bottom billion," seeking to draw attention to the billion or so people living in extreme poverty, on less than US$1 a day. A flurry of international non-governmental organizations (NGOs), global philanthropic foundations and global campaigns today target poverty, the largest of them commanding resources, power, and influence that far exceed the scope of most nation-states. Also present is a global terrain of social action and mobilization that fiercely protests the status quo of development and trade, and calls for an overhaul of global economic and governance systems. Often billed as anti-globalization, these movements are better understood as seeking to articulate the ideas and practices through which, as the World Social Forum motto reads, "another world is possible" (unpaginated). "Millennial development" then is an ensemble of complex and often contradictory forces, but one that is unified by a global conscience about poverty and the call for global forms of action to alleviate poverty.

This chapter takes a closer look at millennial development, this ensemble of ideas and institutional forces that has sought to globalize the mandate to alleviate poverty. Although there are important questions to be asked and answered about whether or not millennial development works and whom it benefits, I am concerned here with a different set of questions. Instead of asking whether poverty is being alleviated, or whether the policies of millennial development are a success, I ask some fundamental questions that must come first: What are the dominant ideas about poverty and poverty alleviation? Whose ideas are these, and how did they become dominant? Are there alternative ideas and, if so, how may we learn about and from them? In other words, this chapter is concerned with the politics of knowledge, with how "ideas are also weapons."

In particular, my research, and this chapter, examines one idea that has acquired significant popularity and recognition: microfinance, the practice of providing tiny enterprise loans and other financial services to very poor people, mainly women, without collateral, at high interest rates but with a proven record of high repayment.[2] Microfinance is a development concept that originated in the global South, specifically in the Grameen Bank of Bangladesh founded by Muhammad Yunus in 1976, but which has rapidly spread. Today, microfinance is a ubiquitous idea, lauded and deployed by development institutions of all stripes and varying ideologies as an important antidote to poverty. The United Nations celebrated 2005 as the year of microcredit. The Grameen Bank and Muhammad Yunus, its founder, won the 2006 Nobel Peace Prize, with the Prize committee recognizing this effort:

> to create economic and social development from below. Lasting peace cannot be achieved unless large population groups find ways in which to break out of poverty. Micro-credit is one such means. Development from below also serves to advance democracy and human rights.
>
> (Mjøs 2006, unpaginated)

In this chapter, I analyze the "globalization" of the microfinance idea, the mainstreaming of microfinance, and the implications of this hegemony. But I am also concerned with formations of counter-hegemony and how these other interpretations of microfinance may present an alternative, and possibly more productive, engagement with poverty. In short, exploring the case of microfinance leads us to a broader story about the structure of development and the politics of knowledge. It is important to note that microfinance is not the development concept on which the most money is spent (here, infrastructure still rules). Nor is it the sector comprising the most international or local NGOs (many other issues are more common – health, human rights, women). But microfinance is everywhere; it exists in the sub-terrain of almost everything in development. This chapter then is an archaeology of ideas, with microfinance providing the occasion to burrow deep into the sub-terrain of hegemony and power.

## A WASHINGTON CONSENSUS ON POVERTY

The globalization of microfinance has been under way for a while now. In the 1980s, as the legend of the Grameen Bank spread, so there was an intriguing reversal of development practices both in the global South and in North America, with "First World" leaders like Bill Clinton advocating the adoption of this "Third World" model in poverty alleviation efforts. In the world of development, the Grameen Bank is today a household name and microfinance is seen as a "fail-safe" product. The Grameen Bank itself has actively promoted the replication of its microfinance model, often directly financing and supporting such programs across the world, from Egypt to the Philippines. But, more recently, the globalization of microfinance has taken on a distinctive form, one that wrenches microfinance away from the Grameen Bank context and rebrands it as "financial services for the poor." Microfinance can thus be understood as a chip or microprocessor in the circuits of capital and truth that constitute development.

Although microfinance was already a popular idea among US presidents, especially Clinton, its adoption by the World Bank indicates a legitimacy for this Southern idea in the Northern institutions of development. This adoption is marked by the formation, in 1995, of an unusual development institution: the Consultative Group to Assist the Poor (CGAP). A consortium of mainly Northern bilateral and multilateral donors, CGAP is housed in the World Bank and wholly focused on microfinance. CGAP is an interesting articulation of World Bank priorities under Wolfensohn. First, it marks a formal commitment to the poverty agenda. It also signals the ways in which Wolfensohn sought to consolidate the role of the World Bank as a "knowledge bank." Although Wolfensohn's Comprehensive Development Framework was meant to prioritize poverty as well as local participation in, and country ownership of, poverty reduction strategies, it also promoted the World Bank's monopoly on developmental knowledge (Cammack 2004). CGAP was thus to provide "donor coordination" in microfinance (Wolfensohn 2000: 5), a rather bureaucratic turn of phrase for what is in fact a formidable apparatus of knowledge production, more concerned with agenda setting than with actual budget allocations. Today, CGAP produces and disseminates authoritative knowledge about microfinance globally. It is the CGAP agenda and its "key principles of microfinance" that are endorsed at G8 summits; it is CGAP that establishes "performance-based benchmarks"; it is CGAP best practices that are taken up by practitioners around the world; in short, it is CGAP that creates what is tantamount to a "Washington consensus" on poverty. The term "Washington consensus" derives from Williamson's (1990) depiction of the self-evident nature of free-market truths. The term is more broadly interpreted to mean a period of neoliberal hegemony exercised by Washington-based institutions such as the International Monetary Fund (IMF) and the World Bank and manifested in policies such as structural adjustment, privatization, and deregulation. Thus, the Wolfensohn years of the World Bank, with their concern for poverty and human development, came to be known as the "post-Washington consensus" (Stiglitz 1998; Fine *et al.* 2001). I argue that agenda-setting institutions such as CGAP control the portals of knowledge for a new global order, millennial development, which must therefore be understood as a Washington consensus, this time focused on poverty rather than on the free market. I also argue that this Washington consensus on poverty revives and reworks certain "key truths" about "the market," thereby extending rather than eroding neoliberal hegemony.

The hallmark of the Washington consensus on poverty is the financialization of development, the effort to turn development practices such as microfinance into sites of financial investment and profit. CGAP argues not only that access to financial services is critical for poverty alleviation, but also that such access is possible primarily through financial markets, that finance for the poor must be fully integrated into mainstream markets. Although the CGAP mission statement emphasizes the role of "local, deposit-driven markets," it is clear that the broader context is one in which lending to the poor is increasingly imagined as a "global financial markets instrument."[3] Indeed, microfinance can be thought of as a sub-prime market, with high interest lending to the otherwise financially "untouchable" poor. Yet as other sub-prime markets, such as the redlined US housing mortgage market, have collapsed, microfinance, with its high repayment rates and skilful management of risk, seems to be of growing interest to Wall Street and other financial markets (Parker 2008). Thus, in a World Bank interview conducted in 2006, Elizabeth Littlefield, the Executive Director of CGAP, noted the following:

> Microfinance has actually matured into one of the most successful and fastest-growing industries in the world. In Africa alone, its growth is probably second only to that of cell phone use . . . Worldwide, these leading microfinance institutions are nearly twice as profitable as the world's leading commercial banks.
>
> (World Bank 2006, unpaginated)

In the year of the "bottom billion," the billion dollar question then is whether microfinance will become an "asset class." Will it be what Paul Wolfowitz (2007, unpaginated) – the neo-conservative architect of the Iraq War, appointed to the World Bank presidency by George W. Bush, and then forced out of office on corruption charges – in his resignation statement, termed "frontier markets"?

But building an "asset class," and constructing markets, takes work. Here the knowledge-producing role of CGAP is central. For example, in order to forge new frontiers of capital accumulation, to mobilize these emerging markets of sub-prime borrowers, it is necessary to map risk. The microfinance model of the Grameen Bank is predicated on a very careful management of risk through peer groups, gendered discipline, and the presence of a massive NGO in village life. To develop new financial markets that are no longer embedded in such institutional forms, it is necessary to also invent new technologies of risk management. Through institutions such as the Microfinance Information Exchange (MIX), through "performance-based benchmarking," through the data transparency provided by information technology, and more generally through an emphasis on financial sustainability, CGAP seeks to map and minimize risk. Such risk management techniques are applied not only to individual consumers but also to microfinance organizations (MFIs) themselves, rating them through various performance indicators in order to chart their potential as investment sites for global funds. As new financial vehicles, viz. microfinance investment funds, have emerged to seize the opportunity of this "frontier market," so the pace of ratings, benchmarkings, and rankings has intensified. Standard & Poor's Managing Director for Latin American Corporate & Government Ratings puts it thus:

> In the past, the lack of consistent, globally accepted metrics for analyzing MFIs has hindered investment at a time when microfinance has been growing at a substantial rate. To unlock these sources of capital in both international and domestic markets, investors require transparent and globally accepted credit analysis.
>
> (PR Newswire 2008, unpaginated)

Ironically for a sector that targets the poor, the terms of this "credit analysis" are much less about impacts on poverty than they are about financial capacity. Thus, a recent Forbes ranking of the world's "Top Microfinance Institutions" focused on four categories: scale, efficiency, portfolio risk, and profitability (Swibel 2007). In this "wild, wild West" of finance and development the big players are inevitably Wall Street players, the investment banks that can manage and profit from a global "asset class."

But whereas the neoliberal rhetoric of the 1980s emphasized the efficiency benefits of a lean and mean free market in contrast to a bloated public sector, the rhetoric of millennial development is as much concerned with equity as it is with efficiency. The CGAP mission statement, while insisting on the role of financial markets, also insists on the need to achieve both equity and efficiency. Crucially, the financialization of development proceeds today in the name of the "democratization of capital," and thus presents a microfinance "revolution" (Robinson 2001). It is worth taking a closer look at these claims and the key analytical ideas that undergird them. One in particular stands out: a theory of markets.

## MARKETS WORK (SORT OF)

The shift from the neoliberalism of the 1980s to the millennial development of the 1990s is marked by a transition in ideas within international development institutions – from "market fundamentalism" to "market failure." Epitomized by the work of Joseph Stiglitz, the Washington insider turned critic, this transformation of the intellectual landscape is significant. Stiglitz's Nobel Prize-winning work in institutional economics is concerned with the information problems of markets – the argument that incomplete information, asymmetries in information, and incomplete contracts are all features of markets; that markets are not perfect; and that market failure must be considered seriously in economic theory and policy. But in his commentaries on development, Stiglitz goes further, rejecting the Washington consensus of the 1980s as "market fundamentalism." He argues that markets fail, and that they particularly fail in providing "global public goods" (Stiglitz 1999). Not only does this stunt economic growth, it also creates severe inequities in the distribution of income. For Stiglitz, development is not simply an increase in GDP; it also entails "democratic, equitable, and sustainable development" (Stiglitz 1999: 587). And he is clear: markets alone cannot deliver these outcomes. A similar conception of market failure attends the work of Jeffrey Sachs (2005), for whom a Keynesian or Rostowian-style "Big Push" is necessary to end the "poverty trap."

At first glance, the emphasis on "market failure" seems to indicate a sharp rupture between the free-market ideologies of the neoliberal 1980s and the "kinder and gentler" ethos of millennial development. Is millennial development then a post-neoliberal global order? Is it a radical break with the faith in markets? My discussion of CGAP and microfinance markets clearly indicates that this is not the case. Rather than a *rejection* of markets, millennial development is more appropriately understood as a *reform* of markets. Thus, an especially popular concept in the world of microfinance is the "double bottom line," the idea that microfinance can produce both social returns and financial returns (Tulchin 2003). Here then is a sense of "embedded" markets, markets that, following Polanyi (1944), can be understood to be subject to social control and scrutiny, a "society with markets" rather than a "market society." How is this social logic to be theorized and named? As Fine (2001: 136) notes, for this new consensus, "social capital" is the dream concept; understood as institutions or customs or culture, it is seen to be "the non-market response to market imperfections." Whereas the French sociologist Bourdieu put forward a theory of social capital as a logic of hierarchy, exploitation, and stratification, for the theorists and practitioners of millennial development it is a benign, enabling set of rituals, norms, and exchanges (Rankin 2002). The World Bank defines social capital as:

the institutions, relationships, and norms that shape the quality and quantity of a society's social interactions. Increasing evidence shows that social cohesion is critical for societies to prosper economically and for development to be sustainable. Social capital is not just the sum of the institutions which underpin a society – it is the glue that holds them together.

(World Bank undated, unpaginated)

The success of microcredit is thus ascribed to social capital and the ability of MFIs to mobilize it in order to create institutional structures (Woolcock 1998).

But the frontiers of millennial development are in fact also concerned with "market societies." Robinson's argument about the "democratization of capital" is not one that is concerned with the reform of markets or with forms of collective action that remedy market failure. Rather, it is an argument about the virtues of markets, including financial markets. Microfinance is seen to be a "revolution" simply because it indicates that these markets can also work for the poor. Such ideas of market populism are most authoritatively expressed in C. K. Prahalad's highly popular treatise *The Fortune at the Bottom of the Pyramid* (2004). The subtitle, "eradicating poverty through profit," departs from the idea of the "double bottom line" and Polanyi's sense of socially embedded exchange. Rather, this is an unadulterated assertion of the market, and an authorization of the people's economy in the register of free markets: "If we stop thinking of the poor as victims or as a burden and start recognizing them as resilient and creative entrepreneurs and value-conscious consumers, a whole new world of opportunity will open up" (Prahalad 2004: 1). Such ideas are echoed in the work of William Easterly (2006). Dismissing Sachs as a "Planner" with a "Big Western Plan," Easterly calls for "Searchers" who can find incremental, grassroots solutions to poverty. His celebration of markets – "free markets work" (ibid.: 60) – is also an argument about the democratization of capital: "The rich have markets; the poor have bureaucrats" (ibid.: 165).

What are we to make of such seemingly contradictory ideas, this battle of ideas within millennial development? As I have noted earlier, millennial development can be understood as an ensemble of complex, and often contradictory, ideas. The ambivalence about the role of the market is a key feature of this ensemble. So is the interest in equity, resource distribution, and poverty alleviation. But it would be a mistake to read any of this as a rejection of markets. As expressed in the "Third Way" ideology of US President Clinton and UK Prime Minister Blair, which sought to find a third way between the extremes of state and market, the discussion of market failure is premised on a more general belief in the role and importance of markets:

No one has yet found anything approaching the free market that is as efficient an allocator of goods, services, capital and opportunity. But, the free market left alone . . . will not take account of human needs, not equally distribute human opportunity, not empower people to make the most of what is there and eventually will consume itself.

(Clinton 2006, unpaginated)

As Goonewardena (2003) argues, the Third Way seeks to "modernize" social democracy and the Left by teaching them to trust the market more and the state less. Here, it is worth returning to the concept of social capital and its popularity in millennial development discourses. As Portes and Landolt note:

the notion of social capital has made its appearance, holding the promise of a ground-up alternative to the top-down policies promoted by international finance organizations in the recent past. In the more optimistic versions, the rise of social capital would perform double duty as a counterweight to the unfettered individualism of the market and, simultaneously, as a means to gain advantages in it.

(2000: 530)

This precisely is the promise of "democratized capital" put forward by CGAP and the Washington consensus on poverty.

However, the significance of the Washington consensus on poverty lies not only in its central idea of "frontier markets" but also in the fact that it is a "consensus," one that is carefully constructed and maintained. If ideas are weapons then there is a distinctive geography to the production of authoritative knowledge. It is at the World Bank that the authorized experts establish benchmarks and best practices, draw up the "consensus guidelines," and manage "market intelligence." In this context, Stiglitz's (1999: 590) commentary on knowledge seems either naïve or hegemonic: "Knowledge is one of the central international public goods . . . the accumulation, processing and dissemination of knowledge in development, as well as working more broadly to close the knowledge gap, is the special responsibility of the World Bank."

## A BANGLADESH CONSENSUS?

The globalization of microfinance can be seen as the story of the times; that of a grassroots idea appropriated and coopted by institutions of power and thus made neoliberal and commercial, exemplifying the privatization of Third World indigenous knowledges. The deployment of microfinance as the new financial frontier, helping convert the "bottom billion" into profitable markets, seems strong evidence for such a narrative. The "new order" of poverty management can, then, be seen as what Weber (2002) calls a "global development architecture," an order that facilitates financial sector liberalization and the global trade in financial services, in keeping with the mandates of the World Trade Organization. Further, she argues that, in this order, far from devolving power to the grassroots democratically, microfinance is the "neoliberal safety net *for* neoliberal political restructuring" (Weber 2004: 362, original emphasis).

But let me return once again to the idea that millennial development is an ensemble of complex, often contradictory, ideas and practices. Although the Washington consensus on poverty enjoys a certain hegemony, I argue that this consensus is being constantly challenged, and possibly undermined, by counter-hegemonic formations. The terrain of millennial development, and especially the field of microfinance, is a battle of ideas in which ideas are indeed weapons. To better understand this battle we have to turn to a different geography, to Bangladesh, the site of origin of the first model of microfinance. Bangladesh, known for its extreme poverty, is home to some of the world's largest microfinance organizations. Although the Grameen Bank is perhaps the most well-known of these, others have recently received considerable global attention. These organizations, with a massive outreach to millions of people in rural Bangladesh, either fully or partly rely on microfinance as their main instrument of poverty alleviation. For example, the Association for Social Advancement (ASA) is celebrated as a "Fordist" model of microfinance, because of its efficiencies and rapid growth in client base. BRAC, first titled the Bangladesh Rural Advancement Committee and now known as Building Resources Across Communities (Abed and Matin 2007), dwarfs the Bangladeshi state in the provision of services. In addition to microfinance, it runs a vast rural network of primary schools, health centers, poultry farms, and village organizations. Together, these institutions represent a unique conjuncture of development, one where, in a phase of nation-building, middle-class professionals such as Muhammad Yunus (founder of Grameen), Fazle Abed (founder of BRAC), Shafiq Chowdhury (founder of ASA), and Zafrullah Chowdhury (founder of GKSF, a trail-blazing health services NGO) each crafted a unique civil society strategy and style for development. They are in many ways the founding fathers not only of these organizations but also of Bangladeshi civil society in the wake of the country's establishment as a new nation in the 1970s. Although loosely connected to the state, they were able to establish for each of their organizations considerable autonomy from the state; and although funded by international development institutions, they were easily able to minimize any dependence on Northern donors, and were thus rarely bound by aid conditionalities.

What emerged in Bangladesh, therefore, was an unusual landscape of civil society organizations experimenting with development ideas and practices. It is my contention that it is possible to identify a "Bangladesh consensus" that, although not centrally managed or coordinated by any entity, is nevertheless marked by a striking unity of discourse, world view, and purpose. I therefore do not use the term "consensus" lightly, for, in Bangladesh, even the World Bank programs bear more resemblance to the work of the Grameen Bank or BRAC than they do to CGAP best practices. It is also my contention that development planning has a great deal to learn from this Bangladesh consensus. Let me outline some of the key features of the Bangladesh consensus and, in doing so, foreground the differences between it and the Washington consensus on poverty.

First, the Bangladesh consensus is unequivocally committed to poverty alleviation and therefore to reaching the poor. Whereas the Washington consensus tends to valorize financial sustainability, benchmarking the performance of MFIs in relation to profitability and portfolio quality, the Bangladesh institutions give primacy to impacts on poverty. Here there is sophisticated expertise on how to view and understand poverty, the indicators of deprivation, and how to assess and evaluate impacts on poverty. And there also is self-critique and therefore constant experimentation with how best to reach the ultra-poor, the poorest of the poor. Whereas the Washington consensus narrows the field of action to the "economically active" poor (Robinson 2001: 17), arguing that the poorest must be served by charity, not development, the Bangladesh consensus insists that policy innovations can indeed serve the extreme poor. Perhaps the best known of these innovations, one that has now even been put forward as a best practice by CGAP (Hashemi 2001; Hashemi and Rosenberg 2006), is BRAC's Challenging the Frontiers of Poverty Reduction/Targeting the Ultra Poor program. This experiment seeks to serve the ultra-poor through "opportunity ladders," addressing different forms of vulnerability and combining safety net and food security policies with income generation tools. Such interventions can be understood as "protectional" rather than "promotional" strategies, a distinction I borrow from Hulme and Mosley (1996: 107). Despite the rhetoric of credit and entrepreneurship, the Bangladesh institutions seem to be engaged in forms of social protection that allow the poor to smooth consumption and reduce the volatile insecurities associated with extreme poverty. Such protectional strategies are often implemented through mandates and conditions, such as mandatory savings or Grameen's 16 decisions that require borrowers to meet human development targets. These too are frontiers, but the "frontier issues" are quite different in Bangladesh than they are for the Washington consensus.

Second, although not explicitly political and often disavowing active participation in electoral politics, the Bangladeshi institutions are concerned with political and social empowerment. Seeking to avoid the "elite capture" of the benefits of development (Hossain and Matin 2004), BRAC has worked to create village organizations, to empower the rural poor in general and poor rural women in particular to take ownership of these, and to thereby transform the political and social hierarchies of the Bangladeshi countryside. A key part of such a strategy is an asset-based approach to development (Matin and Begum 2002), one that transcends the income and enterprise concerns of commercialized microfinance. Thus, one of Grameen's least-known and yet perhaps most radical programs is its housing loans. As in the case of traditional Grameen loans, the housing loans are given primarily to poor women; but the effects of these loans are particularly far-reaching, with these women becoming bearers of property rights, owners of assets, in a patriarchal context in which this would otherwise be near impossible.

Third, the largest Bangladeshi institutions have set out not to implement projects but rather to create systems. Fazle Abed, the founder and director of BRAC, describes the ethos behind BRAC's work in the health sector thus:

> In health, a microfinance plus approach could range from simple measures such as using the group meetings to deliver health education, to linking up microfinance clients to a health facility on preferential terms, to providing services directly. We believe the problem is the lack of a well-functioning, pro-poor health system at the village level. So we set out to create a new system rather than implement unsustainable, stop-gap projects.
>
> (Microfinance Gateway 2008, unpaginated)

This idea of sustainability is quite different than that promoted by CGAP. It is not simply about financial ratios or profit statements; rather, it aims to create and maintain service delivery systems at a massive scale, with outreach to the poor and ultra-poor in a context of political uncertainty. It is about the capacity to conceptualize and implement systemic change, as in BRAC's "value-chain" initiative or Grameen's "social enterprises" model. Whereas most MFIs provide enterprise loans to the poor, BRAC and Grameen seek to transform the terms on which the poor are integrated into global markets, renegotiating these value chains and how rural producers are inserted into them. These too are "frontier markets" (Microfinance Gateway 2008, unpaginated), but those in which the livelihood needs of the poorest are paramount.

Fourth, in Bangladesh, there is a keen sense of the politics of knowledge. Having spent many decades establishing programs and projects, achieving astounding scale and outreach, maintaining autonomy and legitimacy, the top institutions are now seeking to showcase their work and draw attention to their set of best practices and benchmarks. They, too, are engaged in the globalization of microfinance, but of *their* model, and through circuits that parallel and at times challenge those of the Washington consensus. BRAC has extended its work to Afghanistan and Africa. Grameen runs a formidable network of replication programs and is closely allied with the Microcredit Summit, based in Washington DC, which explicitly and actively promotes a poverty-focused vision of microfinance as an alternative to the CGAP model. BRAC has a long-standing Research and Evaluation Division, a new BRAC University, and a recently launched BRAC Institute of Development Studies. But it is not easy to win the battle of ideas, especially when located at the margins of global power. Grameen Bank founder Yunus provides an unrelenting critique of the hegemony of the World Bank, arguing against such geographies of authoritative knowledge:

> One day I was approached by an American journalist who was openly irritated by my apparently endless carping against "development aid" organizations such as the World Bank. He said in a challenging voice, "Instead of always being so critical, could you tell me what concrete steps you would take if you became president of the World Bank?" I said coolly, "I suppose the first thing I would do would be to move the headquarters to Dhaka." Why on earth would you do that? Well, if the overarching objective of the World Bank is to combat world poverty, then it seems to me the bank should be moved to a location where poverty is at its worst. Also if the headquarters were moved to Dhaka many of the bank's 5000 employees would simply refuse to come. Dhaka is not known for its vibrant social life and is certainly not a choice spot for a World Banker to raise children. I think that many would voluntarily retire or change jobs. This would help achieve two things. First, it would ease out those who are not completely devoted to fighting poverty; second, it would reduce costs, as Dhaka salaries would be much lower than those required in expensive Washington DC.
>
> (Yunus 2007, unpaginated)

Yunus's critique indicates the ways in which regimes of truth are regimes of enunciation, authorizing particular geographic sites at which expertise can form and from which one can speak with power and legitimacy.

The effects of this alternative consensus in Bangladesh are now palpable. Studies show the impacts of such institutions on reducing vulnerability through consumption smoothing (Khandker 2003), through the creation of new forms of associational life (Kabeer and Matin 2005). The World Bank itself has concluded that the effects are now evident at the scale of Bangladesh's macro-economy, with World Bank President Zoellick stating: "Bangladesh has made significant economic and social gains since the 1990s . . . Its human development achievements have been remarkable in reaching a number of the Millennium Development Goals" (World Bank 2007, unpaginated). Such achievements, in one of the world's poorest countries, where there continues to be great political instability, have come to be widely known as the "Bangladesh paradox."

But in making an argument about the counter-hegemonic quality of the Bangladesh consensus, I do not mean to imply that this consensus presents a radical alternative to the global order of development. Rather I see it as fully implicated in this global order, challenging and contradicting it and at the same time constitutive of it. While I am inspired by the strategic positionality of Bangladeshi civil society, I am also acutely aware that the Washington consensus and Bangladesh consensus are possibly perspectival constructs of the same global order of debt, discipline, and development. This counter-hegemonic narrative is constitutive of the master order. As the Washington consensus on poverty valorizes themes of the self-enterprising poor, of responsibility rather than welfare, of social entrepreneurialism as the golden equilibrium that can help navigate the extremes of market failure and state provision, so the Bangladesh consensus remains staunchly opposed to state-led development. Yunus's take on poverty sounds eerily like the brutal Third Way discourses that accompanied the Clintonian dismantling of the welfare state. In a 1998 speech, one of the few statements by him that made it into a CGAP document, Yunus declares:

> Credit without strict discipline is nothing but charity. Charity does not help overcome poverty. Poverty is a disease that has a paralyzing effect on mind and body. A meaningful poverty alleviation program is one that helps people gather will and strength to make cracks in the wall around them.
>
> (cited in Parker and Pearce 2002: 4)

The success of the Grameen model is predicated on discipline, and indeed gendered discipline. The images of Grameen women at weekly meetings, saluting, being ordered and orderly, chanting the Grameen Bank slogan of "Discipline, Unity, Courage" are well known. But this success also depends on the construction of a self-disciplining subject, one who pledges allegiance to self-improvement and self-responsibility, to embody "rational economic woman" (Rankin 2001), in whose name (Roy 2007) the whole microfinance project is engineered. In this sense, poor women are the last frontier not only in the World Bank's project of inclusion (Bergeron 2003), but also in the work of the Bangladesh consensus. Thus, the story of the globalization of microfinance cannot be told in the simple narrative of the neoliberal corruption of alternative, grassroots development. Rather it has to be told as the reconstruction of an ensemble of ideas and practices in which, from the very beginning, poverty alleviation valorized an entrepreneurial subjectivity; in which, from the very beginning, the "empowerment" of women was tied to debt and discipline.

## Twenty-first-century planning

Why is the story of microfinance and millennial development relevant for planning? The most immediate response to such a question of course is that microfinance is an example of twenty-first-century development planning, an increasingly important tool of community development that is seen to generate income, to alleviate poverty, and to empower women. From inner-city poverty in the American metropolis to the reconstruction of Afghanistan, microfinance is widely touted as the panacea for the ills of disempowered communities. But what is at stake in this story is much more than the successes and failures of microfinance; it is the very nature of development practices and planning expertise. This is a story that exceeds the case of microfinance.

In a recent piece, I note that for many planners the debates that animate millennial development may seem remote and irrelevant, a world that does not relate to the everyday business of managing and envisioning cities and metropolitan regions. But I argue that the ideas and practices of millennial development "must be seen as a set of "global norms" that shape the ethical, and thereby practical, forms of planning," as a "global social contract" that "contains the possibility of forcing a rewriting, at least an examination, of many other social contracts" (Roy 2008: 252, 254). The most obvious implication of such "global norms" for planning is to draw attention to one of the most pressing issues of the twenty-first century: persistent poverty and inequality. How will planners tackle poverty? Through what tools, policies, programs, and innovations?

This chapter suggests that, in order to answer such questions, planners must pay attention to the battle of ideas, to the politics of knowledge and the ethics of expertise. Although it is crucial to understand *what* development does to poor subjects, it is also important to study *how* development constructs its subjects, *how* some ideas come to be seen as best practices, and *how* structures of power are perpetuated through such systems of knowledge. Planners play a prominent role in the battle of ideas. They wield ideas as weapons. By managing knowledge they also manage poverty. Their work thus takes place not only in relation to the poor and poorest but also in relation to structures of expertise. It is crucial therefore for planning theory and planning practice to examine what Timothy Mitchell (2002) has called "the rule of experts." Although planners are often concerned with the built environment, economic opportunity and political institutions, they must also be concerned with the space of knowledge, with the entanglement of knowledge and power that Foucault charts so provocatively in his work. For this is the "order of things" (Foucault 1970) implied by the circuits of capital and truth I have detailed in this chapter. Twenty-first-century planning is implicated in such circuits; its possibilities and limits are demarcated by flows of capital and frontiers of accumulation; its repertoire of models is calibrated through ideas about markets; its benchmarks and best practices echo global ideologies. In all of this there is much that can be learned by looking for the counter-hegemonic, through a journey to the margins. Here is revealed not necessarily the pristine alternative to the global order, but planning forms that are unanticipated, struggles that are ongoing, and the sense that the battle of ideas has not been fully lost.

## Notes

1   *Redistribution with Growth* is the title of an important volume published in 1974 and edited by Hollis Chenery *et al*. The text became central to the vision and mission of the McNamara World Bank.
2   I use the term "microfinance" to indicate a broad panoply of financial services among which "microcredit" is perhaps the most important, but not the only, type of service. It is important to note that there is a politics to the use of these two terms. The Bangladesh institutions, especially the Grameen Bank, insist on the term "microcredit," seeing "microfinance" as a term that connotes profit-driven financialization. My use of the term "microfinance," while aware of this politics of knowledge, simply indicates that even the Bangladesh institutions provide financial services, e.g. savings, that far exceed credit.
3   For example, a 2005 conference held in Chicago and sponsored by the University of Chicago was titled "Expanding the Frontier: Transforming Microfinance into a Global Financial Markets Instrument."

## References

Abed, F. and I. Matin. 2007. "Beyond Lending: How Microfinance Creates New Forms of Capital to Fight Poverty." *Innovations*, Winter and Spring, 3–17.

Bergeron, S. 2003. "The Post-Washington Consensus and Economic Representations of Women in Development at the World Bank." *International Feminist Journal of Politics*, **5**, 397–419.

Cammack, P. 2004. "What the World Bank Means by Poverty Reduction, and Why it Matters." *New Political Economy*, **9**, 189–211.

Chenery, H., Ahluwalia, Montek. S., Bell, C. L. G., Duloy, John. H., and R. Jolly, 1974. *Redistribution with Growth: Policies to Improve Income Distribution in Developing Countries in the Context of Economic Growth*. London: Oxford University Press.

Clinton, B. 2006. "Speech: Remarks at Guildhall on Globalization." London. Available: http://www.clintonfoundation.org/032806-sp-cf-gn-gl-gbr-sp-remarks-at-guildhall-on-globalization.htm. Accessed 15 November 2008.

Easterly, W. 2006. *The White Man's Burden: Why the West's Efforts to Aid the Rest Have Done So Much Ill and So Little Good*. New York: Penguin Press.

Fine, B. 2001. "The Social Capital of the World Bank." In B. Fine, C. Lapavitsas and J. Pincus, eds. *Development Policy in the Twenty-First Century: Beyond the Post-Washington Consensus*. New York: Routledge. pp. 136–54.

Fine, B. *et al*. 2001. *Development Policy in the Twenty-First Century: Beyond the Post-Washington Consensus*. New York: Routledge.

Finnemore, M. 1997. "Redefining Development at the World Bank." In F. Cooper and R.

Packard, eds. *International Development and the Social Sciences: Essays on the History and Politics of Knowledge.* Berkeley: University of California Press. pp. 203–27.

Foucault, M. 1970 (1994 edition). *The Order of Things: An Archaeology of the Human Sciences.* New York: Vintage.

Goonewardena, K. 2003. "The Future of Planning at the 'End of History' " *Planning Theory*, **2**, 183–224.

Hashemi, S. 2001. *Linking Microfinance and Safety Net Programs to Include the Poorest: The Case of IGVGD in Bangladesh.* CGAP Focus Note 21. Washington DC: CGAP.

Hashemi, S. and R. Rosenberg, 2006. *Graduating the Poorest into Microfinance: Linking Safety Nets and Financial Services.* CGAP Focus Note no. 324. Washington DC: CGAP.

Hossain, N. and I. Matin, 2004. *Engaging Elite Support for the Poorest? BRAC's Experience with the Ultra Poor Programme.* CFPR-TUP Working Paper Series No. 3. Dhaka: BRAC.

Hulme, D. and P. Mosley. 1996. *Finance against Poverty*. London: Routledge.

Kabeer, N. and I. Matin. 2005. *The Wider Social Impacts of BRAC's Group Based Lending in Rural Bangladesh: Group Dynamics and Participation in Public Life.* BRAC Research Monograph Series, No. 25. Dhaka: BRAC.

Khandker, S. 2003. *Microfinance and Poverty: Evidence using Panel Data from Bangladesh.* World Bank Policy Research Working Paper 2945. Washington DC: World Bank.

Mallaby, S. 2004. *The World's Banker: A Story of Failed States, Financial Crises, and the Wealth and Poverty of Nations*. New York: Penguin Press.

Marcos. 2000. "Do Not Forget Ideas are Also Weapons." *Le Monde Diplomatique.* Available: http://mondediplo.com/2000/10/13marcos. Accessed 15 November 2008.

Matin, I. and S. A. Begum, 2002. *Asset-ing the Extreme Poor: Experiences and Lessons from BRAC Project.* RED BRAC Economic Studies, Vol. XVIII. Dhaka: BRAC.

Microfinance Gateway. 2008. "Microfinance Multiplied: An Interview with Fazle Abed." Available: http://www.microfinancegateway.org/content/article/detail/49562. Accessed 15 November 2008.

Mitchell, T. 2002. *Rule of Experts: Egypt, Techno-Politics, Modernity.* Berkeley: University of California Press.

Mjøs, O.D. 2006. Presentation Speech. Nobel Peace Prize Award Ceremony, Oslo, Norway. Available: http://nobelprize.org/nobel_prizes/peace/laureates/2006/presentation-speech.html. Accessed 15 November 2008.

Parker, E. 2008. "Subprime Lender." *Wall Street Journal*, 1 March.

Parker, J. and D. Pearce. 2002. *Microfinance, Grants, and Non-Financial Responses to Poverty Reduction: Where Does Microcredit Fit?* CGAP Focus Note 20. Washington DC: CGAP.

Polanyi, K. 1944 (2001 edition). *The Great Transformation: The Political and Economic Origins of Our Time.* Boston: Beacon Press.

Portes, A. and Landolt, P. 2000. "Social Capital: Promise and Pitfalls of its Role in Development." *Journal of Latin American Studies*, **32**, 529–47.

PR Newswire. 2008. "S&P Announces Program to Develop Global Ratings Framework for Microfinance Institutions." February 6. Available: http://www.prnewswire.com/cgi-bin/stories.pl?ACCT=109&STORY=/www/story/02–06–2008/0004750914&EDATE. Accessed 15 November 2008.

Prahalad, C. K. 2004. *The Fortune at the Bottom of the Pyramid: Eradicating Poverty through Profits*. Cambridge: Wharton School Publishing.

Rankin, K. 2001. "Governing Development: Neoliberalism, Microcredit, and Rational Economic Woman." *Economy and Society*, **30** (1), 18–37.

Rankin, K. 2002. "Social Capital, Microfinance, and the Politics of Development." *Feminist Economics*, **8** (1), 1–24.

Robinson, M. 2001. *The Microfinance Revolution: Sustainable Finance for the Poor*. Washington DC: World Bank Publications.

Roy, A. 2007. "In Her Name: The Gender Order of Global Poverty Management." In Cabezas, A. *et al.*, eds. *The Wages of Empire*. Austin, TX: Paradigm Books. pp. 28–39.

Roy, A. 2008. "Global Norms and Planning Forms: The Millennium Development Goals." *Planning Theory and Practice*, **9**, 251–74.

Sachs, J. 2005. *The End of Poverty: Economic Possibilities for Our Time*. New York: Penguin.

Stiglitz, J. 1998. "More Instruments and Broader Goals: Moving Toward the Post-Washington Consensus." WIDER Annual Lecture, Helsinki, Finland.

Stiglitz, J. 1999. "The World Bank at the Millennium." *The Economic Journal*, **109** (459), F577–F597.

Swibel, M. 2007. "Forbes Analyzes Microfinance Investment, Releases First-ever List of Top 50 MFIs." *Forbes*, 20 December. Available: http://www.forbes.com/2007/12/20/top-philanthropy-microfinance-biz-cz_1220land.html. Accessed 15 November 2008.

Tulchin, D. 2003. *Microfinance's Double Bottom Line: Measuring Social Return for the Microfinance Industry*. Washington DC: Social Enterprise Associates.

Weber, H. 2002. "The Imposition of a Global Development Architecture: The Example of Microcredit." *Review of International Studies*, **28**, 537–55.

Weber, H. 2004. "The "new economy" and social risk: banking on the rural poor?." *Review of International Political Economy*, **11**, 356–86.

Williamson, J. 1990. "What Washington Means by Policy Reform." In J. Williamson, ed. *Latin American Adjustment: How Much Has Happened?* Washington DC: Institute for International Economics. pp. 5–20.

Wolfensohn, J. 2000. "How the World Bank is Attacking Poverty through Small Enterprise Development and Microfinance." *Small Enterprise Development*, **11** (1), 5–7.

Wolfowitz, P. 2007. Resignation Statement (15 May 2007). Available: http://web.worldbank.org/WBSITE/EXTERNAL/NEWS/0,,contentMDK:21339650~pagePK:64257043~piPK:437376~theSitePK:4607,00.html. Accessed 15 November 2008.

Woolcock, M. 1998. "Social Capital and Economic Development: Toward a Theoretical Synthesis and Policy Framework." *Theory and Society*, **27**, 151–208.

World Bank. Undated. "What is Social Capital?." Available: http://web.worldbank.org/WBSITE/EXTERNAL/TOPICS/EXTSOCIALDEVELOPMENT/EXTTSOCIALCAPITAL/0,,contentMDK:20185164~menuPK:418217~pagePK:148956~piPK:216618~theSitePK:401015,00.html. Accessed 15 November 2008.

World Bank. 2006. "What Will the Nobel Peace Prize Mean for Microfinance?." 16 October. Available: http://web.worldbank.org/WBSITE/EXTERNAL/COUNTRIES/SOUTHASIAEXT/0,,contentMDK:21091923~pagePK:146736~piPK:146830~theSitePK:223547,00.html. Accessed 15 November 2008.

World Bank. 2007. "World Bank President Supports Bangladesh's Future Challenges." 4 November. Available: http://www.worldbank.org.bd/WBSITE/EXTERNAL/COUN-

TRIES/SOUTHASIAEXT/BANGLADESHEXTN/0,,contentMDK:21536081~men
uPK:50003484~pagePK:2865066~piPK:2865079~theSitePK:295760,00.html.
Accessed 15 November 2008.

World Social Forum. Available: http://www.forumsocialmundial.org.br/index.php?cd_lan-
guage=2. Accessed 15 November 2008.

Yunus, M. 2007. "The Littlest Banker." *World View Magazine Online*, **20** (1). Available:
http://www.worldviewmagazine.org/issues/article.cfm?id=200&issue=47.    Accessed
15 November 2008.

# CHAPTER 3

# TRANSNATIONAL PLANNERS IN A POSTCOLONIAL WORLD

## Stephen V. Ward

### Introduction

From 1945 onwards, the former colonies and other territories[1] of Europe's over-seas empires progressively severed their imperial ties in ways that ranged from triumphant liberation struggles to elaborate ceremonies of peaceful handover. Yet, whatever the means by which it came, the first dawn of independence was usu-ally an occasion of gladness and confidence. It also laid a responsibility on each new government to address the symbolic, material and welfare needs of its newly sovereign nation. This responsibility inevitably demanded diverse actions across a broad front. Some, at least, of these actions involved physical and territorial planning, for example managing the urbanisation rush and creating new spaces from which to govern the new states. Yet these challenges soon surpassed the slender technical capacities of the new nations, forcing their governments to reproduce some aspects of the colonial reliance on external expertise with a new dependence on foreign technical aid. This, in turn, underpinned a flowering of international planning practice in the postcolonial world that was more diverse than that of the colonial era.

This chapter is the first of three that take a historical approach to understand-ing global networks of flow in the urban planning field. Planning historians have played an important role in researching these diffusions of planning knowledge. They have done this in various ways, including by focusing on the experiences of individual planners. In this chapter, I apply this approach specifically to the post-colonial world during the first 20 or so years after independence. These years, from the late 1940s to around the mid-1970s, marked an important transition in established global flows of planning knowledge and expertise. Instead of their former almost exclusive dependence on the planning approaches and personnel of the colonial powers, the newly independent states began to seek more diverse external links and to strengthen indigenous planning capacities to varying degrees. They were actively encouraged in this by new international agencies, particularly the United Nations Organization, and the increased number of bilateral material and technical aid programmes, no longer just those of former imperial powers.

To put some limits on this study, my focus will be specifically on urban planning. It is, however, important to recognise that other types of spatial planning were also deployed within the early postcolonial world. These operated more at the broader regional scale, and had economic and social objectives, rather than the more specifically physical and land-use concerns of urban planning. Important though these newer approaches were, however, it is not possible to do justice to them within a short chapter. My focus on urban planning will allow a closer analysis of how far this period saw a real shift towards more indigenous control compared with the colonial period. Or was the imperial experience of external imposition simply being exchanged for another kind of dependence? Many commentators on the postcolonial period have regretted the early independence years as ones when opportunities to move decisively beyond dependence were lost.

Such themes have featured in the work of historians of diffusion flows within colonial and postcolonial urban planning. In 1977 (though appearing in print only in 1980), Tony King suggested that the diffusion of planning to the colonial/developing world constituted a deliberate imperial and postimperial 'export', rather than an 'import' shaped by indigenous actors into forms appropriate to each national setting, as took place among European countries. A set of further reflections on this duality in processes of diffusion became the central theme of an influential seminar organised by Joe Nasr and Mercedes Volait in 1998 (Nasr and Volait 2003). By then, however, there was recognition that, even where (neo-)colonialism ostensibly prevailed, indigenous actors might often moderate, even negotiate, planning outcomes.

Meanwhile, my own typology of planning's international diffusion had also attempted to codify such thinking about the overall 'power relationship' between countries as a key factor shaping planning's international diffusion (Ward 1998, 1999, 2000). The principal distinction within this typology lay between 'borrowing', in which the inward flow of planning knowledge was shaped by indigenous agency, and 'imposition', in which it was shaped by external actors. Each of these types of diffusion was further demarcated into different categories, with the 'imposition' embracing an outrightly 'authoritarian' approach, in which external dominance was complete, through to a 'contested' variant, in which there was a noticeable indigenous challenge. Least investigated at the time was the postcolonial, aid-dependent context, which I typified as 'negotiated imposition'. This chapter is, in part, a critical reflection on this earlier generalisation. Its central questions are partly about the extent of change in patterns of planning knowledge diffusion that took place during this early postcolonial era. But, in doing this, the chapter also probes where control of the emergent diffusion processes rested in comparison with the previous colonial era. How far, in other words, were newly independent countries, particularly their politicians and professionals, able to take control of the new, more diverse flows of exogenous planning expertise? Or was this simply a new form of dependence?

I begin by considering the colonial legacy and how it shaped the planning cultures of newly independent states. Next examined are the larger trends and institutional changes that affected the relationships of these former imperial territories with foreign expertise. Some examples of work by the rapidly widening group of international planners will then be used to strengthen the general picture. This will allow an evaluation of the significance of the postcolonial work of these transnational planners to the international diffusion of planning knowledge. Finally, there will be a brief consideration of the more recent evolution of planning within the increasingly varied postcolonial world.

## THE COLONIAL PLANNING TRADITION

The imperial world was one of the principal test beds for modern Western-style urban planning. A striking example was in the French world, where the new imperial protectorate of Morocco pioneered the notion of planning as a state function from 1912. Several years before any equivalent in France itself, the Moroccan planning law of 1913 launched a national programme of urban planning (Wright 1991: 73–160). Over the following years this template was widely applied, with variations, throughout the French Empire (Wright 1991: 161–300; Çelik 1997; Davie 2003).

The British also used their own new ideas of town planning from a very early stage in various colonial territories (Home 1997). Particularly notable were the planning of the new imperial capital for India at New Delhi from 1911, under Sir Edwin Lutyens (Irving 1981), and measures to facilitate renewal of the major port cities of Bombay (1898) and Calcutta (1912). Again, these early initiatives were applied more widely to other parts of the Empire between the wars. By 1939 a growing number of British imperial possessions, including Malaya, Northern Rhodesia, Nigeria, Transjordan and Trinidad, had planning powers directly based on British legislation.

Nor were the French and British alone. In Germany's short-lived global empire, the most notable exercise of its planning capacity was at Qingdao in China after 1897. Japan's emergent empire in Taiwan (from 1895), Manchuria (1905) and Korea (1910) also became an arena in which planning skills only newly acquired from the West could be tested (Hein 2003; Tucker 2003). This was especially so in Manchuria during the 1930s, where innovations that would have a profound impact on post-1945 reconstruction in Japan itself were rehearsed. Even that self-defined enemy of old-style formal imperialism, the United States, indulged in colonial planning in the Philippines, where the famous Chicago planner, Daniel Burnham, drew up a notable plan for Manila (Hines 1974). The Dutch East Indies (present-day Indonesia) became the scene of an ambitious programme of planning between the wars (Van der Heiden 1990; Van Roosmalen 2004). Similar tendencies were evident in the erstwhile Italian East African Empire and in Libya during the later 1930s (Fuller 2006).

Twentieth-century imperialists' motives for turning to planning varied. In part, certainly, a simple need was perceived for the creation of spaces for imperial governance and spacious residential districts for colonial elites. But imperial planning was also about more systematic exploitation of colonial resources through improved physical infrastructure. This same concern also drew colonial administrations into health and welfare matters, to combat both economic disruptions caused by disease in the slums and, especially after 1945, the proliferation of informal housing on the fringes of cities. At a symbolic level, planning also helped promote the notion of imperialism as a benevolent force. The widely accepted self-image of urban planning as a movement for social progress could help portray imperialism itself as an enlightened project of modernisation when deployed in a colonial context. Ordered colonial cities were a tangible twentieth-century elaboration of the idea that imperialism extended civilisation to barbarous and backward lands.

Yet, despite sometimes impressive physical results, planning in the colonies was inherently a less progressive project than when it took place at the hearts of the various empires. What made the colonies such important test beds for planning innovation was the opportunity they presented for planners to act ambitiously, facing little political opposition or pressure to compromise their proposals. Although colonial governance varied hugely over time and between places, it was never, even at its best, more than a bounded form of democracy, subject to the ultimate authority of the imperial power.

For much of the colonial era, governance was a good deal worse than this. It was far easier for colonial governments to override the rights of imperially governed peoples than for national governments in the imperial 'mother countries' even to attempt to do the same to their own citizens. The inequality was particularly pronounced in connection with the treatment of citizens of the mother country resident within the colonies, who consequently enjoyed privileged expatriate status. By contrast, indigenous land rights and customary usages could be extinguished more easily. Civil checks on state power were less developed than in the imperial homelands. In extreme circumstances, colonised peoples might violently contest colonial planning's subversion of their own valued places. More usually, they changed the intended meanings of imperially planned and regulated spaces by the way they used them (e.g. Yeoh 1996: 243–311). Such contestations did not, however, alter the overarching reality that imperial authorities were using planning to entrench their dominance.

The actual technical process of giving specific form to planning intentions was also, as has already been noted, usually led by professionals from the colonial power, and in earlier periods completely dominated by them. In India, a very small number of indigenous professionals were, from the 1920s, becoming sufficiently qualified to join the London-based Town Planning Institute (TPI) (there being no equivalent organisation in India until 1949). TPI membership registers and other evidence from this period also show a similar trend evident in neighbouring Ceylon (present-day Sri Lanka) (TPI 1949; Sri Lanka Institute of Architects undated). At the time, planning schools did not exist anywhere in the colonial territories. Some long-term patterns of overseas training dependence began to appear, with important impacts on international flows of thinking. These early Indian and Sinhalese planners, for example, were trained at Liverpool University's Civic Design Department and at University College, London.

At least some of this trickle of indigenous professional planners was finding employment with colonial governments, albeit still in relatively junior roles. There were, however, stronger signs of growth of indigenous professionalism within related fields such as architecture and engineering, where there were more opportunities for private practice. By the 1930s, for example, sufficient numbers of Indian architectural firms had been established to begin to challenge the dominance of British offices (Evenson 1989: 166). Nor were they necessarily in peripheral roles. Between 1917 and 1942, the Indian Institute of Architects had 11 presidents, of whom five were Indian and six British.

A handful of indigenous professionals held official planning roles in other empires, albeit mostly still in minor capacities. These became more common after 1945, for example in Morocco (Johnson 1971: 37) and the Dutch East Indies (Van Roosmalen 2004: 9). Even so, precious few indigenous actors held significant professional roles in most late imperial settings, especially in the colonies proper. Indeed, in some territories, the post-war building boom and apparently successful peacetime renewal of colonial rule after 1945 encouraged a numerical strengthening of European professionals that partly counteracted indigenisation. This trend was noticeable in Malaya and Singapore (Yeang 1992: 222–44), and in Morocco. In the latter, the modernist *urbaniste* Michel Ecochard brought a French team that entirely (and enduringly) re-cast the planning system between 1946 and 1953 (Johnson 1971: 20–40; Rabinow 1992: 179–81). An exceptional (but very singular) case was the future Israel. Here, nation-building capacity was strengthened by the arrival of many well-trained Jewish professionals fleeing fascism in Europe during the 1930s and 1940s (Troen 2003: especially 112–59).

## MOVING BEYOND COLONIAL PLANNING

With independence, most imperial incumbents of official posts were soon superseded by indigenous planners. This was often associated with an exodus of former officials and professionals. What they left behind were the legal systems, policies and working practices of the colonialists. Moreover, to a varying but sometimes surprising extent, some former professionals from the late colonial era also remained. One who retained his senior official position during the first years of India's independence was Otto Koenigsberger (Kalia 1999: 25; Windsor-Liscombe 2006). Yet he was no typical British servant of the Raj. A stateless German Jew, he had left Germany in 1933 when the Nazi party came to power. He then worked as an archaeologist in Egypt before returning to his first profession. In 1939 he was appointed Chief Architect and Planner to the Princely State of Mysore, before becoming Director of Housing for the Government of India in 1944, a post he retained after Independence until his resignation in 1950. As will be shown, he played an important role in the newly independent country and, later, in the wider elaboration of planning policies for the developing world (see Chapters 4 and 7 in the present book).

Many colonial planning officials who remained occupied advisory or academic roles. This often helped meet the shortfall in expertise that was apparent everywhere in former colonial territories. One such example was Jacob Thijisse, head of Dutch colonial planning efforts in Indonesia until 1949, who in 1950 took a senior position at the new state university (Van Roosmalen 2004: 9–10). Depending on local prospects, expatriate private practices with relevant expertise in the bigger cities often continued their work, although there was also an indigenisation of these, albeit more gradual. These various developments typically produced transitional professional cultures in former colonial territories. Local professional arenas (such as the overseas branches or affiliates of the British Town Planning Institute) brought together indigenous and remaining expatriate professionals, further encouraging continuities with late colonial planning approaches (Cherry 1974: 236–9).

Increasingly, however, declining imperial links were overlaid, or at least supplemented, by new opportunities for international exchange. In some cases, links were forged through personal contacts. Alongside such individual cases, however, there were also some larger changes that facilitated this growing diversity. Most important was the United Nations Organization, founded in 1945. From 1948–9 it became (and has remained) deeply involved in Palestinian housing and resettlement issues associated with the creation of the state of Israel. In 1951 these concerns with a specific region were widened and a small UN Housing and Town and Country Planning section was formed, later known as the Centre for Housing, Building and Planning (Ciborowski 1980). It was headed by the Croatian Yugoslav Ernest Weissmann, who had worked in Zagreb, in Vienna and with Le Corbusier in Paris, before moving to the United States to work on the Yugoslav pavilion for the 1939 New York World's Fair (Blau and Platzer 1999: 362; Mumford 2000; Watts 1997: 115; Harris and Giles 2003). He subsequently worked for the refugee agency set up in 1943, the United Nations Relief and Rehabilitation Administration, before heading the new UN planning section from its inception.

Weissmann had a multinational but numerically small team of staff (even in 1963 there were only 12 permanent professional officials), drawn from both the developed and developing worlds. These included Oliver Weerasinghe, a distinguished planner from Ceylon who joined the office in 1956 (Liyanage 2003). He was one of a handful of Sinhalese professionals who had qualified in England during the 1930s. In Ceylon, he planned the new town at Anuradhapura, advised by his former teacher at Liverpool, Sir Patrick Abercrombie. Other colleagues were Wilson Garces, an American architect-planner; Joe Crooks, literally the only planner in Trinidad when he had joined the British TPI in 1952, and who in 1965 succeeded Weissmann; and the British planner Kenneth Watts (Watts 1997: 114–17).

Weissmann's officials acted as intermediaries, linking up foreign experts with newly independent countries in need of planners. His own nationality helped because Yugoslavia, although a communist state, followed a line distinct from both Moscow and the West. This helped allay suspicions among political leaders in the developing world that UN planners were simply instruments of one or other of the two power blocs. It also made it easier for planners from both sides of the Iron Curtain to participate in UN ventures. In fact, Weissmann's mastery in this respect was most completely evident in his orchestration of the multinational approach to re-planning Skopje in (Macedonian) Yugoslavia following a 1963 earthquake (Senior 1970). In the postcolonial world, his staff typically evaluated national requests for assistance, found suitable experts to work for and advise postcolonial countries, and generally promoted knowledge transfer and sponsored demonstration projects. Over time, the office's status grew to reflect the increasing importance of urban issues. In 1978 it was comprehensively re-launched as the much higher-profile UN Human Settlements Programme (UN-Habitat), which continues to play an important role in managing the international flow of funds and expertise from various sources, mainly into poorer countries.

Other international development agencies were also formed alongside the UN during the post-war years (Iriye 2002). Most important among these was the International Bank for Reconstruction and Development (IBRD), established in 1945 and subsequently joined by its several sister organisations – now collectively known as the World Bank Group. The UN also encouraged the growth of international non-governmental organisations (NGOs) and formalised their position in promoting development. Yet the specifically urban planning role of most such organisations in the postcolonial world was not initially very significant. The Ford Foundation, established by the American automobile dynasty in 1936, was the major early exception. In the immediate post-war years the IBRD and most NGOs were preoccupied with problems of relieving and rebuilding Europe and Japan. Nevertheless, along with the UN, they began to create important transnational networks in the wider world during later years.

More immediately important were programmes of financial aid and technical assistance. In some cases, these sustained former imperial links into the postcolonial era. However, there were also important new national contributions that reflected the new balance of power. In 1947 the US government had sanctioned the Marshall Aid programme to Europe. Two years later, President Truman launched the first US programme to assist poorer countries, the Point Four Program, with India amongst the initial recipients (Truman 1950). Alongside this, the Ford Foundation played a direct part in promoting transnational flows of planning knowledge and expertise. In recognition of the ideological importance of this kind of international presence, the Soviet Union and its satellites also became significant suppliers of aid and, to some extent, planning assistance. Over succeeding decades, as their own economies recovered, almost all affluent democratic capitalist countries launched aid programmes, greatly increasing the volume and variety of international planning contacts.

In general, although with important exceptions, donor countries supplied expertise from their own nationals during the early years. Some recipient countries maintained connections largely along the lines of imperial relationships, or at least found a new primary source of aid and assistance to replace the imperial 'mother'. Elsewhere, however, and quite apart from the work of the international organisations, the proliferation of bilateral aid could produce diversity in the nationalities of foreign planners working within individual postcolonial nations. This diversity was related to government policies in recipient countries towards donor nations, which allowed them to 'pick and mix'. It was common also to find shifts over time, as certain aid relationships grew unsatisfactory or tired in various ways, and others began to seem more promising. For example, such trends were clearly apparent in countries such as Ghana and Tanzania, both of which had leaders intent on avoiding neocolonial dependence, but which were also countries subject to major regime changes at national and regional levels (Armstrong 1987a).

Meanwhile demand for technical expertise was growing throughout the postcolonial world. Almost all former colonial territories were experiencing urban growth at unprecedented rates, usually resulting in extensive informal urbanisation. This was compounded in some countries by ethnic and other tensions, which reflected the way that national boundaries were drawn, and produced major refugee resettlement problems. As noted above, it was this that first drew the UN into the planning arena to try to make provision for Palestinian refugees among Israel's neighbours, especially Jordan (which gained independence in 1946) and Lebanon (independent from 1943). The partition of India in 1947 also triggered huge population movements that necessitated various kinds of planned solutions.

At the same time, the process of accelerating the supply of indigenous planners within newly independent countries proved painfully slow. In 1961, for example, it was calculated that, whereas the UK had one planner per 17,000 people, India had only one per 750,000, Pakistan one per million, and Nigeria only one per two and a half million (Home 1997: 201). The training of planners soon became a significant outlet for financial and technical aid, both to support in-country training and to bring trainees to well-established planning schools in the more developed worlds. Planning schools such as Liverpool University, University College, London, the Institut d'Urbanisme in Paris, American schools such as Cornell and the Massachusetts Institute of Technology (MIT), and several schools within the Soviet Union, such as the Moscow and Kiev Institutes of Architecture, educated many future planners from late and former colonial countries. Over time, the numbers of countries and of individual training institutions burgeoned, often reflecting linguistic affinities established under colonialism. At best, however, this offered only a longer-term solution, contributing little to immediate needs in the early years of independence.

## AMERICAN PLANNERS IN THE POSTCOLONIAL WORLD

These various factors encouraged the emergence of a new transnational group of planners who operated substantially in the postcolonial world. The phenomenon of planners working outside their own countries or imperial systems was not actually new (Ward 2005). The major arena for such activity had been the historically postcolonial region of Latin America. Here, before about 1940, many European, mainly French, urban planners had worked with local professionals and political leaders (Almandoz 2002). After then, however, Latin America was an area where planners from the United States increasingly worked, often within bilateral American aid programmes. A pioneer was the New York-based Town Planning Associates, which worked in Venezuela, Brazil, Cuba, Peru and Colombia from 1943 to 1956 (Mumford 1997; de Ventós 1997). Another notable later instance was the team led by Lloyd Rodwin from the MIT, which from 1960 planned the new city of Ciudad Guayana in Venezuela (Rodwin 1969).

More appropriate to the present concern with postcolonialism after 1945 was the work of American planners in India, a country led by Anglophones but no longer tied to Britain (Banerjee 2009). The American connection largely coincided with US President Truman's aid programme, but the planner who actually pioneered the links, Albert Mayer, had already made his own personal connections (Kalia 1999: 31–2). Mayer had worked building airfields in India for American forces during the Second World War. While there, he developed a strong affinity with the country and its people, including future prime minister Jarawarhal Nehru. These early contacts brought him several significant commissions in the newly independent country. These included his first role, advising the city of Kanpur; the Point Four-funded Etawah rural development programme; and working with the Indian municipal engineer N. V. Modak on preliminary studies for the Greater Bombay master plan (Emmett 1977; Evenson 1989: 209).

His most important commission was, however, as planner of the new capital for the partitioned East Punjab at Chandigarh (Kalia 1999: 20–69). Mayer's associates on this project came from his partnership with the American firm of Julian Whittlesey. The Polish American architect Maciej Nowicki was also brought in to oversee detailed designs to implement the plan; but his death in an air crash in 1950, as well as highlighting the perils of transnational working, led to the introduction of the well-known Swiss French architect-planner, Le Corbusier (Kalia 1999: 70–120). Le Corbusier's team, which included his cousin Pierre Jeanneret and the British architects Maxwell Fry and Jane Drew, significantly altered the Mayer plan, to the extent that it is now seen largely as Le Corbusier's own.

Nehru wanted a modern, planned city to move India forward (Kalia 2006; Chapter 4 in the present book). The prime minister strongly backed Mayer to deliver this, although the fee was being paid from India's meagre dollar reserves and not, in this case, by US aid. It has been suggested that Nowicki's death, coming at a time when India was already borrowing massively from the United States to prevent widespread famine, presented an opportunity to pursue a cheaper European option for the project (Kalia 1999: 38–44). Even before Mayer was appointed, the Indian government had considered the least costly option of seconding their chief planning official, Otto Koenigsberger, to plan Chandigarh. Koenigsberger was, however, very busy planning other new towns for refugees, as well as new state capitals at Bhubaneswar (Orissa) and, to a much smaller extent, Gandhinagar (Gujarat). So his involvement was never practicable (Kalia 1999: 31–2, 1994: 130–55, 2004).

Le Corbusier's arrival did not, however, mark the end of Mayer's or indeed other Americans' involvement in Indian planning. Another important contributor during the same period was the Boston firm of Frederick Adams, John Howard and Roland Greeley (Cody 2003: 141). Supported by the US State Department, they took over Koenigsberger's initial work to prepare the 1952 master plan for another new town in Gujarat, Gandhidham, built for refugees of partition. Another feature of these years was that American philanthropic and other agencies became especially important in financing such connections. Thus the Ford Foundation funded the American planning team led by Mayer, which collaborated in preparing a master plan for the newly formed Delhi Development Authority from 1957 (Emmett 1977: 54–67; Banerjee 2009). The Foundation, together with the World Health Organization (which, like most major international bodies, was largely funded by the United States), also contributed to the preparation of a plan for Calcutta during the early 1960s.

American planners worked in other postcolonial settings. Mayer, for example, worked on the design for Ashdod in Israel, while Adams, Howard and Greeley played a central role preparing the 1960 Bangkok master plan.[2] During the 1970s, there were also notable American involvements in Africa. The new Nigerian capital at Abuja was planned by International Planning Associates (IPA), an American consortium in which the well-known Philadelphia firm of David Wallace, Bill Roberts and Tom Todd did the main city planning work (WRT Design, undated; Mabogunje 1990: 146–7). In Tanzania, James Rossant, closely guided by UN advisers, prepared the plan for the national capital (i.e. government) centre within the new capital city, Dodoma (Rossant 1996).

Yet if Dodoma reflected the granting of planning assistance to a rather poor country, Abuja sprang from the optimism of a country flush with oil revenues, hiring Western expertise on a commercial basis. This was to be a growing trend, creating a strong market for various kinds of planning and related expertise in more affluent parts of the postcolonial world, especially in the oil-producing states. Typically, this would be linked with major contracts for American (and other Western) construction firms to build infrastructure. As well as being extremely profitable, this trend also consolidated strategically and economically important relationships with the oil-dependent West. American highway planning firms such as Parsons Brinckerhoff or de Leuw Cather were among the first to benefit from these new possibilities (Cody 2003: 140). As early as 1955, Parsons Brinckerhoff was planning highways in Bahrain (still a British protectorate at the time).

## TRANSNATIONAL PLANNERS FROM THE SOVIET BLOC

The other superpower also saw the postcolonial world as an arena in which it could extend its influence. Indeed, communist insurgents were at the forefront of anti-colonialism in some territories. The result was that several postcolonial governments looked first to the Soviet bloc for aid and technical assistance. This was especially so in new nations where communist governments were actually in charge. The Soviet Union took a somewhat imperious line in dealing with these new communist states, especially in planning matters.

Eastern European satellites of the USSR, which became communist controlled after 1945, are not directly comparable with the former colonies of Western empires. Not least, several of these Eastern European states had comparatively well-developed urban planning capacities that, in relative terms, were at least equivalent to those of the Soviet Union. Nevertheless, the typical Soviet practice of promoting 'appropriate' planning approaches within these new satellites still provides grounds for some comparison (Åman 1992, especially 60–2).

One method for achieving this control was to rely on indigenous planners who had lived in the Soviet Union and were thus seen as having unimpeachable ideological soundness, qualifying them to provide professional leadership. The other was a process of re-education, whereby significant planners from satellites such as Poland and East Germany were called to Moscow to be instructed in socialist realist planning as favoured during the Stalin years. This distinctive approach to urbanism involved creating grand avenues lined with big buildings, impressive vistas and spaces, monuments lauding the regime, and architecture that was functionally modern but clothed in historicist national detailing. Planners from the new Soviet satellite states then returned from Moscow to apply and disseminate these principles, adding national historicist detailing appropriate to their own countries. Soviet 'advisers' rarely participated very directly in urban planning within Eastern Europe, although their role was occasionally significant, for example in Sofia's 1944 development plan (Åman 1992: 61, 68, 141).

Yet direct participation was more typical of the Soviet approach to former colonial, or in China's case semi-colonial, countries. After the 1949 revolution, Soviet planners were quickly despatched to Beijing to guide the preparation of an appropriately communist plan (Sit 1996). Within a few years, however, this somewhat overbearing approach, symptomatic of the whole Soviet attitude towards the new People's Republic, prompted Chinese resistance to direct involvement. With North Vietnam from 1954 and the whole country from 1975, however, connections proved more enduring (Logan 2000: 183–219). French colonial planning had been a major influence on Vietnamese cities, but the Soviet impact between 1955 and 1991 was also important. In 1955, a framework for economic aid and technical assistance for Vietnam from the Soviet Union was formalised, including training many tens of thousands of professionals in the Soviet bloc. It was not simply that there were few existing indigenous professionals; an additional problem for a communist regime was that those there were had been trained by the colonialists. One consequence was that communist-bloc architects, planners and other experts made direct contributions to Vietnamese planning. These professionals came mainly from the Soviet Union, with occasional contributions from elsewhere, including the first such planning contact, a Polish expert in 1955 (Logan 2000: 210). During the first half of the 1960s, there were also stronger links with China than with the Soviet Union (Logan 2000: 197). However, the 1962 and 1973 plans for Hanoi (approved in 1965 and 1976 respectively) were largely Russian efforts, with some participation by local planners. The second (and more important) of these was led by Sergei Ivanovich Sokolov, head of Leningrad's Institute of Urban Research and Planning, and Chief Architect of Leningrad from 1986 (Ruble 1990: 89–91; Logan 2000: 211). Sokolov, an expert on designing sub-urban *microrayons* (equivalent to Western residential neighbourhoods), had also led planning efforts for several cities in Siberia and Kazakhstan, but Hanoi was the Institute's first such involvement with a tropical, postcolonial city.

The international contribution of planners from some Eastern European countries was also significant. Particularly notable was the Polish technical agency, Polservice. Its planning arm comprised planners from the city of Warsaw, whose reconstruction efforts after 1945 had won widespread international acclaim (Ciborowski 1969). Although Polservice was best known for its planning work following the Skopje earthquake (Senior 1970), it was also involved in the post-colonial world. In Iraq, a former imperial territory that had gained independence relatively early in 1932, Polservice prepared an important comprehensive plan for Baghdad in 1973 and a national housing survey in 1977 (Abu-Dayyeh 2004: 82). It also worked on development projects (not always involving urban planning) in Africa and elsewhere. A key figure associated with Polish international work was Adolf Ciborowski, who had been City Architect of Warsaw from 1956 to 1964, and then directed the multinational team at Skopje on behalf of the UN. Ciborowski later served as a UN special planning adviser on projects including the planning of Dodoma (Watts 1997: 129–30; Rossant 1996).

There were other instances of planners from communist countries working in postcolonial countries at the behest of radical socialist or revolutionary governments. Thus, from 1963 to 1969, the Hungarian planner Karoly Polónyi worked for the state-owned Ghana Construction Company, assisting the training of Ghanaian planners (Team 10 Online, undated). Between 1977 and 1980, Polónyi also prepared plans for Addis Ababa, capital of Ethiopia.[3] He covertly maintained good relations with some Western modernists and, like several transnational Soviet-bloc planners, seems to have used international work partly to leave his own country when the political climate was unfavourable.

Elsewhere, the socialist state of Tanzania also received much interest from the Soviet bloc, although the mainland – the former Tanganyika, which had gained independence from Britain in 1961 – tended to rely on planners from Western countries. The other part of the Tanzanian republic, however, the islands of Zanzibar and Pemba, pursued a different course. Following a revolution that overthrew the Sultan in 1964, the Zanzibar government looked to communist countries for guidance, inviting planners from the German Democratic Republic (GDR) to help shape a suitably radical vision (Myers 1994). Their proposal was to re-house the entire population of the islands in ten new towns comprising ideal socialist neighbourhoods. Later, in 1968, a larger GDR team led by Hubert Scholz prepared Zanzibar City's first detailed postcolonial plan, proposing massive reconstruction of the poorest part of the city, with over 200 vast apartment blocks fronting wide avenues in the manner then favoured in the Soviet bloc. A later plan for the city was also prepared by planners from the People's Republic of China.

## PLANNERS FROM OTHER COUNTRIES

From what has been written so far, it is tempting to equate this international export of planning expertise to the postcolonial world directly with the new, cold war contours of global hegemony. Yet, although there is some truth in this formulation, the picture is too crude. Ultimately, leaders of new nations would be more fondly disposed towards one superpower rather than the other because of the tangible economic and military aid it provided, rather than because of its city development plans. This left more possibilities for important planning assistance roles to be provided by less powerful countries from the affluent world. Often, foreign planners were a tiny part of a wider package of assistance. Nor did a foreign planner's country of origin necessarily reflect the primary source of planning funds. Through both its sponsorship of international agencies and its own bilateral aid programmes, the United States in particular often funded the work of expatriate planners from other countries.

A specific example was the remarkable Greek planner, Constantinos Doxiadis (Sarkis 1998; Bromley 2003; Constantinos and Emma Doxiadis Foundation 2003). Doxiadis became adept at securing American aid and negotiating the emergent networks of international planning while heading Greece's post-1945 reconstruction efforts. From 1951 until his death in 1976 he established himself as one of the foremost international planning consultants. The postcolonial/developing world countries where his firm worked included Ghana, India, Iraq, Jordan, Lebanon, Pakistan, Syria, Sudan and Venezuela. Some of his best-known projects, such as the new Pakistani capital at Islamabad, planned from 1959, were funded directly by national governments or with UN assistance. Yet many others were funded either by American agencies such as USAID (the United States Agency for International Development, founded in 1961) or the Ford Foundation. Or they were funded by international agencies that were substantially American controlled, such as the IBRD or the Inter-American Development Bank.

Although Doxiadis was unique in his global 'reach', he was not the only planner from a less prominent country to become an early presence in postcolonial planning. Thus, the Swiss planner Werner Moser planned the new West Bengal town of Kalyani from 1947 (Kalia 1999: 26). Even more such planners entered the field as bilateral aid programmes proliferated in the 1950s and 1960s. For example, Danish planners were at work in Jakarta in 1962 (Watts 1997: 106–7), while, in Tanzania, Canadian planners PPAL, led by Macklin Hancock, prepared the Dar es Salaam master plan in 1968 (Armstrong 1987b). In 1975, PPAL also prepared the above-mentioned Dodoma master plan (Mabogunje 1990: 146–7). Japanese planners also began to work widely across the world, often on urban infrastructure planning, in association with their government's generous overseas aid programme. In 1978, for example, the Tokyo-based International Engineering Consultants Association undertook a Japanese government-funded study for central Amman in Jordan (Abu-Dayyeh 2004: 95–8).

Even though their previous imperial supremacy was rapidly ending, European former colonial powers remained major providers of international expertise. Occasionally, the legacy of colonialism soured relations, such as the major hiatus in Dutch–Indonesian contacts during the later Sukarno years. By 1970, however, several Dutch planners and institutions were deeply involved once again, aiding the evolution of the important Jabotabek metropolitan plan for Jakarta (Giebels 1986). The main former imperial players in the wider field were, however, the British and the French. Both countries (like the Netherlands) enjoyed high international reputations for the expertise of their planners. Both, especially Britain, also had private consultancy sectors that were facing shrinking domestic markets because of the great institutionalisation of planning within government after 1945. International opportunities were thus seized upon with alacrity. In Britain the Town Planning Institute actively promoted the role of the 'British planner abroad' during the 1950s (e.g. TPI 1956).

Many major British planning consultants of the post-war years practised to some extent in late colonial and postcolonial developing world settings (largely those that had belonged to the British empire). For some, such as Sir Patrick Abercrombie, such work was to dominate the twilight of their careers, in his case in Ceylon, Ethiopia, Malta and Cyprus (Build Sri Lanka.com 2001; Ethiopian Telecommunications Corporation, Office for the Revision of Addis Ababa Master Plan 2002; Dix 1981: 123; Zewdou 1998). The next generation, for whom the shrinkage of domestic consultancy work was more acute, was rather more active. Amongst others, these included Max Lock, who worked in Jordan (1954–5), Iraq (1954–6) and Nigeria (1965–7 and 1972–88) (MLCERG 1996).

Another such practice was that of Anthony Minoprio, Hugh Spencely and Peter Macfarlane. With plans for two British new towns to their firm's credit, they prepared a plan for Kuwait (then still a British protectorate) in 1951, and five years later were responsible for the important Baghdad master plan (Marefat 2007). In 1959 they were commissioned to plan the small provincial city of Dhaka as the capital of then East Pakistan (which became the independent state of Bangladesh in 1971) (Palmowski 2008). The same consultants also prepared a plan in 1962 for the main East Pakistani port of Chittagong, which underwent rapid growth after partition. By this time, new consultancies were also entering the field, particularly those of Richard Llewelyn Davies, Colin Buchanan and others (Bruton 1981: 213; McCulloch 2002: 119). All were able to capitalise on the reputation of their British work, notably in new town master plans or traffic planning, to gain work abroad. Oil-producing states were major clients for both of these areas of expertise.

International activity by French planners showed similar tendencies, mainly but not exclusively played out in their country's former colonies. As in earlier times, some individual *urbanistes* stand out, such as Ecochard, who, apart from his work in late imperial Morocco, produced plans for Beirut immediately after independence in 1943 and again in 1963 (Ghorayeb 1998). Another was André Gutton, who produced an important plan for Aleppo, Syria, in 1954 (later notorious for its destruction of the historic fabric) (Bianca *et al.* 1980).

Yet the era of the individual global *urbaniste* ended during the 1960s. There was a marked shift in manner of French delivery of planning expertise to developing world clients, away from individuals, and towards using major public planning offices for such roles. The Institut d'Aménagement et d'Urbanisme de la Région Parisienne (IAURP, renamed IAURIF in 1976 when the region became the Ile de France), for example, was responsible for preparing the famous 1965 Paris regional structure plan. Over the following years, it began to provide planning expertise to other countries, mainly funded by French and/or international agencies (IAURIF undated; Lortie 1995: 225–32). The first such venture was in 1967, when Buenos Aires renewed the historic Latin American connection with Paris by inviting IAURP to prepare a plan (which appeared in 1971) for its metropolitan region. Similar ventures followed for many other cities, including Beirut (1972–9 and 1982–5), Tunis (1975–8), Agadir (1977–80) and Cairo (1981–4), and the work has continued up to the present day. The Paris city planning office (APUR), although less attuned to overseas work, has also prepared more detailed plans for Beirut and Phnom Penh.

## EMERGING DYNAMICS IN POSTCOLONIAL FLOWS OF PLANNING KNOWLEDGE

Sufficient cases have now been discussed to allow some broader reflections on the question I posed at the outset about changes in the patterns of planning knowledge diffusion during the early postcolonial era. In particular, how far did the locus of control over the receipt of overseas ideas and practices shift to the former imperial territories themselves? Or was it a different form of dependence? It was this that would determine how far introduced elements would simply be transferred to the new contexts, and how far used selectively or synthetically with other ideas and practices (cf. Banerjee 2009). Under colonialism, there was never any doubt that imperial authorities were the more powerful player. As noted, there was some contestation of their externally imposed solutions, but these were usually reactive spasms of frustration on the part of those excluded from the colonial planning process, rather than constituting an element deeply integrated within decision-making.

In theory, at least, the political distance between external planner and indigenous client should have lessened after independence, but did it? There were important signs that it did. At Chandigarh, for example, Nehru was absolutely clear that he wanted a modernist planned city, both to signal a change from the Raj and to point out a new direction for traditional India (Kalia 2006). It was not a crudely imposed Western formula. Even where external funding was dominant, Indian leaders were also able to influence what actually happened. Truman's programme might have funded the Etawah rural development project, but Mayer also sought (and took) Gandhi's advice about working with the local communities.

Elsewhere, there would typically be very high-level interest in projects of major national significance and questioning of foreign proposals. Indonesia's first leader, President Sukarno, had trained as an architect and had a good grasp of urban planning issues, taking a direct interest especially in plans for Jakarta (e.g. Watts 1997: 105). In Tanzania, President Julius Nyerere personally queried James Rossant's plans for places of sociability amongst the government ministries of Dodoma, fearing it would be difficult to keep civil servants at their desks (Rossant 1996: 686). Vietnamese architects and planners also successfully challenged the more overbearing aspects of the plans proposed by Soviet experts, notably the planning of Bah Dinh Square and the Ho Chi Minh mausoleum in Hanoi (Logan 2000: 200).

Yet not every planning project could benefit from personal involvement by a Nehru, Sukarno, Nyerere or top indigenous expert. Such instances need to be set alongside the generality of experience. Local political and professional actors dealing with foreign planners were less powerful or fewer in number, and more easily swayed by exotic expertise. On occasion, foreign experts might also compound this. The young Indian architects and planners eager to work with the legendary Le Corbusier at Chandigarh found that he treated them like children (Goldenberg, 'Chaos Creeps up on India's "City of the Future" ', *Guardian*, 12 January 1999). Over time, however, such attitudes changed. By the 1970s, planners from aid-recipient countries became noticeably more assertive (Safier, 3 October 2008, personal communication), and foreign planners went to great lengths to draw on local planning expertise. For example, Max Lock was actively recruiting Nigerians, and a Nigerian subsidiary with local directors was established in 1978 (MLCERG 1996).

There is also a larger point, beyond these shifts in relative levels of deference. In the negotiation of foreign planners' proposals, involvement was confined to local political and professional elites (Safier 1972). Wider engagement with the publics of the postcolonial world was much less in evidence. For them, the outcomes of planning were often no less imposed than they had been under colonialism. By the 1960s, of course, voices of complaint about 'top-down' governance and planning were growing across the West and, more cautiously, even in the communist world. But the failure of mainstream forms of planning to address the real needs of the developing world was on an altogether different scale. From the 1950s, this had encouraged thinking about different approaches, especially for the planning of housing and social development.

This rethinking came directly from the individual experiences of transnational planners who were aware of the mismatch between their initial templates and what they encountered in postcolonial countries. Other planners had travelled this road before, particularly Patrick Geddes, who between 1914 and 1924 pioneered a more 'organic' approach to Indian planning than the crude urban renewal approaches favoured by British colonial administrators (Meller 1990: 202–63; Home 1997: 141–51). Geddes became an inspirational figure for some post-1945 transnational planners (e.g. Tyrwhitt 1947), although few approached his capacity for innovation. None of the new generation of transnational planners from the West was entirely unchanged by their experiences. Generally, though, those with reputations in their own countries, and who saw home as their primary sphere of operations, shifted their views less in these new settings. Not surprisingly, in contrast, it was the figures most completely immersed in the problems of the postcolonial world who shaped and implemented the new thinking.

One was Otto Koenigsberger, who, after leaving India in 1951, worked extensively as a UN consultant and (from 1957) as a London-based academic. He began to see the need for different solutions for the postcolonial world. Instead of a presumption in favour of major direct public housing provision, ruinous for most developing countries, he (and others) increasingly advocated a 'site and services' approach to planning, allowing self-building (Harris 1998). This became part of a growing shift in favour of various more streamlined, less technically oriented, forms of planning during the 1960s. An altogether more radical but hugely influential voice was that of John Turner, an anarchist British architect (much inspired by Geddes) who worked in Peru (Harris 2003). Turner is partly associated with the switch to 'site-and-services' approaches. But in fact he considered even this too much of an imposed solution – an appropriation by planners, foreign or otherwise, of too many decisions about housing and the living environment. He advocated giving more control to poor people to create and regulate their own environments, seeing informal settlements not as a planning problem but as the beginning of a solution.

Such thinking was being endorsed by the UN by 1970, and became the basis of a new orthodoxy for planning in the developing world, especially its poorest parts. In 1973, Koenigsberger established the Development Planning Unit at University College, London, perhaps the first planning school to fully embrace this new approach, which he labelled 'action planning' (Koenigsberger 1974; Safier 1974; see also Chapter 4 in the present book). From the mid-1970s, as the managed global economy of the post-1945 period itself began to unwind, these principles also began to be endorsed by the World Bank, anxious to minimise the debts of developing countries and foster their embrace of market disciplines (Harris and Arku 2006).

## CONCLUSIONS AND POSTSCRIPT

Yet it is important not to project later developments back onto the immediate postcolonial period. The most obvious shift during these years was a widening and intensification of international flows of planning ideas and practices. Before independence, rather like an occasional train chugging slowly from a mainline station at the heart of an empire along a sleepy colonial branch line, parcels of planning knowledge trundled occasionally to each imperial territory. Imperial urban planners took back something of what they learnt, but the place where this colonial experience interacted with other flows of planning knowledge remained within the heartlands of empire. After independence, the former imperial territories remained peripheral, but with, if they made use of them, more connections to other mainline stations and to each other. For most former imperial territories, knowledge began to travel more frequently and from more diverse locations. As more professionals from the postcolonial world became internationally active, they also played a growing part in sending out knowledge.

The planning knowledge that came to the better-connected, postcolonial world inevitably became less distinctive than it had been in colonial times, on the more isolated branch lines. Whereas distinctively 'French', 'British' or 'Dutch' planning approaches had been implanted in the territories of their empires, the new received approaches became more generic. Of course, the legacy of empire remained: imperial legal codes and administrative cultures persisted within the process by which the newly sourced knowledge was applied. But now which country the new generation of transnational planners were from mattered less than it had in the past. At least during the years considered here, the dominant model of urban planning was either an increasingly homogenised Western modernist or a Soviet-bloc planned city. The former had the familiar features of strict land-use zoning, big highways, central business districts with big office buildings, cellular residential structures, and so on. Beneath an ideological relabelling, and with some tangible differences in emphasis, Soviet-bloc planning actually showed many similar features, but placed greater emphasis on central symbolic spaces and major avenues as design features.

Both visions were assembled from a wide repertoire of individual ideas and practices that had diverse international (mainly European and North American) roots. Over earlier decades, their constituent ideas and practices had been widely diffused, modified and re-diffused. They had, effectively, been reinvented in modified forms at different locations. Although there might be national idiosyncrasies in the way that post-1945 planners drew on this internationalised repertoire, these were far less marked than previously. What planners now brought to former colonial countries, whether it was neighbourhood units to Chandigarh, a green belt to Addis Ababa, or satellite towns for Hanoi, were not simply exotic transplants from American or British or Soviet planning. Although these countries were the immediate sources, each concept had a complex international history that reflected more than one national tradition; they were synthesised products of an international planning community.

On the issue of control, the term *negotiated imposition*, coined in 1998 by the present author, still perhaps has some value in understanding the processes of flow, especially in the early postcolonial years. Compared with imperialism, the coercive element was lessened but not eliminated. The amount of external funding needed to pay for planning expertise inevitably qualified the autonomy of indigenous decision-making. But even when the newly independent countries were themselves funding the foreign planners, the palpable weaknesses in indigenous technical capacity and, to varying degrees, of wider civil society's ability to challenge and mediate planning proposals inevitably strengthened the foreign expert. A tradition of widespread deference to the perceived superior technical knowledge of 'advanced' economies and societies persisted long after independence. This was not necessarily challenged by growing numbers of indigenous professionals, as they themselves were benefiting somewhat from this same sense of deference. Those who had been trained abroad almost invariably took precedence in their own countries over those who had not. Yet there were, as noted, real possibilities for *negotiation* as well as for *imposition*. Within the general parameters of the relationships between exotic expertise and indigenous authority, some political and professional leaders were assertive and effective in dealing with foreign planners.

The weakness of this characterisation lies, however, in its static nature. The indigenous assertiveness glimpsed intermittently in dealings with transnational planners in the 1940s and 1950s has become more widespread since the 1970s. There are now many more knowledge networks and flows within the postcolonial developing world (see Sharp and Briggs 2006; McFarlane 2006). At best, these give voice to genuinely marginalised, 'subaltern' groups within the emergent civil societies of developing nations. They offer the possibility of transcending any lingering deference to foreign professional knowledge, drawing on it but selectively and critically, and synthetically with local knowledge and experience. Although it is still possible to identify interactions that could be described as 'negotiated imposition', the balance has shifted markedly.

Today, in a world that is postcolonial and effectively post-communist, and in which market principles have everywhere been ascendant, the former imperial territories are far more diverse than they were even at independence. The most basic human needs certainly remain widely unmet in the cities of many countries. Yet other countries have begun, very partially and unevenly, to achieve sufficient economic growth to begin to resemble the developed world. In such places can be glimpsed the beginnings of new professional flows of expertise that echo some of those which emerged in the more affluent world when other countries and cities sought the expertise that underpinned their perceived success.

The most striking example is Singapore, a British colony until 1965, which then experienced an initially troubled independence. Today, the country's record of astonishing economic success, political stabilisation and social discipline is widely envied by its larger neighbours. Its urban planning (which, incidentally, reflected ideas almost as different as was possible from those of John Turner – see Harris and Giles 2003) has been a key factor in this success (Perry *et al.* 1997: 191–285). Singapore's planners, pre-eminent amongst them Liu Thai Ker of the RSP consultancy, now export expertise across Asia and beyond (Tan 2002). A former Chief Executive of Singapore's Urban Redevelopment Authority and its Housing and Development Board, Liu has lately worked in India, Taiwan, Vietnam, Myanmar, Malaysia, Indonesia, Thailand, the Philippines and China, where he is currently planning advisor to ten Chinese cities, including Beijing.

Liu's work highlights emergent trends in transnational practice and suggests new flows of ideas that could eventually replace traditionally dominant, one-way flows from the developed to the former colonial world. A limited 'reverse flow' of planning ideas and practice from the emergent cities of the developing and former colonial world to the developed world has been apparent for some years (e.g.

Sanyal 1990; Hall 1988: 269–72). To date, however, the carriers have mainly been practitioners from the developed world, repatriating their transnational experience. It remains to be seen how far and how soon planners from the postcolonial world will themselves start to sell their expertise to nations that were their former colonisers or aid donors.

## NOTES

1   The term 'colonial' is widely used in this chapter, although many territories referred to have never been directly governed colonies in the strict legal sense. These were various imperial protectorates or mandate territories that enjoyed some measure of self-government even before independence. Yet, although the degree of imperial dominance of such territories was generally lower, neither were they fully sovereign states, remaining ultimately subject to power exercised by another state. The greater administrative capacity and technical supremacy of the imperial authorities also heightened the unevenness of their relationship with indigenous authority.

2   Note that Thailand, never having been brought within any colonial empire, was not strictly a postcolonial nation. Its post-1945 problems were, however, directly comparable with those of its neighbours.

3   Apart from a brief Italian occupation from 1936 to1941, Ethiopia was never colonised in the manner of other African countries. However, during its brief annexation, the Italian imperial administration did plan Addis Ababa as the future capital of its East African Empire.

## REFERENCES

Abu-Dayyeh, N. (2004) 'Persisting Vision: Plans for a Modern Arab Capital, Amman, 1955–2002'. *Planning Perspectives*, **19**, 79–110.

Almandoz, A. (ed.) (2002) *Planning Latin America's Capital Cities 1850–1950*, London: Routledge.

Åman, A. (1992) *Architecture and Ideology in Eastern Europe during the Stalin Era: An Aspect of Cold War History*, New York/Cambridge, MA: The Architectural Foundation/ MIT Press.

Armstrong, A. M. (1987a) 'Tanzania's Expert-led Planning: An Assessment'. *Public Administration and Development*, **7**, 261–71.

Armstrong, A. M. (1987b) 'Master Plans for Dar-es-Salaam, Tanzania'. *Habitat International*, **11**, 133–46

Banerjee, T. (2009) 'U.S. Planning Expeditions to Postcolonial India'. *Journal of the American Planning Association*, **75**, 193–208.

Bianca, S., David, J.-C., Rizzardi, G., Beton, Y. and Chauffert-Yvart, B. (1980) *The Conservation of the Old City of Aleppo*, Paris: UNESCO.

Blau, E. and Platzer, M. (eds) (1999) *Shaping the Great City: Modern Architecture in Central Europe, 1890–1937*, Munich: Prestel.

Bromley, R. (2003) 'Towards Global Human Settlements: Constantinos Doxiadis as Entrepreneur, Coalition-Builder and Visionary', in Nasr, J. and Volait, M. (eds) op. cit., pp. 316–40.

Bruton, M. J. (1981) Colin Buchanan 1907 – [sic], in Cherry, G. E. (ed.) *Pioneers in British Planning*, London: Architectural Press, pp. 203–23.

Build Sri Lanka.com. (2001) 'City of Colombo Development Plan'. Available: www.buildsri-lanka.com/CDP. Accessed 4 February 2009.

Çelik, Z. (1997) *Urban Forms and Colonial Confrontations: Algiers under French Rule*, Berkeley: University of California Press.

Cherry, G. E. (1974) *The Evolution of British Town Planning*, Leighton Buzzard: Leonard Hill.

Ciborowski, A. (1969) *Warsaw: A City Destroyed and Rebuilt*, Warsaw: Interpress.

Ciborowski, A. (1980) 'United Nations Center for Housing, Building and Planning', in Whittick, A. (ed.) *Encyclopedia of Urban Planning*, reprint edn, Huntingdon, NY: Krieger, pp. 1084–9.

Cody, J. W. (2003) *Exporting American Architecture 1870–2000*, London: Routledge.

Constantinos and Emma Doxiadis Foundation. (2003) 'Constantinos A. Doxiadis'. Available: www.doxiadis.org. Accessed 4 February 2009.

Davie, M. (2003) 'Beirut and the Étoile Area, An Exclusively French Project?', in Nasr, J. and Volait, M. (eds) op. cit., pp. 206–29.

de Ventós, M. R. (1997) 'Cities in Latin America: The Work of Town Planning Associates 1943–1956', in Costa, X. and Hartray, G. (eds) *Sert: Arquitecto in Nueva York*, MACBA: Barcelona, pp. 76–101.

Dix, G. (1981) 'Patrick Abercrombie 1879–1957', in Cherry, G. E. (ed.) *Pioneers in British Planning*, London: Architectural Press, pp. 103–30.

Emmett, R. C. (1977) *Guide to the Albert Mayer Papers on India*, Chicago: University of Chicago Library.

Ethiopian Telecommunications Corporation, Office for the Revision of Addis Ababa Master Plan. (2002) Home page. Available: www.telecom.net.et/~aamp/. Accessed 4 February 2009.

Evenson, N. (1989) *The Indian Metropolis: A View Toward the West*, New Haven, CT: Yale University Press.

Fuller, M. (2006) *Moderns Abroad: Architecture, Cities and Italian Imperialism*, London: Routledge.

Ghorayeb, M. (1998) 'The Work and Influence of Michel Ecochard in Lebanon', in Rowe, P. and Sarkis, H. (eds) *Projecting Beirut: Episodes in the Construction and Reconstruction of a Modern City*, Munich: Prestel, pp. 106–21.

Giebels, L. J. (1986) 'JABOTABEK: An Indonesian-Dutch Concept on Metropolitan Planning of the Jakarta-Region', in Nas, P. J. M. (ed.) *The Indonesian City: Studies in Urban Development and Planning*, Verhandelingen van het Koninklijk Instituut voor Taal-, Land en Volkenkunde 117, Dordrecht: Foris, pp. 101–15.

Goldenberg, S. (1999) 'Chaos Creeps up on India's "City of the Future" ', *Guardian*, 12 January.

Hall, P. (1988) *Cities of Tomorrow: An Intellectual History of Urban Planning and Design in the Twentieth Century*, Oxford: Blackwell.

Harris, R. (1998) 'The Silence of the Experts: "Aided Self-Help Housing", 1939–1954', *Habitat International*, **22**, 165–89.

Harris, R. (2003) 'A Double Irony: The Originality and Influence of John F.C. Turner', *Habitat International*, **27**, 245–69.

Harris, R. and Giles, C. (2003) 'A Mixed Message: The Agents and Forms of International Housing Policy, 1945–1973', *Habitat International*, **27**, 167–91.

Harris, R. and Arku, G. (2006) 'Housing and Economic Development: The Evolution of an Idea Since 1945', *Habitat International*, **30**, 1007–17.

Hein, C. (2003) 'The Transformation of Planning Ideas in Japan and Its Colonies', in Nasr, J. and Volait, M. (eds) op. cit., pp. 51–82.

Hines, T. S. (1974) *Burnham of Chicago: Architect and Planner*, Oxford University Press: New York.

Home, R. (1997) *Of Planting and Planning: The Making of British Colonial Cities*, London: Spon.

IAURIF (Institut d'Aménagement et d'Urbanisme Ile de France). (Undated) Home page. Available: www.iaurif.org/en/projects/sharing/index.htm. Accessed 4 February 2009

Iriye, A. (2002) *Global Community: The Role of International Organizations in the Making of the Contemporary World*, Berkeley: University of California Press.

Irving, R. G. (1981) *Indian Summer: Lutyens, Baker and Imperial Delhi*, New Haven, CT: Yale University Press.

Johnson, K. M. (1971) *Urbanisation in Morocco*, New York: The Ford Foundation.

Kalia, R. (1994) *Bhubaneswar: From a Temple Town to a Capital City*, Carbondale: Southern Illinois University Press.

Kalia, R. (1999) *Chandigarh: The Making of an Indian City*, 2nd edn, New Delhi: Oxford University Press.

Kalia, R. (2004) *Gandhinagar: Building National Identity in Postcolonial India*, Carbondale: Southern Illinois University Press.

Kalia, R. (2006) 'Modernism, Modernization and Postcolonial India: A Reflective Essay', *Planning Perspectives*, **21**, 133–56.

King, A. D. (1980) 'Exporting Planning: The Colonial and Neo-colonial Experience', in Cherry, G. E. (ed.) *Shaping an Urban World: Planning in the Twentieth Century*, London: Mansell, pp. 203–26.

Koenigsberger, O. (1974) 'Habitat for Development: An Action Planning Approach', *Town and Country Planning Overseas Summer School Proceedings*, 72–9.

Liyanage, J. (2003) 'Oliver Weerasinghe's 23rd Death Anniversary Tomorrow: The Father of Sri Lanka's Town Planning', *Sunday Observer Magazine* (Colombo), 19 January.

Logan, W. S. (2000) *Hanoi: Biography of a City*, Sydney: University of New South Wales Press.

Lortie, A. (1995) 'Des Exportations à Géométrie Variable', in Lortie A. (ed.) *Paris s'exporte: architecture modèle on modèles d'architecture*, Paris: Picard/Pavillion de l'Arsenal, pp. 218–32.

Mabogunje, A. L. (1990) 'Urban Planning and the Postcolonial State in Africa: A Research Overview', *African Studies Review*, 33, 121–203.

McCulloch, A. (2002) 'Work Overseas', subsequent contribution to Buchanan, C. (1993), *Told You So*, London: privately published, pp. 119–20.

McFarlane, C. (2006) 'Transnational Development Networks: Bringing Development and Postcolonial Approaches into Dialogue', *Geographical Journal*, **172**, 35–49.

Marefat, M. (2007) '1950s Baghdad', *TAARII (The American Academic Research Institute in Iraq) Newsletter*, **2**, 1–7.

Meller, H. (1990) *Patrick Geddes: Social Evolutionist and City Planner*, Routledge, London.

MLCERG (Max Lock Centre Exhibition Research Group) (1996) *Max Lock 1909–1988: People and Planning – An Exhibition of His Life and Work*, London: University of Westminster.

Mumford, E. (1997) 'CIAM and Latin America', in Costa, X. and Hartray, G. (eds) *Sert: Arquitecto in Nueva York*, Barcelona, MACBA, pp. 48–75.

Mumford, E. (2000) *The CIAM Discourse on Urbanism, 1928–1960*, Cambridge, MA: MIT Press.

Myers, G. A. (1994) 'Making the Socialist City of Zanzibar', *Geographical Review*, **84**, 451–64

Nasr, J. and Volait, M. (eds) (2003) *Urbanism – Imported or Exported: Native Aspirations and Foreign Plans*, Chichester, Wiley.

Palmowski, J. (2008) *Bangladesh, A Dictionary of Contemporary World History*, Oxford: Oxford University Press. Oxford Reference Online. Oxford University Press. Oxford Brookes University. Available: http://www.oxfordreference.com/views/ENTRY.html?subview=Main&entry=t46.e190. Accessed 9 February 2009.

Perry, M., Kong, L. and Yeoh, B. (1997) *Singapore: A Developmental City State*, Chichester: Wiley.

Rabinow, P. (1992) *French Modern: Norms and Forms of the Built Environment*, Chicago: University of Chicago Press.

Rodwin, L. (1969) *Planning Urban Growth and Regional Development: The Experience of the Guyana Program of Venezuela*, Cambridge MA: MIT Press.

Rossant, J. (1996) 'The Making of the National Capital Center', *Conference Proceedings: The 7th International Planning History Conference: The Planning of Capital Cities*, Vol. II, pp. 678–94.

Ruble, B. A. (1990) *Leningrad: Shaping a Soviet City,* Berkeley: University of California Press.

Safier, M. (1972) 'What is to be Done? A Preface to Planning in an Age of Accelerated Urbanisation', *Architectural Association Quarterly*, **3**, 4–16.

Safier, M (1974) 'Habitat for Development: An Action Planning Approach', *Town and Country Planning Overseas Summer School Proceedings*, London: TCPOSS, pp. 72–9.

Sanyal, B. (1990) 'Knowledge Transfer from Poor to Rich Cities: A New Turn of Events', *Cities*, **7**, 31–6.

Sarkis, H (1998) 'Dances with Margaret Mead: Planning Beirut since 1958', in Rowe, P. and Sarkis, H. (eds) *Projecting Beirut: Episodes in the Construction and Reconstruction of a Modern City*, Munich: Prestel, pp. 187–201.

Senior, D. (United Nations Development Programme) (1970) *Skopje Resurgent: The Story of a United Nations Special Fund Development Project*, New York: UNDP.

Sharp, J. and Briggs, J. (2006) 'Postcolonialism and Development: New Dialogues?', *Geographical Journal*, **172**, 6–9.

Sit V. (1996) 'Soviet Influence on Urban Planning in Beijing 1949–1991', *Town Planning Review*, **67,** 457–84.

Sri Lanka Institute of Architects. (Undated) 'History'. Available: www.slia.lk/history.html. Accessed 4 February 2009.

Tan, B. (2002) 'Liu Thai Ker', reproduced from Singapore Pages, Infopedia, National Library of Singapore. Available: http://infopedia.nl.sg/articles/SIP_584_2005–01–22.html. Accessed 4 February 2009.

Team 10 Online. (Undated) 'Karoly Polonyi'. Available: www.team10online.org/team10/
   members/polonyi.htm. Accessed 4 February 2009.

TPI. (Town Planning Institute). (1949) *Register of Members*, London: Town Planning Institute.

TPI. (1956) *The British Planner Abroad*, London: Town Planning Institute.

Troen, S. I. (2003) *Imagining Zion: Dreams, Designs, and Realities in a Century of Jewish
   Settlement*, New Haven, CT: Yale University Press.

Truman, H. (1950) 'Address before the Annual Convention of the American Newspaper
   Guild'. Available online via The American Presidency Project: http://www.presidency.
   ucsb.edu/ws/?pid=13542. Accessed 4 February 2009.

Tucker, D. (2003) 'Learning from Dairen, Learning from Shinkyo: Colonial City Planning and
   Postwar Reconstruction', in Hein, C., Diefendorf, J. M. and Ishida Y. (eds) *Rebuilding
   Urban Japan after 1945*, Basingstoke: Palgrave, pp. 156–87.

Tyrwhitt, J. (ed.) (1947) *Patrick Geddes in India*, London: Lund Humphries.

Van der Heiden, C. N. (1990) 'Town Planning in the Dutch Indies', *Planning Perspectives*,
   **5** (1), 63–84.

Van Roosmalen, P. K. M. (2004) 'Expanding Grounds. The Roots of Spatial Planning in
   Indonesia', paper presented at 1st International Urban Conference, Surabaya.

Ward, S. V. (1998) 'Re-examining the International Diffusion of Planning', in Freestone, R.
   (ed.) *The Twentieth Century Urban Planning Experience*, Conference Proceedings, 8th
   International Planning History Conference, Sydney: University of New South Wales, pp.
   935–40.

Ward, S. V. (1999) 'The International Diffusion of Planning: A Review and a Canadian Case
   Study', *International Planning Studies*, **4** (1), 53–77.

Ward, S. V. (2000) 'Re-examining the International Diffusion of Planning', in Freestone, R.
   (ed.) *Urban Planning in a Changing World: The Twentieth Century Planning Experience*, London: Spon, pp. 40–60.

Ward, S. V. (2005) 'A Pioneer "Global Intelligence Corps"? The Internationalisation of Planning Practice 1890–1939', *Town Planning Review*, **76**, 119–41.

Watts, K. (1997) *Outwards from Home: A Planner's Odyssey*, Lewes: Book Guild.

Windsor-Liscombe, R. (2006) 'In-dependence: Otto Koenigsberger and Modernist Urban
   Resettlement in India', *Planning Perspectives*, **21**, 157–78.

Wright, G. (1991) *The Politics of Design in French Colonial Urbanism*, Chicago: University
   Press.

WRT Design. (Undated) 'Abuja Master Plan'. Available: http://www.wrtdesign.com/project-
   Abuja-Master-Plan-for-the-New-Federal-Capital-of-Nigeria-13.html.      Accessed     4
   February 2009.

Yeang, K. (1992) *The Architecture of Malaysia*, Amsterdam/Kuala Lumpur, Pepin Press.

Yeoh, B. S. A. (1996) *Contesting Space: Power Relations and the Urban Built Environment in Colonial Singapore*, Kuala Lumpur: Oxford University Press.

Zewdou, F. (1998) 'The Capital and its Planner: Addis Ababa and Patrick Abercrombie',
   paper presented at the Seminar on Urbanism: Imported or Exported?, Beirut.

CHAPTER 4

# REIMAGINING THE AMERICAN NEIGHBORHOOD UNIT FOR INDIA[1]

SANJEEV VIDYARTHI

## INTRODUCTION

This chapter asks: How do planners construe the same planning idea to be a good fit with vastly different contexts? I trace how the American concept of the neighborhood unit traveled to India, in order to highlight the different imaginations of planners at the places of its conception and destination. This line of enquiry helps me demonstrate how distinct sets of imaginations enabled the planners to argue that the same concept addressed disparate planning concerns in the two contexts.

In the first part of this chapter, I briefly describe the American social anxieties, theoretical influences, and practical concerns that shaped the conception of the neighborhood unit idea in the 1920s. The aim here is to explain how the contemporary context influenced the imagination of Clarence Perry, who conceptualized the neighborhood unit as a physical planning tool intended to address a particular set of social and civic concerns. In the second part of this chapter, I describe the concept's introduction to India. Here, the objective is to highlight a different set of concerns, such as national development and modernization, which underpinned pioneering planners' imaginations that the neighborhood unit concept suited the Indian context as well.

My strategy for fleshing out the importance of imaginations in aiding the journey of the neighborhood unit is to compare Perry's idea of it with the adapted versions produced by pioneering planners in India. By juxtaposing the original and adapted versions of the neighborhood unit, I demonstrate how planners in India substituted the original concerns and anticipated outcomes of the American neighborhood unit to argue that the same concept also suited the disparate Indian context. Such a repositioning of the American neighborhood unit in distant India highlights how ideas are first imagined and produced in one context, and then become susceptible to processes of reimagination and reproduction that appropriate their originality, but also facilitate their ability to travel to other contexts.

## CLARENCE PERRY AND THE NEIGHBORHOOD UNIT

The origin and first applications of the neighborhood unit concept are well documented (Perry 1929, 1939; Gillette 1983; Banerjee and Baer 1984; Silver 1985;
Schubert 1995; Patricios 2002). In this section, my focus is on highlighting the
influence of the contemporary American context on the conception of the neighborhood unit. The expression "neighborhood unit" was first employed by New
York planner Clarence Perry in the 1920s to refer to his proposal of a physical planning concept for designing neighborhoods. In suggesting this concept,
Perry drew upon several sources of knowledge such as his own professional and
personal experiences, recent theoretical advancements, and his association with
other like-minded individuals concerned with the design and planning of cities. An
understanding of these influences is important because it helps us comprehend
how American social and civic concerns of the times were a wellspring for Perry's
imagination.

Clarence Perry spent most of his professional life at the Russell Sage Foundation in New York, where he worked from 1909 to 1937. The Sage Foundation
was a leading philanthropic organization of the times, founded in 1907 to work in
the areas of social and civic reform. Concerns about improving American urban
communities were emerging in contemporary social sciences and humanities,
motivating turn-of-the-century reformist thinking. For example, American intellectual elites were concerned that the speeding up of urbanization ruptured the
traditional ties between individual, place, and community. Although some commentators were deeply pessimistic about the future of modern cities (e.g. White
and White 1962), other reformists approached the developing metropolis with a
combination of pragmatism and optimism, believing that a restoration of the links
between family, neighborhood, and community might offer a possible solution.
For instance, Jane Addams, who founded a settlement house, and the influential American philosopher and educationist John Dewey subscribed to this view
(Banerjee and Baer 1984). The basic tenet of these social reformers was not to
defy or ignore the city, but to work toward promoting community and social communication, and inculcating neighborliness in the seemingly inchoate and hostile
urban environment.

These concerns were probably best articulated in the literature that came out
of the new field of urban sociology. Louis Wirth, the "Chicago School" sociologist,
laid out the primary characteristics of the contemporary metropolis in his essay,
"Urbanism as a Way of Life" (1938). Here, the grimmer side of his argument
raised the specters of "anomie" and "alienation" in an imagined "mass society,"
and the brighter side evoked the prospect of a new, progressive era of urbanity,
tolerance, and cosmopolitanism. Perry was exposed to this emerging literature,

and at various times in his career acknowledged the influence of Professors Charles Cooley, Robert Park, and Herbert Miller, who emphasized the importance of neighborhood institutions to social welfare (Perry 1929: 126). In his 1909 book, *Social Organization,* Cooley had argued that neighborhoods were the nurseries of "primary ideals," which he identified as loyalty, truth, service, and kindness. Park and Miller's works were also underpinned by similar concerns, and influenced Perry:

> It is only in an organized group—in the home, the neighborhood, the trade union, the co-operative society—where he is a power and an influence, in some region where he has a status and represents something, that man can maintain a stable responsibility. There is only one kind of neighborhood having no representative citizen ... the slum; a world where men cease to be persons because they represent nothing.
>
> (Park and Miller, cited in Perry 1929: 127)

Such influences catalyzed Perry's vision that, in ever-growing and increasingly differentiated cities, citizens needed a comprehensible and accessible focal point, such as a neighborhood school, to base daily activities around. He also imagined that the school's centrality would be further strengthened if the neighborhood, with the school at its heart, became the basic unit for planning, and if the logical definition for a neighborhood derived from the distance a child could easily walk to school.

Apart from such expansive social concerns, a second set of influences on the neighborhood unit concept came from Perry's interest in physical planning. He lived in the planned community of Forest Hills Gardens, a spacious suburban development sponsored by the Sage Foundation, and subscribed to the contemporary belief that physical changes in the urban fabric could improve social life and enhance the spirit of citizenship. In advocating the use of neighborhood schools as a focal point to foster a spirit of civic community, Perry was also influenced by the 1907 St. Louis Plan (Gillette 1983: 423). This was one of many plans prepared following the Columbian Exposition of 1893, most of which copied the "city beautiful" ideas of the Burnham plan of Chicago in their focus on centralized civic centers (see Smith 2006). The St. Louis Plan, however, was unique in that it suggested the construction of half a dozen civic centers in different parts of the city. These civic centers were envisioned as a combination of facilities around a common center such as a park.

A third distinctive set of influences that shaped Perry's design imagination, apart from his personal experiences and exposure to recent theoretical advancement, came from his interactions and collaborations with other like-minded individuals who were concerned with the design and planning of cities. These technical milieux provided Perry with an opportunity not only to learn from other scholars and professionals, but also to showcase his work within diverse institutional networks. For instance, Perry collaborated with Clarence Stein and Henry Wright in the design of the planned community of Radburn (Mumford 1954). He also worked as a team member of the Regional Plan Association of America (RPAA) alongside Lewis Mumford and Catherine Bauer, who had written in support of the neighborhood unit concept (Mumford 1933; Bauer 1934). Additionally, Perry's presentations in a variety of institutional settings helped him accommodate wider concerns into his argument in favor of neighborhood units. For instance, Perry presented the outlines of his concept, tentatively named "community unit," at the National Conference of Social Work in 1924, where he argued that

> with its physical demarcation, its planned recreational facilities, its accessible shopping centers, and its convenient circulatory system—all integrated and harmonized by artistic designing—[the neighborhood] would furnish the kind of environment where vigorous health, a rich social life, civic efficiency, and a progressive community consciousness would spontaneously develop and permanently flourish.
>
> (Perry 1924: 421)

Here, Perry explicitly links the contemporary social concerns that preoccupied his audience with spatial means that could address those concerns, in accordance with the popular belief that appropriate urban planning could reinvigorate and sustain the links between the individual, family, and community. He is also, however, offering a unique imagined program for how these relationships could be restored in practice, through distinct neighborhood boundaries, road networks, and parks. These initial arguments, in an improved format and accommodating a broader range of concerns, matured into the neighborhood unit concept, which Perry presented in the *Regional Survey of New York and its Environs* in 1929.

As evident in Figure 4.1, Perry's proposal for the neighborhood unit was strictly residential in character, in line with the zoning principle, and pivoted around a centrally placed community open space to reinforce civic pride because it contained the school: "The public school . . . [is] in [a] real sense a civic institution. It flies the national flag . . . is found in every local community . . . and deserves a dignified site" (Perry 1929: 72). Apart from the school, which occupied the heart of the neighborhood unit, Perry's concept contained three other basic design elements: small parks and playgrounds, small stores, and a hierarchal configuration of streets that allowed all public facilities to be within safe pedestrian access. To define the relationship between these design elements, Perry (1929: 34) prescribed six simple planning principles in detail:

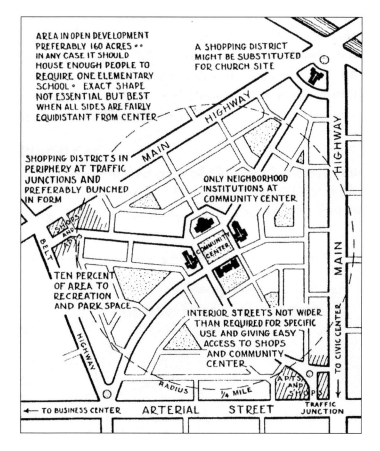

**Figure 4.1**   Clarence Perry's neighborhood unit concept. Source: Perry, C. 1929. *Regional Survey of New York and its Environs*, Vol. VII, p. 88.

1   Size: A residential unit development should provide housing for that population for which one elementary school is ordinarily required, its actual area depending upon population density.

2   Boundaries: The unit should be bounded on all sides by arterial streets, sufficiently wide to facilitate bypassing through traffic.

3   Open spaces: A system of small parks and recreation spaces, planned to meet the needs of the particular neighborhood, should be provided.

4   Institution site: Sites for the school and other institutions having service spheres coinciding with the limits of the units should be suitably grouped about a central point.

5   Local shops: One or more shopping districts, adequate for the population to be served, should be laid out in the circumference of the unit, preferably at traffic junctions and adjacent to similar districts of adjoining neighborhoods.

6 Internal street system: The unit should be provided with a special street system, each highway being proportioned to its probable traffic load, and the street net as a whole being designed to facilitate circulation within the unit and to discourage its use by through traffic.

Perry's concept made its way into the American planning profession within a couple of years of publication, and his simple design principles quickly became general guidelines for planning neighborhoods (Gillette 1983: 427). For instance, the neighborhood unit concept achieved special prominence at President Hoover's 1931 National Conference on Home Building and Home Ownership, where it was cited as a potential solution by each of the four committees formed at the conference (focusing on city planning and zoning, subdivision layout, large-scale building and development, and housing and community; Banerjee and Baer 1984). Over the following years, the concept was not only one of the most "widely discussed urban planning ideas" but also eventually became the "stock planning item" for designing neighborhoods in the post-war years (Silver 1985: 165, 170). Tridib Banerjee and William Baer acknowledged this when they wrote of the neighborhood unit: "Even when not specifically invoked, its premises and constructs have guided residential planning and design. Its credentials are impeccable, its position pre-eminent, and its use ubiquitous" (1984: 3).

However, the establishment of the neighborhood unit concept as the leading physical planning model in America did not occur without some criticism. The concept was attacked on two principal grounds. First, some scholars argued that it was premised on a notion of physical determinism, attempting to force interaction and congeniality upon neighborhood residents. For example, Jane Jacobs (1961) contended that multiuse, unplanned, and diverse neighborhoods are instilled with vitality in contrast with Perry's imagination of a static and exclusively residential community, and Herbert Gans (1968) argued that "spatial units" were not a prerequisite for "social units" and people's lives were not influenced by the physical environments of their residential locations to the extent posited by Perry. Second, and perhaps more seriously, the concept was accused of encouraging neighborhoods as a means of social division. This criticism stemmed from Perry's labeling of neighborhood units as "self-contained," which Christopher Silver later identified as a code word for enforcing social boundaries between neighborhoods, while encouraging homogeneity within them: "The neighborhood unit plan sought to insulate affluent city residents from the disruptive influence of forced interaction with supposedly incompatible social groups" (Silver 1985: 166).

Indeed, Perry had experienced what he would refer to as the "benefits" (1929: 110) of homogenization at first hand while living in the successful suburb of Forest Hills Gardens, which "attracted people with similar tastes and living standards" (ibid.: 94). He was convinced that neighborhoods required high levels of social capital. He envisioned the formation of a kind of club of people with similar tastes. He considered this desirable because "the whole [neighborhood] body would acquire a homogeneity that would facilitate living together and make possible the enjoyment of many benefits not otherwise obtainable" (ibid.: 110). This notion of homogeneity was criticized by scholars such as Chicago-based planner and community activist Reginald Isaacs, who denounced Perry's model because it sought to obliterate his own ideal of heterogeneous neighborhoods (1948). Isaacs believed that heterogeneity was a most important characteristic of successful neighborhoods. Philadelphia planning consultant Henry Churchill seconded Isaac's critique because the neighborhood unit, in his view, was not a natural urban form, and the planner's role should be to control, not obliterate, "the urban pattern of confusion" (cited in Silver 1985: 169).

After the publication of his idea in 1929, Perry grew more confident about its feasibility, and, in his 1939 work *Housing for the Machine Age*, he repositioned the concept as "The Neighborhood Unit Formula." This offered "principles and standards in definite, objective terms which the professional planner could apply in preparing a plan suited to the topography and other characteristics of a particular site" (Perry 1939: 49). The tone of this work is strikingly different in comparison with his 1929 essay. By now, he stood convinced that the new neighborhood units needed to be planned and executed "comprehensively." Perry therefore devoted an entire chapter of the book to urge local governments to start compulsory acquisition of private property rights for assembling land in order to plan new neighborhood units (Perry 1939: 159). However, Perry retired from the Russell Sage Foundation in 1937 and, by the time this later text was published, his direct influence was waning (Gillette 1983: 432). A few years later, he died before seeing the widespread influence of his idea in other parts of the world, including India. The overseas popularity of the neighborhood unit would have probably surprised him, because he had come up with the concept primarily as a remedy for the perceived ills of contemporary American cities.

I now describe how a different set of concerns influenced the imaginations of pioneering planners in faraway India.

## Introducing the neighborhood unit to India

In India, the imaginations of pioneering planners sprang from a totally different set of concerns about national development and modernization. To elucidate the relationship between contemporary Indian concerns and the imaginations of pioneering planners, I will focus on an empirical analysis of the ways in which these planners adapted the neighborhood unit concept. However, before I do so, an understanding of the role of Indian elites and their influence on the contemporary development and planning agenda is important. The modernizing aspirations of these elites were not only pivotal to the development agenda of independent India, but also critically informed the imaginations of pioneering planners that the neighborhood unit was an appropriate model for independent India.

Under British colonial rule in India, a new indigenous elite had arisen that was unconnected to historical sources of authority such as the feudal order, and was instead committed to social reforms, modernization, and development. These elites were largely metropolitan in education and orientation, and were employed in modernized occupations such as teaching, law, or medicine. Recent scholarship has pointed out that these elites, who had played important roles in the struggle for independence, then inherited formal national power when the British departed (e.g. Chakrabarty 2002; Chatterjee 2004). Most of these elites did not own landed property and thus lacked close connections with village society, which, in their view, needed to be reformed and modernized quickly in order for India to progress. They imagined a "modern" society to be wealthy, just, democratic, orderly, and in full control of its own affairs – in short, akin to those found in Western Europe and North America. In contrast, they perceived India and especially its villages and the historical parts of cities to be a "traditional" society: poor, inequitable, repressive, violent, and dependent.

Development, in this schema, was seen as a process of moving from the latter type of society to the former, and became the prime index for measuring efforts toward modernization. Mainstream development theory in the period immediately following India's independence in 1947 argued that development was a social, political, economical, cultural, and physical process. Not only were new physical contexts needed, such as the ones produced by the neighborhood unit concept, but also new political institutions (such as legislatures and courts), cultural mores (individualism and self-orientation), and social structures (the nuclear family and a casteless society). Pioneering planners and their elite clients in India saw in the neighborhood unit an appropriate instrument to advance this developmental agenda, which had quickly emerged as the "most powerful influence structuring social and economic transformations in the non-Western world in [the twentieth] century" (Sivaramakrishnan and Agrawal 2003: 2). None other than Prime Minister Jawahar Lal Nehru spearheaded the formulation and advancement of the development and planning agenda of independent India. Planning, as is well documented, played an important part in Nehru's scheme for India. It would be no exaggeration to describe Nehru as a planner's planner, as was exemplified when the Institute of Town Planners, India (ITPI) voted him its first ever "unqualified" fellow in 1958.[2] At one point of time, Nehru had exclaimed: "You know how attached I am to the concept of planning" (NIUA 1991: 52).[3]

As early as 1938, a good nine years before India's independence, the National Planning Committee chaired by Nehru had defined the concept of planning: "Planning under a democratic system may be defined as the technical co-ordination by disinterested experts, of consumption, production, investment, trade, and income distribution in accordance with social objectives set by bodies representative of the state" (cited in Prakash 1999: 198). Thus, in recommending tools such as the neighborhood unit, the planner was essentially a "disinterested expert" merely facilitating "technical co-ordination," and her recommendations were strictly outside the domain of politics (Chatterjee 1993: 202) because the plans were presented to bodies staffed by technical experts, not public representatives. This also implied that the technical expertise of planners could be trusted to select the right tools, such as the neighborhood unit, for achieving the desired social objectives, and the merits of such a decision were not open to discussion in a political forum. Nehru believed that "under modern conditions we must have experts. If we want to utilize them to the full we must allow them a free hand and there should be as little interference as possible with their work" (NIUA 1991: 71).

The processes used to design and carry out such a planning agenda were facilitated by the state. Sunil Khilnani has identified that the key success of Nehru's premiership was the "establishment of the state at the core of Indian society" (1999: 41). In Nehru's India, the state aimed to be the final articulator of what constituted a "good life" for its citizens. In the field of urban development, this meant the setting up of provincial town planning departments in order to prepare master plans; Nehru commented that "what I should like in regard to every city is a clear plan of what a city will be like, say, 20 or 30 years later" (NIUA 1991: 116). To realize these master plans, it was acceptable for the state and local governments to make liberal use of police powers for acquiring private property rights in order to facilitate the planning and construction of new cities and city extensions. Nehru justified this strategy with statements such as:

> in the India of today, the growth of cities, big and small, is quite anarchic. It is ugly, it is horrible, in fact, it is painful to see. I am surprised at how it is tolerated by large corporations and city municipalities,

(ibid.: 26)

The land acquired in this way was to be used for housing a civic and happy community of citizens through deploying expert-recommended tools, such as the neighborhood unit. Nehru considered a happy community to be vital for the mission of building a secular and casteless society, as part of the wider project of building an independent nation-state. For instance, while laying the foundation stone in 1948 for the new capital city of Orissa state, Bhubaneswar, he was glad to note that "the architect and the chief engineer have thought of this future city in terms not of a few palatial buildings but of a happy community" (ibid.: 117).

The acceptance of the neighborhood unit in India was also aided by the fact that not only did the concept share several characteristics with the established typology of Civil Lines, but it also promised to improve its perceived shortcomings. British colonists had developed the Civil Lines, a euphemism for the sequestered European quarter in South Asian cities, during the nineteenth century. These were, typically, residential settlements of broad and regular streets with bungalows set among vast lots, occupied by the families of expatriate civilian officials. The introduction of Civil Lines was a significant event in the narrative of Indian cities, as it represented a decisive break from the indigenous city, which was seen by the colonial British as unhygienic, chaotic, and incomprehensible (Hosagrahar 2001). Importantly, the Civil Lines typology had gradually permeated the aspirations of the indigenous elite, who, by the early twentieth century, had begun to plan their own residential areas emulating the landscape of the Civil Lines (Khan 1994). Nehru, however, subscribed to more egalitarian ideals and had once sarcastically remarked: "Nearly all the Big Noises and Little Noises live in the Civil Lines" (NIUA 1991: 102). In this respect, the employment of neighborhood units in India represented a compromise between the aspirations of the elites and Nehru's vision of a modern socialist state for the mass of the people.

The elites' interpretation of the potential of the neighborhood unit was made easier as the concept shared several design features with the colonial Civil Lines, such as setback of building lines, regular and wide roads, parks and open spaces, and a certain spatial discipline and order, which created a tidy appearance. These similarities meant that the neighborhood unit typology did not revolt outright against the aspirations of the indigenous elite, who, like the colonial British, continued to harbor a fear of the indigenous city.[4] A contemporary booklet published by the Town Planning Organization of the state of Uttar Pradesh expressed the indigenous elite's fears crisply: "Today, one has an opportunity to choose between planning and no planning, slums and ill-ventilated colonies on the one hand and well-planned and ventilated ones with wide roads, playgrounds and other public amenities, etc., on the other" (Uttar Pradesh Town Planning Organization 1952: 4). Thus, in accordance with Anthony D. King's assertion that the Civil Lines and its bungalows were not just a spatial form but also an attitude of the mind, which persisted long after colonial rule (King 1976), the modern neighborhood unit promised to fit neatly into the post-independence elitist space vacated by the colonial Civil Lines.

The neighborhood unit typology, especially after its adaptation by pioneering planners, also contained several design features that promised to improve the perceived shortcomings of the colonial Civil Lines. For example, unlike the vast lots of the Civil Lines, the neighborhood unit's much smaller lots were more economically viable. They also promoted the high-density development deemed helpful in preserving "our valuable agricultural land in the interest of the nation" (ITPI 1955: 23). The neighborhood unit concept also fitted well with Nehru's secular prerogatives, as Indians of all religions would live together in the new neighborhood units, rather than segregated, as was the case in traditional quarters of Indian cities. The neighborhood unit also appealed to Nehru's progressive and nationalistic sentiments because it promised to house the school in the center, with the nation's flag flying high.

In the following section, I explain how pioneering planners such as Otto Koenigsberger and Albert Mayer reimagined the neighborhood unit concept, adjusting its original American concerns and anticipated outcomes to address the developmental and modernistic concerns of their Indian clients (see Chapter 3 for a further comment on the work of these planners).

## REIMAGINING THE NEIGHBORHOOD UNIT

Otto H. Koenigsberger's convictions and design philosophy, which made him amenable to the neighborhood unit, were a reflection of his formal training in the enlightened and modernistic traditions of the Weimar Republic.[5] His mentor at his alma mater, the Technische Hochschule, Berlin, reputed Weimar architect Ernst May, was famous for the design of public housing in Frankfurt am Main. May's own architectural education had included study in Britain, where he worked with Raymond Unwin, absorbing the lessons and principles of the garden city movement. May's portfolio was thus ahead of its time, including features such as semi-independent houses well equipped with community elements such as playgrounds, schools, and common washing areas. These facilities also featured in the neighborhood unit concept. May's influence on Koenigsberger was profound and lasting, as is evident in the latter's writings on his works in India.

Koenigsberger's activities in India reflect two major convictions that underpinned his planning philosophy. Both are evident in his sustained faith in the neighborhood unit. The first was a belief in the universalist dimension of modern architecture and planning, which could transcend boundaries and be equally valid in all locales (Koenigsberger 1952). His second tenet was an extension and reinforcement of the first. Koenigsberger believed that non-sectarian and

standardized solutions, such as the neighborhood unit, could swiftly alleviate religious–political strife and the tensions around the scarcity of housing in
post-independence India (Liscombe 2006). These beliefs are most evident in his
partially successful effort to set up a factory in Delhi for producing prefabricated
housing units. These houses were to be erected quickly across India, along the
lines of the privately built American suburbs of Levittown, which were constructed
in the early 1950s.[6]

In 1944, Koenigsberger moved from his planning position in the princely state
of Mysore to the government of India as the Director of Housing in the Ministry of
Health. The next seven years saw him working feverishly, supervising the planning
of several new towns to accommodate refugees migrating from the newly created
Pakistan, and designing Bhubaneswar.[7] Designed in 1948 as the new capital for
the state of Orissa, this city was Koenigsberger's most prestigious assignment
in India. For him, as would be the case a little later for Albert Mayer, designing a
brand new capital city from scratch was an unrivaled professional milestone.

In designing Bhubaneswar, Koenigsberger assumed that the neighborhood
unit was an appropriate fit with the planning concerns of post-independence India
(as Mayer would for Chandigarh). In his mind, the origins of the neighborhood unit
in the United States did not matter at all because the concept was a universally
applicable modern typology, especially suitable for the development agenda of
newly independent nations. This position is made explicit in his assertion that the
neighborhood unit had a "special appeal to the people of under-developed countries" and, with some adaptations, it fitted the Indian context well, because the
concept extended India's ancient tradition of rural self-government (the so-called
"village panchayats") into the modern age: "the neighborhood units of the new
towns form the best possible links with the type of community life they [Indians]
know from their villages" (1952: 105).

However, Koenigsberger adapted the neighborhood unit in line with the modernistic and nationalistic agenda of his elite clients. For instance, he extended
Perry's original objective of creating social capital into an attempt to inculcate
secularism and castelessness. This becomes evident in the plan for Bhubaneswar,
in which Koenigsberger adapted the neighborhood concept in two ways. The first
was groundbreaking for India, repositioning the neighborhood unit as a means
to produce a secular and casteless society—a suggestion that anticipated by
several years the proposal of the Interim General Plan for Delhi to use neighborhood units to prevent "ghetto-formation" (Town Planning Organization 1956:
18). Koenigsberger believed that, given the caste traditions of India, there was
a real threat that the neighborhood units could become insular pockets, each
populated by a single socio-economic and/or religious group. The solution, in
his view, lay in "the attempt to provide in each neighborhood a cross-section

of the population, taking good care to have each social and professional group represented in it roughly in accordance with the relative strength in the whole community" (Koenigsberger 1952: 107).

Koenigsberger's adaptation of the concept to dissolve caste barriers is instructive because it stood in contrast to Perry's advocacy of socially similar neighborhood units. Although, in the US, Perry's claims about the virtues of homo-geneity had eventually led to the branding of the neighborhood unit concept as an instrument for segregation, Koenigsberger's argument that they could create mixed communities was largely accepted in India. Despite occasionally success-ful resistance from the hierarchal Indian bureaucracy, which desired homogeneity in accordance with seniority among officials, Koenigsberger's approach was largely adopted in Indian cities, as is evident in the plans of administrative cities such as Bhubaneswar and industrial cities such as Bhilai. Most city extensions across urban India planned after the 1960s aimed at mixing up different economic sections of the society. Later, the Housing and Urban Development Corporation (HUDCO) played a major role by institutionalizing this idea (interview with M. N. Joglekar, Executive Director of HUDCO, on 24 April 2006).

In this respect, the application of the neighborhood unit in India shows that, far from traveling planning ideas always being stripped of their radical intent (as described by Whitzman and Perkovic in Chapter 10), they can also sometimes be employed to achieve a more radical outcome than originally envisaged. The suggestion that the neighborhood unit should create casteless and secular neigh-borhoods was indeed drastic, given that caste and religion in India, historically, served as the main criterion for organizing residential quarters. Koenigsberger's proposition also appears daring and somewhat counter-intuitive in hindsight, but, in agreement with the aspirations of his clients, he positioned the secular and modern concept of the nation in order to replace caste and religious affiliations as the social "glue."

The idea that neighborhood units should house different class, religious, and caste groups also demonstrates the imagination of pioneering planners and their elite clients that the units would have a civilizing effect on the residents, a majority of whom were recent immigrants from villages or the historic quarters of Indian cities. This marks a second major difference between the application of the neigh-borhood unit concept in the American and Indian contexts. In India, the elites who signed up to Nehru's vision visualized the disciplined spatiality of neighborhood units as a crucial design feature that would reduce the enormous cultural gap among neighbors – between the educated and civilized few, and the illiterate and uncivilized many – once they began to live together. This belief in the power of the physical environment to exert a civilizing impact comes alive in this quote from Nehru:

> You should not accept or tolerate ugliness anywhere, in your life, in your activities, in your buildings. The worst type of ugliness of course is ugly behavior of individuals and groups. But to some extent, the environment reflects itself in the behaviour of the individual, as a beautiful environment helps in developing a sense of beauty in the people who live there. It is desirable, therefore, that what we build, however simple and humble it may be, should have some artistic value. And mind you, do not connect artistic value with money.
>
> (cited in NIUA 1991: 30)

This quote highlights Nehru's belief that the spatial environment could improve ugly behavior among individuals and groups – while emphasizing the role of a certain type of aesthetics that is not achieved by large or expensive features, such as big bungalows or ostentatious settings, but comes about by building a simple and disciplined physical environment such as that of the neighborhood unit. Nehru is once again articulating a relationship between the spatial aspects and the social outcomes of a physical environment: ugly and uncivilized behaviors can be controlled, and even obliterated, by the spatiality and constituent design features of a residential environment. The neighborhood unit, in this scheme, was imagined as a vehicle that promised deliverance by hauling the "uncivilized" into a planned realm, whose envisaged spatiality also served an auxiliary pedagogical purpose. Thus Perry's imagination that the spatiality of the neighborhood unit would help to repair deteriorating links between the individual, the family, and the community was substituted, in India, by the equally curious imagination that the disciplined spatiality of neighborhood units would "civilize" their residents.[8]

However, Koenigsberger was not the first to imagine that the neighborhood unit concept could be employed to house a cross-section of society. In his native Germany, a housing estate had been planned in the early 1940s to reflect the National Socialist Party's ideology of *Volk ohne Raum*, which meant breaking the class barrier and uniting the workers and farmers as one "people." Koenigsberger might have been familiar with this project. The plan for this estate, catering for a population of 7,000, resembled Perry's concept closely, but the German planners insisted that the idea was an inherently German solution (Schubert 1995: 34). It is perhaps ironic that Koenigsberger, himself a Jew persecuted by the Nazis, imagined that the same idea could dissolve caste and religious barriers in India.

Koenigsberger's second major adaptation, which he called the "band-town" formation, used the scalability feature of the concept to arrange a single row of neighborhood units, not more than half a mile in depth, on both sides of a motorized traffic artery (Grenell 1972: 101). He found these "chains of neighborhoods strung to an arterial road, like pearls on a string" (Koenigsberger 1952: 109) a sensible arrangement for two reasons. First, it ensured that all units were designed with walking distances in mind, which was appropriate as most residents lacked cars and would therefore use public transport. Second, this arrangement consolidated the number of small and scattered open spaces within the units into a compact space, which was sensible as they were difficult to maintain in India's dry climatic conditions, easily becoming "brown patches of dusty desert" if left as scattered pieces of parkland (ibid.: 109). Consolidating these areas was intended to refashion Perry's small central square, embellished with a "monument, fountain or other ornamental feature" (Perry 1929: 40), on a grander scale, to be used for community activities. This large focal space could also be useful for civic or nationalistic functions such as the new nation's Independence Day (15 August) or the Republic Day (26 January). In combination with the cross-sections of society represented in the new neighborhoods, this underlined the fact that the pioneering planners and their elite Indian patrons not only imagined the neighborhood units to be compatible with their project of nation-building (see Stephen Ward's discussion in Chapter 3) but also visualized them as a microcosm of the nation.

Thus, Koenigsberger's adaptations of the neighborhood unit reflected many aspirations of his most important patron, Prime Minister Nehru, who unequivocally endorsed Koenigsberger's plan and commended it while laying the foundation stone of Bhubaneswar – once again underlining its role in reinforcing the new national identity among its residents:

> The new town will be grouped in self-contained neighbourhood units, each comprising about 850 families. This will enable the town to grow without losing its community and neighbourly character. In each area residential houses will surround the schools and shopping centres and will be near to open fields and recreation grounds. In the centre of the town will be a group of public buildings with a Gandhi memorial pillar symbolising the life and teachings of Gandhiji.
>
> (cited in NIUA 1991: 118)

Nehru, however, was aware of the inherent contradiction of deploying Western models in the post-independence context. On the one hand, these models fitted well with the ideals of a secular, modern, and democratic polity, and therefore appeared necessary for the nation's progress. On the other hand, they violated the nationalistic concerns of the indigenous elite who wished to see a confident and self-reliant nation purged of both colonial legacies and Western influences. Nehru tried to balance both demands. For instance, while inviting the American planner Albert Mayer to "build up community life [in India] on a higher scale without breaking up the old foundations" in 1946, asking him to utilize Western ideas and fit them "into Indian resources and Indian conditions," he cautioned that it was not "an easy matter, for the resources are limited at present and the conditions are often very different from those in Western countries" (cited in Kalia 1987: 47). Nehru's cautionary advice both implicitly encouraged planners to employ Western models and emphasized that they should be carefully combined with local cultural and social practices.

Albert Mayer and his assistant Matthew Nowicki also took Nehru's advice seriously, as evident in their report entitled *Supplementary Notes to the Architectural Study of Superblock L-37,* prepared in 1950. Here, Nowicki's detailing of the neighborhood plan exhibits a conscious effort to adapt the neighborhood unit to Indian conditions, in accordance with Nehru's comments. For instance, the houses were designed around courtyards to provide an internal space that was private and sensitive to the climate, and they also had a provision for terraces to enable the residents to sleep outdoors during the summer nights. Most importantly, the plan tried to capture the essence of the heart of an Indian urban quarter: the bazaar (Kalia 1987: 68).

Albert Mayer, like many other Westerners, was fascinated with the oriental bazaar and therefore envisaged the new neighborhoods as being "intimate," so that the bazaar's modern avatar, the shopping center, could preserve and encourage "as far as we can in a reasonably orderly way do so . . . the marvelous excitement and gaiety of the bazaar, the people in their sociable pre-occupation with shopping and visiting undisturbed by traffic" (Mayer 1950: 174). This imagination is manifested in Nowicki's detailed plan of the shopping center, in which shops had provisions for everyday local practices such as shopping and negotiating while sitting on the floor. Nowicki also incorporated the possibility of installing a seasonal canvas roof, an idea borrowed from the thatch overhangs in indigenous bazaars, to protect the merchandise and provide shade to the pedestrians. He also proposed including a separate area for street hawkers.

Mayer's works in India, like Koenigsberger's, reveal his ideological moorings. For instance, his employment of the neighborhood unit in the master plans of Kanpur and Bombay, which he completed before planning the iconic Chandigarh, reflected his past experiences in the field of what is now called community planning and development (Kalia 1987: 53). Mayer had gained insights into community housing through a decade of planning experience. In the late 1920s and the early 1930s, he worked for and collaborated with leading architects and planners of the times, including such stalwarts as Clarence Stein and Henry Wright, both of whom made use of the neighborhood unit concept. His experience designing the planned community of Greenbrook, United States, during Roosevelt's second administration, as a member of the team along with Henry Wright, Allen Kamstra, and Henry Churchill, had also prepared him for planning new towns and neighborhoods. These previous experiences and the modernistic development agenda of India's elites informed Mayer's imaginations that the neighborhood unit suited the Indian context even better than its own place of origin, for reasons which he summed up succinctly to a gathering of planners in Washington DC in October 1950: "However useful the neighborhood concept is here [in the United States], it is more valid in India, where most people are still villagers and small-community people at heart, and fairly recently by origin" (Mayer 1950: 174).

Such generous advocacy of the neighborhood unit, and the quick employment of it in iconic projects such as Chandigarh, Bhubaneswar, and Gandhi Nagar (Kalia 2004, 1995, 1987), helped it become institutionalized into Indian planning practice. In India, as in the United States, the neighborhood unit concept eventually became the prototype for designing city extensions and new towns (Dutt 1993: 365). Its penetration and popularity can be gauged from the fact that, in 1966, M. C. Krishna Swamy reported about 50 such new towns in an article for the *Journal of the Institute of Town Planners, India*. Krishna Swamy commented that "irrespective of the developing agency the main concept and the basic planning principle dominant in these new towns is the self-contained neighborhood unit" (1966: 42).

This brings us to a suitable point to recapitulate the two sets of imaginations that enabled the neighborhood unit concept to become the recurrent theme of plans for new towns and city extensions in both the United States and India.

## CONCLUSION

During this research, I found not even one reference in Koenigsberger's or Mayer's Indian publications to the American urban context in which the concept of the neighborhood unit originated, or to the social anxieties that had prompted its invention in the first place. The focus of these documents, rather, was oriented solely towards India's planning concerns and the development agenda of their clients. I believe the pioneering planners did not even once invoke the American social concerns and urban context for two reasons. First, because the concept in their imaginations was universally valid, the neighborhood unit did not have a monogenic allegiance towards any particular locale, including the one in which it was produced. Yet its "universe" was actually the United States. Second, the Indians perceived the neighborhood unit as "modern" and not specifically American and thus the planners did not need to bother about its US origins. In line with the ideals of "high modernism" (Scott 1998), Mayer and Koenigsberger believed that planning concepts such as the neighborhood unit were justly transferable, and cities such as Chandigarh, Bhubaneswar, and Brasilia could be built anywhere in the world.

However, Mayer and Koenigsberger had to reconcile a remarkable contradiction in order to facilitate the introduction of the neighborhood unit concept to

India. On the one hand, they imagined the neighborhood unit as an appropriate physical instrumentality for producing modern citizens who, for instance, would be secular and caste-neutral in orientation. On the other hand, they imaginatively linked the neighborhood unit with a romantic vision of India's historical villages in order to satisfy the nationalistic concerns of the indigenous elite. To Koenigsberger, this latter perspective was self-evident in the fact that the neighborhood unit extended the ancient tradition of self-government in India's villages into the future. To Mayer, as described above, the concept was a better fit in India, even than in its place of origin, because of Indian's inherent neighborhood tendencies.

Interestingly, pioneering planners also inverted the conundrum that had prompted the invention of the neighborhood unit concept in the first place. Perry's aim in conceiving the neighborhood unit was to inculcate "neighborliness" by creating a village-like state in American cities. Mayer and Koenigsberger, on the other hand, faced a more complicated situation because they wanted to create "neighborliness" by preserving the best elements of existing village life while modernizing Indian cities. However, in doing so, they were ironically aiding the very processes of urbanization that, to Perry, were the root of the problem.

Finally, although Mayer and Koenigsberger were successful in reimagining and reproducing adapted versions of the neighborhood unit, their success was predicated on subverting the original aims and desired outcomes of the concept. This provides a point of reference for today's planners to ponder how current trendy ideas, such as "new urbanism," are increasingly popular in planning contexts far removed from the places of their conception.[9]

## NOTES

1  This research was supported by a Junior Research Fellowship from the American Institute for Indian Studies (AIIS), Chicago. I am also thankful to Aseem Inam, Gavin Shatkin, and William Glover for helpful comments and discussions about this article.

2  The significance of this accolade can be gauged from the fact that, in its almost 50 years of history, ITPI has elected only three "unqualified" fellows. Bhagwan Das, who was involved in the first master plan of Delhi, and was later a Lieutenant Governor of Delhi, was another.

3  A greater emphasis is generally placed on the economic and technological aspects of Nehruvian planning. However, for Nehru, planning was a tool to encourage progress in all of the fields of national life: "[India's problems] call for planning on a national scale, encompassing all aspects of economic and social life, for efforts to mobilize resources, to determine priorities and goals and to create a widespread outlook of change and technological progress" (Nehru, cited in NIUA 1991: 50).

4  Dipesh Chakrabarty has succinctly described this phenomenon: "It would be unfair . . . to think of this perception as simply Western. What it speaks is the language of modernity, of civic consciousness and public health, even of certain ideas of beauty related to management of public space and interests, an order of aesthetics from which the ideals of public health and hygiene can not be separated. It is the language of modern governments, both

colonial and postcolonial, and, for that reason, it is the language, not only of imperialist officials, but of modernist nationalists as well" (2002: 66).

5  Koenigsberger's career is described in Aldhous *et al.* (1983) and in a brief biographical note published online by the Development Planning Unit at University College, London (undated – see References for details).

6  The failure of this production project and the subsequent political fallout was a principal reason for Koenigsberger's departure from India (Liscombe 2006). However, the factory was taken over and renamed by the government of India in 1953, and continues to function today (see Hindustan Prefab Limited, undated.)

7  Koenigsberger's article "New Towns in India" (1952) describes nine such new town projects. Some were designed by him, such as Bhadravati and Bhubaneswar; for some towns, such as Faridabad and Rajpura, he collaborated with various planners; and others, such as Nilokheri and Kalyani, were designed by other planners under his supervision.

8  The civilizing mission also employed methods such as neighborhood-wide bodies, called Vikas Mandal ("Development Councils"), which were intended to sensitize and "educate" the local population in accordance with the neighborhood unit's civic aims (see Clinard and Chatterjee 1962). The miserable failure of this civilizing mission comes alive in the lamentations of an erstwhile HUDCO chairman (Bijlani 1988).

9  The Congress for the New Urbanism (CNU), for example, already identifies projects that derive their inspiration from the principles of new urbanism in locations as disparate as Nicaragua, Saudi Arabia, and India (CNU 2007).

## References

Aldhous, W., Groak, S., Mumtaz, B., and Safir, M. (Eds.). 1983. "Otto Koenigsberger." *Fetschrift, Habitat International*, **7** (5/6), 337–46. Oxford: Pergamon Press.

Banerjee, Tridib and William C. Baer. 1984. *Beyond the Neighborhood Unit.* New York: Plenum Press.

Bauer, Catherine. 1934. *Modern Housing.* Boston: Houghton Mifflin.

Bijlani, H. U. 1988. "Urban Social Facilities." In *South Asian Urban Experience.* Edited by R. C. Sharma. New Delhi: Criterion Publications. pp. 57–74.

Chakrabarty, Dipesh. 2002. *Habitations of Modernity: Essays in the Wake of Subaltern Studies.* Chicago: University of Chicago Press.

Chatterjee, Partha. 1993. *The Nation and its Fragments: Colonial and Postcolonial Histories.* Princeton, NJ: Princeton University Press.

—— 2004. *The Politics of the Governed: Reflection on Popular Politics in Most of the World.* New York: Columbia University Press.

Clinard, Marshall and B. Chatterjee. 1962. "Urban Community Development." In *India's Urban Future.* Edited by Roy Turner. Berkeley: University of California Press. pp. 71–93.

Cooley, C. 1909. *Social Organization.* New York: Charles Scribner's Sons.

CNU (Congress for the New Urbanism). 2007. "Projects." Available: http://www.cnu.org/search/projects. Accessed 2 October 2008.

Development Planning Unit, University College, London. (Undated). Available: http://www.ucl.ac.uk/dpu/Otto%20Koenigsberger/OHK.htm. Accessed 23 March 2006.

Dutt, Ashok K. 1993. "Cities of South Asia." In *Cities of the World—World Regional Urban Development.* Edited by Stanley D. Brunn and Jack F. William. New York: HarperCollins. pp. 331–71.

Gans, Herbert J. 1968. *People and Plans.* New York: Basic Book Publishing.

Gillette, Howard, Jr. 1983. "The Evolution of Neighborhood Planning: From the Progressive Era to the 1949 Housing Act." *Journal of Urban History,* **9** (4), 421–44.

Grenell, Peter. 1972. "Planning for Invisible People: Some Consequences of Bureaucratic Values and Practices." In *Freedom to Build.* Edited by John F. C. Turner and Robert Fichter. New York: Macmillan. pp. 95–121.

Hindustan Prefab Limited. Undated. "Memories." Available: http://www.hindprefab.com/english/memories.html. Accessed 9 February 2006.

Hosagrahar, Jyoti. 2001. "Mansions to Margins: Modernity and the Domestic Landscapes of Historic Delhi." *Journal of the Society of Architectural Historians,* **60** (1), 26–45.

Institute of Town Planners, India (ITPI). 1955. "Autumn Planning Seminar and State Planning Officials' Conference at Lucknow." *Journal of the Institute of Town Planners, India,* November 1955, 8–28.

Isaacs, Reginald R. 1948. "The Neighborhood Theory." *Journal of the AIP,* Spring, **14** (2), 15–23.

Kalia, Ravi. 1987. *Chandigarh: In Search of an Identity.* Carbondale: Southern Illinois University Press.

—— 1995. *Bhubaneswar: From a Temple Town to a Capital City.* Carbondale: Southern Illinois University Press.

—— 2004. *Gandhi Nagar: Building National Identity in Postcolonial India.* Columbia: University of South Carolina Press.

Khan, Masood. 1994. "Cultural Transfers: The Repossession of Architectural Form." *Environmental Design: Journal of the Islamic Environmental Design Research Centre,* **1–2**, 84–103.

Khilnani, Sunil. 1999. *The Idea of India.* New York: Farrar Straus Giroux.

King, D. Anthony. 1976. *Colonial Urban Development: Culture, Social Power, and Environment.* New York: Routledge and Kegan Paul.

Koenigsberger, Otto H. 1952. "New Towns in India." *Town Planning Review,* **23**, 94–131.

Liscombe, Rhodri Windsor. 2006. "In-dependence: Otto Koenigsberger and Modernist Urban Resettlement in India." *Planning Perspectives,* **21**, 157–78.

Mayer, Albert. 1950. "The New Capital of Punjab." *Journal of American Institute of Architects,* **14**, 166–175.

Mayer, Albert and Matthew Nowicki. 1950. *Supplementary Notes to the Architectural Study of Superblock L-37.* Albert Mayer papers on India, University of Chicago Library, Box 18, Folders 30–3.

Mumford, Lewis. 1933. "The Planned Community." *Architectural Forum,* **58**, 253–4.

Mumford, Lewis. 1954. "The Neighborhood and the Neighborhood Unit." *Town Planning Review,* **24**, 256–70.

National Institute of Urban Affairs (NIUA). 1991. *Jawahar Lal Nehru on Building a New India.* New Delhi: NIUA.

Patricios, Nicholas N. 2002. "The Neighborhood Concept: A Retrospective of Physical Design and Social Interaction." *Journal of Architecture and Planning Research,* **19** (1), 70–90.

Perry, Clarence A. 1924. "Planning a City Neighborhood from the Social Point of View." *Proceedings of the National Conference of Social Work* (Chicago), p. 421.

—— 1929. *The Neighborhood Unit, a Scheme for Arrangement for the Family-Life Com-*

*munity. Monograph One in Neighborhood and Community Planning, Regional Survey of New York and its Environs.* New York: Regional Plan of New York and its Environs.

——1939. *Housing for the Machine Age.* New York: Russell Sage Foundation.

Prakash, Gyan. 1999. *Another Reason: Science and the Imagination of Modern India.* Princeton, NJ: University of Princeton Press.

Schubert, Dirk. 1995. "Origins of the Neighborhood Units Idea in Great Britain and Germany: Examples from London and Hamburg." *Planning History,* **17** (3), 32–40.

Scott, James C. 1998. *Seeing Like a State.* New Haven, CT: Yale University Press.

Silver, Christopher. 1985. "Neighborhood Planning in Historical Perspective." *Journal of American Planning Association,* **51** (2), 161–74.

Sivaramakrishnan K. and Arun Agrawal (Eds.). 2003. *Regional Modernities: The Cultural Politics of Development in India.* Stanford, CA: Stanford University Press.

Smith, C. 2006. *The Plan of Chicago: Daniel Burnham and the Remaking of the American City.* Chicago: University of Chicago Press.

Swamy, M. C. Krishna. 1966. "New Towns in India." *Journal of the Institute of Town Planners, India,* **49–50**, 40–51.

Town Planning Organization (TPO). 1956. *Interim General Plan for Greater Delhi.* New Delhi: Ministry of Health, Government of India.

Uttar Pradesh Town Planning Organization (UPTPO). 1952. *Progressive Uttar Pradesh: Town Planning.* Lucknow: New Government Press.

White, M. and L. White. 1962. *The Intellectual versus the City.* New York: Mentor Books.

Wirth, L. 1938. "Urbanism as a Way of Life." *American Journal of Sociology,* **44** (1), 1–24.

# CHAPTER 5

## CITIES IN TRANSITION
### EPISODES OF SPATIAL PLANNING IN MODERN CHINA

**BING WANG**

This paper examines three critical episodes of Chinese spatial planning in the context of the country's urbanization and modernization process from the late nineteenth century to the mid-twentieth century. It focuses primarily on the significance of the diffusion and assimilation of borrowed ideas and techniques in planning applications for the construction of urban landscape. The multitude of channels that transferred this planning knowledge base to China – which ranged from the translation of imported techniques into local operations, and direct implantation of imaginary physical identities, to the interpretation of spatial planning as a component of macro-economic development and resource allocation – have all contributed to form the hybrid layering of the spatial and social fabric of urban neighborhoods in Chinese cities, and to record changes in urban history.

Ever since the concept of modern planning first appeared in the late 1910s in China, and was adopted as an effective tool by the founding father of the Nationalist government, Sun Yat-sen, to reconfigure the industrial ports along China's coastline based on scientific rationalization principles (Sun 1922), the assimilation of ideas and operational principles for spatial planning from outside China has been utilized frequently by successive governments to create political and ideological legitimacy, and as part of massive reformating measures to advance economic development. The aim of this paper is to trace multiple episodes of transformation in institutional organization and operative principles of spatial planning in the Chinese context, and to analyze how the trajectory of spatial planning in China was influenced by deposited cultural and contemporary political ideologies and functioned in a country that experienced dramatic turbulence in the wake of its delayed modernization.

This paper is organized both chronologically and thematically. The intended structure interweaves a horizontal dimension that chronicles three episodic spatial planning "moments" in China with a vertical dimension, consisting of the borrowed institutional characteristics of planning practice. This twofold structure is intended to address the dual nature of continuity and discontinuity in the spatial planning of modern China, and its transitional nature, which have established crucial unspoken premises for the contemporary discourse on urban planning in Chinese society.

## PREMISES OF CULTURAL ASSIMILATION AND DIFFUSION IN SPATIAL PLANNING

A few key premises regarding cultural assimilation and diffusion in spatial planning must first be established. Notably, spatial planning itself is a complex and loose term, denoting deposited results of thought, vision, and action. Spatial planning helps to establish the framework of urban fabrics for the daily lives of human beings, weaving layers of history, selective forms, and the collective memories of a particular culture together, based on rationalization of knowledge and execution. The multitude of critical operative elements encompassed in spatial planning includes planning techniques, guiding principles, institutional frameworks, regulatory mechanisms, and resultant formal representations. The different natures of these operative components entail essential variations in the nature of assimilation and diffusion, as well as in the resultant time span for planning processes. On the one hand, it is critical to evaluate the capability of the recipient environment to accommodate and absorb outside cultural and operative elements. On the other hand, it is also essential to examine the intrinsic nature of the operative elements to be borrowed and transferred, as they are indeed the contents and thus a key factor that defines their own capacity to travel through the boundaries that exist between cultures and nations.

Because the application of spatial planning responds to both formal institutional frameworks and informal conventions, and as the execution of spatial planning itself is always site-defined and agent-specific, interpretations of ideologies and cultural norms that have penetrated through the planned form and spatiality vary greatly. Some of the operative planning components mentioned above can be appropriated and borrowed relatively easily, thus providing selective paradigms for constructing new norms of planning practice in a different context. Some, however, are intrinsically culture- and location-bound.

Over the course of the twentieth century, the trajectory of spatial planning in China has proven to be anything but a straight course. Within the three episodes discussed below, a dynamic instance of cross-cultural borrowing at varying levels presents itself at every critical juncture of the Chinese experience. In each instance, what was appropriated came via multiple channels and functioned as a new knowledge base, an unprecedented institutional framework, the construction of new ideologies, or other tangibles or intangibles, which, in turn, were assimilated over time until they eventually became part of the localized Chinese spatial planning fabric.

Because of the complexity and wide coverage of theories and practices related to spatial planning, and its multi-directional involvement with the flow of ideas, capital, and people, delineating a clear path for its processes of diffusion and assimilation is a rather difficult task. In fact, the process of assimilation has never been linear or cohesive. Instead, it has always been a discursive formation through multiple layers, conducted by various agents, be they architects/planners, politicians, academics, or others.

In the three episodes discussed below, each time a disparate model and framework was borrowed from Western practice into the Chinese context, it represented a historical juncture that was followed by waves of nationalistic reactions. The tumult that occurred with each shift of political ideology, and the various interpretations given to the concept of traditional Chinese culture following these shifts, have contributed to the complexity and ambiguity of the process of assimilation and diffusion. This has, in many ways, defined the characteristics and consequences of the ideas and practices of spatial planning in modern China.

## THREE EPISODES OF DIFFUSION AND ADAPTATION IN SPATIAL PLANNING

### EPISODE 1: CREATION OF INSTITUTIONAL AND SOCIAL INFRASTRUCTURE

China has a long history of applying the power of spatial planning. The belief that the formal configuration of the physical environment permeates everyday life through visual display as it shapes the mindset of ordinary people is well reflected in the master planning of traditional cities, through which the established hierarchies in spatiality are conveyed with a clear sense of order, strict social stratification, and the inward nature of family-oriented planning culture.

The modern sense of urban planning in China emerged within the broad socio-political context of a transitional society, which developed from the 1860s to the 1940s. Planning's initial appearance and early, sporadic applications were concentrated largely within a few coastal cities, most of which shared a common trajectory of urbanization and a temporal sequence of opening up to outside cultures. Among these, Shanghai, which was experiencing accelerated modernization during the period, represented the most intense exchange in the realm of spatial planning, including the formation of institutional frameworks, the application of planning techniques, and a realization of spatial representations of planning as a form of publicity and an instrument for the establishment of modern government. What is interesting, and indeed intellectually stimulating, in the

Shanghai case is that the city itself, at that time, was administered simultaneously through two markedly different cultural and political systems. One was a transitional Chinese system from the feudal period to the initial modern stage, and the other was the semi-colonized, extra-territorial governance established by the West on Chinese soil. The emergence of spatial planning in the modern sense in China thus developed amid the influences, conflicts, and confusions of these two distinct political and cultural milieux, wherein exchange and unspoken competition prompted each side onward, with strong nationalistic sentiments rendered by the specific context.

In fact, the arrival of spatial planning in China as a practical and intellectual discourse, largely through Shanghai, was no accident. During the twentieth century, Shanghai distinguished itself in many ways from other port cities with foreign concessions. Compared with other cities such as Guangzhou and Tianjin, where established local culture, centralized government, and hierarchical urban spatial frameworks had already been formed, Shanghai's relatively brief history entailed its porosity to outside customs and cultures. As a fishing village and then a concentrated trading center, Shanghai was a "melting pot" even within China, where a mixture of cultures and guild organizations were prevalent in the eighteenth and early nineteenth centuries. Its geographic location at the mid-point along China's coastline, and at the estuary of one of the country's most active rivers, which linked it to the major settlements of the hinterland, also enhanced Shanghai's attraction to both Chinese and Westerners searching for a "land of opportunity."

Since the signing of the Treaty of Nanking (Nanjing) in 1842, the establishment of the British concession marked the opening of Shanghai as one of the five "Treaty Ports," forced to open up to residence and trading activities by foreign citizens.[1] Originally, trading was the foremost concern of the Western occupiers and "the concept of creating or even planning a city was utterly absent" (Denison and Ren 2006: 34). Only when conflicts between foreign concessions and the Chinese government, as well as fissures among the different concessions, caused numerous social problems, among which land ownership and property use rights were the most pressing, were a rationalized administrative body and an effective governing strategy called for, and the initial effort of "surveying the ground, drawing the plans, marking out the roads, defining the boundaries of lots, etc" began (ibid.: 46). The need for spatial planning as a means of governance and political control became increasingly evident as the foreign concessions continued to transform into a localized community. When a local riot led by the "Small Sword" Society and the subsequent Taiping Rebellion resulted in an influx of affluent Chinese people to the concessions, seeking refuge in Shanghai, rents for landowners in the area soared, and a new building typology of Lilong housing,[2] as well as a nascent modern real estate market, were born. Improvements in building construction as well as in overall city infrastructure and urban hygiene conditions followed. Roads of 20–25 feet in width were constructed in the foreign concessions, compared with those of only 6 feet in the walled Chinese city. Public utilities, such as electricity and water, and a tramway transport service became available within the confines of the concessions. By the 1880s, the governing body of the British concession area, the Municipal Council, had already transformed a large area of barren swamp along the riverbank into the prosperous new urban center for the emerging Shanghai (later known as "the Bund"). In so doing, the coordinated planning efforts for civic improvements, spearheaded by the Municipal Council of the British concession, were established as the de facto administrative exemplar for the Chinese government of urban construction and management. Modern spatial planning emerged naturally and imperatively in Shanghai, based on local necessity, with civic improvement as its initial focus.

The Municipal Council's seemingly efficient organizational structure, together with its systematic enactment and implementation of laws and regulations, offered an administrative model for the Chinese government. Moreover, it placed pressure on its Chinese counterpart to improve correspondingly its performance in coping with construction activities in the context of rapid urbanization. In 1895, the first district-level Chinese government agency, known initially as the South City Bureau of Roadworks, was established in response to the need for the planning and construction of the road networks within the district. In 1905, 10 years later, after obtaining approval from the municipal official of the Qing Court (the circuit intendant or *daotai*),[3] and financial support from a member of the local gentry, Li Zhong-jue, a citywide governmental agency – the Shanghai Bureau of General Works – was formed. This agency was given responsibility for building infrastructure and "manag[ing] all matters connected with roads, lighting, and policy in the city and its suburbs" (Henriot 1993: 10–11). Under the leadership of local elites, similar administrative agencies were soon created in 1906 in two other local sub-districts of Shanghai: the Zhabei Bureau of Roads, Public Works and Patrols, as well as the Pudong Bureau of Dike Maintenance. As predecessors of Shanghai's governing institutions for managing the construction of physical infrastructure in different constituencies within the city, all of these agencies were to be amalgamated into the Bureau of Public Works of Shanghai Municipality in the 1920s.

Cognizant of the successful administration of the Municipal Council within the International Settlement, and indeed pressed into competition by it, the Bureau of Public Works under the jurisdiction of Shanghai's municipal government proceeded to develop a similar operative and regulatory framework. This accordingly became one of the first Chinese governmental agencies founded at the municipal level to oversee urban infrastructure and planning activities for the physical environment. Its purview differed from that of the traditional Chinese municipal institutions of the feudal dynasties in that the scope of its management covered not only the construction of official edifices, but also wider-ranging physical production efforts, such as public infrastructure and open spaces, as well as the development of zoning policies and regulations for private residences that shaped and had an impact on the cityscape as a whole (Shanghai Bureau of Public Works 1937). Instead of focusing on the construction of individual edifices of official agencies, often on a monumental scale, now the focus of government intervention was civic improvement on an urban scale, facilitated by a knowledge of scientific engineering and spatial planning strategies. This resulted in their improved ability to systematically manage construction activities amidst the urban chaos and disorder brought about by Shanghai's rapid urban growth.

By 1928, under the Nationalist government, the Shanghai Bureau of Public Works had developed into a central agency consisting of five departments, with a total administrative staff of 123. It was in charge of the planning and construction management of bridges, docks, roads, and canals, and the renovation of dilapidated neighborhoods (including both private and public buildings). A department of urban planning was added the following year, and an additional department responsible for the management and procurement of construction materials was created in 1933. The Bureau, in addition to managing physical building and construction activities, also oversaw the administration of registered individual practitioners in the field. It was the first Chinese government agency to introduce and administer open bids and public competitions among design-planning professionals. The Bureau's municipal administrative system soon expanded into each district of the city to provide a disciplinary and bureaucratic structure for conducting building inspections and issuing permits, as well as for managing professional associations in various geographic areas.

By the 1920s, several other large cities had followed the example of the Shanghai Bureau of Public Works by establishing similar governmental agencies. For instance, the Bureau of Public Works in Beijing was established in September 1928 and was charged with the management of public and private building activities under the Beijing municipal government. Cities such as Tianjin and Qingdao also followed with similar agencies. By the late 1930s, under the unified administration of the Nationalist government, the Bureau of Public Works and the Bureau of Land were listed as municipal agencies under the dual supervision of the municipal governments and the Ministry of the Interior at state level. The specific function of the Bureau of Land was to survey and classify land extensions and record land transactions, as well as to allocate land for public buildings and to utilize public land as a governmental resource to finance the construction of public infrastructure.

Construction techniques for building wide and flatlaid asphalt roads that were suitable and durable enough for urban growth, with street lamps aligned, were in fact just one example of many Western methods adopted by the Chinese government in Shanghai for the improvement of civic infrastructure. Overall, borrowing detailed construction techniques and importing building materials contributed physically to the rapid transformation of Shanghai into a metropolis in a relatively short period. More importantly, however, the International Settlement's Municipal Council presented the Chinese government with a model of an effective institutional framework, with the application of scientific knowledge in dealing with the rapidly expanding urban territory. The effectiveness of the emerging modern municipal agencies, such as the Bureau of Public Works and the Bureau of Land, highlighted the important role that the construction and management of the physical environment played as an instrument for reinforcing the stability of modern governments. The administration of land use, the spatial planning of urban infrastructure, the construction of buildings, and the management of independent design and planning professionals gradually became critical components in the development of a modern Chinese government.

The profound changes that accompanied the development of spatial planning in Shanghai were multi-layered. Not only was the basic and fundamental governing structure established; laws and regulations were also adopted as the guiding foundation for urban interventions by the government. A new methodology for spatial planning that focused on civic improvement and modern infrastructure functioned for the first time as the leading factor to steer the growth of the city. New professions that specialized in creating the spatial order and forms of the physical environment were born: first the architect, followed later by the urban planner. Both were to become groups understood to have the professional knowledge and expertise needed to guide urban development.

Traditionally, educated Chinese (the *literati*) had been Confucian generalists with scholarly expertise in the fields of classics, history, and literature. From the 1920s on, the foreign architects practicing in Shanghai, together with the foreign-educated Chinese returnees who studied and trained abroad in disciplines such as architecture and civil engineering, became one of the first groups of emerging professionals in China. Those who had trained overseas represented a new breed of educated Chinese (Wang and Rowe 2010). Together with foreign practitioners, they functioned as one of the forces for the diffusion of planning ideas and techniques, as well as the promoters of new aesthetic architectural standards. Their knowledge and skills were oriented far more pragmatically in everyday life, and were more grounded in scientific rationalization, than those of the former *literati*. Possessed of technical expertise and, gradually, cultural and moral authority, these new groups soon became the agents of cultural exchange and assimilation, helping to transform the fundamental social structure of traditional Chinese society.

Compared with the reality that it took roughly half a century for the professional status of architects to be officially acknowledged by governing authorities in China, the official recognition of "urban planning" as a modern discipline and a professional practice surfaced relatively promptly in China, taking place in line with the formation of this profession elsewhere. Planning expertise was elevated publicly by a government announcement on the front page of a popular Shanghai newspaper on 29 December 1927, in an article entitled "Urban Building": "The prosperity of a country, to a large extent, depends on highly specialized professional elites" (*Shanghai Newspaper*, 29 December 1927). Three points were addressed in the article: first, that a rational physical planning process was a key component of civic design, and that the public sector should aim at building an environment to provide, above anything else, convenience for urban dwellers; second, that public buildings and open spaces should be the primary focus of large-scale civic design and spatial planning; and third, that zoning should be adopted as an effective approach to the enhanced management of private residences in urban planning. Thus, the article constituted an early public policy address, highlighting rational planning and functionalist thinking, as well as the concept of zoning (an increasingly popular planning instrument at the international level).

This declaration acknowledged in a public manner that the expertise offered by spatial/urban planning was viewed eagerly by the government, and was considered an indispensable and effective means to accelerate the nation's modernization. The concept of professional urban planning and zoning vis-à-vis the government's intervention in creating a livable urban environment for the public was unprecedented in China. If early adoption of regulations and control through the specifics of a rational planning process had shared the top-down notions implicit in traditional Chinese city planning, as is evidenced by the development and administration of government entities such as the Zhabei and Pudong Bureaux mentioned above, the 1927 newspaper announcement made clear that, for a modern China, scientific zoning and efficient land-use allocation were to occur – a planning system based on a knowledge of engineering and on functional thinking, rather than on the social hierarchies of the old feudal system.

## EPISODE 2: FORMAL REPRESENTATION IN SPATIAL PLANNING

Soon after these events, spatial planning was utilized to construct new civic centers for Shanghai and Nanking (Nanjing), the latter as the capital of the Nationalist government. The political connotations of these two planning efforts were highlighted when the first large-scale and comprehensive documents of spatial planning of modern China, the Greater Shanghai Plan of 1930 and the Nanking Capital Plan, caught the public's attention.

Both projects attached significant symbolic and political implications to the physical representation of planning. The new centers were intended to celebrate China's past glory as well as its future modernity. Straddling such a duality necessarily required the effort of spatial planning to combine a formalized, traditional Chinese architectural style with the application of new building technologies, and the representation of rationalized planning principles. Formal Western aesthetic and spatial organization principles were borrowed to represent the essence of modernity, which the new government was keen to promote. As pointed out succinctly by Sun Ke, one of the Nationalist Central Committee council members, who had studied city planning and politics at UCLA in Los Angeles and at Columbia University in New York, "the planning of the projects [should] follow Western scientific principles and Chinese artistic expressions" (Zhang 2004: 13).

The influence of the American "City Beautiful" movement, and the emphasis on comprehensive planning for the public good and on the "science" of engineering in city building, became evident in both the Shanghai Plan and the Nanking Capital Plan. The classical geometric composition of the road networks, the idea of processional boulevards with a decorated urban landscape, a large public gathering space, as well as the highlighted importance of architectural expressions for the monumental civic buildings, reflected the guiding principles of the plans of Chicago and San Francisco drawn up at the beginning of the twentieth century by renowned figures such as Daniel Burnham. Functionalist urban planning principles, such as hierarchical road classification and zones of separated land use – administrative, industrial, commercial, and residential, as well as zones for the port facilities in Shanghai and for a proposed airport in Nanjing – all reflected the surging modernistic and functionalistic thinking of the spatial planning that was growing in popularity in contemporary US cities. The intended monumentality of the civic centers highlighted by the two Plans was conveyed not only through the building layouts and proposed scales, but also by the specificities of zoning ordinances and the provision of open public spaces (Figures 5.1 and 5.2).

The Nationalist government, as a close ally of the United States, encouraged and invited the participation and leadership of American architects and experts in the two projects, along with other foreign professionals. Each project went through a nationwide design competition that was open to both domestic and foreign architects. The Planning Commission of the Shanghai Plan consisted of Chinese returnees and select foreign advisors. Among these, Shen Yi was the director of the Commission, a German-trained hydraulic engineer and Commissioner of Public Works in Shanghai for 10 years (Shen 1985: 99–134). Dong

**Figure 5.1**   The master plan of Greater Shanghai, 1931. Source: Society of Chinese Architects
(1933: 4).

**Figure 5.2**   The new civic center of Shanghai, 1933. Source: Society of Chinese Architects
(1933: 5).

Dayou, the architectural advisor, was trained at the University of Minnesota and
at Columbia University, where the Beaux-Arts system dominated. Three foreign
experts, invited as advisors and consultants, included Asa E. Phillips, an American
city planner; Dr. Carl E. Grunsky, a civil engineer from San Francisco, who had
worked on a committee advising infrastructure planning and construction for Chicago; and Hermann Jansen from Berlin University, who was involved at the time

in the planning of the modern Turkish capital of Ankara. For the Nanjing Plan, the American architect Murphy Henry acted as the chief architectural advisor to the Capital Planning Office, and Ernest Goodrich, a fellow American, as the engineering advisor.

Promulgated in around the same time period as China's first municipal law (MacPherson 1990), both Plans also sought to reassert traditional values and maintain "Chinese-ness" in their spatial consequences. Nationalistic sentiments, and traditional calls for the elite group to lead the conscience of the country's future, were reflected through the planning process, while Chinese cultural values were represented through both the orientations of the spatial order and the design of individual architectural style. The strong axis leading north–south, with a symmetrical organization of governmental edifices located in the middle of the planned city center, evidently spoke to a typical tradition of Chinese city layout. Most of the individual buildings were designed to revive a style traditional for Chinese official buildings, with gable roofs and stone podiums.

Specifically, the Greater Shanghai Plan, with the new civic center as the focus, reiterated the initial positioning of Shanghai as the largest port in East Asia – as had been proposed by Sun Yat-sen in his 1922 book *The International Development of China*. The exercise focused on the planning of a partial new territory of Shanghai. The Plan did not include either the concession area or the high-density, original walled city. Rather, in the Plan, the strategic location of the new city center of Shanghai was designated to be independent from the Chinese past and the Shanghai urbanism of foreign construction, and thus situated between the foreign concessions and the Wusong Port, a potential strategic industrial port of the city. According to the Mayor of Shanghai at that time, Huang Yu, this was intended to reduce the dependence of Shanghai on the Yangtze River, along which the International Settlement was located.

For the Nanking Plan, Nanking's capital status imbued it with importance as "an icon of nationalist political ideals" (Cody 1996: 357). Its planning effort focused on the highlighted efficiency of government operations and its symbolism for transparency and nationalistic pride. The government buildings were grouped around different functions of governmental branches and were visually aligned along the axis of the mausoleum of the founding father of the Nationalist government, Sun Yat-sen (Figure 5.3). Using zoning as a basis for development control and for guiding the master plan, the government enacted the National Government Enabling Act for Municipal Planning and Zoning nationwide, which was patterned upon New York's Zoning Act of 1916 (ibid.: 362).

Unfortunately, with the breakout of the Sino-Japan war in 1937, the implementation of both Plans came to a complete halt. However, the evident interest in integrating modern planning rationales with China's traditional aesthetic

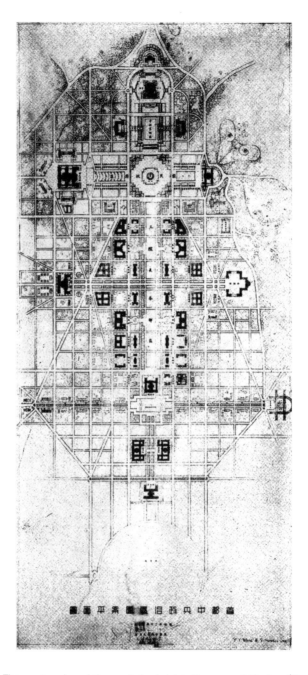

首都中央政治区旧署平面圖

**Figure 5.3** The master plan of the central administrative area of Nanjing (Nanking), 1929. Source: Capital Planning Technical Personnel Office (1929: 14).

sensibilities, the application of new building materials, and the use of unprec-edented construction techniques had been clearly reflected in the eclectic style of a few buildings that had been completed, and in the overall planning layouts of these first comprehensive Chinese planning documents. More importantly, the drawings of the master plans functioned as a national development strategy both politically and strategically, and formed the guiding principle for the first modern spatial planning of land use in both Shanghai and Nanjing. The process of com-bining institutional efforts for organizing functions of the city based on rationalized land-use analysis, and then imbuing them with spatial representations, reflected the true essence of modern spatial planning as a discipline, and initiated a new discourse in understanding and planning cities in China.

## EPISODE 3: THE CENTRALIZED PLANNING SYSTEM AND SOCIALIST PLANNING PRINCIPLES

When the Communist government came to power in 1949, China was largely an agrarian society, with an urban population of only 7 percent and a nationwide non-agricultural rural population of 20 percent. Shanghai alone, which accounted for approximately 9 percent of the entire urban population in 1949, produced 20 percent of China's industrial output. The urgent pressure on the government to rebuild society highlighted a critical need for the expertise of spatial planning to help a country devastated by years of warfare. Spatial planning was to prove a strategic and essential instrument for the new government to achieve a balance between the constructions of socialist idealism and of economic advancement.

Eminent architect-planner representatives were appointed to important official posts as spokesmen for the national government, their professional expertise serv-ing to ratify the critical planning decisions made by the governing entity. Although the building of an administrative structure was important, the gaining of legitimacy in the eyes of the population was even more urgent, as the new government had risen to power largely through the support of the majority agrarian populace. Thus, as Benedict Anderson argues, nationhood was an "imagined community" before it became a political reality (Anderson 1983). The newly formed communist gov-ernment utilized spatial planning fully to help fill in the broad contours of a newly envisioned China, and to disseminate that vision to the public. On the one hand, planning was increasingly becoming a component of macro-economic policy, because there was now a planned economy. On the other hand, physical planning was invited to help the government project a vision of a near-utopian communist society, using concrete forms of buildings and monumental public spaces that spoke to an ideologically and politically engaged "imagination."

The ideological link between China and the Soviet Union at the time welcomed a wholehearted adaptation of Soviet theories and practices of spatial planning to China. One example of the government's keenness regarding the Soviet model was reflected in the task assigned to all available Russian language instructors at the People's University in Beijing, the country's newly established educational center for training Communist leaders. Between September 1950 and August 1955, these instructors translated more than 2,000 course syllabi, lecture notes, and related textbooks from Soviet technical materials. A total print run of 7.65 million copies of these translations was subsequently distributed in more than 100 institutions of higher learning (Hsu 1964).

Spatial planning shifted from the original focus on physical improvements to large-scale reconstruction and reorganization of the urban environment, having descended from the initial Anglo-American concepts to become a means of distribution of social products for the purpose of advancing the national economy and the industrialization effort. With financial aid and technical support from the Soviet Union, 156 large-scale industrial projects were launched in 1953, functioning as the focus of China's first Five-Year Plan.[4] The planning and construction of these projects were to become catalysts of the first organized efforts of nationwide industrialization, as well as for initiatives of urban renewal and city-building activities. The State Planning Commission organized personnel from various ministries, together with Soviet engineers and planners, to visit sites and investigate the feasibility of building cities around these potential 156 industrial sites. There was a planning committee for each site, comprising between five and seven architect-planners under the guidance of Soviet advisors. Between 1955 and 1957 alone, the state approved more than 20 General Plans for cities that contained multiple industrial projects. Based on the principles of these General Plans, cities became mere containers of industrial sites for economic production. And the shift from "cities of consumption" to "cities of production" was one of many strategies employed by the government in response to the challenge of building up a socialist state both physically and mentally. Projected demographic growth and urban expansion, as well as the calculation of wind strength and direction in deciding the location of industrial sites, etc., were all based on either quota systems or formulae provided by Soviet technical advisors and the newly translated instruction books. Spatial planning became just one of many integrated components in the overall establishment of a centralized economic planning system.

Standardization and the hierarchical organization of neighborhoods along Soviet planning principles that were pervasive throughout many East European cities were ardently embraced in China (see also Ward's chapter in the present book). However, changes in the operational frameworks of spatial planning did not necessarily guarantee a dramatic and intrinsically different formal representation of the cities. The Master Plan of Shanghai of 1953 still revealed strong continuities from the Shanghai Master Plan of 1930, such as the geometrically highlighted civic center, and the classically composed road system. The only exception was that, in contrast to the strict land-use separation based on zoning in the Plan of 1930, the Master Plan of 1953 embraced the idea of collective living, based on the organization and physical location of working units (*danwei*). Houses were grouped around factories, with schools and convenient shopping facilities – their size based on population quota – located within walking distance.

Soviet experience in industrialization and urbanization was actively sought after, not only through the organized effort for the translation of Soviet technical books, but also through measures including the establishment of exchange programs, the invitation of Soviet experts to act in advisory roles in decision-making processes, and even the mandatory teaching of Russian in high schools and universities. These all reflected the Chinese government's belief in a need to "catch up," and a confidence in the Soviet system. At the same time, the widely spread planning ideas of satellite towns and garden cities, influenced by the UK new town and garden city movement, were also adopted in many General Plans for cities, and were incorporated into detailed plans for neighborhood design.

The physical planning system of the time relied heavily on national government as the centralized organizer, responsible for determining what was in the public's best interests and acting as a spokesperson for client satisfaction. Expressed through the government's centralized planning agenda, the so-called "collective will of the people" became the most critical element in the decision-making process. This further restricted the participation of individual architect-planners in many aspects of spatial production, reducing their role to that of mere technicians and government functionaries.

Following the gradual implementation of nationalization strategies, all spatial planning and construction activities were eventually subsumed into the country's overall central planning system for economic development and distribution. The framework provided by this for the development of the planning profession and the building industry in general consisted of four major aspects. The first was a systematic macro-projection of future building activities at every administrative level, whereby respective government agencies determined the total buildable areas in each administrative region, city, and town over a fixed period of time. The second aspect of the new planning and construction framework was a macro-projection of budgets allocated for building and spatial planning activities, overseen by the China Construction Bank, which was established specifically for this purpose. The third aspect of the framework was the centralized operation of state-owned design/planning institutes and construction enterprises, which incorporated a dual system of corporate governance consisting of a professional management team and a Party organizational team within each corporate entity. The fourth aspect was the unification of design guidelines across all of China, standardized periodically to conform to changing economic circumstances and the introduction of new political initiatives.

Spatial planning became, as a consequence, the product and the effective channel of redistribution of urban growth and economic production, both geographically and socially. The policy incentives that encouraged the growth of smaller cities and de-densification of regional cities all aimed at reorganizing the national economy through achieving maximum efficiencies within the shortest possible span of time. As a critical and integral part of economic planning, spatial planning became the ends and the means for establishing and realizing visions that were believed to be aligned with the goals of a socialist society. In the absence of private market forces, planning simply acted as the fundamental instrument for coordination between the state and its various agencies, as well as between the central government and local forces.

As a result, planning activities themselves were positioned economically and ideologically at the forefront of the national reconstruction project. Spatial planning functioned as a discourse that focused only on the macro level and the long term. General Plans usually covered periods of 20–30 years, even though (in theory at least) they were subject to five-year reviews. However, the physicality of micro-level place-making principles appeared to have lost out to the less sophisticated practice of creating monumentality, and the construction of symbolic edifices as political statements.

## CONCLUSION

Three critical historical episodes were depicted above to illustrate how modern spatial planning originated as a borrowed discourse in China, how it evolved, and how it was interpreted and utilized by various governments to facilitate the twentieth-century modernization of the country.

Within each episode, borrowing and learning from others has been a characteristic intrinsically embedded in the developmental trajectory of the spatial planning agenda in China. On the one hand, this certainly is not unique to China alone. Plans, ideas, and innovations for achieving an orderly society have been interchanged repeatedly among cultures and countries throughout history. Formal representations of spatial planning principles and architectural images often inspire those beyond the boundaries of a nation. On the other hand, given China's delayed entry into the modern era, which saw its industrialization lag far behind that of other countries in the international arena, borrowing from existing models that had been tested elsewhere seemed to be a particularly obvious and efficient method for catching up quickly.

There have been a multitude of exchanges and assimilations in the process of China's development of spatial planning, from the original conception of spatial planning to its administrative structure, regulatory framework, and final physical implementation. The composition of each essential element for the functions of planning, in turn, has reflected the interconnectedness of spatial planning in terms of both its disciplinary practice and its theorization.

China's borrowing of multiple operative planning elements, through multilayered channels, combined the actions of what I would like to call both *passive* and *active* borrowing. The boundary between the two was often not clear-cut. For our purposes, *active* borrowing means the conscious adaptation of foreign models on the part of either the government or influential sectors/agents of society in systemic efforts to develop new organizational operations and rational forms of execution. In contrast, *passive* borrowing takes place by way of a discursive formation, and accumulates through informal cultural interactions over time.

From 1845 to the mid-1920s, Shanghai evolved from a small, walled Chinese town to become a modern Asian metropolis. Within these 70 years of urban growth, spatial planning gradually evolved from its initial form as the government's response to pressures from the International Settlement, into a means of dealing simultaneously with land use, population mobility, and the speculative growth of urban development. The initial focus on civic improvement in early Chinese spatial planning, which was no different from spatial planning's original concerns in the West near the end of the nineteenth century, expressed an understanding of planning as a necessary form of disciplinary control[5] to deal with deteriorating urban conditions and intensifying social tensions caused by rapid industrialization. In the Chinese case, these issues were triggered and expedited by the opening of the treaty ports by the Western military powers, and their desire for trade. Spatial planning brought to Shanghai not only the modernized road system, faster tramways, and new building typologies and construction techniques, but also a mentality of rationalization through scientific knowledge, and disciplinary organization in the processes of the production and management of physical space and rapid urban growth. With this, a modern model for the municipal government was born.

This process of borrowing in spatial planning practice was channeled by multiple means, and gradually permeated every part of everyday life in China. This occurred through the physical reality of the built urban area produced within the foreign concessions on Chinese soil, through the practices of foreign architects and foreign-educated Chinese, through the engagement of foreign advisors, and through publications translated from foreign sources for general circulation. Such borrowing and cultural exchanges were initially not pursued systematically or cohesively. Instead, this was the choice of "no choice," after the previous half-century of struggle by the Chinese government and by the intellectual elite in search of a direction for a country that was deep in nostalgia for its glorious past and had consistently suffered military defeats and economic stagnations since the late Qing dynasty (1644–1911). However, the beneficial effects that borrowing brought to cities was soon evident, although it was accompanied by tremendous national humiliation and moral dilemmas linked with foreign interference and extra-territoriality. From then on, this established evidence for the potential of borrowing from outside propelled the government's pursuit of organizing, operating, and expanding the large-scale appropriation of multiple elements within the realm of spatial planning and beyond. Spatial planning gradually became a sustaining armature for change, as well as an effective instrument for governing entities to legitimize the new regime and to claim uniqueness in its ideological construction.

Political chaos and institutional fragmentation in China's modern history, from the nineteenth century to the mid-twentieth century, often followed social changes that challenged entrenched cultural values, fomented considerable confusion around traditional norms, and thus promptly established a backdrop for the frenzied copying and diffusion of Western models. However, it is also evident that copying and borrowing did not always guarantee a successful application amid the specificities of each locality. In fact, the process of borrowing has never been a smooth journey in China or anywhere else. The concrete contents of active borrowing, and the rates of subsequent assimilation, always vary at different periods of history according to the associated macro-political and economic conditions, and are based on the nature of the specific elements being appropriated.

In the field of modern spatial planning in China, borrowing was first initiated for the institutional structure of the governmental system, and technical, rationalized reasoning. This was followed by an acceptance of a formal realization of new spatial orders, through the physical construction of buildings and cities that were seen as necessary catalysts for rapid economic progress and as instruments of political proclamation. The first action of appropriation – establishing institutional infrastructure – was less intangible than the second borrowing, although still fundamental, and was thus appropriated without a great deal of public confrontation. Shortly after, however, once the borrowing was represented in tangible form through the physical environment, the act of borrowing was revisited in an analytical process of ideological justification by both the government and the public. During this time, intellectuals often led debates that involved various interpretations of a growing nationalism. This second stage of borrowing, then, encompassed a struggle for Chinese identity within the borrowing process that frequently led to a re-examination of various aspects of Chinese culture, and a reinterpretation of cultural progress. For example, in the late Qing dynasty, the famous quotation by Zhang Zhi-dong, "Chinese learning for essential principles,

Western learning for practical functions" (Teng and Fairbank 1979), reflected a clear strategy and an explicit compromise, arrived at by both the government and the elites in their attempts to justify the process of active borrowing. Under the Nationalist government, the building of the new government centers in Shanghai and Nanjing combined Western planning principles with distinctly traditional Chinese visual building styles. This desire to blend Chinese and non-Chinese elements in the new physical forms was a tangible manifestation of the ideological struggles taking place, and the consequent compromise. After 1949, active borrowing from the Soviet Union initially proved less troublesome as the models being adopted at least conformed to a jointly embraced Marxist political ideology; soon after, however, both the public and the government went through the same process of struggle, calling for a reinterpretation of Chinese ideological and cultural identity, a cycle that was repeated throughout history.

It was not until the 1990s, arguably, that the conflict between borrowing and the quest for an ideological identity was subdued in China, because of a strong sense of pragmatism that has permeated this recent reform era. This pragmatism has been combined with a growing understanding of the detrimental nature of the largely superficial political and ideological struggles that characterized previous periods. The acceptance of borrowing as a primary tool for China's rapid modernization, along with a final acknowledgment that such borrowing would not efface the fundamental nature of Chinese culture or its distinctive identity overnight, have helped to build a new confidence in both the spatial planning discourse and beyond.

Therefore, in the development of spatial planning discourse in China, borrowing has constituted both an introductory step in efforts to find a means of progress, and a unique way of repositioning Chinese culture in contemporary time and space. Active borrowing has often been a deliberate practice that is subsequently followed by a series of refusals, ideological struggles, justifications, and an extended process of trial and error, after which a final stage of assimilation occurs, and the receptive capacity of Chinese culture itself is tested and broadened. With increased globalization, the channels for the exchange of ideas and operational techniques become more complex and often defy old premises. Complexity and contradictions, actions of borrowing, and multiple layers of both importing and exporting thoughts and innovations can all exist at the same time and within the same locality.

## NOTES

1  Between 1842 and 1844, the British, French, and Americans were granted extra-territorial rights to reside for 100 years, with their respective independent governing bodies, police, and judicial systems, in a designated territory along the Huangpu River in Shanghai. The

British concession later merged with that of the Americans to become the International Settlement, which was governed subsequently by the Municipal Council. It was in 1943 that
both the International Settlement and the French concession were abolished in Shanghai.

2  Lilong housing is a unique housing typology that originated in the foreign concessions of
Shanghai at the end of the nineteenth century. Built initially as mass commodity housing
for the purpose of commercial profits by speculators residing in the foreign settlements,
Lilong housing soon became a popular residential type in Shanghai between the 1910s
and 1940s. It boasts the combined architectural characteristics of south-eastern Chinese
traditional courtyard housing and European rowhouses. As a specific residential typology,
Lilong housing was intended to suit the traditional Chinese living style and the demand for
high density in contemporary Shanghai. In Chinese, *li* means "neighborhoods," *long* means
"lanes."

3  The local *daotai*, or circuit intendant, was the most senior official in Shanghai's local administration during the Qing dynasty, the equivalent of a modern-day mayor of Shanghai.

4  The Five-Year Plans of China were a series of economic development initiatives. The concept was initially developed by the Soviet State Planning Committee based on the Marxist
Theory of Productive Forces, and was adopted by China in the early 1950s to guide centralized economic planning.

5  According to Foucault, disciplinary control works to compose a productive force within the
dimension of space–time whose effect will be greater than the sum of its component forces
(see details in Foucault 1995).

## REFERENCES

Anderson, B. (1983) *Imagined Communities: Reflections on the Origin and Spread of
Nationalism* (New York, Verso).

Capital Planning Technical Personnel Office (1929) *Planning of the Capital*, vol. 1 (Nanjing,
Capital Planning Technical Personnel Office).

Cody, J. (1996) "American Planning in Republican China 1911–1937," *Planning Perspectives*, **11** (4), 339–77.

Denison, E. and Ren, G. Y. (2006) *Building Shanghai: The Story of China's Gateway*
(Chichester, Wiley-Academy).

Foucault, M. (1975, 2nd edition 1995) *Discipline and Punish: The Birth of the Prison*,
translated from the French by Alan Sheridan (New York, Vintage Books).

Henriot, C. (1993) *Shanghai, 1927–1937: Municipal Power, Locality and Modernization*
(Berkeley, University of California Press).

Hsu, C. Y. (1964) "The Reorganization of Higher Education in Communist China 1949–61,"
*China Quarterly*, **19** (July–September), 139–45.

MacPherson, K. (1990) "The Greater Shanghai Plan, 1927–1937," *Planning Perspectives*,
**5**, 39–62.

Shanghai Bureau of Public Works (1937) *Brief History and Evolution of Shanghai Bureau
of Public Works* (Shanghai, Wenhai Publisher).

*Shanghai Newspaper* (*Shen Bao*) (1927) "Urban Building," 29 December.

Shen, Y. (1985) *Shen Yi tzu-shu* [Autobiography of Shen Yi] (Taibei, Chuan Qi Wenxue
Publisher).

Society of Chinese Architects (1933) "Vision for the Greater Shanghai," *Chinese Architecture*, **1** (6), 4–6.

Sun Y. (1922) *The International Development of China* (New York, China Cultural Service).

Teng, S. and Fairbank, J. K. (1979) *China's Response to the West: A Documentary Survey, 1839–1923*, 2nd edn. (Cambridge, MA, Harvard University Press).

Wang, B. and Rowe, P. G. (2010) "Formation and Re-formation of the Architecture Profession in China, The Professions in China," in Alford, W. S., Kirby, W. and Winston, K. (Eds.) *The Professions in China* (New York, Routledge).

Zhang, F. H. (2004) *Proceedings of Chinese Architecture History International Conference in 2002* (Beijing, Tsinghua University Press).

# CHAPTER 6

# URBAN SUSTAINABILITY AND COMPACT CITIES IDEAS IN JAPAN
## THE DIFFUSION, TRANSFORMATION AND DEPLOYMENT OF PLANNING CONCEPTS

**ANDRÉ SORENSEN**

Urban sustainability and compact cities have recently become prominent public policy issues in Japan, with several major new national government initiatives being introduced, and best-selling books on the topic appearing in major bookstores. In 2005 the Comprehensive National Land Development Act was replaced by the National Land Sustainability Planning Act, and in 2007, then Prime Minister Fukuda's foremost urban policy was to promote "compact cities."[1] This promised to include stronger urban growth boundaries, and the revitalization and intensification of city centers in an attempt to change patterns of urban growth and promote sustainability.

This paper examines the recent emergence of ideas of "urban sustainability" and "compact cities" as major policy approaches in Japan, in order to consider the role of ideas in policy change, the ways in which policy ideas travel and diffuse at the global scale, and the ways in which they are selectively adopted and transformed when they are taken up in a specific governmental context. Japan provides an interesting case study of the diffusion of planning ideas, as it is a nation famously "open" to ideas from elsewhere, and has built a reputation as a consummate borrower and improver of ideas and technologies during its period of modernization and rapid economic growth. It is a cliché of Japanese studies that Japan has always borrowed and learned from other countries, and that many of the characteristic features of Japanese culture – from the Chinese writing system and Zen Buddhism, to transistors and cars – were first borrowed from elsewhere, and then greatly improved upon.

Also, far more than countries such as the United States, Japanese policy-makers and people are highly aware of developments outside Japan. This reflects, in part, the perennial insecurity of Japan, which is highly dependent on the rest of the world not only for food, energy, and raw materials for industrial use, but also for national security and export markets. This sense of insecurity and precarious dependence on world markets has been a constant, except for the brief euphoria of the bubble economy period in the 1980s, when economic triumphalism prevailed

(Pempel 1998). Intense scrutiny of the rest of the world occurs at all levels in Japan, from government to industry to academia to popular study clubs. Academics – including planning academics – often make major contributions towards disseminating new ideas through their expertise in another country's practices, and through importing knowledge, ideas, and experts from abroad. Books and concepts are translated into Japanese, with a huge publishing, translating, and academic industry devoted to the observation and interpretation of foreign expertise. Subdiscipline shelves in major bookstores invariably include translated works from abroad, and survey and synthesis works by Japanese scholars that interpret foreign ideas into the Japanese context. A common academic career path in many policy-related disciplines is to become an expert in a particular new idea developed elsewhere, to translate and interpret key works, and to propose policies for Japan based on those findings.

Despite this embrace of ideas from elsewhere, there was a considerable time lag between the identification of sustainability as a crucial global issue in the late 1980s – an event that, in Europe, produced major debates about the roles of cities in sustainability, and significant urban policy moves, from the early 1990s on – and the emergence in Japan of serious policy attempts to address sustainability as a spatial planning issue. This stands in striking contrast to Japan's immediate response to issues of global warming and the Kyoto Protocol, and also to Local Agenda 21 after the Rio Earth Summit, in which Japanese municipalities were world leaders in implementation (Barrett and Usui 2002; ICLEI 2002). Why the long delay in this case?

This chapter shows that the diffusion of planning ideas is contingent on local factors, and that ideas are translated, interpreted, and negotiated by multiple actors to serve ongoing struggles and conflicts over development, priorities, and visions. Ideas from elsewhere can be used strategically, with actors borrowing not only a concept or analysis, but also its legitimacy and moral authority, to serve quite varied agendas. So planning institutions, actors, and issues play a key role in the dissemination of planning ideas, which can grow and evolve in unanticipated ways. Understanding the ways in which the idea of urban sustainability has been translated into the Japanese context provides some insight into the Japanese political economy and planning culture as well as into the nature of planning ideas and their processes of diffusion. Whereas the global discourse on sustainability has become increasingly diverse and hard to summarize neatly, a smaller subset of ideas has been brought into Japanese debates, and a yet more select group has been incorporated into policy. That process of selection provides a guide to the priorities, constraints, and interpretive frames of policy-makers in Japan. This chapter, therefore, examines those elements of the original ideas that survive the processes of translation and policy development, how they are formulated, and how they are put into practice.

In this examination of the impacts of the idea of sustainability on urban policy in Japan, the main questions are: Why have ideas of sustainability and compact cities recently risen to public policy prominence in Japan? How do different actors interpret and deploy ideas of sustainable cities, and how are those ideas transformed in the process? Which aspects survive the process of borrowing, which do not, and why? What can we learn about the diffusion and transformation of planning concepts from this case?

The next section outlines the approach taken here to the role of ideas in policy. The following section sketches several characteristics of Japanese political culture that have shaped ideas of sustainable cities, and a fourth section details the emergence of policies linking sustainability and urban space at central and local government levels. The final section draws together the main findings.

## THE ROLE OF IDEAS

City planning has always been highly international, with the studying, borrowing and transplanting of planning ideas and practices between places forming a core activity since the early days of modern planning at the end of the nineteenth century (see Sutcliffe 1981; Hall 1988; Ward 2002). During the past decade, the study of ideas as independent causal variables in policy change has received considerable attention (Legro 2000; Blyth 2001; Kisby 2007). Many agree that ideas are influential, but it is not so easy to pin down how they are influential, and to what extent any particular idea can be credited with policy change. Attempts to show the impacts of ideas in politics have been criticized for a lack of empirical evidence linking ideas to particular policy changes (Blyth 1997; Campbell 1998).

Such a causal link would be particularly difficult to determine in the case of the idea of sustainable cities, the meaning of which is contested. Interpretations range from the ideas of deep ecology, arguing that contemporary industrial society is fundamentally unsustainable, to the view that the goal of sustainability is to sustain current levels of consumption. The application of the term "sustainability" to cities has provoked especially varied interpretations but, as most approaches to urban sustainability require some significant changes to "business as usual," solutions are politically contested. Perhaps even more than some other areas, borrowed ideas of urban sustainability will, therefore, be subject to transformations by different political cultures of planning. Such transformations can range from something as minor as a slightly different emphasis on which aspects of the concept are the most important, to such radical reinterpretation that the idea becomes quite different, even while employing the same terminology and reasoning. The approach here is to look at particular policies justified by ideas of sustainability and compact cities, and so the emphasis is more on practice than on discourse; but it is still important to have a conception of the ways in which ideas may influence policy.

Ideas clearly don't do any work on their own; they need what Kingdon (2003) has described as "policy entrepreneurs" to take an idea and deploy it politically. So the influence of ideas is not direct, but works through multiple processes, in which influential actors see an opportunity to use the idea to push forward a policy change. As Campbell puts it, ideas allow policy-makers to "construct frames with which to legitimize their policy proposals," and "ideas facilitate policy-making action not just by serving as road maps, but also by providing symbols and other discursive schema that actors can use" to sell their policies (1998: 398, 381). Sometimes the policy proposal that actors are deploying the idea to support is generated by the idea; sometimes it is an old policy that is newly legitimized by it. Either way, ideas need proponents who perceive their value, and have the capacity and opportunity to deploy them.

Kingdon (2003) identifies three major processes through which the US federal government sets its agenda: problem recognition, the formation and refining of policy proposals, and politics. These are broadly similar in Japan, albeit with some distinctive characteristics discussed below. Problem recognition is the process through which problems are identified and gain the attention of people in and around government. In the case of urban sustainability, the Rio Earth Summit, the Kyoto Protocol, and the ongoing climate change crisis have undoubtedly put the problem of urban sustainability on the agenda everywhere. But, as the issue of urban sustainability is so broad, the question remains, what problem is identified? Is it pollution? Resource consumption? Solid waste production? Urban sprawl? Social polarization? There are a virtually unlimited number of problems that might fit under the general heading of urban sustainability, and so it is revealing to identify which of these become the focus of policy attention and are linked with the issue of "sustainable cities" in any particular case. This is attempted in the penultimate section of this chapter.

The second agenda-setting process identified by Kingdon is the development and refining of policy proposals. There are multiple policy-relevant ideas in circulation at any given time, yet only some ideas generate policy-making activity; so it is also important to understand why some policy issues attract attention. In Kingdon's view, most decision-making does not follow the rational, comprehensive ideal of first defining problems, then researching possible responses, and finally evaluating different policy options to select and implement the most effective solutions. Instead, "solutions search for problems. People work on problems only when a particular combination of problem, solution, and participants in a choice situation makes it possible" (Kingdon 2003: 86). Policy windows open when pressing problems are linked to solutions, and both are swept up in a political moment when political will is generated for implementation.

In an urban application of this thesis, Rodgers (1998) argues that, in city planning, the process of problem recognition is closely related to the availability of solutions, as solutions often make problems comprehensible and action imaginable. With no solutions at hand, even issues that are clearly problematic won't necessarily generate much policy activity. He illustrates this with the invention of flush toilets and water-carried sewage systems in Britain in the mid-nineteenth century. Human waste had been a critical issue in large cities for a very long time, but had generated little policy intervention until the major burst of sewer-building activity in the second half of the century. So although the larger analysis of a crisis is important, particular actionable solutions may be a more proximate influence on policy than the general identification of a problem, especially one as complex as sustainability.

The development of policy is not the same as the development of solutions. In the case of human waste disposal in cities, the solution was toilet technology and the water-carried sewer system. The policy questions, on the other hand, were how they would be financed and built, who would maintain them, what changes to building regulations were needed, and what penalties for non-compliance were to be enforced and by whom. Kingdon identifies a cluster of policy specialists – bureaucrats, political staff, academia, interest groups, and researchers – who generate and refine policy proposals in the United States. In Japan the players are similar, but with the lead role played by central government bureaucrats, who have retained a pre-eminent role in policy development and coordination. Divided into policy areas, each ministry section is intensely competitive in generating policy proposals, the adoption of which can ensure budget growth or make a career. The Japanese government is famously vertically divided, with intense competition not only between ministries, but also between sections of the same ministry. Local governments are also active in policy development and the innovative application of tools developed at the center. So in Japan there is a continuous stream of well-developed policy proposals available for political processes to seize upon.

In Kingdon's model, the third, political process "is composed of things like swings of national mood, vagaries of public opinion, election results, changes in administration, shifts in ideological distributions in Congress, and interest group pressure campaigns" (Kingdon 2003: 87). As a democratic country, a similar list would apply to Japan, except for the fact that, during the past 50 years, the Liberal Democratic Party (LDP) has been out of power only for little more than a year up (over 1993 and 1994 and since the elections of September 2009) – so election results have seldom resulted in dramatic shifts in government. Nevertheless, most

analysts of Japanese politics agree that the Japanese government is quite politically responsive; even though the LDP is perennially in power, it is frequently at
risk of losing its majority, and must work hard to maintain public support (Pempel
1982; Calder 1988; Muramatsu 1993). Also, as city planning is in part a local
government responsibility, the division of powers and responsibilities between
central and local authorities has important impacts on policy processes. In Japan,
each level of government has different priorities and approaches to issues of
urban sustainability, as is shown in my fourth section.

In Japan, as elsewhere, political processes are a key factor that structure the
ways in which ideas of urban sustainability have been engaged. It is, therefore,
important to review briefly several contextual factors that shaped the emergence
of sustainable city policies.

## THE CONTEXT OF SUSTAINABLE CITIES IDEAS IN JAPAN

There are several key aspects of the Japanese context that have played a major
role in shaping the ways in which sustainable cities ideas have emerged. In a
limited space, it is not easy to summarize a planning culture and context, but four
themes stand out: issues of translation, the developmental state, its technocratic
orientation, and imminent population decline.

### TRANSLATION

One issue in importing concepts of sustainability and sustainable cities to Japan
is the difficulty of translating the word "sustainable" into Japanese. The most common translation of "sustainable city" is *Jizoku Kanô na Toshi,* in which *toshi* is the
common word for city. The adjective *Jizoku Kanô* (持続可能) is constructed
of the character pair *Jizoku*, meaning "continuation" or "durability," and the pair
*Kanô*, meaning "possible," "practical," or "feasible." So the full word literally means
"possible to continue" or "can be durable." Perhaps as a result, one theme in
Japanese writing about sustainability is on equilibrium, as is exemplified by the
conceptual framework offered by Aoki (2006) in a major collection of work by
Japanese scholars on the topic of "sustainable cities." Aoki outlines a "plastic
bucket model" in which a sustainable system is conceived as one that has the
same inflow of water from a tap as outflow through a hole in the bucket. His chapter, therefore, posits "sustainability" as "equilibrium" or continuity. Aoki goes on
to extrapolate a range of interesting mathematical examples of dynamic and sto-
chastic equilibria, making crude analogies with urban processes. He concludes
that such conditions are directly analogous with changes in urban land use, and
proposes that urban zoning should be eliminated in order to make cities more

sustainable (Aoki 2006: 68). Without attempting to evaluate the merits of this specific proposal, it is notable that the paper starts from first principles, and cites no research on the topic of urban sustainability other than the Brundtland report. It seems that, although the word "sustainability" itself can be translated directly, the larger cluster of ideas that surround it in the environmental, development and planning literatures do not necessarily inhere in the Japanese phrase "sustainable cities," and have only developed over time as the Japanese literature employing the term has become richer and more nuanced.

## THE DEVELOPMENTAL/CONSTRUCTION STATE

Although Japan's era of rapid economic growth is now long past, there are several major institutional legacies of the developmental state period that continue to be influential. Perhaps most fundamental is the basic assumption that growth is the ultimate solution for most problems, and that the promotion of economic growth is the basic task of society as a whole – not just for the state and market, but also for citizens, whose private interests may be considered selfish and antisocial if they hinder its pursuit (see Sorensen 2005). Although this conception has been increasingly challenged during the past decade (see, for example, Yamamoto 1999), the Japanese system of government is still oriented overwhelmingly toward the promotion of economic development and investment, not its restraint.

The relative power of central government has been reinforced by vast spending on public works over the past 15 years, particularly by the Ministry of Land, Infrastructure, and Transport (MLIT – formed in 2001 through a merger of the Ministries of Construction and Transport and the National Land Agency). Japan's enormous spending on roads, highways, bridges, railways, airports, ports, and flood protection is legendary. For example, in 1992 contruction investment was 18.2 percent of GDP, more than double the level of the United States (Woodall 1996; Feldhoff 2007). This investment in infrastructure was also highly effective in inducing cooperation among local governments that compete for subsidies from Tokyo. The system that linked the long-ruling LDP with the construction and land development industries in a mutually profitable embrace has been labeled the "construction state" (*Dokken Kokka*) (McCormack 1996, 2002), and has proven extraordinarily hard to dislodge. Even the popular Prime Minister Koizumi largely failed in his promise to break the grip of the public works debt spiral through ending the exclusive use of gas tax funds for highway building, privatizing the Japan Highways Public Corporation, and privatizing the Post Office savings system. This last institution supplied money for Japan's "second budget,"[2] spent by central ministries largely outside the scrutiny of parliament (McCormack 1996; Vogel 2006; Feldhoff 2007).

Central government policies have been profoundly shaped by the pathology of the construction state nexus, which has linked together politicians, bureaucracy, the building industry, and localities, not only in their dependence on continued flows of public money, but also in the pervasive corruption of politicians, bureaucrats, and firms that profit from bid rigging, as has been exposed almost weekly in the Japanese press over the past decade. So, for the central state, policies of spatial planning, development, and infrastructure building have a strongly pro-growth character, and powerful vested interests seek their continuation. These enduring patterns have tainted spatial development planning, so that policies to shape patterns of urban development, in particular, are viewed skeptically as opportunities for private profit rather than as measures to promote the public good. Such new urban policies certainly do not present themselves as obvious first-choice solutions for either climate change or energy consumption issues. Despite recent reforms, budget cuts, and downscaling, massive public works projects continue, and are accepted as more or less unstoppable. Put simply, although the Japanese state has policy levers for national spatial planning and development that have often been envied, these have been so badly distorted by construction state networks that they do not appear to lend themselves easily to the promotion of more sustainable development patterns.

And, of course, there can be little that is more incontestably unsustainable than the massive central and local government debts that have been created in large part by public works spending. At almost 200 percent of annual GDP, total debt is now far past the 75 percent of GDP that has usually been seen as a state of emergency in other developed countries. The Japanese government has literally been mortgaging the future of the Japanese nation, and has drastically limited the policy options of future governments in doing so.

## TECHNOCRATIC ORIENTATION

Another legacy of the developmental state is an enduring preference for technological solutions as a substitute for regulation (Imura 1994; OECD 1994). Although Japan has tended to have relatively weak land-use planning regulations, it has a very strong tradition of regulating industrial pollution, encouraging capital investment in industrial plants, and achieving energy efficiencies and input–output synergies in industry. The Japanese building industry is also one of the most technologically advanced in the world, and Japan has very high standards of green building construction, including its own equivalent to the LEED certification in the CASBEE system.[3] Most opinion leaders in their fifties and sixties today came of age during the environmental crisis of the 1960s, and saw the dramatic success of the pollution regulations of the early 1970s that relied primarily on end-of-pipe technologies rather than market mechanisms or taxes. Whether the task is to reduce greenhouse gas emissions, reduce energy consumption, or consume fewer raw materials, the obvious solution is to re-engineer industrial production, and particularly the way that electricity is produced, rather than to change the way that cities are built. As Fujita and Hill show, Japan is a leader in "lean production" and the application of the principles of industrial ecology, in which industrial waste products from one process become inputs for a subsequent process. Japan is also one of the world's most efficient users of industrial energy, second only to Sweden amongst the Organization for Economic Cooperation and Development (OECD) members in its ratio of GDP to $CO_2$ production; and Japanese manufacturers lowered energy use per unit of output by 40 percent during the three decades after 1973. France and Germany use 50 percent more energy than Japan per unit of GDP, while Britain uses double, the United States triple, and China eight times more (Fujita and Hill 2007).

This preference for an industrial engineering, rather than a city planning, approach to sustainability was reinforced by the fact that Japanese policy-making, political and economic power, media, and academia are all highly concentrated in Tokyo. Throughout the twentieth century, these forces have tended to create policy approaches based on Tokyo's problems and solutions, allowing peripheral areas relatively little autonomy to develop or implement local policies and solutions (although this has been changing gradually over the past 30 years). For policy-makers in central Tokyo, the first round of Western approaches to sustainable cities – the "compact cities" formula of increased densities, more public transit, more vibrant, walkable mixed-use areas, and the orientation of buildings to benefit from solar heating in the winter – presented little that was of immediate use, as it all described Tokyo quite precisely. Tokyo was already a very high-density, mixed-use, walkable place, with the best public transit system in the world (with 90 percent of trips to the central area being made by heavy rail), extensive use of solar hot water panels, and the solar orientation of buildings. If anything, the Western literature on the desirability of compact cities and the problems of sprawl appeared to indicate that Japanese urban planning approaches and priorities had been very successful, and that urban form changes could not contribute much towards making Japanese cities more sustainable (Sorensen et al. 2004).

## POPULATION DECLINE

A major sustainability issue for Japan is long-term population decline, which has been experienced by rural areas for 50 years, by most medium-sized cities since the 1990s, and by the country as a whole since 2004. The Japanese population grew from 44 million in 1900 to 72 million in 1945, and to a peak of about 128 million in 2004. Because of steep declines in fertility during the past 40 years, however, in the absence of major changes in fertility or immigration, the population is projected to decline to 117 million in 2030, and to 100 million by 2050. A second crucial consequence of the end of population growth is population ageing. The share of the population over 65 years has increased from 4.9 percent in 1950 to 19.5 percent in 2004, and is expected to rise to 29.6 percent by 2030 (see Japan Ministry of Internal Affairs and Communications 2005; Ogawa 2005). Such decline and ageing is distributed very unevenly geographically, with peripheral towns and cities experiencing much more serious population loss and ageing than the major metropolitan areas (Sorensen 2006). This pattern has greatly influenced thinking about urban sustainability. The prospect of massive population decline has focused minds on "sustainability," and one topic of papers on urban sustainability is the challenge of maintaining population levels in particular places (Tamagawa and Ehara 2006).

## SUSTAINABILITY AND COMPACT CITIES IDEAS IN JAPAN

In Western developed countries the concept of sustainability has had a major impact on planning discourse, lending a renewed sense of purpose both to the planning project and to its underlying normative agenda of embedding long-term environmental, quality of life, and social justice concerns into spatial policy processes. Low *et al.* (2005) describe the idea of sustainability as the greatest change in human thought and behavior in 3,000 years, from the assumption that progress means an increasing mastery of nature, to a realization that progress means a radical reduction of our impact on the natural world in order to survive. The Brundtland report in particular (World Congress on Environment and Development 1987) fostered a new understanding of the global interrelatedness of issues of development, poverty, environmental decline, and long-term processes. The report's core definition of sustainable development – "development that meets the needs of the present without compromising the ability of future generations to meet their own needs" – has been hugely influential in many fields. It is not, however, so simple to translate that imperative into an urban planning program, and a wide range of policy approaches have been developed in different countries to pursue it. The focus here is on the contribution envisaged for city planning in attempts to achieve more sustainable cities, and how those ideas have influenced policy and practice in Japan.

Even with that narrower focus, in developed countries the range of ideas and proposals linking sustainability and cities is vast. It is possible, however, to identify a core set of concepts relating the idea of sustainable cities to city planning. These start with the assumption that high energy use is a key problem and that patterns of built form can have a significant impact on energy use, both for mobility and for heating and cooling (Owens 1986; Newman and Kenworthy 1989). Low-density urban fringe and exurban development that requires extensive automobile travel was identified early on as a problem, particularly as this was the dominant form of most new development in many wealthy countries (Cervero 1986; Breheny 1992a). Very quickly, policy approaches emerged that advocated more compact development, intensification and revitalization of city centers, restrictions on out-of-town shopping, and integrated public transit and land-use development (Commission of the European Communities 1990; Elkin et al. 1991; Calthorpe 1993). This set of ideas soon came to be known as the "compact city" approach (Burgess 2000; Miller et al. 2000; Neuman 2005).

Possibly in part because of the early adoption of policies supporting intensification (e.g. by the EU), debates on sustainable cities and urban form have focused significantly on questions of whether compact cities really are more sustainable (Breheny 1992b; Jenks et al. 1996); whether they are achievable given current trends (Bourne 1996; Breheny 2001); or whether they are desirable (Gordon and Richardson 1997; Neuman 2005). Nevertheless, many agree that lively, compact, walkable, and transit-oriented cities, with high-density mixed-use transit centers, reorienting growth away from greenfield sites on the fringe to underused sites within existing built-up areas, would be a more sustainable urban form. This would permit an increased share of trips to be made by transport modes other than automobiles, and allow an increased role for district heating and cooling, and combined heat and power generation (Ewing 1997; Roseland et al. 1998; Jenks et al. 2000; Nelson et al. 2004).

In Japan, ideas of compact, sustainable cities have recently become major elements of government policies, as noted above. Central government and local governments, however, tend to have quite different conceptions both of the challenges of sustainability and of the role of spatial policy in achieving more sustainable urban areas.

The central government is still influenced by the salience of public works spending in the Japanese political economy. Although it is difficult to paint large-scale public works as a contribution to future sustainability, it is not impossible, as suggested by the recent changes in 2005 that replaced the Comprehensive National Development Act with a new National Land Sustainability Plan and an accompanying National Land Sustainability Planning Act. The last Comprehensive National Development Plan was the fifth in a series of plans begun in 1962 to coordinate national spatial development and investment. The fifth plan, titled "Grand Design for the 21st Century," was prepared during the peak of public works spending in the mid-1990s, and was approved in 1998. The plan deployed all the well-known levers of public investment to promote "balanced" growth throughout the national territory, including new railway lines, expressways, airports, bridges between major islands, dams and nuclear stations, and the relocation of the capital city to a new site, all at a cost of trillions of debt-financed yen (Japan Ministry of Land, Infrastructure, and Transport 1998; McCormack 2002: 14). The new "sustainability" plan does not drop most of these infrastructure proposals, but changes the emphasis in the plan to participation and cooperation, qualitative rather than quantitative development goals, the participation of stakeholders in the planning process, and greater regional autonomy (Ministry of Land, Infrastructure, and Transport 2005).

Still, the main central government approaches to sustainability lie not in spatial development but elsewhere. The Japanese government wishes to be seen as a responsible and fair player on the international stage, takes very seriously its role in international organizations such as the UN and OECD, and welcomes occasions to demonstrate its global citizenship. Japanese governments are very sensitive to the political imperatives of globalization, trade, and treaty obligations, in part because of an enduring sense of insecurity that has made Japan susceptible to diplomatic pressure from abroad.[4] There is thus little likelihood of Japan adopting the recent US strategy of thumbing its nose at the international consensus about the seriousness of global warming. Japan appears to have signed the Kyoto Protocol with the full intention of achieving its targets. In contrast to Canada and the United States, who did nothing for most of the decade after Kyoto, the Japanese ministries immediately got to work producing a viable strategy for reducing greenhouse gas emissions. Within 6 months of Kyoto, the government announced Japan's strategy: a doubling of the output of nuclear electricity within 12 years, in order to shut down oil-fired electrical generators. This would have achieved Japan's Kyoto targets at one stroke, even assuming a resumption of economic growth, and promised the added benefit of reducing dependence on imported oil. As it happened, the building of new nuclear plants has been much slower than planned, primarily because of opposition to plant siting, drawn-out processes of negotiation and compensation with nearby residents, and the cancellation or relocation of several proposed plants (Lesbirel 1998; Aldrich 2008).[5] The Rio Earth Summit and Kyoto processes also had a more subtle impact, making the issue of sustainability and global environmental burdens a foreign affairs issue, not a land planning issue. The Ministry of Land, Infrastructure, and Transport was not directly involved, and land-use planning did not play a significant part in the government's sustainability framework until the much later adoption of compact cities ideas.

The "compact cities" idea has emerged relatively recently as a key central government policy that links sustainable cities ideas and urban spatial planning, and has been paralleled by an emerging academic planning literature. The first mention of "compact cities" in the Japanese urban planning journals *City Planning*

*Review* and *City Planning Annals,* published by the City Planning Association of Japan, appeared in articles that evaluated the possibility of reduced energy consumption for travel in compact cities (Morimoto and Koike 1998; Hori *et al.* 1999; Matsuhashi 2000). These were soon followed by more wide-ranging papers that reviewed Western literature and debates about compact cities, particularly those in the UK (Kaidô 1999; Suzuki 2001). Kaidô presents the arguments in favor of compact cities thoroughly, including arguments for inner-city regeneration and intensification with mixed-use development, to prevent greenfield development and reduce car use – arguments that are extended in his subsequent book on compact cities (Kaidô 2001). Suzuki (2001), however, presents a wide-ranging review of both sides of the Western compact cities debate, including the views of more skeptical analysts who question whether compact cities are achievable or will deliver the promised benefits. These initial papers were soon followed by detailed case studies of the potential application of compact cities ideas to medium-sized cities (Kitahara 2002; Shimaoka *et al.* 2003; Nakamichi *et al.* 2004). More recently there has been a surge of books published advocating compact cities, and elaborating policy approaches to achieving them in Japan (Matsunaga 2005; Yamamoto 2006; Kaidô 2007; Suzuki 2007). The Ministry of Land, Infrastructure, and Transport engagement began with a small research project and policy initiative in 2002, looking at the possibilities of compact city policies, especially for regional cities.[6] That program gradually expanded, and in 2007 was designated as a priority of the central government by the incoming Prime Minister Fukuda. Repeated demands from regional local governments for effective ways of managing sprawl had resulted in policy research on "compact cities" being prioritized; this, in turn, became an opportune theme for Prime Minister Fukuda to adopt in 2007 as his signature contribution to urban policy. In this way, the compact city solution became linked to a pressing urban problem, and was caught up in a gust of political opportunity.

Local governments have a very different perspective on land, urban growth, and sustainability from that of central government, partly because local governments have long been directly responsible for solving the urban infrastructure deficits created during and since the rapid growth period, and partly because they are unavoidably closer to their residents – many of whom see issues of livability as a primary responsibility of municipal governments. Sustainable cities and compact cities ideas also fit well with long-term municipal priorities of limiting sprawl and promoting downtown revitalization. They also provide the promise of an approach for making cities more livable for an ageing population, dealing with population decline, and slowing the boom of out-of-town shopping centers, the most recent engine of urban sprawl. Local governments have long been strong proponents of better regulation of development, primarily to ensure that new urban areas are provided with infrastructure at the time of urbanization, instead of retroactively. In contrast, until 2000 central government refused to give local governments legal authority to create their own stricter regulations, and national city planning laws have always been subject to loopholes and periodic deregulations that limited their effectiveness in development control (Sorensen 2002).

Although only recently identified as issues of urban sustainability, the issues of urban growth management and sprawl have been central to Japanese local planning practice since the mid-1960s. During the rapid urbanization of the 1950s and 1960s there were virtually no restrictions on land development. Developers could build anywhere within commuting range of growing cities, without requirements to contribute towards the costs of the infrastructure their development made necessary. Because so much urban development proceeded without any contributions to public goods, Japanese suburban areas face major shortfalls of roads and sidewalks, parks, public facilities such as libraries and community centers, and especially sewers. The environmental crisis of the 1960s was thus closely linked with issues of urban sprawl (called *supurôru* in Japan, borrowed from English); sprawl and environmental deterioration became linked, and were joint drivers of planning reform in 1968 and the early 1970s. Huge investments have been made into retroactively building such municipal infrastructure over the past 30 years, but the frontier of unplanned development has continued to move outwards.

From the 1980s, the expanded construction of expressways and their associated uses transformed the urban periphery, as did exponential growth in car ownership. Propelled by the property development boom of the bubble years, a new, extended pattern of metropolitan mobility emerged. This included a new phenomenon: large-scale, automobile-oriented resorts throughout the archipelago, typically golf courses, but also hotels, spas, etc. Although the resort boom went bust in the early 1990s, changes in the late 1980s to the Large-Scale Retail Stores Law (*Daiten Ho,* LRSL) prompted a boom of exurban retail development along peripheral arterial highways and arterial roads from the early 1990s. So urban sprawl has continued during the whole period since 1970, although in evolving forms and in an ever more dispersed pattern.

The LRSL and its impacts on location of retail facilities were a key factor in the emergence of local governments' current "compact cities" policies, and are revealing of central/local relations, and so exploring this in more detail is useful. Since 1974 the Ministry of International Trade and Industry (MITI) had used the LRSL to regulate the location of any retail store with over 1,500 m² of floor space. The LRSL is an excellent example of the traditionally loose fit between Japanese laws and their implementation by ministries, as MITI created a "consultative council" system not provided for in the law to compel negotiations between prospective entrants to retail markets and existing store owners. As a result, many new entrants were blocked, and existing merchants were often able to extract a range of concessions on the sizes of stores, parking requirements, and co-located space for local stores in new developments. Retail location was regulated, not to prevent sprawl, but to prevent competition with existing small and medium retailers, who were an important constituency for the reigning LDP party (Upham 1993: 271).

During the 1980s, increasing trade friction with the United States was a major foreign policy issue for Japan. The United States complained that its ballooning trade deficit with Japan was caused by a deliberately undervalued yen, and multiple non-tariff barriers to imports. One outcome was the Plaza Accords of 1986, which revalued the yen sharply upwards, and yielded a promise by MITI in 1990 to reform the LRSL to make it easier for large retailers (both domestic and foreign) to build stores. Immediate steps were to be taken to make it easier to open large stores, and a major re-evaluation of retail location policy, including the possibility of complete deregulation, was promised within two years (Upham 1993: 285).

In 1991 the Diet passed a series of laws effective in 1992 that fundamentally changed the way that the retail sector was regulated, abolishing the consultative councils, and bringing the decision-making process into the ministry itself. The number of applications for permission to open large-scale stores jumped from 794 in 1989 to 1,987 in 1990 and peaked at 2,269 in 1996 (Japan Ministry of Foreign Affairs 2008). This boom had multiple impacts: it produced strips of big-box stores, gas stations, chain restaurants, and automobile dealerships along exurban arterials in unregulated zones, it prompted major increases in automobile use and traffic congestion in outer urban areas, and it contributed to the sudden decline of traditional retail districts in small and medium-sized cities throughout Japan. It did not have such a major impact on central city retail in the largest cities, because the urban fringe was too far away for convenient car access. The collapse of downtown shopping areas was a disaster for small and medium-sized cities, and strongly reinforced the existing trend of depopulation and decline of the walkable, transit-oriented, vibrant city centers. This prompted intense lobbying by local governments for policies to support their commercial centers and to regulate urban fringe development.

That the LSRL is the responsibility of MITI, a ministry with few ties with or responsibilities to local governments, is illustrative of a major problem of city planning in Japan. This major reform of urban policy was undertaken without consideration of the impact on patterns of development or on consumers, either by cartelizing existing merchants in the first instance, or by promoting retail dispersion into the least-regulated areas of the urban fringe after deregulation. MITI proved responsive primarily to elements of the business sector, and secondarily to foreign threats of restrictions on Japanese exports, whereas local governments had little negotiating power with the ministry. Although US pressure was decisive in forcing action, deregulation was strongly supported by domestic interests as well, prominent among which were a new generation of large-scale Japanese retailers that wished to expand their operations (Upham 1993).

Deregulation of retail location was such a disaster during the 1990s that a policy consultation council (*shingikai*) was formed by MITI in 1997, and a new LRSL was enacted in 1998, applicable in 2000. The new law passed the responsibility for regulating retail location to municipal governments. It states explicitly that it is not to be used as a way for retail interests to negotiate between each other, as had occurred in the 1980s, and as had continued in a transformed way in the 1990s. Instead, the new LRSL's goal is to "foster the sound development of the retail sector as a whole," and protect the living environment in the vicinity of large stores (Japan Ministry of Economy 2008). Explicitly mentioned are traffic problems and parking standards. The key change is that decisions are now made by local governments, several of which are using the system to prevent new large stores from opening in suburban and peripheral areas, curtailing the dominant trend of the 1990s (Takami 2006: 140). Instead, an incentive system was introduced in 2002 to induce large retailers to locate in city center locations. These changes have brought retail location into the local sustainability debate, and the LRSL is now referred to as one of the Three Town Planning Laws (*Machizukuri Sanpo*), along with the City Planning Law and the Building Standards Law.

More recent moves towards policies to create more compact cities have been led by a number of regional cities that are faced with ageing and declining populations, reduced municipal revenues, dispersed development patterns, and central city decline. An excellent example is the prefectural capital Aomori, located in the snow belt of northern Japan, which suffered from all of these issues. In addition, however, extensive development patterns were creating a crisis for the snow-removal budget, as Aomori receives between 10 and 20 meters of snow each winter, and had an ever-growing road network to clear. The municipality was also forced to spend a large and growing share of its budget on infrastructure in the outer suburbs. Central city population fell from 5,200 in 1975 to 2,300 in 2000, prompting fears of inner-city hollowing out, before recent measures pushed the population back up to 3,200 in 2004. Aomori has created a range of ways to promote compact city development. These include a three-tier zoning system of inner city, mid-city, and outer city, with improvements in public facilities, retail development, and housing projects supported in the inner area, and strongly discouraged in the outer area. Other improvements in the central area include the creation of pedestrian zones and investments in public transit services. Service reductions are also proposed for the outer area, especially snow clearing (Terasawa 2007).

Although there is no abstract argument about sustainability underlying the compact city approach in Aomori, there is no doubt that concerns about the long-run viability and livability of the city are the motivations here, and the major goals of reduced sprawl, decreased auto dependency, and inner-city revitalization are similar to those in other developed countries.

For medium-size regional cities in Japan, the "compact city" and "sustainable city" ideas borrowed from Europe provided a new, integrated planning policy framework that brought together global environmental concerns, municipal infrastructure and services management strategies, a local economic revitalization agenda, and a proactive approach to problems of an ageing and declining population. The fact that the policy comes from abroad, and is endorsed by bodies as varied as the UN, EU, and UK, lends legitimacy to the program. And in fact, as with Smart Growth in the United States (Porter *et al.* 2002; Downs 2005; Dierwechter 2008), the "new" agenda is mostly a repackaging of long-term municipal planning goals, with a new rationale, and in response to admittedly stronger recent pressures of decline.

## CONCLUSIONS

The Japanese case suggests that ideas can be important, but that they do not always have the impacts that their originators intended, and they are particularly unlikely to mean the same thing when they have been translated into a different cultural setting, political system, and policy context. The ways in which urban sustainability issues are perceived and the solutions that make sense in different contexts are strongly influenced by the available and effective policy levers, and by past patterns of institutional development. These factors create both capacities and preferences among relevant actors. As sustainable cities ideas are so varied, and possible policy approaches so diverse, it is not surprising to find that different actors will interpret the imperative to promote sustainability differently, and will adopt those aspects of the idea that best fit their own situation.

The Japanese case shows that the borrowing of planning ideas can occur simultaneously at multiple scales, with different actors pursuing varied aims. In line with its strong technocratic tradition and orientation towards urban infrastructure projects, the main initial response of the central government to its Kyoto commitment was to launch a program of doubling Japan's nuclear electric-generating capacity. A similar but more wide-ranging approach has been the development of green building technologies and standards by the engineering, architecture, and construction industries, which, given Japan's rapid turnover of building stock, promises to have significant impacts in lowering energy consumption and waste production. A more opportunistic deployment of sustainability ideas appears to be the promotion of "urban renaissance" policies that are designed primarily to enhance development profits in Tokyo, and the rebranding of the National Comprehensive Development Plan as the National Land Sustainability Plan.

On the other hand, serious efforts at adopting sustainable cities policies and ideas have been made by local governments, which are struggling with inner-city hollowing out, population decline, ageing, and continuing suburban sprawl (particularly of retail functions). A major influence of sustainable cities ideas in Japan has been the emergence of compact cities ideas as an important policy direction during the past 10 years. It also seems fair to suggest that the efforts of local governments to promote sustainability are not just lip service, or political posturing, but a serious and long-term response to enduring municipal governance issues. Compact city policies promise lower municipal infrastructure building and maintenance costs, and also promise to contribute to more livable cities that work better for older residents, and to revitalize inner cities. These goals are core priorities for Japanese local governments. In this sense, although the sincerity of the efforts of local governments are not in doubt, and the energy efficiency and sustainability impacts may be significant, it appears that sustainability and compact cities ideas are being used primarily as a way of framing and legitimizing existing long-term planning goals, not necessarily as a way of fundamentally challenging existing policy orientations.

So, in considering the case of ideas about urban sustainability in Japan, the word "diffusion" may not be quite right; rather than a neutral process, such as the even diffusion of a drop of colored dye into a glass of water, the process is more active, contested, and political. Some actors in some places will be receptive, finding real value in a new planning idea and a political opportunity to deploy it, whereas elsewhere the idea will fall on barren ground, will be actively resisted, will be transformed into something quite different, or will be simply misunderstood. So the spread of planning ideas occurs in varied ways depending on the context. As Kingdon suggests, ideas must find advocates and be linked to problems and political opportunities in order to have a significant effect on policies. This often produces delays in the spread of ideas, and can also mean that ideas can be used to support policies that would be quite surprising to their originators. Ideas get harnessed to serve ongoing struggles over policy priorities, jurisdiction, and resources, and can be transformed in the process in big or small ways. Even if a similar terminology and rationale for policy adoption is presented, the real reasons for policy adoption may be quite different from those in the place where the idea originated. Policy arenas are subject to the play of power relations; ideas can be used strategically; policy legitimacy can be borrowed; and the credibility of a respected idea can be hitched to quite different agendas from those originally imagined.

Particularly evident in the Japanese case discussed here is the value of the borrowed legitimacy of ideas authored and endorsed elsewhere. Such borrowed legitimacy may be particularly important in Japan, given the respect for multilateral commitments and institutionalized attention to "outside pressures" (*gaiatsu*), but is probably applicable elsewhere also, especially in less powerful places that routinely experience the wash of new ideas, technologies, and capital outward from metropolitan centers.

Ideas from elsewhere can be useful because they arrive with ready-made expert analysis, and/or moral authority that enables policy entrepreneurs to frame credible, legitimate solutions to pressing local problems. The borrowed legitimacy of imported planning ideas may be especially important for smaller actors, who are politically and economically weaker, and who lack the ability either to impose ideas or solutions on other actors or even to pursue them autonomously without permission or aid. For such weaker actors, the endorsement, credibility, and imaginaries of proponents elsewhere may be key to being taken seriously. This is likely to be particularly true for advocates of improved urban conditions and greater sustainability and livability, who are so often weaker politically and economically than those pursuing profit through urban development or redevelopment. Planning ideas, then, can be deployed as strategic resources by actors engaged in struggles over the control of urban development and change processes.

Finally, it is significant that key elements of ideas can be lost in the process of translation. For example, during the processes of translating, disseminating, and adopting urban sustainability ideas into policy in Japan, the issues of intergenerational, transfrontier, and social equity that are such a central part of sustainability debates elsewhere have been almost entirely lost. The most influential elements of the sustainable cities and compact cities ideas in the Japanese context have been those that promise to solve major Japanese spatial and economic problems, and that can be implemented within the frameworks of existing policy tools and programs.

## NOTES

1  The phrase is written in the phonetic Japanese Katakana script, used primarily for words and ideas borrowed from other languages: コンパクトシチイ (pronounced *konpacuto shitii*, directly borrowed from the English).

2  The Fiscal Investment and Loan Program (FILP) was created during the rapid growth period as a way of financing infrastructure development to boost economic growth. Within it ministries and public corporations borrow money from the postal savings account system at low interest rates. As spending is, in theory, for capital investment, not current expenditure, it is not included in the national budget.

3  CASBEE stands for Comprehensive Assessment System for Building Environmental Efficiency. See Japan Sustainable Building Consortium (2006).

4  Commonly referred to as *gaiatsu*, literally "outside pressure," which the United States, as Japan's largest foreign market and military protector, has been most effective at exploiting.

5  Public opposition to nuclear plants was greatly strengthened by a series of minor and major accidents that repeatedly escalated into major political incidents because of inept disaster management responses, and recurring attempts at cover-ups. These produced a major loss of credibility for the claims of safety and transparency made by both the nuclear industry and its regulators, and several facilities were shut down for extended periods to fix leaks. Most prominent were, first, a major fire and leak at the Monju fast breeder reactor and nuclear fuel reprocessing facility, which was intended to reduce Japanese dependence on imported uranium, and, second, an uncontrolled nuclear reaction at a nuclear fuel processing facility in Ibaragi near Tokyo, which caused a major release of radiation. This latter incident, caused by poorly trained workers who were mixing uranium in a bucket instead of the mixing machine, was the first self-sustained nuclear reaction to occur outside a nuclear reactor in the history of civilian nuclear power.

6  See Ministry of Land, Infrastructure, and Transport (Undated).

## References

Aldrich, D. P. (2008). *Site Fights: Divisive Facilities and Civil Society in Japan and the West*. Ithaca, NY, Cornell University Press.

Aoki, Y. (2006). "Formulating Sustainable Systems," in H. Tamagawa (Ed.) *Sustainable Cities: Japanese Perspectives on Physical and Social Structures*. Tokyo, United Nations University Press. pp. 50-69.

Barrett, B. and M. Usui (2002). "Local Agenda 21 in Japan: Transforming Local Environmental Governance," *Local Environment*, **7** (1), 49–67.

Blyth, M. (1997). "Any More Bright Ideas? The Ideational Turn of Comparative Political Economy," *Comparative Politics*, **29** (2), 229–50.

Blyth, M. (2001). "The Transformation of the Swedish Model: Economic Ideas, Distribution Conflict, and Institutional Change," *World Politics*, **54**, 1–26.

Bourne, L. S. (1996). "Reurbanization, Uneven Urban Development, and the Debate on New Urban Forms," *Urban Geography*, **17** (8), 690–713.

Breheny, M. J. (Ed.) (1992a). *Sustainable Development and Urban Form*. London, Pion.

Breheny, M. J. (1992b). "The Contradictions of the Compact City: A Review," in M. J. Breheny (Ed.) *Sustainable Development and Urban Form*. London, Pion. pp. 138–59.

Breheny, M. (2001). "Densities and Sustainable Cities: The UK Experience," in M. Echenique and A. Saint (Eds.) *Cities for the New Millennium*. London, Spon Press. pp. 39–51.

Burgess, R. (2000). "The Compact City Debate: A Global Perspective," in M. Jenks and R. Burgess (Eds.) *Compact Cities: Sustainable Urban Forms for Developing Countries*. London, E. & F. N. Spon. pp. 9–24.

Calder, K. E. (1988). *Crisis and Compensation: Public Policy and Political Stability in Japan, 1949–1986*. Princeton, NJ, Princeton University Press.

Calthorpe, P. (1993). *The Next American Metropolis*. New York, Princeton Architectural Press.

Campbell, J. L. (1998). "Institutional Analysis and the Role of Ideas in Political Economy," *Theory and Society*, **27** (3), 377–409.

Cervero, R. (1986). *Suburban Gridlock*. New Brunswick, NJ, Centre for Urban Policy Research.

Commission of the European Communities (CEC) (1990). *Green Paper on the Urban Environment*. Brussels, Commission of the European Communities.

Dierwechter, Y. (2008). *Urban Growth Management and its Discontents: Promises, Practices, and Geopolitics in U.S. City-Regions*. New York, Palgrave Macmillan.

Downs, A. (2005). "Smart Growth: Why We Discuss it More than We Do it," *Journal of the American Planning Association*, **71** (4), 367–80.

Eisenstadt, S. N. (1996). *Japanese Civilization: A Comparative View*. Chicago, University of Chicago Press.

Elkin, T., D. McLaren, and M. Hillman (1991). *Reviving the City: Towards Sustainable Urban Development*. London, Friends of the Earth.

Ewing, R. (1997). "Is Los Angeles Style Sprawl Desirable?," *Journal of the American Planning Association*, **63** (1), 107–26.

Feldhoff, T. (2007). "Japan's Construction Lobby and the Privatization of Highway-Related Public Corporations," in A. Sorensen and C. Funck (Eds.) *Living Cities in Japan: Citizens' Movements, Machizukuri and Local Environments*. London, Routledge. pp. 91–112.

Fujita, K. and R. C. Hill (2007). "The Zero Waste City: Tokyo's Quest for a Sustainable Environment," *Journal of Comparative Policy Analysis*, **9** (4), 405–25.

Gordon, P. and H. Richardson (1997). "Are Compact Cities a Desirable Goal?," *Journal of the American Planning Association*, **63** (1), 95–106.

Hall, P. (1988). *Cities of Tomorrow*. Oxford, Blackwell.

Hori, Y., A. Hosomi and T. Kurokawa (1999). "Study on the Effects of Energy Consumption by Vehicle Trips in a Compact City: Using the 1975 and 1992 Person Trip Data of Utsunomiya City," *Collected Papers of the Japanese City Planning Association* (*Nihon Toshi Keikaku Gakkai Ronbun Shu*), **34**, 241–6.

ICLEI (2002). *Local Governments' Response to Agenda 21: Summary Report of LA21 Survey Response with Regional Focus*. Toronto, International Council for Local Environmental Initiatives.

Imura, H. (1994). "Japan's Environmental Balancing Act: Accommodating Sustained Development," *Asian Survey*, **34** (4), 355–68.

Japan Ministry of Economy, Trade, and Industry (2008). *Outline of "Daiten-Ricchi Ho": Law Concerning the Measures by Large-Scale Retail Stores for Preservation of Living Environment*. D. I. Division. Tokyo, Ministry of Economy, Trade and Industry. pp. 1–5.

Japan Ministry of Foreign Affairs (2008). *Regulatory Reform: Japan Fact Sheet*. Tokyo, Ministry of Foreign Affairs.

Japan Ministry of Internal Affairs and Communications (2005). "Statistical Handbook of Japan, Chapter 2 Population." Available: http://www.stat.go.jp/english/data/handbook/c02cont.htm. Accessed 13 November 2005.

Japan Ministry of Land, Infrastructure, and Transport (2005). *New National Land Sustainability Plan*. Available: http://www.mlit.go.jp/english/2006/b_n_and_r_planning_bureau/01_duties/New_NLSP_060515.pdf. Accessed 12 June 2005.

Japan Ministry of Land, Infrastructure, and Transport (undated). *5th Comprehensive National Development Plan 1998* [*Dai 5ji Zenkoku Sôgô Kaihatsu Kekaku*]. National Planning Division, Ministry of Land, Infrastructure and Transport. Tokyo, Japan Ministry of

Land, Infrastructure, and Transport. Available: http://www.mlit.go.jp/kokudokeik/2s5-e/index.html.

Japan Ministry of Land, Infrastructure, and Transport (Undated). "Compact City: Compact Cities for Better Living." Available: http://www.thr.mlit.go.jp/compact%2Dcity/. Accessed 15 January 2009.

Japan Sustainable Building Consortium (JSBC) (2006). "An Overview of CASBEE." Available: http://www.ibec.or.jp/CASBEE/english/overviewE.htm. Accessed 15 January 2009.

Jenks, M., E. Burton, and K. Williams (1996). *The Compact City: A Sustainable Urban Form?* London, E. & F. N. Spon.

Jenks, M., K. Williams, and E. Burton (2000). *Achieving Sustainable Urban Form*. London, E. & F. N. Spon.

Kaidô, K. (1999). "The Compact City and Revitalization of City Center: Introducing the Argument in Britain and Comparing with Urban Form of German City" ["Conpacuto Shitii Ron to Chûshin Shigaichi Saisei: Eikoku de Rongi oyobi Deuch Toshi to Hikaku kara"], *City Planning Review (Toshi Keikaku)* **220**, 13–16.

Kaidô, K. (2001). *Compact City: Looking for an Urban Form for a Sustainable Society* [*Conpacuto Shitii: Jizoku Kanô na Shakai no Toshizô wo Motomete*]. Kyoto, Gakugei Shuppansha.

Kaidô, K. (2007). *Compact City, Planning and Design*. Tokyo, Gakugei Shuppansha.

Kingdon, J. W. (2003). *Agendas, Alternatives, and Public Policies*. New York, Longman.

Kisby, B. (2007). "Analysing Policy Networks: Towards an Ideational Approach," *Policy Studies*, **28** (1), 71–90.

Kitahara, K. (2002). "An Essay on Possibilities and Problems of the Downtown Living in the Local City for Making the Compact City a Reality," *City Planning Review (Toshi Keikaku)* **240**, 25–8.

Legro, J. W. (2000). "The Transformation of Policy Ideas," *American Journal of Political Science*, **44** (3), 419–32.

Lesbirel, S. H. (1998). *NIMBY Politics in Japan*. Ithaca, NY, Cornell University Press.

Low, N., B. Gleeson, R. Green, and D. Radovic (2005). *The Green City: Sustainable Homes, Sustainable Suburbs*. Abingdon, Routledge.

Matsuhashi, K. (2000). "A Study on the Compact City in View of Regional Trip Energy in Osaka Metropolitan Area," *City Planning Review (Toshi Keikaku)*, **35**, 469–74.

Matsunaga, Y. (2005). *New Wave of Machizukuri: Compact City/New Urbanism/Urban Village*. Tokyo, Shokokusha.

McCormack, G. (1996). *The Emptiness of Japanese Affluence*. Armonk, NY, M. E. Sharpe.

McCormack, G. (2002). "Breaking the Iron Triangle," *New Left Review*, **13** (1), 5–23.

Miller, D., G. de Roo, and International Urban Planning and Environment Association (2000). *Compact Cities and Sustainable Urban Development: A Critical Assessment of Policies and Plans from an International Perspective*. Aldershot, VT, Ashgate.

Morimoto, A. and H. Koike (1998). "Evaluation of Measures for Transportation Energy Reduction and Urban Forms" (in Japanese), *Collected Papers of the Japanese City Planning Association (Nihon Toshi Keikaku Gakkai Ronbun Shu)*, **33**, 181–6.

Muramatsu, M. (1993). "Patterned Pluralism under Challenge: The Policies of the 1980s," in G. Allinson and Y. Sone (Eds.) *Political Dynamics in Contemporary Japan*. Ithaca, NY, Cornell University Press. pp. 50–71.

Nakamichi, K., M. Taniguchi, and R. Matsunaka (2004). "Development and Application of the Practical Evaluation for Urban Consolidation Projects," *Journal of the City Planning Institute of Japan*, **39** (3), 67–72.

Nelson, A. C., R. J. Burby, E. Feser, C. J. Dawkins, E. E. Malizia, and R. Quercia (2004). "Urban Containment and Central-City Revitalization," *Journal of the American Planning Association*, **70** (4), 411–25.

Neuman, M. (2005). "The Compact City Fallacy," *Journal of Planning Education and Research*, **25**, 11–26.

Newman, P. and J. Kenworthy (1989). "Gasoline Consumption and Cities – A Comparison of US Cities with a Global Survey," *Journal of the American Planning Association*, **55** (1), 24–37.

OECD (1994). *OECD Environmental Performance Reviews: Japan*. Paris, Organization for Economic Cooperation and Development.

Ogawa, N. (2005). "Population Aging and Policy Options for a Sustainable Future: The Case of Japan," *Genus*, **61** (3–4), 369–410.

Owens, S. E. (1986). *Energy, Planning and Urban Form*. London, Pion.

Pempel, T. J. (1982). *Policy and Politics in Japan: Creative Conservativism*. Philadelphia, Temple University Press.

Pempel, T. J. (1998). *Regime Shift: Comparative Dynamics of the Japanese Political Economy*. Ithaca, NY, Cornell University Press.

Porter, D. R., R. T. Dunphy, and D. Salvesen (2002). *Making Smart Growth Work*. Washington DC, Urban Land Institute.

Rodgers, D. T. (1998). *Atlantic Crossings: Social Politics in a Progressive Age*. Cambridge, MA, Belknap Press of Harvard University Press.

Roseland, M., M. Cureton, and H. Wornell (1998). *Toward Sustainable Communities: Resources for Citizens and Their Governments*. Gabriola Island, BC, New Society Publishers.

Shimaoka, A., M. Taniguchi, and T. Ikeda (2003). "Guideline for Local Cities to Develop Consolidated Residential Areas," *Collected Papers of the Japanese City Planning Association* (*Nihon Toshi Keikaku Gakkai Ronbun Shu*), **38**, 775–80.

Sorensen, A. (2002). *The Making of Urban Japan: Cities and Planning from Edo to the 21st Century*. London, Routledge.

Sorensen, A. (2005). "The Developmental State and the Extreme Narrowness of the Public Realm: The 20th Century Evolution of Japanese Planning Culture," in B. Sanyal (Ed.) *Comparative Planning Cultures*. New York, Routledge. pp. 223–58.

Sorensen, A. (2006). "Liveable Cities in Japan: Population Ageing and Decline as Vectors of Change," *International Planning Studies*, **11** (3–4), 225–42.

Sorensen, A., P. J. Marcotullio, and J. Grant (Eds.) (2004). *Towards Sustainable Cities: East Asian, North American and European Perspectives*. Aldershot, Ashgate.

Sutcliffe, A. (1981). *Towards the Planned City: Germany, Britain, the United States and France, 1780–1914*. Oxford, Basil Blackwell.

Suzuki, H. (2007). *Japanese Version Compact City: Creating Local Cyclable Urban Form*. Tokyo, Gakuyo Shobô.

Suzuki, T. (2001). "A Review of the Compact City as a Sustainable Urban Form," *City Planning Review* (*Toshi Keikaku*), **232**, 11–14.

Takami, K. (2006). "Car Use and Sustainability: Reflection on Retail Development Control Systems," in H. Tamagawa (Ed.) *Sustainable Cities: Japanese Perspectives on Physical and Social Structures*. Tokyo, United Nations University Press. pp. 139–66.

Tamagawa, H. and N. Ehara (2006). "Population Stability and Urban Area," in H. Tamagawa (Ed.) *Sustainable Cities: Japanese Perspectives on Physical and Social Structures*. Tokyo, United Nations University Press. pp. 167–205.

Terasawa, M. (2007). "Compact City Formation and Aiming at Downtown Revitalization" ["Conpacuto shitii no keisei to chûshin shigaichi no saisei wo mezashite"], *New Cities* (*Shintoshi*), **61** (5), 105–9.

Upham, F. (1993). "Privatizing Regulation: The Implementation of the Large Scale Retail Stores Law," in G. Allinson and Y. Sone (Eds.) *Political Dynamics in Contemporary Japan*. Ithaca, NY, Cornell University Press. pp. 264–94.

Vogel, S. K. (2006). *Japan Remodeled: How Government and Industry are Reforming Japanese Capitalism*. Ithaca, NY, Cornell University Press.

Ward, S. V. (2002). *Planning the Twentieth-Century City: The Advanced Capitalist World*. Chichester, Wiley and Sons.

Woodall, B. (1996). *Japan under Construction: Corruption, Politics and Public Works*. Berkeley, University of California Press.

World Congress on Environment and Development (1987). *Our Common Future*. Oxford, Oxford University Press.

Yamamoto, K. (2006). *Compact City: Challenge of City of Aomori*. Tokyo, Gyôsei Shuppan.

Yamamoto, T. (Ed.) (1999). *Deciding the Public Good: Governance and Civil Society in Japan*. Tokyo, Japan Center for International Exchange.

# CHAPTER 7

# WHEN PLANNING IDEAS LAND

MAHAWELI'S PEOPLE-CENTERED APPROACH

**NIHAL PERERA**

The Mahaweli Development Project, Sri Lanka's largest-ever single development project, aimed to harness the water resources of the country's longest river, the Mahaweli, and six allied river basins (Figure 7.1).[1] At its start in 1963, this long-term project was expected to irrigate vast tracts of land, more than double the nation's electricity production,[2] and radically transform its economy and society. It also involved the voluntary and compulsory resettlement of large numbers of families to new and redeveloped towns. Typically for a development project, the Mahaweli Project primarily depended on Western capital, knowledge, direction, models, and skills; yet it also represents an instance of planners engaging in an inside-out planning effort, defying the top-down imposition of planning ideas.

I joined the project in 1981 as a young architect who wanted to use his design skills to serve regular people. Its planning and design office was far from encouraging. It had only a couple of architects who barely produced anything new, mainly issuing blueprints of typical buildings on demand. Most planners diligently discharged their duties, but with hardly any power or will to improve the towns they were creating. The locations of settlements and towns were determined by the irrigation infrastructure, planning largely followed Western models, and the towns hardly functioned for a decade. Two years later, however, I was involved in the founding of the Mahaweli Architectural Unit (MAU), which adopted an inside-out, people-friendly approach, and created towns that functioned from the outset. This chapter focuses on MAU's planning approach and interventions, from its formation in 1983 to its reabsorption into the mainstream in 1989.

MAU is not unique in having challenged the supremacy of incompatible Western expertise. Adapting, complementing, and questioning mainstream planning, select planners and designers in other places have also developed tools that are more appropriate for their particular communities. In South Asia, these have included action planning, support systems for housing, and critical vernacularism in architecture (Koenigsberger 1982; Perera 1998). In a global context where

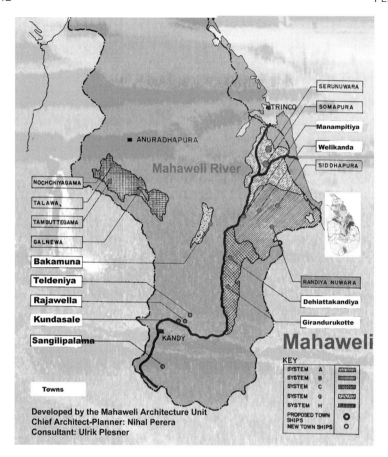

**Figure 7.1** Mahaweli area and towns (MAU towns highlighted with a white background).

formal development and planning discourses are rooted in Western modernity, and development is premised upon a deficit between the current state of people's lives and how they should be, "local knowledge" is largely produced through learning by doing, that is, learning about local cultures and environments through the application of "Western planning." Yet we know very little about these reflective, locally produced practices, especially how planning and development are viewed, managed, resisted, transformed, and practiced by those at the receiving end. This is largely because of the external vantage points of inquiry adopted in mainstream scholarship; although there is no lack of claims to represent weaker actors, whether the working class or the colonized, these self-appointed attempts hardly ever adopt a viewpoint empathetic to the practices of these groups (Perera 2009).

My research interest here is in examining the "local" production – within a transnational context – of development and planning approaches, frameworks, methods, and tools specific to this particular society and project. Almost every present-day community is subject to external influences but, in these encounters, recipients bring their material and cultural resources to process, express, and refashion external forces, such as capital and modernity, in local communities (cf. Appadurai 2002: 166; Escobar 1995: 98–9). My focus is on the transformative capacity of subjects to familiarize the strange, making ideas useful for their own society (cf. Ashcroft *et al*. 2002; Holston 1989; Yeoh 1996; Perera 1998; Zhang 2001). The goal is to make visible the production and implementation of new culture- and place-specific planning ideas in the cracks and interstices and at the margins of assumed structures of hegemony and domination. The specific production of the resulting planning and spaces is best understood from a vantage point empathic to subjects, particularly their local contexts and world views at the place of production (Perera 2009).

In particular, this chapter will examine the planning and development of towns by MAU in the 1980s. Although MAU's story is long, complex, and includes many shortcomings, the main concern of this paper is the planning approach that MAU developed within a nationally significant, internationally funded, and highly-structured project, through which it nonetheless managed to carve out a high level of autonomy in planning and design for both itself and the people it represented.

Methodologically, the chapter will rely on my own experience in this project, mainly as the Chief Architect-Planner from 1983 to 1989. The main aim is to revisit my planning and design experience in MAU, and view it through contemporary analytical frameworks. I will also draw on archival material, various studies and evaluations, my own observations made in each town over the past 10 years, and interviews with those who were involved in the planning, design, and construction of Mahaweli towns in the 1980s. I will examine this from a vantage point empathetic to MAU.

## FROM IRRIGATION PROJECTS TO THE ACCELERATED MAHAWELI

Sri Lanka boasts a history of over 2,000 years of irrigation. Yet the concepts underlying contemporary irrigation-based development projects were largely shaped during the British colonial period in the then Ceylon (Sri Lanka from 1972). According to Muller and Hettige:

> concerted efforts at the restoration of major irrigation tanks and the reclaiming of
> long abandoned tracts of rice fields with the objective of returning to the "roots" and

establishing dense peasant settlements were ... [undertaken after] a considerable measure of self-rule was conceded by the British ... to the indigenous political elite in the early 1930s.

(1995: 1)

These "roots" were the ancient Lankan irrigation technology, which the British had considered a wonder, and the rural practice of irrigation-based rice paddy cultivation. The new settlements were, however, more production oriented, larger, denser, and more diverse than the former more self-sufficient and spread-out rural communities (Perera 1998). In this, the late colonial administration incorporated irrigation-based cultivation into the modernity it was building in Ceylon, both dehistoricizing and defamiliarizing it for Sri Lankans. After independence in 1948, such projects were promoted as national development and reinforced by foreign aid.

The Mahaweli Project, which began in the 1960s, both continued and marked a significant break from this colonial past. The Mahaweli was the most ambitious of these post-independence irrigation projects, marking the high point of development initiatives in the 1960s and accounting for 22 percent of national capital expenditure (Moore 1985). At the time of writing, according to the Director General of the Mahaweli Authority, Dharmasiri Susith de Alwis, 160,000 ha have so far been cultivated and 144,000 farming families have been resettled under the project (cited in Wedaarachchi 2009). Most of these settlers went through a selection process, received land, and voluntarily moved into the project area. Others were compelled to relocate from their own fertile lands in the upstream valleys, which were flooded by newly built reservoirs. The project has been perceived as highly effective: rice paddy production rose from about 450,000 tons in 1953 to 3.13 million tons in 2007 (FAO 2009) and, in 2005, the Minister of Agriculture, Anura Kumara Dissanayake, claimed that – at 2.2 million tons – the country was now self-sufficient in rice production (Oryza Sri Lanka Rice Market Report 2005, unpaginated).

The Mahaweli Project also marked a significant break from previous approaches: "it permanently [linked] together a large part of the country through its extensive network of upstream reservoirs and downstream conveyance and distributory canals . . . This is unprecedented" (Muller and Hettige 1995: 2). Moreover, it integrated a number of otherwise unconnected hydrological basins by means of transbasin canals. Signaling a further break from the past, the government of 1977 "accelerated" the project for completion within six years. The Accelerated Mahaweli Project, completed in 1991, comprised five major dams and fed 130,000 ha of already and newly irrigated land. Each of the five major dams was financed and built by aid agencies and contractors from different donor countries: Kotmale Dam by Sweden, Victoria Dam by the UK, Randenigala and Rantambe by Germany, and Maduru Oya Dam and the transbasin canal by Canada. The accelerated project was anticipated to provide farm employment for 500,000 people and off-farm employment for another 50,000 (Karunaratna 1988: 31). The acceleration required the construction of a large number of urban centers and buildings within the remaining six years, turning planning and design offices into assembly lines that mass-produced stock blueprints and standard plans.

## CONSTRUCTION, NEGOTIATION, AND REPRESENTATION

Although it was not evident to us at the time, in hindsight, the Mahaweli Project was never a single comprehensive project, but a discursive construction that created the project through the negotiation of various components – donors, experts, and politicians. Planning ideas, whether these were from the West, the national government, or project administrators, did not smoothly materialize into regions, towns, and buildings. The project comprised many layers and components, and politicians, technocrats, and bureaucrats – the whole development coalition of the project – used this room for maneuver to assert their agency to negotiate their interests. They simultaneously represented Mahaweli as an integrated and comprehensive project, thus consolidating their own positional superiority within it.

The combining thread was development. The sponsors, funding agencies, consultants, and government largely shared the idea of a "universal" approach to development. Although this hegemonic development discourse urged "underdeveloped" countries to "catch up" with Western industrialization, the effects of the Mahaweli Project were nevertheless to reinforce Sri Lanka's role as an agricultural producer, and its position at the periphery of the capitalist world economy. This also took place during a period when Sri Lanka's social indicators of development were far ahead of the so-called Third World (Sen 2000: 46–8, 96–7).

The politics of national development and economic growth, argues Timothy Mitchell, was a politics of techno-science, which claimed to bring the expertise of modern engineering, technology, and social science to improve the defects of nature, to transform peasant agriculture, to repair the ills of society, and to fix the economy (Mitchell 2002: 15). Despite praising ancient Lankan hydraulic schemes, the consultants on the Mahaweli employed Western models such as that of the Tennessee valley development (Selznick 1949), which had also been followed in the Gal-Oya irrigation project in the Eastern Province (Ministry of Defence 2008). Other Western theories such as central place theory and post-War master planning were applied in conceiving the physical layout of urban centers.

Substantively, the project was developed through numbers, maps, images, texts, and external ordering systems useful for the understanding of regions and populations from a distance, overlooking the individuals, their desires, livelihoods, and spaces. As Arjun Appadurai highlights:

> number, by its nature, flattens idiosyncrasies and creates boundaries around these homogeneous bodies as it performatively limits their extent . . . Statistics are to bodies and social types what maps are to territories: they flatten and enclose . . . the unruly body . . . [which] is recuperated through the language of numbers that allows these very bodies to be brought back, now counted and accounted, for the humdrum projects of taxation, sanitation, education, welfare, and loyalty.
>
> (1998: 133)

The project leaders viewed locality and inhabitants as the background setting, rather than as the figures animating the scene, "recognizing neither their fragility nor their ethos as a property of social life" (Appadurai 1998: 182). The consultants, politicians, and professionals involved assumed the role of agents of change who could "modernize" the peasants. The settlers were considered the recipients of better life, the target population, the object of development, with no agency or voice. For the purposes of planning, they were bodies in space that needed to be ordered and organized.

As a career, development provides both livelihoods and social status for a significant population across national boundaries, in both donor and recipient countries. According to Edward Said, since colonialism, "to be interested in the East was something bright young Westerners would find to be an all-consuming passion" – a major advantage of which has been the positional superiority that places development "experts" in a whole series of relationships without ever losing them the relative upper hand (2004 [1978]: 4, 7). In the Mahaweli Project, foreign experts' "positional superiority" was manifested through relationships with Sri Lanka, the project, and the home country.

Development provides more opportunities than colonialism did for citizens of donor countries to work in consulting and construction. It also provides significant opportunities for intermediaries in recipient societies, particularly technocrats, bureaucrats, building contractors, and material suppliers. These groups depend for their livelihoods on aid-based projects, promoted by international growth coalitions made up of aid agencies, governments, entrepreneurs, political leaders, newspapers, and leading professionals, most of whom have made development a career and/or a business.[3] According to Frank Dunnill, even

Mahaweli field staff were more concerned with their own careers, and with their own status and financial interests, than with the welfare of the settlers and their families. A "we and they" attitude soon grew up; and it was too often assumed that "they" were essentially inferior.

(1995: 176)

It is coalitions of select groups of powerful actors like these that create development projects through the negotiation of their interests.

On the Mahaweli Project, the principal actors projected the image of a single comprehensive project. Any difference between plans and outcomes were largely attributed to "human error," usually a lack of coordination or an implementation problem; that is, the human conveyor belt did not transfer ideas smoothly from one stage, office, or component to another. Yet the Western science applied by the consultants and the engineers is effective only in solving small problems that can be separated from complex phenomena – their context, in particular. As Charles Lindblom (1959) argues, it is impossible to apply a comprehensive method to complex problems. Advanced scientific procedures, operations research, statistical decision-making theory, and systems analysis remain largely appropriate techniques for relatively small-scale problem-solving, in which the total number of variables considered is minimal and value problems are restricted. Five decades ago, Jane Jacobs highlighted that, within science, human settlements are not a "problem" of simplicity or of disorganized complexity, the two approaches in which the strengths of science lay, but belong to the category of organized complexity, like the human body. Science has no full understanding of organized complexity, only aspects of it (1961: 428–43). Moreover, human settlements involve multiple perspectives. As communicative planning theorists have recognized:

we are diverse people living in complex webs of economic and social relations, within which we develop potentially very varied ways of seeing the world, of identifying our interests and values, of reasoning about them, and of thinking about our relations with others.

(Healey 2003: 239)

There is much research demonstrating that the actual practice of planning in Western countries is rarely comprehensive, but is largely incremental (see Flyvbjerg 1998). In scientizing development, as Escobar diligently argues with regard to development economists (1995), "experts" have constructed their own discourse and object. Similarly, the Mahaweli Project was made up of multiple components, some of which were at odds with others.

It was the social power of Eurocentrism and the authority of the national state that created such hegemony for the project, particularly its goals, both among ordinary citizens and among those of us who worked on it. Although many young Sri Lankan professionals had heard stories about how the settlers and those affected by the project were dissatisfied with it, many, like me, opted to dedicate themselves to the greater good. As James Scott highlights, such projects are "driven by utopian plans and an authoritarian disregard for the values, desires, and objections of their subjects" (1998: 7). For me, my initial optimism received its biggest shock much later when I saw some graffiti on the side of a ruined house that had been flooded by the Victoria Reservoir, but had resurfaced when the water level receded: it read *gangak gamakata kala hadiya* – "What a river has done to a village!" It was clearly not the river, it dawned on me, but the project actors. It brought flashing back the many complaints I had heard, including those that the project was relocating people from fertile valleys to barren land in the Dry Zone. Yet the hegemonic notion that "rapid economic progress is impossible without painful adjustments" was far too strong for me to even hear such voices (United Nations 1951, cited in Escobar 1995: 3).

Despite its overarching influence, the hegemony of Western development reproduced by the national state and the technocrats was incomplete. People are not passive recipients of external ideas and initiatives. They tend to transform select materials and ideas that come their way into something familiar and useful for them within their immediate context and constraints (Appadurai 1998; Goh 2002; Perera 2009). As I have argued elsewhere (Perera 2009), the familiarization of space involves both the adaptation of the subject to his/her new position and space, and the subject's own, reciprocal modification of these to make meaning for him/herself. This is not unique to "developing" contexts; it can be seen in regard to the circulation of planning ideas within the West as well. For example, Jill Grant highlights this "familiarization" regarding New Urbanism in Canada:

> [Although within] the ultimate New Urbanist scenario, home owners live next to renters and the merchants live above the shops ... [in reality] both apartments and houses ... are [mostly] occupied by owners; few are rented. Stores, with false stories above, are leased to franchises. These new "towns" are in danger of becoming caricatures of a real community: a theme park.
>
> (2005: 26, drawing on Hutchinson 1998 and Saunders 1997)

As Partha Chatterjee argues with regard to modern governments, exceptions are as important as rules for the functioning of both social systems and the rules themselves (2007). The fact that a particular order works for municipal or state authorities (or an international agency) is no guarantee that it works for citizens (Scott 1998: 58). Very often, ordinary people's understanding of a norm at local level is quite different, with local standards of measurement tied to practical needs (Scott 1998: 29); yet "it is only by recognizing that norm at the local level that . . . the larger structure will survive" (Chatterjee 2007, unpaginated). This foregrounds a paradox: if people practice a norm or a law differently from how the state defines it, it is a failure; yet the successful transmission of an idea depends on its being understood by "recipients," who do so through interpreting and modifying it within their local contexts. Exceptions, then, are significant, allowing room for local interventions into systems, structures, and processes, whether they are global, regional, or national in scale. In fact, "formal schemes . . . are parasitic on informal processes that, alone, they could not create or maintain" (Scott 1998: 6). Even in the legalistic United States, planning incorporates both formal mechanisms (regulations, public hearings, mandated checklists) and informal mechanisms (lobbying, advocacy reports, recourse to the media); and these two approaches coexist as projects progress (Birch 2005). Projects, especially large ones, depend on a host of informal practices and improvisations that can never be codified.

The acceleration of the project also expanded the room available for maneuver in several ways (Perera 1988). First, being multipurpose and multifunctional, the project required a range of actors from different professions to contribute and cooperate (see also Muller and Hettige 1995). The different perceptions and approaches that they employed required considerable internal negotiation. Second, the project extended across half the country and it was impossible to maintain strict control over its organization and activities from one center. It took over eight hours of fairly uncomfortable driving from Colombo to reach the furthest sites, and the telephone service to most distant offices was weak. Third, the compression of the project's duration required simultaneous action on many fronts, across a large area, requiring project staff to make a large number of (small) decisions very quickly, and resulting in a degree of complexity that was far beyond the total control of any centralized authority (see also Muller and Hettige 1995). All of these factors made it impossible for a hierarchical organization and a centralized management system to operate perfectly. This difficulty was apparent in the increasing number of agencies and offices created by the Mahaweli Authority to handle various aspects of the project – which in themselves created more gaps within the structure and processes, and provided even more room for potential intervention. As I will now outline, government officials, consultants, engineers, and planners had their own ideas about what development should mean, how it should be pursued, and how to make use of various opportunities to meet their own institutional, social, and personal needs, wants, and aspirations.

The room for maneuver was amply used by the national government and its powerful members to generate political, social, and personal capital. Along with the key ministers of the 1977 government, who were competing to highlight their achievements through mega-projects such as *Gam Udawa*, *Mahapola*, and the new capital built by and named after the President (Vale 1992; Perera 2005), the Mahaweli Minister also made substantial political capital out of the project. Accelerating the visible components of the project such as dams, major canals, and the irrigation infrastructure, his ministry packaged it as a spectacle.[4] The Minister also built more overt monuments for himself: in addition to one of the major dams in his electorate, Kotmale, he constructed a giant concrete stupa right next to the dam,[5] striking a comparison between himself and significant ancient Sinhalese kings who built massive stupas and reservoirs.

While various agents employed the room for maneuver to enhance their own agendas, businesses, or livelihoods through the project, they also strengthened and hegemonized the notion of development on which they depended. Being a lead project of the government, the Mahaweli scheme received enormous political and financial backing and publicity. Nor did the left-oriented political opposition question the idea of development behind the project, despite criticizing members of the government for corruption.

Extracting personal benefits from the public project was also evident among the donors and consultants. Most of the aid was spent by companies of donor countries and their staff. Staff on the Victoria (dam) Project, for example, were largely British, employees of Sir Alexander Gibb and Partners (the consultants), Balfour Beatty Construction, and Edmund Nuttall (the contractors). These firms bought vehicles and equipment and hired people from the UK, thus using most of the project money to support the British economy. The locally apparent aspect of personal gain among foreign staff was the lavish lives they led in a gated community in Rajawella, with huge comforts they could not afford in their home countries, such as domestic workers. In Sri Lanka, only a few in Colombo could afford such lifestyles. Local people in the area worked in expatriates' gardens and homes (in addition to various sites and the housing complex), and sometimes, allegedly, in their beds. Whereas some locals were angry about this exploitation, others were envious of the salaries these workers drew and of expatriates' lifestyles. Sri Lankan employees who lived in smaller houses in the gated community, especially engineers and professionals, were viewed indifferently by the nearby villagers. Enhancing their difference and assumed power, these professionals largely spoke in English, used jeeps for transportation, played tennis, used swimming pools and clubs for recreation, and sent their children to international schools that their counterparts working in Colombo or other places could not afford. Although I was not an employee of the dam construction project, I too lived in this gated community.

Bureaucrats and technocrats working on the Mahaweli Project also used the available room to maneuver to establish their own positional superiority. In this mini-battle, the engineers succeeded in defining the project's implementation. The two crucial arms of the Mahaweli Authority were the Mahaweli Economic Agency and the Mahaweli Engineering and Construction Agency. Although the Economic Agency held the power to allocate funds and monitor the progress and the direction of the project, it was the Engineering Agency, which carried out design and construction, that established its dominance. This occurred because, first, irrigation engineers directed the physical growth process of the project (see Muller and Hettige 1995). Second, the politicians and the media used engineering feats – major dams and canals – to represent the project. Third, the engineers' hold had historic roots: the project was first undertaken by the Irrigation Department, of which the Engineering Agency was an outgrowth. Finally, engineering designs were seen as objective, scientific, truthful, economical, and unchangeable; their hegemony marginalized other forms of questioning. A well-respected engineering educator, A. Thurairajah, observed that "the Mahaweli Programme gives the impression of being mainly directed towards construction rather than actual settler development" (1985: 34).

The project thus constituted an abandonment of Sri Lanka's historical culture of irrigation and cultivation; the engineers incorporated ideas and elements from ancient irrigation systems, such as reservoirs, but modified these into a new modernist project represented in civil engineering achievements. This is precisely why it is important to emphasize the human aspects of the project, reinjecting the social values excluded by a technocratic perspective, and exploring the ways in which the project benefited some actors, affected others, and was adapted by still others.

The separation of engineering and science from social values in contemporary irrigation-based projects in Sri Lanka is a Western imagination infused during the British colonial rule, argues Bryan Pfaffenberger (1990). According to his observations, social values and engineering designs were integrated in historic Lankan irrigation systems. Modern-day "colonization" schemes, as such works are suggestively called by the Irrigation Department, have

> almost uniformly failed to achieve their social goals . . . [and are] inclined to reproduce (rather than ameliorate) the worst aspects of Sri Lankan peasant society, such as indebtedness, land fragmentation, sharecropping on a massive scale, socioeconomic differentiation, and low agricultural productivity.
>
> (Pfaffenberger 1990: 361–2)

He notes that the "social design" of these systems – their effects upon the settlers – was firmly a creation of British public servants, rather than engineers. But this approach was adopted without question and promoted zealously by Sri Lanka's postcolonial elite (ibid.: 365), and technocrats.

Later, on the Mahaweli Project, this irrigation infrastructure continued to determine the form and structure of settlements. The engineers approached planning from a physicalist–scientific standpoint, giving primacy to factors such as soils, elevations, slopes, and the water flow in an environment assumed to be cultureless and timeless. Engineering in Mahaweli was mainly about the design and construction of a physical infrastructure, for the purposes of collecting and distributing the maximum possible quantity of water for irrigation and the production of a large quantity of electricity. Engineers designed roads using the same principles, largely along ridges and canal bunds, thus fixing the access, connectivity, and circulation systems. Instead of beginning from where people are, or could be, and working upwards, the infrastructure was supposed to determine these aspects, as well as settlement planning, which were all seen as less significant.

Even sensitivity to the environment and society was not valued. The rejection of my first ever travel request to visit a site by my then boss provides an example. My first assignment concerned a town on the east of the central mountains unfamiliar to me, and I wished to visit the site. The Deputy General Manager of the Design department told me that I should instead consult the topographical and land-use maps. When I told him that I wanted to develop a feeling for the site, his response was that Mahiyangana hills were much smaller than Kandyan hills.[6] The abstract–physicalist considerations in regard to settlements not only maintained a clear distance from social concerns, but also paid very little attention to the physical qualities of the site, such as land forms, hills, reservoirs, vegetation, and existing land uses – thus rejecting the local physical factors that made each site unique. The development of human settlements was never accorded the same level of importance as engineering works in terms of expert involvement and resource allocation (Muller and Hettige 1995: 2).

The engineers relied on map information that had already reduced physical realities into points, lines, and areas. Settlement planning was thus subsumed into the irrigation design, and was viewed merely as the logical next step to complete it. Engineers used the same modernist logic employed by Western analysts, largely viewing the world as a homogeneous place that can be understood and managed using science. Although defending their own "turf" at times, they accepted most of what came from the West as objective, believing that this offered ways for locals to achieve the higher standard of living enjoyed in the West. In creating their own position within the project, the engineers institutionalized a linear process of development planning, subordinating subjects, and hierarchically placing planning and architecture directly under the Deputy General Manager for Design of the Engineering Agency.

In short, the politicians, the technocrats and other agencies exercised their limited autonomy to shape and develop the project in ways that mattered to them and constructed social power for them. Collectively, they operated within and reinforced the hegemonic notion of development promoted by donors and consultants, and imported Western technical ideas through the consultants. By employing civil engineering spectacles as the project's representation, the government highlighted the connections between both the glorious hydraulic systems of the past and the modern future it was creating; and the engineers turned this vision into a physical design project. While, in reality, Sri Lankan authorities and technocrats were negotiating their plans with donors and consultants, the members of the development coalition were careful to present Mahaweli as a single project, with a hierarchical structure and top-down linear processes that ended up on site.

## Neglected settlers and landscapes of uncertainty

Before MAU's formation, the physical planners took their cues from the norms set by consultants and the physical layout created by engineers. For the Engineering Agency, settlement planning was a straightforward, scientific, low-skilled activity. No experienced planners were employed;[7] instead, the settlement phase was used to provide on-the-job training for graduates in Estate Management and Valuation.[8] In preparing plans for regional structures, urban centers of various scales, and hamlets, planners followed the respective norms recommended by each of the consultancy firms. In the process, the planners were both socialized into the engineering mode of thinking and trained to complete the next step of physical development. In the end, the settlers were neglected and the intended towns hardly materialized on the ground.

The foreign consultants recommended an evenly distributed, hierarchical settlement structure based on central place theory (Pieris 1996: 185). Although many precedents were set by an early study carried out by Sogreah, a French consultancy, for a large area west of the river (System H) (MDB and Sogreah 1972), preliminary studies for the development of each hydrological system – those fed by either a large reservoir or a major canal – were carried out individually by consultancy firms from the country that had funded it.[9] As recommended, the smallest settlement unit, a "block," was served by a single irrigation channel, and consisted of about 100 farming families. A couple of these, comprising 250–300 families, made up a hamlet. Local services were systematically planned at block, hamlet, village, area, urban, and sub-district levels (Figure 7.2), with town centers intended to serve about 8,000–10,000 farming families. Within this highly ordered hierarchy, the planners "blocked out" hamlets and service centers, and the architects simply issued drawings for each type of building.

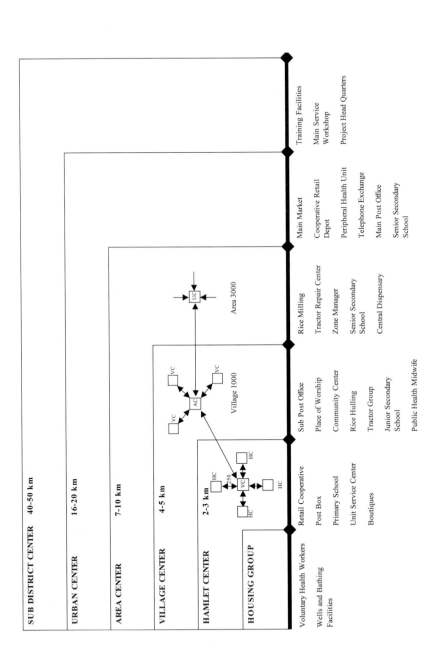

**Figure 7.2**  The hierarchical organization of service centers.

Planning – or blocking out – is not just the application of theoretical knowledge, Escobar argues aptly, but was also the instrument through which economics became useful in a direct way to policy and the state (1995: 85). By applying the central place and allied theories, consultants on the Mahaweli Project not only disregarded the local social, cultural, and environmental context, but also opted to transform it to fit into a perception developed in the environmentally and culturally different Germany and other Western states. Evidently, the consultants did not see much value in studying Sri Lankan settlements and culture in depth. Alongside the few studies carried out by foreign consultants themselves, there are hardly any references to Sri Lankan studies: one consultant's report (Hunting Technical Services 1980: Q.83–4) refers to a PhD dissertation (Gunewardene 1964) and a published Master's thesis focusing on growth poles and corridors (Mendis 1973).[10] Instead of developing plans to suit the place, consultants applied their knowledge onto the Mahaweli area, transforming it into a familiar context for their knowledge, doing so perhaps to an even greater degree than the colonial administration.

This raises the issue of legitimate knowledge. Susantha Goonatilaka (1984: 111) argues that the legitimization of knowledge takes a different form in the periphery. In the center, knowledge is legitimized through debate and social negotiation of scientific issues by scientists of the center, and through publication in relevant peer-reviewed journals. In the dependent periphery, however, significant knowledge accretions are built up through the diffusion of ideas from the center, and legitimization occurs through recourse to writings from it. Scientific reputations within a peripheral country are often based not on scholarly achievements, but along personal–political lines. Hence, "in the periphery, the dependent structures give rise to mimicked knowledge or to knowledge legitimized on nonscientific criteria; knowledge no longer portrays reality . . . it acts as a suppressor of creativity" (ibid.: 111). On the Mahaweli Project, the consultants' reports achieved just this: most physical planners referred to them only for the few pages that provided planning and design standards and were totally detached from the development process.

The consultants did not completely ignore local society, but were hardly conversant with it. For example, Sogreah's idea of the fundamental "manageable and comfortable social unit" being clusters of 100 families was derived from *purana gam,* "old villages" (MDB and Sogreah 1972: 5). This is one of the few deep insights provided by a consultancy firm on the project, adopting a Sinhala term first employed on the earlier Chandrikawewa Project to describe traditional villages of around 50–60 people (Amunugama 1965). Yet there are fundamental differences between the scientific and capitalist worldviews in which these "blocks" were conceived, and the lived environments of the inhabitants of *purana gam*. First, *purana gam* were largely "self-sufficient" and subsistence oriented, existing on the margins of mainstream society. They were highly incompatible with the production-oriented Mahaweli Project. This is evident, second, in the notion of "blocks" – a term implying the various shades of neighborhood unit popular among Western planners (see Vidyarthi's account in Chapter 4) – which implies a lack of appreciation for traditional experiences. In the Mahaweli blocks, each lot is a privately owned, separate parcel of land, with many inhabitants having no previous relationship with their neighbors. This contrasts with traditional Sri Lankan villages – *purana gam* or otherwise – which are socially cohesive and collaborative. The blocks, in contrast, are not communities, but made up of individuals. In fact, communities and "the things that only community life can engender and protect: the care for the old, the care . . . of children, family life, neighborly work, the handing down of memory . . . respect for nature and the lives of wild creatures" (Berry 1990: 157, cited in Prakash and Esteva 2008: 7) were also destroyed in the process.

Moreover, Sogreah's bonafide reference to *purana gam* was made in the early 1970s; later, following the project's acceleration, the consultants made little further effort to connect to local realities. The continued use of the term *purana gam* thus appears to express more of an attempt to gain local acceptance for the project than any intention to connect with local society. To its credit, Sogreah also discouraged the use of terms such as "colonies" and "tracts" and numbers to identify the settlements, recommending instead the use of names (1972: 199). These recommendations were carried out in the 1980s, but this was still far from an attempt to construct the towns around local settlers' realities.

The physical planners working from Colombo also treated Mahaweli areas as familiar, or as *tabula rasa,* without much reference to deeper local realities. They spent most of their time in the office and largely relied on map information and numbers that had already been abstracted. The strength of external ideas, socialization into such thinking, and planners' own education enticed them to conceive of townships in rectangular, grid-iron forms built on leveled and cleared land. As the EU liaison officer Dunnill stresses, an academic in Colombo can be as alien to the inhabitants of rural Sri Lanka as one in Chicago (1995: 182).

Most neglected of all were the settlers. Neither the engineers, nor the planners, nor the architects paid much attention to social and cultural needs and wants of the settlers, particularly their dwellings and urban environments. The project leaders focused on the means – dams and canals – rather than the stated ends – the amelioration of living conditions for everyday Sri Lankans, in whose name the project was supposedly taking place. Development colonized reality and became the reality (Escobar 1992). Each settler was given a plot of land and a meager 1,500 rupees (approximately US$50) in compensation for resettlement, which was inadequate to construct a dwelling. Jaap Jan Speelman and G. M. van der Top observed that, in the mid-1980s, many settlers lived in "huts" on the verge of collapse (1985). Although their concerns might be a bit exaggerated, concern for settlers on the Mahaweli Project was much less than on earlier irrigation initiatives; for example, the government provided core houses for settlers of the Uda Walawe Project in the 1960s and this was recommended for Mahaweli settlers by Sogreah (1972). MAU went on to develop a program to improve settler housing, but this paper focuses on its role in urban development. As I will now explain, before MAU's establishment, the larger urban centers created on the project remained largely "ghost towns," populated by a few institutional buildings spread across scrub jungle. It was in the construction of later towns in the 1980s that MAU's relatively small intervention managed to make an enormous difference.

The key issue that instigated the creation of MAU was the recognition by its founders of the lack of a sense of place in Mahaweli settlements, particularly the towns. Despite the bona fide intentions of the former physical planners, there was a substantial gap between the way that the towns were conceived and the way that they materialized. They adopted a post-War, master-planning style, established under the guidance of consultants, particularly Hunting Technical Services (1980). This failed to acknowledge local needs and contexts. Each town was totally planned with regard to the delineation of land for various uses, suggesting that it was expected to be completely built. Yet, with very little funds allocated each year, the "towns" became just a few dispersed buildings, with mini-jungles between them. As the settlers were moved into areas before even the irrigation water became available, this meant they had few social and economic services for over a decade.

Various factors led to the towns taking so long to materialize, but fundamentally the time lag reveals a basic mismatch between the plan and the context. First, there was very little funding for town building; the priority was irrigation structures. Each year, the Economic Agency funded the construction of a few select buildings in each town, for example two Mahaweli offices and 12 dwellings for Mahaweli staff in the first year, and a school and a hospital in the second year. The dispersed location of these, based on the master plan, gave towns and service centers an abandoned feel. Second, responsibility for the towns' development was meant to be shared between the government, responsible for the construction of institutional (service) buildings such as schools and post offices, and businesses and private individuals, who were expected to build on land allocated by Mahaweli. In reality, the private sector usually held off, reluctant to invest until secure markets were established for the goods or the services they expected to sell. This meant that, for at least a decade, only a handful of shops would be operating in a town, based in temporary shacks. The plans were thus incapable of guiding the town-building process, and the partly-built "towns" represented landscapes of uncertainty.

Moreover, there was the lack of infrastructure or vegetation in these towns. The sites earmarked for towns and roads were cleared by bulldozers. Road reservations were very wide, marginalizing pedestrians, and the lack of shade made it impossible for people to walk on them in the tropical heat. The roads were unpaved within the city and were washed away each rainy season. The towns were thus vastly spread out, requiring a lot of resources for maintenance – not a forte in Sri Lanka. Once the project was completed, the towns were expected to be the responsibility of local authorities, whose resources were very limited. Even the town center of Girandurukotte, which is highly compact compared with others, is currently not well maintained (Scudder 2005).

Mahaweli towns had the potential to offer farmers a place to sell their produce, buy consumer goods and agricultural supplies, and obtain health and banking services (Perera 1986: 11), yet this had failed. As Jane Jacobs (1961: 238) points out in regard to American cities, towns can provide something for everybody only when they are created by everybody. Mahaweli towns clearly fell short of allowing people to create their own places and develop a sense of belonging; this was the major underlying issue to which MAU responded.

In sum, the plans did not produce towns on the ground. For us, failure of towns to be "leaders" rather than "followers" of development, as strongly advised also by the Hunting consultancy group (1980: 86), began not with "implementation" issues but with a shortcoming in planning approach and method; effectively, the plans had been unable to transform small but significant state investments into functioning urban environments. Although MAU profoundly redistributed resources through planning, in the Mahaweli context, we felt, planning should become less about resource allocation in an ideal sense, and more about the utilization of available resources to guide the development of functioning towns. It was, therefore, necessary to develop an approach that addressed local concerns. This required the understanding of issues, needs, operational mechanisms, and the context, rather than simply a knowledge of models.

## REFLECTIVE LEARNING, THE INSIDE-OUT APPROACH, ACTION PLANNING

MAU's main goal was to create towns that functioned from the outset and supported the local populace in their daily activities and cultural practices, particularly through the production of spaces and places for these. This required the decentering of processes that were reproducing hegemonic planning practices. The crucial first step was to create a separate institution outside of the structure of the Engineering Agency, and to move out of the direct path of the outside-in imposition of ideas (see also Perera 1988: 9, 1990). People cannot be empowered instrumentally by interventions; but their own empowerment can be facilitated. MAU's success in this facilitation was built upon its capacity to read the cracks in the project structure and processes, in order "to see the opportunity for 'doing things differently', and to be able to widen a crack into a real potential for change" (Healey 1997: 270). Using this space, MAU seized opportunities to exercise its agency and actually used these to enable people's own processes. For this, it adopted a "loose-fit" planning method that produced significant results (see Heath 2009).

MAU's emergence was made possible through the fact that, in 1983, the architect Ulrik Plesner joined the project through the Mahaweli Ministry as a consultant. Originally from Denmark, Plesner is well-known in Sri Lanka for having co-developed, alongside the leading Sri Lankan architect Geoffrey Bawa, a hybrid architecture both suitable for contemporary institutions and functions and culturally comfortable for Sri Lankans, which I call "critical vernacular" (Perera 1998). Early in his career, in 1957, Plesner moved from Denmark to Sri Lanka, largely because of his interest in Buddhism, partnering with Bawa from 1959 to 1965. Although he later moved to Israel, he continued his involvement in projects in Sri Lanka. A Sri Lankan in many ways, he understands the country and its citizens well.[11] Plesner and I shared similar interests with regard to planning and design, and had complementary strengths. We were able to develop new ideas about how to improve Mahaweli towns, which resulted in the creation of MAU.

In formulating a better collaboration between people and institutions, MAU opted to ensure that the settlers received most of the benefits possible within the project. Acknowledging that town building is largely a political act and that implementation is integral to planning,[12] its leaders relied on their social networks for political and financial support and on the energy of construction agencies and inhabitants to shape the towns. Plesner and I employed our complementary strengths: his experience, external connections, and access to upper administration, and my knowledge of local conditions, local connections, social capital, and the willingness to take risks. It also helped that I was Sri Lankan and he was foreign and "white." We convinced the Cabinet Minister and the Director General of the perhaps inadvertent marginalization of settlers, settlement planning, and town building within this nationally significant project. A change in the method of planning, we conveyed, was capable of extending more benefits of the project to the settlers.

With the Minister accepting our approach to planning, MAU came into existence in 1983. While I was appointed the acting head (Chief Architect-Planner), Plesner was appointed Acting Director. After playing a leading role in establishing

MAU, he then took on more of a consultancy role, visiting three times a year. Impressed with our proposals for downstream towns, which were to serve farmers in newly irrigated areas, the Minister charged the Unit with also planning upstream towns built to replace urban facilities that had been flooded. Whereas downstream design and construction were carried out by the Engineering Agency, upstream, where all the major dams were located, was under the direct jurisdiction of the larger Mahaweli Authority. The construction of the dams themselves was carried out by foreign firms and coordinated by a different engineering organization: the Central Engineering Consultancy Bureau (CECB). Although the MAU staff belonged to the Engineering Agency, the upstream commissions and responsibilities to the larger Mahaweli Authority made MAU semi-autonomous in regard to its operations and responsibilities. By making use of the room for maneuver this afforded, MAU planned, designed, and built 12 towns – mostly new, but also some restructured – over the course of the 1980s. All but one of these grew much faster than expected.

MAU concentrated on the immediate scale, where it saw that the (abstract) project was both affecting and being shaped by people. This is where larger ideologies, structures, and processes touch the ground and interface with human beings. From a local vantage point, the project was interpreted, modified, and constructed in this (trans)locality. "Local" is also the scale that corporate executives, political leaders, professionals, and scholars who engage in larger-scale processes ignore the most. For MAU, for example, the (abstract) EU and its transnational aid network was represented in its (concrete) liaison officer, Frank Dunnill. While he carried out EU projects, MAU leaders also convinced him of their good work and needs, and Dunnill eventually obtained EU funds for two consultants for MAU and the building of stores in Girandurukotte.

From MAU's perspective, the ability of the resettled farming families to make a living – economically, socially, and culturally – in the downstream area was the most crucial condition for the success of the whole Mahaweli Project, particularly its agricultural component. MAU thus approached planning from the settlers' vantage point. The settlers needed social and economic opportunities and a sense of security and belonging to begin this journey. The original United Nations Development Programme/Food and Agriculture Organization (UNDP/FAO) feasibility study had recommended that certain facilities be available to them at the time of resettlement (cited in MDB and Sogreah 1972). Besides the settlers' own homesteads and farms, town environments with the necessary amenities are highly significant in facilitating the settlement process. Planning is most successful when the inhabitants are able to relate to the environment and familiarize their spaces and places with minimal transformation of their daily activities and cultural practices.

MAU took account of local realities such as funding, implementation conditions, and the interests of local and international agencies. Leaving a large area of land for future consideration in each town, it organized initial service buildings into a contiguous and dense urban core that would grow outward in specified directions. In contrast to earlier Mahaweli towns, these cores were actually built. The institutional buildings were complemented with public amenities, open spaces, a dozen stores and restaurants, and a transportation node that connected each town to other places. This concentration of buildings, activities, and people, all brought together in an integrated urban center, created a sense of place that was radically new in Mahaweli; and the two-storied buildings gave the towns a unique physical identity and character, new to this previously rural area.

The initial buildings were organized around a main street complemented by, where possible, a few squares along it (Figure 7.3). The storefronts and the fronts of office buildings, all built up to and facing squares and the main street, were connected by a covered sidewalk that runs around the squares and along the main street, joining up the various parts of the town. In contrast to pre-MAU Mahaweli towns and city centers elsewhere that directly adopted Western standards (e.g. wide roads), such as Anuradhapura, which lack any clear identity, MAU towns have a strong identity. They represent a locally produced modernity, rather than an abstract or imposed modernity.

Upstream towns posed different challenges. Here, the government offered land and money as compensation for flooded property, and building activity was left in the hands of the resettled population. Yet it is not individual buildings but the relationship between these and the supporting infrastructure that makes towns, neighborhoods, and places. The Minister got MAU involved before any of these towns were built, and, as with the downstream areas, the Unit suggested organizing the initial urban facilities into urban cores. The Mahaweli Authority agreed to replace public buildings, but would fund only buildings of the same area as those that had been flooded. MAU lobbied for extra facilities including verandas (arcades) for buildings, sidewalks, paved roads, public toilets, bus stations, and trees, enabling the resulting collections of buildings to become town centers. Once these were sanctioned, and so organized, the upstream towns began functioning effectively much faster, because they had far more initial buildings, especially stores and restaurants. The occupants were from nearby areas, and the flooded towns already had a population that depended on them.

As the authorities realized the value of MAU's approach, funds became available to build more complete urban cores both downstream and upstream. A major selling point, however, remained cost-effectiveness, a language that the authorities understood and the technocrats could not refute. Our studies of Telhiriyawa, a downstream town that had already been planned, revealed that it was six times as expensive as the "concentrated towns" we proposed.[13] Once convinced, the

**Figure 7.3** Urban services provided from the outset: Teldeniya town.

Mahaweli Authority allocated funds to pave roads, plant trees, build bus stations, tile roofs, and build shells for a limited number of stores in the towns that we designed – in short, to build complete town centers and access roads.

Working for and with settlers meant intervening as little as possible, in order to generate optimum enablement and enhancement of people's own processes.[14] Comprehensive planning or planning for the long term was not on MAU's agenda. What MAU relied on instead was a framework, a loose-fit plan, which could guide the development of each town. Instead of prescribing the input of partners in building, such as the Electricity Board, we tapped into their energy and potential creativity and got them involved in building attractive and vibrant towns. The engineering offices that coordinated the construction of towns, especially the CECB office at Rajawella, became highly excited about MAU's approach, and closely collaborated as equals. It is important to note that not all engineers strongly adhered to the hegemonic engineering approach; many, especially young engineers, were more socially conscious. It was the engineer at the Rajawella office who suggested planting trees between the new town and the bypass. As the towns grew rapidly and people moved in, MAU also accepted citizens' interventions. All of this was coordinated and facilitated through loose-fit plans, which were frequently updated to incorporate and adapt to changes. As the initial set of stores and restaurants began functioning faster than expected in Dehiattakandiya, for example, we added more of these and organized them in clusters around open courtyards. Thus MAU was cyclically amending the plans, both accommodating and directing the occupants' interventions as required, and blurring the separation of plan making and plan implementation.

In addition to responding to the growth of towns, MAU brought Sri Lankan sensibilities into planning and design by tapping into the experience of its planners and conducting special studies. Usually, Sri Lankan people visit the nearest urban center very frequently – daily if possible – to buy fresh vegetables and food. Public transportation is central to this, and towns are filled with pedestrians. As people carry out a multitude of tasks while in town, walking from one facility to the other, each town is compact and made up of various (mixed) land uses and functions that are not separated out in the way that cities are understood in Western land-use discourse. MAU opted to create urban centers similar to these, but with select improvements, such as making them safer (as I will describe below).

Yet these towns were not conceived as "Sri Lankan" or "traditional" within an opposition between "Western" and "non-Western." MAU's aim was to create towns for the people, who were not either in any pure sense, and had no problem drawing from Western, rural, traditional, or any other experience in creating their contemporary livelihoods and identities, or "local (hybrid) modernities." Young and energetic members of the team, for example, grew up in semi-urban or rural Sri Lanka, but were educated in the university system within a Western curriculum. There were also consultants from the UK, Denmark, and Israel who were interested in learning about the Sri Lankan culture. MAU employed the most appropriate and useful elements from all of these traditions, creating "modern" towns that were nonetheless functionally and culturally comfortable for their inhabitants to carry out their daily functions and cultural practices. Urban cores thus consisted of an array of hybrid spaces with a blend of uses and functions. These simultaneously afforded polysemic, multiple uses and identities for places and streets, safety to users, and an economy of scale for the town.

MAU was concerned about the traffic situation. We wanted the urban centers to be busy, as in other Sri Lankan towns, but sought to prevent vehicles from dividing up and blocking off the centers, as has occurred in small towns elsewhere such as Kegalla and Mawanella. These towns have grown into continuous urban strips on either side of a narrow main road, full of buses, trucks, and cars, which pass dangerously through, separating the town in two, and intoxicating inhabitants with fumes (Plesner 1986). MAU was equally determined, however, to avoid the opposite: the dispersed towns with wide roads, such as Ampara and Anuradhapura, which lack urban vitality.

To make people dominant and the towns safe, MAU opted to separate through traffic from its towns. These were thus located away from the bypass, while still maintaining visibility from the road. Buses were brought right into the town, and the bus station was centrally located. The two-lane narrow streets made pedestrians dominant, and the residential areas were connected to the town center with a hierarchical system of streets ending in cul-de-sacs and pedestrian paths. Thus houses and homes were located on quiet streets where children could play and walk safely to school, and the distances from houses to shops were still short (Figure 7.4).

Zoning was used, but not for the purpose of land-use regulation – instead, as a tool to conceptualize what was being developed. Besides, there were no planning authorities to regulate usages; what mattered was the leadership. MAU did not separate out land uses unless they were strongly incompatible. "Loose" zoning within built-up areas was limited to commercial, institutional, and residential uses, thus broadly defining segments of the towns. A more significant separation was between the areas allocated for immediate construction, and those for future development. The industrial area was reserved for future light industries such as rice mills. Rather than simply allocating land for shops and leaving it up to inhabitants to construct them, MAU designed and built these with an upper floor for living and/or storing goods. This is the model used along many main roads in Sri Lanka, but in the new towns we built only the shells, leaving flexibility for the store owners to personalize the shops. This was one way of responding to the risk of homogeneity among Mahaweli towns, as they were planned and designed by the same office. In upstream towns, the stores were all occupied and had sufficient business within a year of building. Convinced by the success of this strategy, the

Figure 7.4    Action planning: Dehiattakandiya town.

EU funded the building of a series of shops in Girandurukotte with apartments on the upper floor, kitchens at the back, and a courtyard in between.

Different combinations of buildings, based on funding, and the personalization of these lent different identities to the urban cores, but so did their locations and the terrain. In contrast to the previous positioning of towns away from environmental features, on flat land, and in a uniform, grid-iron layout, MAU embraced nature, building from the ground up and blurring the towns' separation from the natural environment. The plans combined the built elements with natural features such as hills, rocks, valleys, and reservoirs, enabling these to create unique physical characters for towns. The main street of Teldeniya, for example, is between two hills, with a dominating mountain at the backdrop of the entrance and the Victoria Reservoir at the other end; the rest of the town runs around the two hills on either side. Sangilipalama is developed on the slope of a mountain (Figure 7.5).

Replacing the machine-oriented approach of clearing away vegetation before construction, MAU staggered the location of houses to save as many trees as possible. In hot and flat downstream areas, trees provided the settlers with shade and the towns with character. This policy was also extended to highway construction, where contractors had previously cleared the whole reservation, often 100 meters across, for a carriageway of just 12 meters. MAU persuaded the Authority to clear only the strip needed for construction. Similar environmental protection measures were adopted in town building, where only the necessary trees and the underbrush were removed, leaving most trees untouched, and sometimes shifting buildings to accommodate them. In addition to making the towns more habitable, this vegetative backdrop enhanced the character of the town centers.

In the towns it designed, MAU was able to focus on the built environment as a central element to provide and enhance a sense of place and belonging. The key was to design buildings and spaces to which people could relate, which could support the towns' functions, and which could also provide the towns with a strong identity. MAU had a head start through Plesner's involvement and his "critical vernacular" approach. The MAU designs incorporated culturally familiar spatial elements such as verandahs, courtyards, and overarching roofs, scales

**Figure 7.5**    Each town has a unique character.

that were not overwhelming, and ordinary building materials such as bricks and tiles. In particular, the provision of sidewalks enhanced the people-friendly nature of the environment, as did the stores, with their living quarters above and arcades in front. The users adjusted to these familiar environments very quickly, adapting them to their own practices and functions. All but one of the towns were busy, concentrated with people, and many held weekly farmers' markets.

MAU towns were not perfect, but were "modern," contemporary people's towns. As a planning unit, MAU was responsible for mediating between the goals of various stakeholders of the project and the needs of those involved in building these towns, and for bringing in external experiences; and it addressed issues ranging from planning towns to designing buildings and spaces. Yet it did not pre-determine complete towns on a drawing board, nor did it control their growth.[15] Its loose-fit planning, social learning, and active, on-site working with other agents involved in the building process, particularly the residents themselves, opened up more space for people's activities, rather than aiming to determine them. MAU focused more on the process than the ends; it captured every bit of people's energy, and used the cracks in the structure and processes of the project to develop towns with them.

## A PEOPLE-CENTERED PROCESS

In sum, MAU approached planning from a people's perspective, one that both was empathetic to them, and considered them the primary resource and agents of development. In familiarizing physical environments, it is people who provide meaning and identity to these, thus creating social spaces and places. MAU both acted as an advocate of the farmers and urban dwellers, and opened up space for their actions. Familiarization is much stronger in most non-Western states where people are relatively more powerful and states and private companies are com-paratively weak. As the growth of pre-MAU towns was slow, and the plans failed, people began using the land for their own activities, such as temporary shops, in ways different from those imagined in plans. MAU embraced their creative energy and the new hybrid spaces they created, at the same time directing this energy toward building technically sound, vibrant towns. For example, it fought hard against the Engineering Agency's proposal to develop Manampitiya new town away from the existing town, proposing instead to consolidate and expand the ways that inhabitants had adapted the old town. With the new towns, as they were being designed from scratch, it was even more important for MAU not to lay claim to totally predetermined outcomes, but to leave sufficient room for future occupiers to adapt the spaces and to update the plans as they familiarized them. In short, MAU honored the dignity of people and trusted them to define their

homes, commercial activities, and community settings in a way that was meaningful to them, rather than being dependent on the system.

In hindsight, among others, this method relates to the reflective practice that
allows experience to become transformed into knowledge, as discussed by Don
Schön (1983), which Otto Koenigsberger calls "action planning" (Koenigsberger
1982; see also Chapters 3 and 4 in the present book). Action planning was
developed in a different context – in large Asian cities such as Singapore – but,
like the MAU approach, it emerged in response to the failure of post-War master planning based on blueprint utopia. One major problem that action planning
addressed was the statistical projections developed in Europe and the United
States, which always fell short of, for example, real population growth. In its own
context, MAU, too, recognized the shortcomings of projections and the unpredict-
ability of the future. Focusing instead on the present, it opted to carry out real-time
planning, and create a future together with residents.

In a larger sense, MAU effectively subverted the linear flow of hegemonic ideas
and social power that claimed to operate along a hierarchical structure across
geographical scales, from large to small. Intercepting the processes by which
powerful actors determined town planning, and through which the international
growth coalition shaped the lives and lived spaces of its subjects, MAU made
space for its own interventions at the town-planning level and employed this to
enhance inhabitants' processes of building new livelihoods in Mahaweli. Instead of
making plans, MAU built towns; instead of planning ideal towns, based on abstract
scientific views, which might or might not succeed if and when materialized, MAU
created urban cores that functioned from the outset. Instead of using plans as a
tool of control, MAU employed these to enhance people's processes and took
its lead from these; instead of allocating resources, it deployed them to create
better towns for ordinary people; instead of fixing uses, it enabled settlers' own
interventions. MAU's inside-out approach gave rise to community action planning built on social learning, in which the planners design, implement, observe,
reflect upon, and update plans cyclically, without separating these processes into
distinct phases.

This experience demonstrates that structures never fully determine the roles of
actors, nor does policy design at a larger scale determine local activities. Projects
are not monolithic, but are negotiated by actors and have gaps between their
components. Nor are the plans complete; they provide potential room for intervention. Yet capitalizing on these opportunities requires social agents (including
planners) with the capacity to read the cracks in the assumed processes, structures, and systems, to learn by doing, and to create opportunities to ground the
practice in people. Bringing Mahaweli towns into existence required planners to
be vigilant, open, flexible, and active. Interventions of weaker actors such as MAU

may not last long; they will either be coopted or marginalized by the system – that is, by its main actors. At the same time, nor do they disappear; the memory and meaning they construct will continue to influence future planning, design, and space-making activities. It is these bottom-up interventions that eventually accumulate to cause transformations in larger structures and processes.

## NOTES

1 The initial surveys were carried out by the Huntings Survey and UNDP/FAO. For a list, see Mahaweli Authority Library at http://www.mahaweli.gov.lk/Other%20Pages/Library/Pre%20Mahaweli.html, accessed on June 15, 2009.

2 By the end of 1993, 52 percent of power generated in Sri Lanka (1,442 Gwh) came from the Mahaweli (Kajander 2001, unpaginated).

3 See Logan and Molotch (1987) for a discussion of growth coalitions.

4 He also successfully raised funds to build these capital-intensive projects.

5 A stupa is a large, hemispherical mound, built to house Buddhist relics and as a funerary monument; it is now a sacred object of veneration.

6 He did eventually listen to my reasoning and approve my request.

7 Previously, it was architects who drew up plans; planners were not even considered significant.

8 This should not underestimate the enthusiasm and ability of individual planners; some received graduate degrees in Town and Country Planning from the University of Moratuwa and went on to become professional planners.

9 The original feasibility study was carried out by UNDP/FAO.

10 Mendis himself became one of the most respected planning educators in Sri Lanka.

11 In 2008, his contribution was acknowledged through Honorary Membership of the Sri Lanka Institute of Architects.

12 For a discussion of the significance of plan implementation, and the politics of planning, see Verma (2002).

13 MAU's approach would have reduced the length of roads by 60 percent, which alone would have saved 772,000 rupees (approximately US$29,000). Reducing services along these roads promised to bring down the costs substantially.

14 Although there were no direct influences between the two projects, minimal intervention for optimal effect was the key theme of the support systems policy practiced by the National Housing Development Authority in its Million Houses Programme (Sirivardana 1984).

15 It is important to note that, at the level of towns, there were no big growth coalitions trying to make their fortunes; most pre-MAU towns hardly grew at all during the first five to ten years.

## REFERENCES

Amunugama, Sarath. 1965. "Chandrikawena: A recent attempt at colonization on a peasant framework," *Ceylon Journal of Historical and Social Studies*, **8** (1,2): 130–62.

Appadurai, Arjun. 1998 [1996]. *Modernity at Large: Cultural Dimensions of Globalization* (Minneapolis, MN: University of Minnesota Press).

Appadurai, Arjun. 2002. "Disjuncture and Difference in the Global Cultural Economy." In Susanne Schech, Jane Haggis (Eds.) *Development*, pp. 157–67 (Minneapolis, MN: Wiley-Blackwell).

Ashcroft, B., Griffiths, G., and Tiffin, H. 2002 [1989]. *The Empire Writes Back: Theory and Practice in Postcolonial Literatures* (New York: Routledge).

Berry, W. 1990. *What Are People For?* (San Francisco: North Point Press).

Birch, Eugenie. 2005. "U.S. Planning Culture under Pressure: Major Elements Endure and Flourish in the Face of Crisis." In Bish Sanyal (Ed.) *Comparative Planning Cultures*, pp. 331–58 (New York: Routledge).

Chatterjee, P. 2007. "Towards a Postcolonial Modernity: AsiaSource Interview with Partha Chatterjee," *Asia Source: A Resource of the Asia Society*, available online at http://www.asiasource.org/news/special_reports/chatterjee.cfm, accessed 10 January 2007.

Dunnill, Frank. 1995. "Control versus Participation." In H. P. Muller and S. T. Hettige (Eds.) *The Blurring of a Vision – The Mahaweli*, pp. 174–83 (Ratmalana, Sri Lanka: Sarvodaya).

Escobar, Arturo. 1992. "Reflections on 'Development': Grassroots Approaches and Alternative Politics in the Third World," *Futures*, **24** (5): 411–36.

Escobar, Arturo. 1995. *Encountering Development: The Making and Unmaking of the Third World* (Princeton, NJ: Princeton University Press).

FAO. 2009. "FAOSTAT: Food and Agriculture Organization of the United Nations," available online at http://faostat.fao.org/site/567/DesktopDefault.aspx?PageID=567#ancor, accessed 31 December 2008.

Flyvbjerg, Bent. 1998. *Rationality and Power: Democracy in Practice* (Chicago: The University of Chicago Press).

Goh, Beng-Lan. 2002. *Modern Dreams: An Inquiry into Power, Cultural Production, and the Cityscape in Contemporary Urban Penang, Malaysia* (Ithaca, NY: Southeast Asia Program, Cornell University).

Goonatilaka, Susantha. 1984. *Aborted Discovery: Science and Creativity in the Third World* (London: Zed Books).

Grant, Jill. 2005. "Mixed Use in Theory and Practice: Canadian Experience with Implementing a Planning Principle." In Bruce Stiftel and Vanessa Watson (Eds.) *Dialogues in Urban and Regional Planning I*, pp. 15–36 (London: Routledge).

Gunewardene, K. A. 1964. "Central Place in Southern Ceylon," PhD dissertation (Cambridge: University of Cambridge).

Healey, P. 1997. *Collaborative Planning: Shaping Places in Fragmented Societies* (London: Macmillan).

Healey, P. 2003. "The Communicative Turn in Planning Theory and Its Implications for Spatial Strategy Formation." In Scott Campbell and Susan S. Fainstein (Eds.) *Readings in Planning Theory*, 2nd edn, pp. 237–56 (Oxford: Wiley-Blackwell).

Heath, Kingston W. 2009. *Vernacular Architecture and Regional Design* (Oxford: Architectural Press).

Holston, James. 1989. *The Modernist City: An Anthropological Critique of Brasilia* (Chicago, IL: Chicago University Press).

Hunting Technical Services Limited. 1980. *Summary and Conclusions. System C Mahaweli Development Project – Feasibility Study Volume 5* (Colombo: MDB).

Hutchinson, B. 1998. "Good Porches Make Good Neighbors (A Back to Basics Movement Called New Urbanism is Threatening the Suburban Model)," *Canadian Business*, 26 June, 120–3.

Jacobs, Jane. 1961. *The Death and Life of Great American Cities* (New York: Vintage Books).

Kajander, Tommi. 2001. "Water Resources, Large Dams and Hydropower in Asia," Master's thesis (Helsinki: Helsinki University of Technology, available at http://www.water.tkk.fi/wr/tutkimus/glob/publications/Kajander/toc.html, accessed 6 January 2009).

Karunaratna, H. N. S. 1988. *The Accelerated Mahaweli Programme and its Impact* (Colombo: Center for Demographic and Socio-Economic Studies).

Koenigsberger, Otto. 1982. "An Action Planning Approach to Possible Pattern and Solution for Accelerated Urbanization." In B. Mumtaz (Ed.) *Reading in Action Planning*. DPU Document Series No. 1, pp. 10–23 (London: Development Planning Unit).

Lindblom, Charles. 1959. "The Science of 'Muddling Through'," *Public Administration Review*, **19**, 79–88.

Logan, John R. and Harvey L. Molotch. 1987. *Urban Fortunes: The Political Economy of Place* (Berkeley: University of California Press).

MDB and Sogreah. 1972. *Mahaweli Ganga Development: Project 1: Feasibility Study for Stage II: Volume VII – Settlement Planning and Development* (Colombo: Mahaweli Development Board).

Mendis, Willie. 1973. *The Planning Implications of the Mahaweli Development Project in Sri Lanka* (Colombo: Lake House).

Ministry of Defence, Sri Lanka. 2008. Available at http://www.defence.lk/PrintPage. asp?fname=20061024_04, accessed 15 September 2008.

Mitchell, Timothy. 2002. *Rule of Experts: Egypt, Techno-Politics, Modernity* (Berkeley, CA: University of California Press).

Moore, Mick. 1985. *The State and Peasant Policies in Sri Lanka* (Cambridge: Cambridge University Press).

Muller, H. P. and S. T. Hettige. 1995. "Introduction." In H. P. Muller and S. T. Hettige (Eds.) *The Blurring of a Vision – The Mahaweli*, pp. 1–22 (Ratmalana, Sri Lanka: Sarvodaya).

Oryza Sri Lanka Rice Market Report. 2005. Available at http://www.oryza.com/asia/srilanka/index.shtml, accessed 31 December 2008.

Perera, Nihal. 1986. "Planning Parameters for Mahaweli Towns" (in Sinhala), *Isura*, **11** (4), 11–13.

Perera, Nihal. 1988. "Scope and Potential of Planning and Architectural Professions in the Mahaweli Project," Mahaweli Architects' Union: Annual General Meeting, Digana, pp. 7–10.

Perera, Nihal. 1990. "The Conceptual Framework Employed in Planning Mahaweli Towns," *The Sri Lanka Architect*, **100** (6), 14–18.

Perera, Nihal. 1998. *Society and Space: Colonialism, Nationalism, and Postcolonial Identity in Sri Lanka* (Boulder, CO: Westview Press).

Perera, Nihal. 2005. "The Making of a National Capital: Conflicts, Contradictions, and Contestations in Sri Jayawardhanapura." In Michael Geisler (Ed.) *National Symbols, Fractured Identities: Contesting the National Narrative*, pp. 241–72 (Middlebury, VT: Middlebury College Press).

Perera, Nihal. 2009. "People's Spaces: Familiarization, Subject Formation, and Emergent Spaces in Colombo," *Planning Theory*, **8** (3), 50–74

Pfaffenberger, Bryan. 1990. "The Harsh Facts of Hydraulics: Technology and Society in Sri Lanka's Colonization Schemes," *Technology and Culture*, **31** (3), 361–97.

Pieris, G. H. 1996. *Development and Change in Sri Lanka: Geographical Perspectives* (New Delhi: Macmillan India).

Plesner, Ulrik. 1986. "Mahaweli Building Program, Sri Lanka," *Living Architecture*, **5**, 88–93.

Prakash, Madhu Suri and Gustavo Esteva. 2008. *Escaping Education: Living as Learning within Grassroots Cultures*, 2nd edn (New York: Peter Lang).

Said, Edward. 2004 [1978]. *Orientalism* (New York: Vintage Books).

Saunders, D. 1997. "Ye New Olde Town," *The Globe and Mail*, 8 March, C 17.

Schön, Donald. 1983. *The Reflective Practitioner: How Professionals Think in Action* (London: Temple Smith).

Scott, James. 1998. *Seeing Like a State: How Certain Schemes to Improve the Human Condition Have Failed* (New Haven, CT: Yale University Press).

Scudder, Thayer. 2005. *The Future of Large Dams.* (London: Earthscan Publications).

Sen, Amartya. 2000. *Development as Freedom* (New Delhi: Oxford University Press).

Selznick, P. 1949. *TVA and the Grass Roots* (Berkeley, CA: University of California Press).

Sirivardana, Susil. 1984. *A Small Housing Loan – Ingenuity and Method: An Inquiry Into a Sri Lankan Implementation Experience* (Colombo: National Housing Development Authority).

Speelman, Jaap Jan and G. M. van der Top. 1985. "Downstream Development in the Accelerated Mahaweli Development Programme," *Economic Review* **2** (4,5), 35–8.

Thurairajah, A. 1985. "How Engineers Could Have Benefitted from Mahaweli Construction," *Economic Review* **2** (4,5), 34–5.

United Nations. Department of Social and Economic Affairs. 1951. *Measures for Economic Development of Underdeveloped Countries* (New York: United Nations).

Vale, Lawrence J. 1992. *Architecture, Power, and National Identity* (New Haven, CT: Yale University Press).

Verma, Gita Devan. 2002. *Slumming India: A Chronicle of Slums and Their Saviours* (New Delhi: Penguin).

Wedaarachchi, Ananda. 2009. "Fillip for Settler Income and Living Standards – DG," *Sunday Observer*, online edition, 31 May 2009. available at http://www.sundayobserver.lk/2009/05/31/new30.asp, accessed 5 June 2009.

Yeoh, B. S. A. 1996. *Contesting Space: Power Relations and the Urban Built Environment in Colonial Singapore* (Kuala Lumpur: Oxford University Press).

Zhang, Li. 2001. *Strangers in the City: Reconfigurations of Space, Power, and Social Networks within China's Floating Population* (Stanford, CA: Stanford University Press).

CHAPTER 8

# WEST–EAST POLICY TRANSFER IN EUROPE

## THE CASE OF URBAN TRANSPORT POLICY[1]

**DOMINIC STEAD, MARTIN DE JONG AND IVETA REINHOLDE**

> Isolation is impossible in the contemporary world, and policy transfer has
> become a fact of everyday life in various countries . . . post-communist
> countries have been especially willing to emulate the West.
>
> (Randma-Liiv 2005: 472)

## INTRODUCTION

Various examples have recently emerged of countries in Central and Eastern
Europe (CEE)[2] seeking to catch up politically and economically by drawing lessons from policies in more developed countries (Rose 1993). The uncertainties of
policy-making in some of these countries have made policy transfer a particularly
attractive option; politicians often see transfer as the quickest solution to many
problems without having to reinvent the wheel (Rose 2005; Tavits 2003). This
chapter explores international policy transfer, focusing specifically on two examples of attempts to transfer sustainable urban transport concepts from Western
Europe to CEE countries. In the two cases examined here, efforts were made to
establish German-style public transport authorities (*Verkehrsverbünde*) in Riga in
Latvia, and in Wroclaw in Poland. In these cases, the social and economic situations in the 'borrowing' and 'lending' countries are very different. So too are the
institutional frameworks. As a consequence, the policy transfer process is much
more complex than mere copying or emulation.

The subject of transferring policy ideas, institutions, models and programmes
between national, regional and local authorities has received significant attention
in politics and policy sciences over recent years, involving terms such as policy
transfer, policy convergence, legal transplantation, institutional transplantation,
institutional transfer, institutional change, imitation and emulation, policy learning
and lesson drawing.[3] Various definitions of policy transfer and its related concepts
exist; one of the earliest and most commonly cited comes from Dolowitz and

Marsh, who define it as 'a process in which knowledge about policies, administrative arrangements, institutions etc. in one time and/or place is used in the development of policies, administrative arrangements and institutions in another time and/or place' (1996: 344).

Policy transfer can involve a number of processes and possible objects of transfer, including policies, institutions, ideologies or justifications, attitudes and ideas, and negative lessons. Transfer can take place across time, within countries, and across countries (Dolowitz and Marsh 1996). There are different degrees of transfer, ranging from direct copying at one end of the scale through to inspiration at the other. Emulation and adaptation fit somewhere in between these two points (Dolowitz and Marsh 2000). Policy transfer can be either voluntary (endogenously driven) or coerced (exogenously driven) (ibid.). Holm-Hansen (2005) suggests that most real examples of policy transfer lie on a continuum somewhere between these two extreme points. Related to this, policy transfer can also be demand led or supply led. According to Randma-Liiv (2005), demand-based policy transfer is based on the initiative and acknowledged need of a recipient administration, whereas supply-led policy transfer is based on the initiative of the donor and the donor's perception of the needs of the recipient (e.g. foreign aid initiatives).

Most previous studies of policy transfer have focused on highly developed countries.[4] Among the theoretical works on the topic, only Rose (1993) makes explicit reference to the new democracies of Central and Eastern Europe, citing these as examples of nations seeking to catch up politically and economically by drawing lessons from highly developed countries (cited in Randma-Liiv 2005). According to Randma-Liiv, in many CEE countries, supply-based policy transfer was more predominant at the start of transition in the early 1990s, whereas by the late 1990s borrowers became more proactive in policy transfer activities. At the beginning of the 1990s, both politicians and senior civil servants in most CEE countries lacked not only know-how about how to build up governmental structures, but also an understanding of the very basic functions of an independent democratic state. The role of foreign expertise in this regard was twofold: it helped decision-makers acquire a grasp of the basics of governmental structures, their functions, and the fields of state intervention, and it also contributed to the analysis of specific fields or policies. In a situation mainly characterised by a lack of policy-making skills combined with low competence on the part of public servants, it was easier to copy or emulate a foreign programme than to start from scratch. In this way, policy transfer provided a means of avoiding 'newcomer costs'; using the experience of other countries was cheaper, because they had already borne the costs of policy planning and analysis, whereas creating original policies required substantial financial resources.

Various common messages can be synthesised from the literature on policy transfer and closely related concepts regarding factors that contribute to success. A number of these messages (mainly derived from de Jong *et al*. 2002) are briefly summarised below, and form a general analytical framework for examining the policy transfer processes in our two case studies:

- Inspiration from several policy examples is better than inspiration from only one. Looking across several examples (either the same sort of policy in different contexts or else different policies in relatively similar contexts) can help to identify the useful and constructive elements of each, and allow the various policy actors to enter into a process of negotiation regarding appropriate policy options.
- Making a literal copy of one example is unlikely to succeed. Generally, this approach is not conducive to generating locally appropriate solutions or implementation mechanisms.
- Strong domestic champions and change agents (or 'policy entrepreneurs') are often necessary to achieve policy change. Their creativity and agility in dealing with other (sometimes more powerful) policy actors can make a big difference to policy outcomes.
- Transferring policies from nations that are legally and culturally akin should in principle be easier to achieve than transferring policies from countries that are very different. However, even similar countries have subtly different preferences, circumstances and institutional arrangements, which are not always fully anticipated.
- Policy ideas, solutions, models, programmes or instruments invariably have to be incorporated in the existing institutional structure of the recipient constituency. Adopting generic ideas or instruments, rather than specific policies, programmes or legislation, provides leeway for making refinements appropriate to the formal and informal institutional environment.
- Ideas, interests, institutions, and individuals are all crucial to policy change, but so too is timing.[5] Windows of opportunity for policy change are only open at certain times. Opportunities for changes in policy or institutional arrangements can increase in periods of crisis or emergency.

## THE CENTRAL AND EAST EUROPEAN POLICY CONTEXT

The past decade and a half has been characterised by profound and ongoing political and economic changes in CEE countries, which have had significant implications for urban transport policy (Lijewski 1996; Pucher and Buehler 2005;

World Bank 2002). For example, there have been substantial shifts in transport modes (decreases in rail transport, rapid increases in car ownership and use), transport flows (more flows to and from Western Europe), passenger travel patterns (more international travel, less subsidised commuting), the types of goods transported (fewer raw materials, more consumer goods), and the organisation of transport companies (decreasing state involvement, and the emergence of the private sector). Even before the events of 1989 (the 'Autumn of Nations'), various political and economic changes had already started across many CEE countries: trade and prices were being liberalised, public expenditure was being cut, and protectionism for public-sector enterprises was being dismantled. The government's role in the economy was being scaled down, and the privatisation of state companies was starting to take place (World Bank 2002). The events of 1989 very much accelerated these processes.

Since the late 1980s, CEE countries have moved towards the decentralisation of decision-making, albeit with large variations in the scope and depth of the transfer of power and resources from the state to the regional and local level (World Bank 2002). In fast-reforming CEE countries such as Poland, city governments were given jurisdiction over the provision of most local infrastructure and services, and the ownership both of local utility companies and of housing and some road infrastructure. This meant that local matters were put into the hands of the local leaders, but had the drawback that there was a mismatch between the local governments' new responsibilities and the funds immediately available. Cities were given the unenviable task of increasing previously very low user fees for various municipal services and infrastructure, for a population whose real incomes had fallen, and/or increasing local taxation in a damaged and fragile local economy. The alternative was to cut services, at the same time as the new electoral democracy made local politicians dependent on voter satisfaction. Most cities failed to resolve this dilemma. This resulted in a gap between costs and revenues for companies providing various municipal services. Over time, underspending led to poorer services, less efficient production, and a decline in equipment and infrastructure. The sudden gap between the total revenue and the aggregate expenditure burden was very difficult to fill, even in the richest cities such as Budapest, Prague and Warsaw, and services faltered across the region.

Until the end of the 1980s, public transport services in CEE countries were generally extensive, frequent and cheap (Pucher and Buehler 2005). Low incomes meant that public transport use was high and car ownership was low. The regulation of the prices and the supply of cars and fuel in most CEE countries ensured that private car ownership and use was extremely expensive and difficult. Consequently, most people simply could not afford cars, particularly for use on a regular basis. Before the 1990s, urban transport service providers were typically state-owned or city-owned enterprises, organised according to vehicle type (e.g. bus, tram, metro) or united into a single company with a monopoly on intra-urban travel. Almost all of these had a range of structural problems, as was the case in most state-controlled sectors: unwieldy management and organisational structures, overstaffing (especially in the administrative departments), incompetence, lack of motivation among the workforce, excessive bureaucracy, and extreme inefficiency (Pucher and Buehler 2005; World Bank 2002).

In the 1990s, public transport systems in CEE countries were in deep decline as a consequence of a wave of macro-economic reforms and a recession. Much of the transport rolling stock was worn out and out of date, and levels of fuel consumption and pollution emissions for most vehicles were very high (Güller 1996; Judge 2002; Suchorzewski 2001; World Bank 2002; Zachariadis and Kouvaritakis 2003). The revenue base of public transport companies collapsed because of inadequate local government budgets and a drop in incomes among the fare-paying public. This caused a funding squeeze that first affected the companies' plans for expansion and replacement. Maintenance and repairs were the next to suffer. With sharp reductions in subsidy, public transport systems were forced to raise fares drastically, both in absolute terms as well as relative to inflation, wages, and the cost of car ownership and use. Not only were public transport fares increased, but services were also curtailed, especially in smaller cities. Although budgets were strained at every level, many central and local governments still devoted considerable expenditure to improving and expanding road networks, focusing particularly on high-speed arterial roads, ring roads around cities, bottlenecks at key intersections, and connections to the main intercity and international routes. Thus the supply of roadway infrastructure was increased, although much more slowly than the rapid increases in car use.

The increasing reliance on private transport, which had already started during the later years of the socialist era, was greatly accelerated in the 1990s. Virtually all restrictions on car ownership were removed, opening up the market in CEE countries almost immediately to foreign car manufacturers. This greatly increased the quantity and quality of cars that residents of former socialist countries could buy. Some central governments (such as those of Poland and the Czech Republic) promoted their own car industries as part of their national economic development strategy, through loans and subsidies for expanding and modernising car production facilities (Pucher 1999; World Bank 2002). In general, local and national government policies in CEE countries became much less favourable for public transport and much more accommodating of private car ownership and use, leading to a vicious downward cycle of declining public transport use (Judge 2002; Pucher and Buehler 2005). Non-segregated public transport services (i.e. those sharing the same road space as private transport), including most bus and trolleybus lines, were hardest hit by traffic congestion generated by the rapid increases in car ownership and use. This then further reduced the attractiveness of public transport services, increased their operating costs, and fuelled the demand for private transport (World Bank 2002).

As a result, while car ownership and use were increasing in the 1980s and 1990s in CEE countries, public transport use plummeted (Lijewski 1996; Pucher and Buehler 2005). Passenger-kilometres by bus and coach, for example, dropped by almost 70 per cent in Latvia between 1990 and 1995 (European Commission 2006). Similarly, passenger-kilometres travelled by train dropped by more than 70 per cent in Latvia and by almost 50 per cent in Poland between 1990 and 1995 (ibid.). After the turbulent decade of the 1990s, the new millennium has brought more gradual changes to CEE countries. Car ownership and use seems set to continue to grow, just as it is continuing to grow throughout the whole of Europe, but the growth is unlikely to be as explosive as during the 1990s. There are some indications that the use of public transport may now have stabilised in CEE countries (ibid.). Throughout CEE, local authorities are now making efforts to expand and improve public transport services, although it is unlikely that usage will return to the extremely high levels of the communist era (Zachariadis and Kouvaritakis 2003).

Substantial land-use changes also took place in CEE countries as a consequence of the major political and economic changes of the past two decades. Many of the changes in land use worked against public transport and in favour of private transport and/or informal transport operators (World Bank 2002). A number of earlier economic activities folded, leaving behind large areas of derelict land in urban centres. New economic activities sprang up, often in 'unplanned' locations in the suburbs, especially along major roads, causing urban sprawl. Although some cities retained strict land-use regulations and building codes, much new suburban and exurban development took place beyond cities' jurisdictions, where land-use regulations were often far less demanding, and where virtually any kind of development was permitted in order to generate local jobs, tax revenues and economic development (Pucher and Buehler 2005). Wealthier urban residents began to move from inner cities to the suburbs. Unlike the high-density apartment complexes of the communist era, most new housing developments were low-density family homes. Shopping centres appeared along the exits of ring roads in most large cities. In Warsaw, for example, nearly 30 out-of-town shopping centres and megastore complexes were built in the suburbs of the city over the space of just 10 years up to 2002 (Transit Cooperative Research Program 2003). These developments were heavily biased towards access by car and put new pressures on the road network, creating bottlenecks in outlying locations. The suburban locations of new businesses generated tangential and circular travel patterns, in contrast to the traditional radial orientation of the existing public transport networks. Transport modes based on rail infrastructure (tramways, metros and suburban railways) were especially hard hit by these shifts in land use and travel patterns.

By the end of the 1990s, the economic, social and environmental problems associated with the sudden increase in private transport and the equally dramatic decline in public transport use were becoming widely recognised in many CEE cities. City authorities realised that their urban transport policies were in need of adjustment (Pucher and Buehler 2005). For the most part, however, political support tended to favour policies that accommodated wider car ownership and use. Thus, policies that inconvenienced motorists or significantly increased the price of driving are still not widespread across cities in CEE countries. In many cities, buses and trams often still do not have traffic priority to insulate them to some degree from the seriously congested streets. Whereas most Western European cities instituted bus lanes and priority traffic signals long ago as a way of ensuring smoother flows of buses and trams, only a few Central and Eastern European cities have begun to adopt such measures. Nevertheless, local governments have at least given more attention to public transport as an essential part of the urban transport system. Sometimes in partnership with Western European officials or other experts, some urban public transport operations in CEE cities have tried to improve the quality of their service, modernise their vehicles and infrastructure, and increase the efficiency of their operations. The case studies examined in this chapter provide two examples of this type of activity.

## WEST–EAST POLICY TRANSFER: TWO CASE STUDIES

> To what extent are transport policy instruments, which have proved to be successful in one urban area, transferable to another, given that the latter has a different historical, cultural or political background, or is in another phase of economic development? Are there 'best practices' which are convertible like currencies? If not, how and to what extent must one take account of specific circumstances?
>
> (Güller 1996: 25)

These questions, posed by Peter Güller in 1996, are just as resonant and valid today, perhaps even more so, and are very closely related to the content of our analysis. Two case studies of West–East cross-city policy transfer are examined: Wroclaw in Poland and Riga in Latvia. Both cities have recently been involved in similar projects funded by the German Federal Environment Agency (*Umweltbundesamt* – UBA) under its advisory assistance programme for environmental protection in Central and Eastern Europe, the Caucasus, and Central Asia. Both projects primarily aimed to establish German-style regional public transport authorities (*Verkehrsverbünde*), or similar cooperative administrative and organisational structures, as a way of promoting public transport and reducing the overall environmental burden of transport both within the two cities and in the wider region around them.[6] The specific outcomes that the projects sought to achieve were: more coordinated public transport services and timetables; common information, communication and marketing for transport services; and integrated ticketing across different transport operators. Although the public transport situation was (and still is) quite different in the two cities, there was nevertheless the belief that changes in the administrative and organisational structures were of central importance to both cities (Seifert 2004). As we show in the two case studies, however, the experiences and outcomes of the projects were quite different.

The information for these case studies was obtained from reports and documents as well as interviews with key players involved in the process of policy transfer. In addition, two of the authors attended workshops in Berlin and Riga at which detailed information was presented on the Wroclaw and Riga projects as well as on other similar projects. Both case studies are presented below, following a broadly similar structure. First, the sources of inspiration for policy transfer are identified, and information about the evolution of the transfer process is outlined. The main actors in the policy transfer process are then identified, both donors and recipients, and their main influences on the process are explored; this is followed by the results of the transfer process.

## WROCLAW

Wroclaw is Poland's fourth largest city and the capital city of Lower Silesia, a region in the south-west of the country. The city's population is currently around 630,000, and the population of the city region is approximately 1.1 million. Car ownership in the city of Wroclaw is significantly higher than the Polish national average: 378 cars per 1,000 inhabitants in Wroclaw (in 2005) compared with 323 cars per 1,000 people in Poland as a whole (Polish Central Statistical Office 2007, unpaginated). The city has an extensive public transport system, consisting of 61 bus routes covering 546 kilometres and 25 tram routes covering 84 kilometres.

From 2000, the German Federal Environment Agency provided support to the city of Wroclaw to improve cooperation and coordination between regional public transport operators. The initial idea was to establish an integrated public transport system based on the German model of regional public transport authorities. Early in the course of the project, however, it became apparent that the German model was not feasible in Wroclaw, although there was a belief that improved cooperation and coordination in public transport could still be achieved by different means. There were several reasons why the German model was considered unworkable. First, integrated public transport authorities in Germany and other Western European countries have recourse to funding that is not available in Poland. As a consequence, Wroclaw had to find a solution that involved fewer costs, but that nevertheless strengthened cooperation between regional transport contractors. Second, after analysing the legal situation in Poland, the study came to the conclusion that a regional public transport authority was not really feasible: too many competing administrative levels would have to be involved, with the consequence that there would be long periods of consultation and coordination, as well as very uncertain project outcomes. Promoting and developing bilateral arrangements between municipalities was considered a more appropriate and realistic option. The project was therefore re-orientated, and a locally adapted solution to the German model was developed (UBA 2006).

Wroclaw is atypical in the sense that, contrary to many other Polish cities, awareness grew early among municipal authorities that public transport was an important part of the urban transport system. One of the reasons why policy-makers and civil servants in Wroclaw were eager to adopt these ideas was a desire to reduce the growth in car traffic and reverse the decline in public transport use that they realised was taking place. They believed that this could be achieved by the step-by-step improvement of an updated tram system in the city, and improved coordination with surrounding municipalities and all transport operators. What made Wroclaw different from many other cities was the presence of forward-looking leadership among these officials, combined with relative political and administrative stability, which ensured that initiatives were not interrupted when other political parties took office.

The project's main source of inspiration was the German *Verkehrsverbund*, and study trips were made to several German regional public transport authorities during the course of the project (including Darmstadt-Dieburg and Hannover). Some Dutch cities were also visited (such as The Hague and Rotterdam). In addition, there was a study trip to Prague, which also inspired officials from Wroclaw and its surrounding municipalities. The visit to Prague helped to convince the Polish officials that, in spite of having only limited resources and experience at their disposal, cities in Eastern Europe were still able to improve the quality of their transport systems. Prague's public transport system was perhaps not the most advanced example, compared with those in many cities in Western Europe, but it was inspiring enough to convince the officials from Wroclaw that reforms and investments were possible in CEE and that these changes could make a difference.

The Wroclaw city government and administration were not able to push through changes without outside support. There were a number of important actors in the process. The main supporting institution was the German UBA (*Umweltbundesamt*), which provided financial support for the project. More active advisory activities were taken up by the German non-governmental organisa-tion (NGO) *Euronatur* (European Nature Heritage Fund), and regular visits took place between *Euronatur* and policy-makers in Wroclaw to exchange information. According to our interviews with various actors, *Euronatur's* approach played a vital role in facilitating the project within Poland because it encouraged local par-ticipation in the project, and did not try to adopt a superior role. In turn, a Polish organisation, the Lower Silesian branch of the Polish Ecological Club (PKE), was crucial in opening doors for *Euronatur*. PKE had less know-how on the subject but enabled *Euronatur* to get in touch with many other players in and around Wroclaw. Because Polish administration relies on personal networks much more than governments in Germany or much of Western Europe, PKE's involvement in the project was crucial. Other key players in the process were the adjacent local authorities, through which the regional services had to be arranged, and the city tram and bus operators, who were responsible for delivering services. In most cases, these players were also supportive of the project's activities. In addi-tion, somewhat against the expectations of most other players, Polish National Railways (PKP) was cooperative in adapting its timetables to fit with the other public transport services, in spite of its reputation for being centralised and highly bureaucratic. PKP also accepted the idea of a single ticket for the Wroclaw agglomeration. This situation can best be explained as a desire on the part of the company to boost its economic performance.

The transfer and learning process took a number of years, assisted by resources from UBA and later from a German–Polish strategic collaboration agreement. Part of this money consisted of donations, and part was a low-interest loan to the city of Wroclaw. After this, *Euronatur* and the city of Wroclaw submitted a proposal for European funding to conduct a feasibility study for the refurbishment of tramline 7, for which a subsidy of €15 million was granted subject to co-funding from the city of Wroclaw. During the whole project, the actors found that Polish legislation and financial constraints made the simple adoption of the German institutional model for regional public transport authorities quite impossible. It was not legally feasible, and it would take far too much time, effort, political manoeuvring and money to go through a process of institutional reform. In addition, the official adoption of local and regional transport plans was considered a far too difficult procedure. A sort of plan was drafted ('Integrated Plan for Public Transport Devel-opment in the City and Agglomeration for the Years 2004–2008') but this was a much more pragmatic document than is produced in Germany, and did not have the official status of German transport plans. In the latter stages of the project, rather than tackling institutional issues, Wroclaw preferred to focus on practical physical improvements and short-term visible achievements such as refurbishing tramlines, improving transfer points and acquiring new rolling stock.

When it came to regional services, as in most other cities in CEE countries, city-owned bus operators had been privatised but their shares were still largely publicly owned. Because these contractors still depended on licences from the local government for their services, their deregulation had a positive effect on their willingness to integrate into the regional system. The way in which regional coop- eration between operators was arranged in Wroclaw was by means of bilateral agreements with neighbouring municipalities. Instead of establishing a regional authority, limited cash transfers between local municipalities were agreed as a way of balancing payments for regional public transport operations. Together with a neighbouring municipality (Swieta Katarzyna), the city of Wroclaw also suc- cessfully managed to set up a tender procedure to select a regional bus operator to provide integrated services between the two authorities. This experience led to plans for similar arrangements with other municipalities.

Overall, the results of the policy transfer process in Wroclaw have been mod- erately positive, even though the initial idea of the project had to be substantially re-orientated. Using relatively limited resources, a brake has been put on the decline in the use of public transport in Wroclaw, which can be considered a success. Another important point is that no significant public transport budget cuts have taken place in Wroclaw in the past few years, which is very much unlike the situation in other Polish cities. Apparently, political and public support for collective passenger transport has increased, and the policy transfer process has perhaps contributed to this. It is more than probable that the pragmatic approach of the partners was a decisive factor. There are plans to improve the new regional ticketing system further using electronic chip cards, as well as proposals for a new type of rail system in the city region that will be fully integrated with other public transport modes. Whether the latter comes to fruition is to some extent dependent on the cooperation of Polish National Railways.

## RIGA

Riga, the capital of Latvia, is the largest city in the Baltic States. The city's popu- lation is currently just over 720,000, and the population of the urban region is approximately 1.1 million – almost half of the national population. Car ownership in Riga is currently close to 290 cars per 1,000 inhabitants, somewhat lower than car ownership in the country as a whole, which is around 315 cars per 1,000 inhabitants (Central Statistical Bureau of Latvia 2007, unpaginated). Riga's public transport network is extensive (comprising 62 bus routes, 21 trolleybus routes and 11 tramlines) and run by a publicly owned body (*Rīgas Satiksme*). A fleet of privately operated minibuses also forms part of Riga's transport system. During the past 15 years, the development of the transport sector (as in all other sectors of industry in Latvia) has been considerably influenced by the triple transformation of politics, economics and administration initiated by the collapse of the Soviet Union. Latvia's present administrative model for public transport was strongly influenced by Western European experience, market pressures and EU requirements. As in the case of most CEE countries, local municipalities in Latvia are now responsible for public transport services (ECMT 2001). The current spatial plan for Riga identifies a number of shortcomings of the city's present transport system: a large proportion of the city's public transport rolling stock is outdated and lacks modern standards of comfort; there are gaps in the coverage of the public transport network; a parking policy has not yet been developed, and the demand for parking spaces in the city centre exceeds supply; and the passenger transport potential of the rail system is underused (Riga City Council 2005a).

In Riga, as in the case of Wroclaw, the initial aim of the project supported by the UBA was to promote regional cooperation in public transport, along the lines of the German regional passenger transport authorities (UBA 2006). The project began in 2000. Key players were Riga City Council's traffic department, two private consulting companies from Riga (one responsible for project management, the other for technical advice), a German transport consultancy (Institute for Transport Ecology) and the city of Bremen as a partner city.[7] Discussions with representatives of Riga City Council, Riga's transport companies and the Latvian Ministry of Transport, however, quickly established that, although the idea of integrated transport was both important and appropriate for the city, public transport within the city and outside the city were two separate and very different things. Against this background, an integrated transport system based on the German model was not considered the appropriate way forward for the activities funded by UBA in Riga. There was, however, great interest in an integrated system at the local level. As a result, the original idea of a regional passenger transport authority was abandoned in favour of a more appropriate local solution, mainly focused around giving greater priority to public transport in the city.

The main elements of the project were new park and ride sites, new priority lanes and signals for public transport, and new public transport routes. None of these individual elements was particularly new to Riga; the issue of park and ride, for example, had been at the centre of public debate for some time. In the mid-1990s, the prospect of Western European transport problems such as traffic congestion, air quality problems and the shortage of parking space (especially in the city centre) was already identified in Riga's Transport Policy for 1999–2003. In 2001, the City Council agreed to a park and ride pilot project in the suburb of Jugla, although this pilot was never implemented. It was not until 2006 that

Riga City Council finally passed a motion to introduce park and ride (Decision 1760) and agreed to acquire land for the development of park and ride sites. The decision also assigned responsibility for the implementation of the park and ride system to the City's Transport Department, the Development Department and the Property Department. On the positive side, a formal decision had finally been passed after years of discussion. On the negative side, three departments were given shared responsibility for the system, which presented administrative problems and complications in implementation.

Although policy transfer in Riga started some time after the project in Wroclaw, there is still remarkably little evidence of impact and few visible outcomes on the ground. There are no new park and ride sites and no new public transport priority lanes or signals. Most recent changes in urban transport have had either an administrative or a regulative nature. Instead of infrastructure improvements, Riga City Council has mainly concentrated its activities on fines for parking in restricted areas and raising parking prices, which has caused public protests as the money collected has not resulted in traffic improvements. In the meantime, the city's inhabitants are inventing their own solutions, for example by parking their cars at shopping centres outside the city centre and taking public transport from there. As a result, some car parks at these out-of-town shopping centres are often full for large parts of the day, thus undermining access to them, and their economic viability.

Residents of Riga have recently faced sharp increases in the price of public transport: the cost of a single trip increased from 20 to 30 santims in February 2007, and from 30 to 40 santims in January 2008.[8] *Rīgas Satiksme*, the enterprise operating public transport in Riga, argued that the increase was necessary to cover increasing production costs. Many passengers, on the other hand, argued that prices have been increasing without visible improvements in the quality of public transport. In fact, increasing traffic congestion has actually led to slower and less reliable services. At the same time, little action to address congestion is evident. The situation is typical of the downward spiral of public transport that has affected many CEE countries: out-of-date infrastructure, public pressure for modernisation, decreasing ridership, increasing operating costs and politicians' fears of taking on responsibility for problems and showing the initiative to resolve them. Regarding this last issue, Abolina and Zilans (2002) contend that Latvian local politics is often tainted by political patronage and vested interests. At a local level, planners frequently have their 'hands tied' when it comes to promoting and implementing new policies. Either it is not practical to go against 'political winds', or political decisions are simply made contrary to adopted planning policies and measures (ibid.). In this case, local politicians in Riga, as in many other cities, have implemented cheaper, short-term measures, or even attempted to raise money, rather than funding expensive, long-term projects such as major infrastructure improvements. In summary, the overall effect of the UBA-funded project in Riga has been limited: there are few visible outcomes on the ground and little evidence of policy transfer.

Although Riga has many of the necessary preconditions for successful policy transfer, inaction prevailed for a variety of reasons. First of all, donor-funded projects in Latvia were (and still are) perceived as separate activities by local authorities, and not part of the general policy framework. Second, development programmes and plans do not necessarily result in implementation. The lack of political and administrative continuity, which is inherent to Latvian public administration, has contributed to this. Third, substantial resources and administrative efforts have been channelled into larger transport projects (such as the southern road bridge over the river Daugava, currently the largest construction project in Latvia), to the detriment of most other schemes.

## CONCLUSIONS

Countries in Central and Eastern Europe have experienced dramatic and rapid economic, social and political changes in the past two decades. As these changes have generally followed Western European development trends, it might be logical to assume that CEE countries should be looking to learn lessons, both good and bad, from Western Europe to help decision-makers prevent problems before they arise, and to avoid newcomer costs. However, there is more to policy transfer and lesson drawing than simple copying or emulation, particularly in the case of West–East policy transfer. What works in one situation does not necessarily work in another: context is crucial. Policy transfer requires the right combination of individuals, ideas, incentives and interests, and the timing has to be right. It also seems apparent that taking preventative action to address problems before they become serious (e.g. parking shortages, congestion) rarely occurs; most administrations seem to have to experience the problems first-hand, and experience them to a critical degree, before taking action. Achieving policy change in the transport sector in CEE countries may also have a psychological dimension. More than in Western Europe, the car is seen in CEE countries as a symbol of social status, wealth and self-confidence – not just as a means of transport. Policies and actions that affect car ownership and use are therefore as unpopular in CEE countries as they are in Western Europe, if not more so. Policies to improve public transport, on the other hand, are unlikely to be considered important.

Both of the case studies examined here help to highlight some success factors of policy transfer. Donor organisations, for instance, should avoid imposing their views or setting the agenda. The existence of a small, close network of participating actors is also extremely important; some of these can serve as talented and motivated champions (in the form of change agents or policy entrepreneurs), and others contribute their personal networks. Strong awareness is vital right from the start that each country and/or city is institutionally different and has different practical circumstances and different preference structures. Flexibility and adaptation in the policy transfer process are beneficial. Moreover, local awareness that pragmatic solutions with shorter time horizons were needed, rather than large-scale institutional transformation, precluded direct copying of the original policy model. A combination of forward-looking individuals, relevant policy ideas, incentives for change and the alignment of various actor interests was in place during the transfer process. These conditions were lacking in the case of Riga, where few visible outcomes of urban transport are evident.

We identify four general key lessons for the transfer of urban transport concepts from Western to Eastern European cities. First, large-scale institutional reform is not a promising route to improving policy system performance, especially when policy actors have to make do with limited resources. Large-scale institutional reform is likely neither to create strong public support nor to appease actors who may stand to lose from institutional change. It is much more fruitful to focus on achievable practical goals that can boost enthusiasm among the parties involved and the wider public. Second, site visits help to create both ideas and inspiration about what alternatives can look like and how they might work in practice. Site visits to other cities in CEE countries can help to develop confidence and reassurance that certain policies or actions can work outside Western Europe. Third, cultural differences are important in the interactions among partners from various countries involved in the transfer process. These are not always predictable, but a high tolerance for uncertainty and ambiguity helps. In the Wroclaw case, the German partners came to understand that structured procedures and solid planning are not features that can be relied upon in Poland, where communication within an organisation is often more top-down. By taking these differences into account, more realistic estimates can be made about which goals are feasible and how these might be achieved. Fourth, policy transfer is likely to be more successful when recipients are able to set the agenda for the transfer process and identify its main priorities. The transfer of shorter-term, practical, visible solutions is often both simpler to achieve and more acceptable than longer-term, less visible institutional changes; the former may also help in paving the way for the latter.

## NOTES

1  This chapter is based on a paper originally presented at the 2007 AESOP Congress in Naples, Italy. The material is partly based on a study funded by the Dutch government through the Habiforum Innovative Land Use Program and by Delft University of Technology through the Delft Research Centre for Sustainable Urban Areas.

2  The term 'Central and Eastern Europe' refers to Albania, Bosnia and Herzegovina, Bulgaria, Croatia, the Czech Republic, Estonia, Hungary, Latvia, Lithuania, Montenegro, Poland, the Republic of Macedonia, Romania, Serbia, Slovakia and Slovenia.

3  See, for example, Bennett (1991); de Jong (2004); de Jong *et al.* (2002); Dolowitz (1999); Dolowitz and Marsh (1996); Evans (2004); Evans and Davies (1999); Greener (2002); Héritier *et al.* (2001); Holm-Hansen (2005); Jacoby (2000); James and Lodge (2003); Knill (2001); Ladi (2005); Radaelli (2004); Rogers (1995); Rose (1991, 1993, 2005); Stone (1999, 2004); Wolman (1992).

4  See, for example, Bennett (1991, 1997); Dolowitz and Marsh (1996, 2000); Majone (1991); Robertson (1991); Rose (1993, 2005); Stone (1999); Wolman (1992); Wolman and Page (2002).

5  Here we draw on Dudley and Richardson's (2000) analysis of key variables influencing policy change: ideas, interests, institutions, individuals and time.

6  Various references in the transport policy literature can be found advocating the benefits of *Verkehrsverbünde* as a means of providing integrated regional public transport services (see, for example, Pucher and Kurth 1995; Wilson and Bell 1985).

7  Although Bremen provided the main source of inspiration for the project, examples from other German cities were also important. Recent documents from Riga City Council's traffic department also mention the German city of Karlsruhe as an interesting example of intermodal transfer (see, for example, Riga City Council 2005b).

8  20 santims was approximately €0.28 in 2006.

## REFERENCES

Abolina, K. and Zilans, A. (2002). 'Evaluation of Urban Sustainability in Specific Sectors in Latvia'. *Environment, Development and Sustainability* **4** (3), 299–314.

Bennett, C. J. (1991). 'How States Utilize Foreign Evidence'. *Journal of Public Policy* **11** (1), 31–54.

—— (1997). 'Understanding Ripple Effects: The Cross-National Adoption of Policy Instruments for Bureaucratic Accountability'. *Governance* **19** (3), 213–33.

Central Statistical Bureau of Latvia (2007). Statistical databases, available: www.csb.gov. lv/csp/content/?lng=en&cat=355, accessed 26 May 2009.

de Jong, M. (2004). 'The Pitfalls of Family Resemblance: Why Transferring Planning Institutions between "Similar Countries" is Delicate Business'. *European Planning Studies* **12** (7), 1055–68.

de Jong, M., Lalenis, K. and Mamadouh, V. (2002). *The Theory and Practice of Institutional Transplantation; Experiences with the Transfer of Policy Institutions*. Dordrecht: Kluwer Academic Publishers.

Dolowitz, D. (1999). *Learning from America: Policy Transfer and the Development of the British Workfare State*. Brighton: Sussex Academic Press.

Dolowitz, D. and Marsh, D. (1996). 'Who Learns from Whom: A Review of the Policy Transfer Literature'. *Political Studies* **44** (2), 343–57.

—— (2000). 'Learning from Abroad: The Role of Policy Transfer in Contemporary Policy Making'. *Governance* **13** (1), 5–24.

Dudley, G. and Richardson, J. (2000). *Why Does Policy Change? Lessons from British Transport Policy 1945–99*. London: Routledge.

European Commission (2006). *European Union in Figures: Energy and Transport 2006*.

Brussels: European Commission Directorate-General for Energy and Transport/Eurostat.

European Conference of Ministers of Transport (ECMT) (2001). *Transport Policy Forum. Transport Policies in the Countries of Central and Eastern Europe. A Decade of Integration: Results and New Challenges.* Report prepared by the Latvian Delegation. Document No 6. Paris: ECMT.

Evans, M. (Ed.) (2004). *Policy Transfer in Global Perspective.* Aldershot: Ashgate.

Evans, M. and Davies, J. (1999). 'Understanding Policy Transfer: A Multi-Level, Multi-Disciplinary Perspective'. *Public Administration* **77** (2), 361–85.

Greener, I. (2002). 'Understanding NHS Reform: The Policy Transfer, Social learning and Path-Dependency Perspectives'. *Governance* **15** (2), 161–83.

Güller, P. (1996). 'Urban Travel in East and West: Key Problems and a Framework for Action'. In: ECMT (Ed.) *Sustainable Transport in Central and Eastern European Cities*, pp. 16–43. Paris: ECMT.

Héritier, A., Kerwer, D., Knill, C. and Lehmkuhl, D. (2001). *Differential Europe: The European Union Impact on National Policy-Making.* Lanham, MD: Rowman and Littlefield.

Holm-Hansen, J. (2005). *The Transferability of Policy Instruments: How New Environmental Policy Instruments Strike Roots in Russia and Latvia.* NIBR Report 2005:16. Oslo: Norwegian Institute for Urban and Regional Research (NIBR).

Jacoby, W. (2000). *Imitation and Politics: Redesigning Modern Germany.* Ithaca, NY: Cornell University Press.

James, O. and Lodge, M. (2003). 'The Limitations of "Policy Transfer" and "Lesson-Drawing" for Public Policy Research'. *Political Studies Review* **1** (3), 179–93.

Judge, E. (2002). 'The Development of Sustainable Transport Policies in Warsaw: 1990–2000'. In: Rydin, Y. and Thornley, A. (Eds.) *Planning in a Globalised Era,* pp. 359–86. Aldershot: Ashgate.

Knill, C. (2001). *The Europeanisation of National Administrations: Pattern of Institutional Change and Persistence.* Cambridge: Cambridge University Press.

Ladi, S. (2005). *Globalisation, Policy Transfer and Policy Research Institutes.* Cheltenham: Edward Elgar Publishing.

Lijewski, T. (1996). 'The Impact of Political Changes on Transport in Central and Eastern Europe'. *Transport Reviews* **16** (1), 37–53.

Majone, G. (1991). 'Cross-National Sources of Regulatory Policymaking in Europe and the United States'. *Journal of Public Policy* **11** (1), 79–106.

Polish Central Statistical Office (2007). 'Wrocław na tle województwa dolnośląskiego i kraju w 2005 r'. ['Wroclaw as Compared with the Dolnośląskie Voivodship and with the Country in 2005']. Polish Central Statistical Office, Warsaw, available: www.stat.gov.pl/wroc/67_1121_ENG_HTML.htm, accessed 26 May 2009.

Pucher, J. (1999). 'The Transformation of Urban Transport in the Czech Republic, 1988–1998'. *Transport Policy* **6** (4), 225–36.

Pucher, J. and Buehler, R. (2005). 'Transport Policy in Post-Communist Europe'. In: Button, K. and Hensher, D. (Eds.) *Handbook of Transport Strategy, Policy and Institutions*, pp. 725–43. Oxford: Elsevier.

Pucher, J. and Kurth, S. (1995). '*Verkehrsverbund*: The Success of Regional Public Transport in Germany, Austria and Switzerland'. *Transport Policy* **2** (4), 279–91.

Radaelli, C. (2004). 'The Diffusion or Regulatory Impact Assessment – Best Practice or Lesson-Drawing'. *European Journal of Political Research* **43** (4), 723–47.

Randma-Liiv, T. (2005). 'Demand- and Supply-Based Policy Transfer in Estonian Public Administration'. *Journal of Baltic Studies* **36** (4), 467–87.

Riga City Council (2005a). *Spatial Plan of Riga for 2006–2018. Explanatory Memorandum*. Riga: City Development Department, Riga City Council.

—— (2005b). *Sabiedriskais transports. Attīstības modelis* [*Public Transport: The Developmental Model*]. Riga: Riga City Council.

Robertson, D. (1991). 'Political Conflict and Lesson-Drawing'. *Journal of Public Policy* **11** (1), 55–78.

Rogers, E. M. (1995). *Diffusion of Innovations*. New York: The Free Press.

Rose, R. (1991). 'What is Lesson-Drawing?'. *Journal of Public Policy* **11** (1), 3–30.

—— (1993). *Lesson-Drawing in Public Policy: A Guide to Learning Across Time and Space*. Chatham, NJ: Chatham House.

—— (2005). *Learning from Comparative Public Policy: A Practical Guide*. London: Routledge.

Seifert, K. (2004). *Establishing Public Transport Executives for Local Public Passenger Transport – Challenge and Opportunity for Environmentally Benign Transport Development in Central and Eastern Europe*. Research and Development Project prepared for the German Federal Environmental Agency (FKZ 201 96 103). Rheinbach: European Nature Heritage Fund (Euronatur) Report.

Stone, D. (1999). 'Learning Lessons and Transferring Policy across Time, Space and Disciplines'. *Politics* **19** (1), 51–9.

—— (2004). 'Transfer Agents and Global Networks in the "Transnationalization" of Policy'. *Journal of European Public Policy* **11** (3), 545–66.

Suchorzewski, W. (2001). *Transport Policy Forum. Transport Policies in the Countries of Central and Eastern Europe. A Decade of Integration: Results and New Challenges*. Document No 1. Paris: ECMT.

Tavits, M. (2003). 'Policy Learning and Uncertainty: The Case of Pension Reform in Estonia and Latvia'. *Policy Studies Journal* **31** (4), 643–60.

Transit Cooperative Research Program (2003). *Transit Operations in Central and Eastern Europe. International Transit Studies Program Report on the Fall 2002 Mission*. Research Results Digest No. 62. Washington DC: Transit Cooperative Research Program.

Umweltbundesamt (UBA) (2006). *Attractive Public Transport through Regional Co-operation: Experiences and Suggestions from Wroclaw*. Dessau: UBA.

Wilson, T. K. and Bell, M. C. (1985). 'Transport Co-ordination and Integration in West Germany'. *Highways and Transportation* **32** (10), 5–12.

Wolman, H. (1992). 'Understanding Cross-National Policy Transfers: The Case of Britain and the United States'. *Governance* **5** (1), 27–45.

Wolman, H. and Page, E. (2002). 'Policy Transfer among Local Governments: An Information Theory Approach'. *Governance* **15** (4), 477–501.

World Bank (2002). *Urban Transport in the Europe and Central Asia Region: World Bank Experience and Strategy*. Report No. 25188 ECA. Washington DC: World Bank.

Zachariadis, T. and Kouvaritakis, N. (2003). 'Long-Term Outlook of Energy Use and $CO_2$ Emissions from Transport in Central and Eastern Europe'. *Energy Policy* **31** (8), 759–73.

# CHAPTER 9

# SUBALTERN SPEAK IN A POSTCOLONIAL SETTING

## Diffusing and Contesting Donor-Engendered Knowledge in the Water Sector in Zambia

**Barbara Mwila Kazimbaya-Senkwe and Peter Lubambo**

## Introduction

Postcolonialism is used as a designation for critical discourses that thematise issues emerging from colonial relations and their aftermath, covering a long historical span including the present (Hoogvelt 2001: 167). It focuses on a conceptualisation of power in which there is a recognition of the relationship between power, discourse, and political institutions and practices, with the aim of casting new light on colonial and postcolonial experiences, and providing for a more comprehensive understanding of how past and present relations of inequality are constructed and maintained (Abrahamsen 2003: 190). A key interest of postcolonialism is a focus on relationships in colonial societies in which the colonisers depend on a discursive creation and normalisation of difference, through cultural classifications and representations of self and others (see Said 1979; Loomba 1998; Abrahamsen 2003; Kothari 2005). This 'othering' and creation of subject identities (Said 1979) was 'based on particular types of knowledge which required the classifications of "other" and "difference", superiority and inferiority in order to justify and sustain colonial power and control' (Kothari 2005: 432). Thus, in *Orientalism*, Edward Said shows how the British created a version of the 'Oriental' as a person who was backward, not very handsome, unintelligent, laid back, incapable of self-rule and therefore deserving to be colonised (see Said 1979). Similarly, Mudimbe (1988) shows how complementary genres of 'speeches' contributed to the invention of a 'Primitive Africa' (see also Chipungu 1992; Hansen 1989; and Kazimbaya-Senkwe 2005 on various representations of Zambians by the British).

This othering leads to the creation of two societies that are not only seen as different, but also diametrically opposed to each other. In colonial parlance, the result is the formation of a social order in which there are two groups, the 'Us' – civilised, normal, Europeans – and the 'Others' – abnormal, 'them', uncivilised, Natives, Orientals or (in the present study) 'Africans'. Edward Said has noted that 'throughout the exchange between Europeans and their "others" . . . the one idea that has scarcely varied is that there is an "Us" and "Them", each quite settled, clear, unassailably self-evident' (Said 1994: xxviii). This leads to the creation of what JanMohamed has called the 'Manichean allegory', in which a binary and implacable discursive opposition between races is produced (see JanMohamed 1985: 60).

The ensuing power relationship between coloniser and colonised was obviously asymmetrical, but not one-sided. Spivak (1985) asks, 'Can the Subaltern Speak?' Indeed he can, and many postcolonial writers point to this fact (see, for instance, Spivak 1990; Qotole 2001; Wolputte 2004; Kazimbaya-Senkwe 2005). Although colonialism entails domination, the colonised also have windows and strategies for contributing to the development of their country or city. Postcolonialism therefore acknowledges the creativity and adaptability of the subaltern in the face of power, as a way of destabilising the hegemonic narratives through which the West has constructed the Other (Abrahamsen 2003: 207). The subaltern is not a helpless victim, but has what Yeoh (1996) describes as 'transformative capacity'[1] – that is, different groups are capable of intervening in any given set of events so as to alter them in some way. This transformative capacity is not a prerogative of the colonialist; the configuration of power in the colonial city is also shaped by the 'strategic conduct' of the colonised.[2]

It is important to note that the strategies of the subaltern may be both overt and 'active', such as riots, protests, etc., but also, more often than not, passive or subtle, whereby the community adopts an outward attitude of apparent acquiescence, but in reality disregards or even thwarts the measures imposed by colonial control. Thus Steven Van Wolputte opts not to refer to these actions as strategies, or an anti-colonial ideology, but rather as 'stratagems' embedded in local subjectivity (Wolputte 2004). This quiet contestation or resistance by the subaltern is captured in the postcolonial notion of 'hybridity', which marks the failure of the colonisers to fully colonise their subjects. As Wolputte states, locals find ways of profiting from colonial stereotypes by hybridising their colonially given identities. This rules out recognition, disrupting differentiation, making the differences that the colonisers rely upon to justify their actions no longer immediately observable. Subalterns must therefore be seen as knowledgeable and skilled agents with some awareness of the struggle for control – not just passive recipients of colonial rule, or, as colonists labelled them, 'ignorant' and 'prejudiced' people whose obstructionist habits were manifestations of a lack of civilisation.

The ability of the subaltern to speak in the present postcolonial era is the main interest of this paper. The reliance of former colonial countries such as Zambia on donor finances for development programs perpetuates a new colonialism in which foreign agencies and experts assume a seat at the policy-making table and use their financial resources to leverage their knowledge to influence policy and development outcomes. Indeed, whereas policy-making in developed countries does not generally involve foreigners, the reverse is true in countries such as Zambia, where such external (mainly Western) knowledge is taken as a given, if not a prerequisite, for development. This is largely perpetuated by the reliance of most former colonial countries on aid from Western governments and loans from multilateral financing institutions such as the World Bank. In the past five decades since gaining political independence in the 1960s, many African countries including Zambia have gone through severe economic crisis, resulting from numerous factors including but not limited to lack of creditworthiness, susceptibility to global financial crises, commodity price shifts and natural disasters, civil wars and poor economic management (see Rakodi 1997 and Simon 1997). Consequently, they have been unable to finance national development from their own resources, but rather depend on external donor and multilateral agencies. Because of the large-scale investments and large technological input required for water and sanitation services, normally far above what most African governments can and/or are willing to afford, financing for the sector is mainly through donor-funded projects or loans from multilateral financing institutions. In Zambia, over 90 per cent of investment funding for the sector has been provided in this way in recent years.

These donor resources come not unattached but rather with a plethora of foreign development experts and policy prescriptions, implying the assumption that development cannot take place without this external knowledge. This happens in part because of the persistent discursive social construction of Africa and other formerly colonised areas as backward areas, inhabited by backward peoples. Arturo Escobar employs a Foucauldian conception of the power/knowledge nexus and politics of representation to show how development and its opposite, underdevelopment, are not self-evident or pre-ordained categories (Escobar 1995). They are, instead, discursive constructs, particular ways of seeing and acting upon the world, that reflect not only the conditions they describe, but also the constellations of social, economic and political forces at the time of their emergence (Abrahamsen 2003: 202). Escobar argues that American President Truman's problematisation of underdevelopment in 1949 led to ordering of social reality into new categories such as 'underdeveloped', 'malnourished', 'illiterate', etc. This then established emerging countries as objects of intervention, and normalised the right of the 'North' to intervene and control, adapt, and reshape the structures, practices and ways of life of the 'South'. Not only are Africa and other non-Western areas described as backward, but development itself is predicated on the assumption that some people and places are more developed than others, and therefore those who are 'developed' have the knowledge and expertise to help those who are not (Parpart 1995: 221), not to mention the right to do so.

This type of development model can be regarded as 'analogous to the realm of "the social" in domestic politics, as through such interventions, the underdeveloped subject becomes known, categorised . . . which in turn legitimates practices and facilitates the emergence of the "disciplined subject"' (Abrahamsen 2003: 202). This othering and 'knowing of the subject' finds practical expression in the donor advisors, experts and specialists whose knowledge and presence at the policy-making table in former colonial countries such as Zambia is taken as a given, if not a prerequisite, for development. These experts are 'identified as such not solely because of the extent and form of their knowledge, but often because of who they are and where they come from' (Kothari 2005: 426). As Kothari goes on to point out:

> It is not only significant what knowledge people possess but who possesses it. As Crewe and Harrison observe, 'the division between indigenous and Western or scientific knowledge is . . . based on ideas about people, rather than on objective differences in knowledge and expertise'. Beneficiaries of aid in developing countries are generally not seen as having expertise, not only because their knowledge and expertise is devalued, but more importantly because the very notion of expertise is socially, culturally and geographically informed.
>
> (ibid.: 428–9, citing Crewe and Harrison 1998: 92)

Thus the Western, donor-funded expert has assumed an apparent right to intervene and provide policy advice in development processes in postcolonial countries, and embodies the unequal relationship between the First and Third Worlds, and between donors and aid recipients.

Not only does the West feel justified to intervene, it is also able to use sanctions to achieve compliance. This disciplinary aspect of development can be seen, for instance, in conditionalities attached to external donor financing. However, as Kothari has argued, these

> development strategies and interventions produce unequal global relations not solely by invoking colonial forms of rule of the past, but also through the construction of expertise . . . [for] the development of tools and techniques designed and controlled by the development expert privileges forms of western knowledge.

> Masquerading as universal and neutral, they pose as 'acceptable' forms of authority
> by mobilising overarching discourses of 'humanitarianism', 'philanthropy' and pov-
> erty alleviation, presented in contradistinction to the exploitative colonial projects.
>
> (ibid.: 433)

This expertise and the power imbalances it engenders are not, however, lost on the local stakeholders, who also have their own knowledge, plans and resources, and invariably more interests at stake than the outsiders. Using the case study of the water sector reforms in the Copperbelt Province of Zambia, this chapter aims to show how those on the receiving end of this unequal power relation-ship continue to question and challenge the development model. It shows how the subaltern continues to speak in today's neo-colonised world. Tracing the failure to establish a regional water utility in the Copperbelt Province of Zambia between 1990 and 2007, the chapter sheds light on the operations of a typical donor-funded project, exposing on the one hand how donor knowledge embodies the unequal neo-colonial power relationship between donors and poor govern-ments, and on the other how this knowledge is neither easily diffused nor easily assimilated, but is rather challenged and sometimes actively thwarted by the local stakeholders. The aim is not to speak on behalf of the marginalised, but rather to mark the space of the silenced in conventional imperial history (Spivak 1990). The chapter is based on the authors' personal involvement with water reform in the Copperbelt specifically and in Zambia broadly, as well as on an analysis of secondary documentation and key informant interviews.

The chapter is organised into five sections as follows. The first section provides a brief overview of the water sector in Zambia. The second section delves into a case study of water reform in the Copperbelt, showing how external agencies and experts sought but failed to influence reform in the area. The third section provides an analysis of how, through a typical donor-funded water project, the World Bank alongside other local stakeholders was provided with a place at the decision-making table. The fourth section highlights the different knowledge that each group of stakeholders brought to bear on the decision-making process. The fifth and final section draws out some analysis, and the policy and theoretical implications of the case study.

## THE WATER SECTOR IN ZAMBIA

A brief account of the current status and history of the Zambian water sector will be useful to orient the discussion. The Republic of Zambia is located in South-Central Africa between latitudes 8 and 18 degrees south and longitudes 22 and 34 degrees east. It has a population of just over 11 million, of whom about 35 per cent live in 18 large urban areas, and the remainder in 54 rural districts. Administratively, the country is divided into nine provinces. Politically, Zambia is a multi-party democracy with an elected central government, and elected local governments in all 72 districts. The Ministry for Energy and Water Development (MEWD) is responsible for water resources management, whereas the Ministry for Local Government and Housing (MLGH) is responsible for water supply and sanitation services. Through the Local Government Act of 1991, the MLGH delegated the function of water supply and sanitation services provision to the 72 local authorities.

Zambia, which until 1964 was known as Northern Rhodesia, was formally a British colony for 40 years from 1924 to October 1964, when it was granted independence.[3] From colonial times to the present, access to adequate clean drinking water in the Copperbelt, as in the rest of Zambia, has been a preserve of only a portion of the population. As in the rest of Africa, Zambia is still struggling to provide clean drinking water and adequate sanitation facilities for its population. Currently, only 53 per cent of the population are said to have access to clean drinking water either in the home or from a public stand post, and only 23 per cent access to sanitation. Even in urban areas, these figures are only 86 per cent access to water and 41 per cent access to sanitation (see WSP 2006). Part of the explanation is to be found in the fact that the domestication of water, which began in colonial times around 1929, has been both incomplete and carried out in a manner that excludes some social groups (see Kazimbaya-Senkwe 2005 and Kazimbaya-Senkwe and Guy 2007 for a more detailed discussion of the construction of water networks and differentiated access in the Copperbelt). In her PhD thesis, Kazimbaya-Senkwe (2005) also shows how the formal process of water domestication in the Copperbelt, including decisions about who was to get what access, was led by foreigners in the British colonial administration, to the exclusion of the native Zambians. However, subalterns also responded to and challenged these exclusionary tendencies, and in their own way influenced the domestication process (ibid.: Chapters 5–10). Foreign domination over water matters in Zambia, and contestation of this dominance by local Zambians – that is, 'subaltern speak' – is therefore not a new phenomenon. The narrative presented in the current chapter aims to draw attention to the continuities and changes from colonial times to the present, with a specific focus on the power relationships attending the domestication of water. As Rita Abrahamsen has argued, 'the post in postcolonialism should not be understood as a clearly dividing temporal post, but rather as an indication of continuity' (2003: 195).

## THE REGIONALISATION OF THE WATER SUPPLY IN THE COPPERBELT

The Copperbelt Province is located in the north-western part of Zambia, sharing an international border with the Democratic Republic of Congo (Figure 9.1). The province is the second smallest in the country, with a land area of approximately 31,217 km[2]. The province is divided into three rural districts and seven urban copper mining districts. The focus of this chapter is on the failure to create a single regional water utility in urban districts in the Copperbelt between 1990 and 2007.[4] (The three rural districts went through a different reform process, not discussed here.) Unlike the other provinces in the country, the Copperbelt Province, because of its copper mining legacy, had from the colonial days developed two parallel systems for the provision of municipal services including water supply and sanitation. Whilst the local authorities provided services to all members of the public, the mining conglomerate Zambia Consolidated Copper Mines (ZCCM) provided services to all mining establishments, including the residential townships that were exclusive to miners and their families.[5] This is why water supply to the Copperbelt is a particularly interesting, and a particularly postcolonial, problem.

In 1993, water sector reforms started during the late 1970s were given impetus by the establishment of the Water Sector Development Group (WSDG)

**Figure 9.1**   Zambia and the Copperbelt. Source: adapted from Kazimbaya-Senkwe (2005: 1).

by the new government formed in 1991 by the Movement for Multi-Party Democracy (MMD). This government advocated a 'neo-liberal' policy agenda, including encouraging the privatisation of public infrastructure agencies. The reforms resulted in the adoption of the National Water Policy in 1994 and enactment of the Water Supply and Sanitation Act of 1997. The Act lays out different ways in which the local authorities can supply water and sanitation. Councils can provide the services directly, or form a commercial utility (CU), either alone or with other councils. Since 2000, a total of 10 commercial utilities have been formed in eight provinces, and the last one is being established in Luapula Province at the time of writing. A key principle of these utilities is commercial viability and the expansion of services to fast-growing cities and towns. As a result, the commercial utilities are registered as private companies under the Companies Act, and are expected to operate independently on a day-to-day basis. The utilities are owned by the local authorities, who are the main shareholders, and who appoint a board of directors who in turn employ the management team.

Before the 1997 Water Act, two commercial utility companies had already been established in the country. The Copperbelt Province was therefore the first to develop commercial water utilities on the basis of the 1997 Act. In 1998–9, a study funded by the Norwegian Development Agency (NORAD) was conducted by consultants Price Waterhouse (now PricewaterhouseCoopers). This recommended a single, provincial-level utility as the most financially viable option for the Copperbelt. Although most stakeholders agreed that commercial viability was important, and that a large utility would profit from economies of scale and probably reduce the unit cost for customers, the idea of a regional utility was, nevertheless, ultimately rejected. How this occurred is the core narrative of this chapter.

The key opponents to the proposal included the then Minister for Local Government and Housing, who argued that creating one utility would be contrary to the government's decentralisation agenda, as the government was also in the process of breaking up other national corporations such as ZCCM into smaller entities. The WSDG asked Price Waterhouse to re-examine the options. Although the revised proposals maintained that one utility was the most viable option, they also suggested scenarios with two, three or four commercial utility companies. These were discussed in a stakeholder workshop, which, on the basis of geographical and historical considerations, opted for the formation of three companies, even though these were not expected to be financially viable. These were established in 2000 (Table 9.1).

The three new commercial utilities initially catered only for the local authority areas because, at the time of their formation, ZCCM was still serving mining

**Table 9.1** The Copperbelt districts with respective water utilities

| Commercial water utility | District grouping |
| --- | --- |
| Kafubu Water and Sewerage Company (KWSC) | Ndola, Luanshya and Masaiti |
| Mulonga Water and Sewerage Company (MWSC) | Chingola, Chililabombwe and Mufulira |
| Nkana Water and Sewerage Company (NWSC) | Kitwe and Kalulushi |

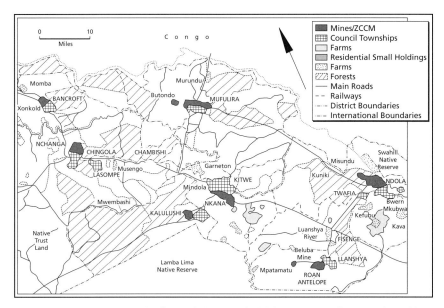

**Figure 9.2** Water supply in the Copperbelt from colonial times to 2000. Source: adapted from Kazimbaya-Senkwe (2005: 127).

establishments. Spatially, the result was that each commercial utility covered two or more districts, but without covering any district in its entirety, as part of each district was still controlled by ZCCM (Figure 9.2). ZCCM, however, was in the process of being privatised, leaving open the question of which body would supply water to its former customers, as we will now describe.

## THE MINE TOWNSHIP SERVICES PROJECT AND THE THIRD FAILURE TO CREATE A REGIONAL UTILITY

In the early 2000s the copper mines in Zambia were privatised. From the onset of the privatisation negotiations, the bidding companies made it clear that they did not intend to continue providing municipal services such as housing to the miners, as ZCCM had done, since the housing stock was being sold off to sitting tenants.

As a result, it was proposed that the local authorities should take over all of the municipal functions, including markets, bus stops and cemeteries, which they did.

However, for fear of dealing with potential clients who had become accustomed to the idea of receiving 'free' water services from the mines, and also because of their own financial and institutional weaknesses and their ongoing project of forming commercial utilities, the local authorities were not ready to take on this responsibility.

Privatisation of the mines being an important national priority, the government asked the World Bank to assist. Thus the idea of the Mine Township Services Project (MTSP) was born, a five-year programme that, among other things, was intended to 'educate' the miners about the importance of paying for services, to wean them gradually from the previous arrangements, and to help turn them into 'normal' water customers.[6] In conformity with the 1997 Act, all ZCCM's water supply and sanitation assets were transferred to the Asset-Holding Company Mining Municipal Services (AHC-MMS), which was created under the MTSP. This continued the system of parallel provision of water services in the region. To ensure that service provision was effective and efficient, and to safeguard the financial investment provided by the World Bank, a management contract was signed between the government of Zambia and the French company Saur for a period of four years (2000–4). Saur was to manage the assets and develop the commercial management capacity of the local staff. This represented the first, and to date the only, truly private sector participation in the water sector in Zambia.

The AHC–Saur arrangement was transitional, requiring the definition of a permanent strategy during the five-year lifetime of MTSP. The MTSP therefore included an 'exit strategy' within the remit of the Ministry of Local Government and Housing, intended to outline modalities for the takeover by the local authorities. The exit strategy comprised various studies, including one on enhanced private sector participation (see GKW with Grant Thornton Associates 2003). It must be noted that from the outset the Bank saw the ability to attract a private operator as a major indicator of success of the MTSP and the exit strategy. Such a successful outcome was a prerequisite for any follow-on Bank operation in the sector. Thus, it can be argued that, from the outset, the bank had locked itself into a particular position, even though the exit strategy was meant to provide alternatives. Although some of the stakeholders did not seem to mind the idea of a private operator, there was resistance to this idea, particularly from the then Minister. However, it was agreed by the central government and the World Bank to try out the management contract for two years, and thereafter to review and determine a way forward. A key objective of the review would be to define ways to merge the AHC and the three utilities into one utility, and to attract a private operator.

Serious discussion on the exit strategy commenced in 2003 after the consultants submitted their 'options report' (BCHOD with Ernst and Young 2003a). Three main options were presented: maintaining the three existing utilities and formalising the AHC as the fourth; creating two utilities; and creating one regional utility. These options were presented to various stakeholders for discussion (see BCHOD with Ernst and Young 2003b). From the outset of the discussions, it became evident that there were two strong and opposing positions. One of these, held by the technicians in central government, the AHC and the World Bank team, preferred the amalgamation of the four utility companies into a single regional utility – 'one commercial utility' or '1CU'. The opposing view, held mainly by the regulator (the National Water Supply and Sanitation Council, NWASCO), the local authorities and the three newly created commercial utilities, was to break up the AHC and divide out its assets amongst the other three companies.

These two camps were fairly entrenched in their respective positions, leading to protracted negotiation and the consequent extension of the Saur management contract and MTSP by one year. By 2005, closure was needed for both MTSP and the exit strategy. Numerous discussions were held between the MLGH, the local authorities, the commercial utilities and the World Bank. In December 2005, the Minister finally agreed to a compromise solution in which the AHC would be taken over in its entirety by Nkana Water and Sewerage Company (NWSC), which was the largest and best-performing amongst the three local authority utilities. The takeover took place in January 2006. Nkana Water was thus enlarged, and began to provide services in districts where the other commercial utilities were also operational. In effect, NWSC became like the former ZCCM or AHC, operating a parallel water system in local authority areas, but on a larger scale. The enlarged Nkana operated successfully for nearly two years, and was acknowledged as the best-performing utility in Zambia. Part of this success was attributed to the large asset and consumer base it gained, together with the commercial systems that had been set up by AHC under the MTSP.

This success, however, received a backlash from the other two commercial utilities in the region, which put pressure on the Minister to break up and share out the assets from AHC. In October 2007, the Minister finally consented and the three utilities were re-established, although with one major difference: for the first time in the history of the Copperbelt, there would no longer be two parallel water systems in the towns. Under this arrangement, each utility company would manage all assets in their respective districts, namely assets from both the local authorities and the mining companies (Figure 9.3). However, this also meant that the Copperbelt remained the one province with three utility companies, rather than one.

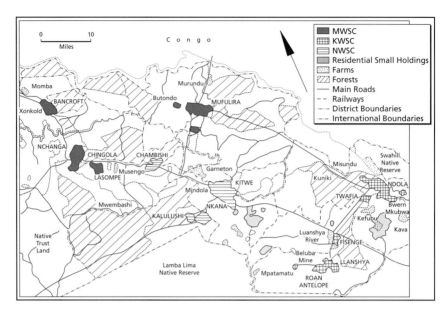

**Figure 9.3**   Water supply in the Copperbelt, 2007–9. Source: adapted from Kazimbaya-
           Senkwe (2005: 127).

These events describe, at the time of writing, the current situation with regard
to the supply of water in the Copperbelt region. We will now go on to explore in
more detail the dynamics and undercurrents that were at play in these events,
investigating the main stakeholders and their claims to a place in the decision-
making process, the different types of knowledge they deployed during the
negotiations, and how the application of postcolonial theory might help make
sense of the failure of what the authors believe was the most rational solution: a
single utility company.

## THE MAIN PLAYERS AND PLATFORMS FOR
## ENGAGEMENT IN THE DECISION-MAKING PROCESS

There were five broad groups of stakeholders who shaped decisions over water
reform in the Copperbelt, namely central government, local authorities, the regulator, the commercial utilities (of which three belonged to the local authorities, and
one was the Asset Holding Company AHC-MMS) and the World Bank. In this
section we explain how the design of a typical donor-funded project provided different places for these stakeholders at the decision-making table.

In the MTSP, as in most typical donor-funded water projects, there was within
the recipient country a group of civil servants and other public officers working as
'counterparts' to and recipient points for the donor support. At central government

level, this took shape in the person of the Director of Infrastructure Support Services of the Ministry for Local Government and Housing (one of the authors of this chapter). The Director is a senior civil servant who acts as a liaison point between the donors and the civil service. The Director and his team are largely responsible for compliance – on one hand that of the government, to meet the requirements of the donor, and on the other hand that of the donor, to meet the requirements of the country. This group of stakeholders therefore gained access to and legitimacy at the decision-making table through their positions as civil servants responsible for implementing government policy. The team reported to the Permanent Secretary, the most senior civil servant, responsible for managing the sector. The Permanent Secretary reports to the sector Minister, who is responsible for policy. This is the group that interacted frequently with the World Bank and which therefore had a platform in decision-making from the inception of the MTSP.

In Zambia, as in most African countries, financial mobilisation for the water sector is highly centralised, but delivery services are highly localised. In the current case, delivery was in the hands of the three local commercial utilities and the AHC-MMS. These entities comprised mainly local staff, except for the AHC-MMS, which had some international staff from Saur. These bodies also represented the seven local authorities who were shareholders of the three commercial utilities, and this group of local-level authorities was expected not only to benefit directly from the World Bank credit, but also to carry out any policy measures agreed between the central government and the Bank. They were also the ones directly affected by real and potential gains and losses from any policy measures. The regulator (NWASCO) was also involved, because it was to be responsible for regulating any new utility companies that would be formed.

For the MTSP, as in most typical donor-funded water projects, on the World Bank side there was an international (read 'foreign') water sector advisor from Washington, the Task Team Leader. This person led the team and was responsible for all key decisions with regards to the project, including project design and decisions on when and how the funds flowed. In an effort to take a bit more account of the local circumstances of different countries, the Bank team, in common with most other donors, included a local specialist to provide advice to the foreign water advisor and also to ensure and assist the government's compliance with project requirements at country level. (The other author of this chapter filled this role.) For the MTSP, as for other projects, there was also provision for consultants paid for with World Bank credit to carry out studies to inform policy outcomes. These consultant water advisors, specialists, and technical assistants acted primarily as the conduits for the knowledge and policy direction espoused by the Bank, taking direction from and at the same time giving advice to the Bank, whilst also assisting the government to implement the project in accordance with donor requirements.

So what forms of knowledge did each of these players rely upon, and how did this contestation play itself out? This is the subject to which we now turn.

## CONTESTING FORMS OF KNOWLEDGE

This section explores the knowledge that each of the stakeholders brought to bear on the process, as well as some of the key interests that drove their participation and positioning. The stakeholders were divided into two broad groups, namely those in favour of forming a single utility (the '1CU' solution), comprising the technicians in central government, the AHC and the World Bank; and those against '1CU', the politicians at central government level, the local authorities, the regulator, and the three local authority commercial utilities. From the discussions between these two groups, it is possible to pull out three main types of knowledge that were used, namely technical rational knowledge; knowledge based on experience of previous reforms, which included experience of reforms in an abstract sense, and experience of previous personal and organisational gains and losses; and knowledge related to the idea of insiders and outsiders or 'us' and 'them'.

### CONTESTED TECHNICAL ASSESSMENT, UNDERPINNED BY ECONOMIC ANALYSIS

Discussions on whether or not to form one utility were by and large based on the studies undertaken as part of the exit strategy, which had depicted the model of a single utility as the only rational choice (see BCHOD with Ernst and Young 2003a). Furthermore, the Copperbelt Province has the highest population in Zambia, and is the second most urbanised and densely populated province after Lusaka. It also has the highest number of water connections in the country, the most located within the smallest geographical spread of any province in the country. The province also has the highest rate of formal employment in the country, and therefore the largest population with access to a reliable disposable income. These factors made the Copperbelt an ideal candidate for pursuing the economies of scale that could result from the formation of a single utility. This rational knowledge and argument was the main basis of the position taken by the World Bank. As far as the Bank was concerned, anything short of '1CU' would constitute an unacceptable sub-standard solution, as it could not be justified in the Bank's dominant logic of technical rationality.

In this regard, the main questions from the Bank in the discussion revolved around issues such as, 'Why would you go for a solution that is more expensive for the government and the consumers? Why would you not build on the gains made by Saur and AHC, by forming one utility and attracting investment into the

Copperbelt?'[7] Furthermore, the Bank could not understand why the government would choose a sub-optimal model that ran the risk of damaging investment gains through a break-up of the assets installed through the MTSP. They could not, for instance, understand how the government would share out assets such as the billing systems, central laboratories, workshops and information management systems without destroying the integrated systems that the project was designed to support. In addition, the Bank staff's technical logic, based on rational economic analysis, dictated that small, unprofitable utilities would lead to a failure to attract private sector investments, and consequently a failure to institutionalise the commercial gains made through the MTSP–Saur management contract.

Holding similar views to the Bank, the technicians in the Ministry, led by the Director, were also convinced that '1CU' was the most rational choice, as the Ministry had been present from the establishment of the three utility companies and the design and rollout of MTSP. Their main point of knowledge was a concern with providing national policy to attain universal utilities coverage for water supply and sanitation services through improved efficiencies and reduced costs. For this group, the formation of one utility presented an opportunity to deliver utilities cost-effectively to the residents of the Copperbelt. As described above, the Copperbelt made an ideal candidate for '1CU', compared with all of the other rural provinces where the '1CU' model was being rolled out. Furthermore, public apprehension over private sector participation was mitigated by the success of the operator AHC, and the exit strategy, which had demonstrated improved service delivery. Therefore, to the Ministry, the '1CU' model seemed simply the rational next step to enhance ongoing reforms. This type of rational knowledge, however, straitjacketed the Bank and the technicians in the Ministry into a commitment to '1CU', and put them on a collision course with the other local stakeholders.

Opponents of '1CU' – politicians at central government level, local authorities, the regulator, and the three local authority commercial utilities – contested the Bank's and the Ministry's rationality, arguing that the '1CU' model was not necessarily more efficient, as smaller commercial utilities could be made efficient with requisite support. Moreover, a single utility company would be too large, leading to inefficiency and bureaucracy (as had been the case with ZCCM). According to this group, it was irrational and contradictory for the Bank and the Ministry officials to call for the setting up of larger organisations, when the government was already going through a process of unbundling large and failed public entities. Furthermore, even though there was no competition between the commercial utilities, the regulator nonetheless took the view that by promoting the '1CU' model the Bank was killing competition in the sector. The mere existence of three commercial utilities was seen as creating room for benchmarking and therefore improving performance. Thus this position was partly contingent on a contestation of technical rationality. The stakeholders also, however, used knowledge from their past experiences.

## KNOWLEDGE BASED ON PREVIOUS EXPERIENCE

Perhaps even more important than these debates within the sphere of technical rationality was knowledge that the decision makers had gained from past experiences. These included experiences with privatisation and retrenchments in general, as well as experiences of personal and organisational gains and losses. The opponents of the '1CU' model drew upon negative experiences, whereas the proponents focused on previous positive experiences of reform.

### EXPERIENCE WITH PRIVATISATION AND RETRENCHMENTS

For the politicians who opposed a single utility company, the knowledge they deployed was linked to previous negative experiences of the economic privatisation and liberalisation programme supported by the World Bank and the International Monetary Fund (IMF). From the birth of the country in the second decade of the twentieth century, until the late 2000s, the Copperbelt Province was the industrial heartland of Zambia.[8] The province houses seven major copper mines, which until March 2000 were owned by the Zambian government through the parastatal company ZCCM. From the mid-1970s, the copper economy had suffered from the oil crisis, a decline in world copper prices, low copper production and deteriorating terms of trade (Gardner 1993; World Bank 1994; Ferguson 1999). In an effort to stem some of the resultant economic problems, the country embarked on a World Bank/IMF-supported Structural Adjustment Programme (SAP). A major part of the SAP was the privatisation of the copper mines, which took place between 1997 and 2000. Resulting from this were a significant number of retrenchments in both ZCCM and many small- to medium-scale suppliers to the mines. At the same time, many parastatal companies were either privatised or liquidated, leading to major job losses. This programme therefore made politicians extremely unpopular, probably nowhere more so than in the Copperbelt, which, historically, had had the largest concentration of formal employment in the country. The politicians thus saw the proposed reform of the water sector in the Copperbelt, especially the linking of the '1CU' model to private sector participation, as potentially risky. They were therefore keen to avoid any decisions on the exit strategy that would somehow link them to job losses.

The brunt of the retrenchments in the water sector had been borne by the utility companies. The 1993 water reform had forced the commercial utilities to take on council employees who could not be laid off, as the government could not afford to pay their retrenchment benefits. Thus, although these redundant employees were not working, the utility companies were still obliged to pay their salaries. The commercial utilities were also, therefore, very worried that the formation of a single utility would lead to more retrenchments, thus doubling their financial burden. There was also a belief amongst the utility companies and the local authorities that the World Bank had reneged on some earlier promise to fund the retrenchments in the Copperbelt. Thus, as far as the commercial utilities were concerned, the World Bank was only interested in getting its way – '1CU' – whilst leaving them to deal with all of the negative after-effects.

For the labour unions, their staff had already experienced a loss of jobs and difficulties arising from the non-payment of retrenchment benefits. Thus, although they were not necessarily against any particular model, they were keen that whichever model was chosen would not lead to job losses and hence a loss of union membership.

On the other hand, the World Bank, the technicians in the Ministry and the AHC saw private sector participation as a good thing. The World Bank in particular drew on its experience in other countries, such as Côte d'Ivoire, Senegal and Guinea Conakry, where private sector participation was being touted as successful (see Menard and Clarke 2000; Menard *et al*. 2000). Similarly, management contracts such as the one designed for AHC and executed by Saur had been implemented with success in other countries. This is why, in the design of MTSP, private sector participation was taken as a given, at least by the World Bank. It is also worth noting that, by the time of the exit strategy, other countries were experimenting successfully with the single utility model, such as Uganda's National Water and Sewerage Company in Kampala.

Similarly, for the technicians in the Ministry, private sector participation was enticing. During the implementation of the MTSP, the Ministry of Local Government and Housing had led a delegation of the chief executives of all of the commercial utilities in the Copperbelt, along with WSDG members, to see firsthand the successes in both Côte d' Ivoire and Senegal. At the same time, the Zambian government was seriously engaged in discussions about the possibility of getting a private operator to work with Lusaka Water and Sewerage Company in the capital city. It must be noted, too, that the 1997 Water Supply Act provides for private sector participation in provision of utilities through the purchase of up to 49 per cent of shares. Thus, for the Ministry technicians, the AHC, which had a more positive financial performance and better projections than the other commercial utilities in the Copperbelt, had sowed the seed to attract private sector investment into the region. The formation of a single utility thus seemed a natural next step.

The AHC, as the only ardent local proponent of the merger into a single regional commercial utility, derived its knowledge from the fact that it had implemented the MTSP and therefore had firsthand experience in arrangements involving the private sector. Having benefited from skills transfer from Saur, they understood the value of partnering with the private sector, even though their appreciation was more linked to the commercial aspects, as they felt strongly that their own engineering skills equalled if not bettered those of Saur (see, for instance, AHC-MMS 2005). Second, having come out of ZCCM, they had the benefit of already having gone through a process of privatisation. Furthermore, unlike the other commercial utilities, they knew that they would not face any retrenchment issues, as all workers on MTSP were employed on a contract basis.

For the World Bank, although the financial burden imposed by the old retrenchments was fairly substantial, it was not insurmountable. At the time of the exit strategy, the Bank was in the process of preparing a follow-on project to the MTSP. Thus it was possible that, with a successful outcome in the Copperbelt, the issue of retrenchments (old, and new, if any) could be resolved through this new project. This was ultimately what happened.

## FEAR OF PERSONAL AND ORGANISATIONAL LOSS

For the local authorities, another important point of knowledge gained through experience was their previous relationship with the three commercial utilities, and the organisational gains and losses involved. As shareholders, they had still not received any dividends from the companies up to this point. These dividends were important as a substitute for the income from water sales, which had been lost because of the formation of the utility companies. Second, the commercial utilities seemed to have little respect and regard for their shareholders, describing them in various fora as having caused the dilapidation of the services and as therefore being 'useless'. Thus the argument for forming one utility was unappealing to the local authorities, as they thought that with the '1CU' model their powers would be eroded even more, as their percentage shares in the new commercial utility would reduce dramatically – from the existing 33 per cent for some of them to as low as 12 per cent.

The boards of the utility companies had enjoyed a certain level of privilege, prestige, status and influence. On average, a board member of one of the commercial utilities may earn about US$480 per year in allowances for attending scheduled quarterly meetings. They also, however, get to attend non-scheduled meetings, as well as committee meetings throughout the year. On average, therefore, a member may earn up to US$1500 per year in allowances. This should be contrasted with an average monthly salary of US$600 for professionals in the water sector in Zambia. All expenses related to these meetings are also paid.

Members may serve for up to three years on a board, and some may be retained after the first term. Thus there is a relatively small, but nonetheless important, financial gain associated with being a board member. More importantly, however, those serving on boards gain prestige, status and influence by sitting at the decision-making table for one of life's most basic needs, that is, water. '1CU' would mean one board, and therefore some members would have to be retired. This potential personal loss of prestige, status, influence and income was therefore a key driver for board members' opposition to the '1CU' model.

Similarly, the management staff of the utility companies understood that the merger would entail a collapse of four management bodies into one, and therefore only one chief executive. Their fear was further strengthened by the fact that they viewed the chief executive of the AHC as the favourite of the World Bank and therefore the 'heir apparent' to leadership of the '1CU'. This potential loss of employment, power and status was therefore a strong incentive for management staff in the commercial utilities to fight the '1CU' model, as it touched on their personal survival.

It is also possible to speculate that those who had been involved with the earlier reform process of 2000, including the regulator, may have perceived the proposal to form '1CU' as an indictment by the World Bank, suggesting that they were failures. The reinvigorated interest in the single utility model may have been understood as the Bank coming back again to 'finally correct what that first team of Zambians' had 'got wrong' in 2000. It is the argument of this paper that this notion of 'the Zambians versus the foreigners' probably played a bigger part in arriving at the final decision than both the contestations of the technical experts and the self-interest of the stakeholders.

## THE LOCAL VERSUS THE FOREIGN

Probably the biggest catalyst for the opponents and finally for the Minister's decision against '1CU' was the perception that it was not the local technical staff who had generated the idea. Rather, the proposal was seen as emanating and being pushed by a foreign consultant, working in collaboration and in agreement with the World Bank. One statement, for instance, that the Minister made a number of times was, 'Why should people from Washington come and tell me what to do? Why are these ideas not coming from my own people?' Thus the message itself may not necessarily have been unwelcome, but the bearer of that message was clearly not very welcome. This discomfort of politicians with the overt role of the World Bank was further strengthened by the fact that the MTSP was designed with private sector participation as a possible end point. This was read to mean that, at the time of establishing the MTSP, the Bank had already decided what outcome it wanted, and was simply going through the motions of pretending to be consultative. Furthermore, the Bank had a great belief in the AHC, because of its apparently better performance, which in turn was related to the involvement of the foreign company Saur. The Bank made quite some hype about this success, leading the AHC team to feel rather superior to the other utility companies, and thus annoying the others even more. Consequently, attempts by the World Bank to explain that the MTSP was successful, and should therefore be safeguarded by the creation of the '1CU' to attract more investments, just infuriated the Minister, rather than impressing her, and only served to entrench suspicions about the Bank's intentions.

Related to this was the fact that the Bank had great faith in its technical analyses and the technical capabilities of its staff. Although there was supervision of the project by senior World Bank staff in Washington, the key players on the ground on the Bank side were fairly young, and therefore had limited years of experience. Fronting this young team of technicians partially led to the Bank being seen as arrogant and removed from the political realities of the nation. This was exemplified, for instance, in a remark from the Minister, in which she wondered 'why junior officers and young girls from Washington' were being sent to discuss this matter with her, rather than the 'more senior' and therefore more experienced and politically savvy country manager.[9]

This feeling of the outside imposing on the inside also found expression amongst the owners of the utility companies, namely the local authorities. Drawing on their knowledge of the decentralisation policy and the Water Supply Act, they were concerned about the role of the World Bank in this matter. As far as the law is concerned, the formation of utility companies, including the choice of whether to partner with other local authorities or the private sector, was the perogative of the local authorities. Thus, even though they appreciated the technical rationale behind the proposal to set up a single utility, they took strong exception to the fact that the '1CU' model was very much a World Bank agenda item. Largely for this reason, they opted to fall back on their right to determine their own destinies, as provided for in national policy and legislation, and chose to keep the three commercial utilities.

Similarly, the boards of the utility companies saw the proposal to form a single utility as an affront to their rights and privileges, and their business acumen. Their main source of knowledge came from their interactions with the affairs of the utility companies. As supervisors of corporate bodies, they felt that they were responsible for the affairs of the companies, including decisions on mergers, privatisation, etc. They therefore did not understand why the government, and in particular the World Bank, were telling them how to run their businesses, especially given that neither was funding the three utility companies. For instance, one statement made by one of the board chairmen during a meeting was that 'the World Bank should leave the government alone to make its own decisions'.

As with the local authorities and their boards, the management of the commercial utilities saw the single utility model as an invention of the World Bank, being forced on them by technicians in the Ministry who had 'sold out' to the Bank. Second, as the studies that recommended '1CU' had all pointed to existing inefficiencies and the unsustainable financial operations of all four commercial utilities, accepting the model would have been an admission of failure. Such an admission, coming on the back of a World Bank-led program, was not acceptable, considering that the MTSP had not extended to the other commercial utilities. The outside, therefore, had to be kept at bay, no matter the consequences.

## DIFFUSING AND CONTESTING KNOWLEDGE: TOWARDS SOME CONCLUSIONS

This chapter has shown how today's Zambia is still affected by colonial-type relations. Through these relations, which are a result of reliance on donor and multilateral financing, Zambia is 'known' through, and therefore expected to take and use knowledge from, the West for its development agenda. We have shown how, by bringing in financial resources, the World Bank got a place at the decision-making table for its technical assistants and advisors. This place assured them space to air their 'ideas' about what the sector and 'development' should be. But, as Marcos (2000, unpaginated) has argued, 'ideas are also weapons'. By offering their financial resources, the donors arrive, in effect, to plan the country's development future. Through its financial, technical and knowledge resources, the World Bank became a participant in the water planning process, seeking to influence policy as well as development outcomes. This participation, which comes with some conditionalities (in this case the need for a 'satisfactory' outcome on the exit strategy – defined as the preservation of the integrity of the assets installed under MTSP, leading to attraction of private sector participation), may be well intentioned. However, this type of development trajectory is akin to interventions in the realm of 'the social' in domestic politics, which, as Abrahamsen describes, help those in power to 'know', create and discipline their subjects (2003: 202). The World Bank's external staff believed that they 'knew' the Copperbelt, and that the water sector needed a single utility to be able to function optimally. It would not do that the local stakeholders had other considerations beyond the rationale of the '1CU' model. The Bank believed that it was right and, if the government was not willing to listen, then it would pay the price by losing out on the follow-on project, which was dependent on the Bank's satisfaction with the final decision of the exit strategy. This attitude coerced the government into taking a decision that it did not believe in, and brings into sharp relief the asymmetry in power in the relationship between donor and recipient.

The case study of the Copperbelt also, however, points to the fact that this type of relationship is not necessarily taken as a given by those on the receiving end. Indeed, this chapter shows that the subaltern continues to speak against postcolonial domination. The case study illustrates tensions between the local and the outside, demonstrating how the actions of those located 'in the local' may be prescribed by those 'on the outside', but not necessarily controlled. In other words, the stakeholders physically located in the Copperbelt were able to 'speak' against external decisions. This can be seen first in their overt actions, which mainly consisted of their consistent rejection of the single utility model. At no point did they ever hide the fact that they did not want the model. Neither did they hide their displeasure with the overt role of the World Bank. By being outspoken about this issue, although the local stakeholders did not entirely displace efficiency and economies of scale from the top of the political agenda, they also focused on ascribing to the debate a value that had nothing to do with economic rationality. Efficiency was important, but there were other things that were important too, such as self-determination, jobs and prestige, which the World Bank, by focusing on economic rationality, was inadvertently underplaying. By being vocal on the subject of their disapproval, the stakeholders also re-emphasised the importance of the decentralisation agenda, and the need for policy-makers to respect those whose job it was to make decisions about the future of the Copperbelt. As they constantly told the government and the World Bank, 'if you don't want to listen to us, then stop asking us what we want and go ahead and make your decision and just inform us'.

Further, the local stakeholders reacted by 'othering' and creating difference between themselves and the proponents of the single utility model. In hyping up the success of the AHC and Saur, the Bank actually created the difference between the AHC and the other commercial utilities, portraying the AHC as the 'normal', civilised 'us', and the other local utility companies as the 'abnormal others' who needed to be reformed and improved. By suggesting the merger of the other utility companies, the Bank was actually implying their normalisation into functional and efficient utility companies 'like AHC'. For the Bank, it was only rational that, if AHC was a success, others should follow, and not the other way round. This culminated in pitting the AHC management against the other three utility companies, leading to a high level of dislike of the AHC, and ultimately the other stakeholders' determination to isolate and annihilate it. In short, there was no room for the other commercial utilities and AHC to coexist. And, as far as the local stakeholders were concerned, AHC was not only the 'misfit', but also the 'foreigner', and thus had to be the one to go. Their reaction also 'othered' the Bank, Saur, the technicians in government and AHC, reinforcing the difference created by the Bank. Capitalising on the very fact that both the Bank and Saur were external agents, local stakeholders tagged them as 'intrusive foreigners', ignored their strengths and good intentions, and thus ultimately turned them into the problem. They thus turned the tables and became the 'normal us', whilst the Bank and its protégés became the 'abnormal others'. In this way, they moved the focus of the discussion from the contestation of rational ideas to an issue of 'outsiders and insiders'. To complete this stratagem, local stakeholders went further and effectively 'foreignised' the local proponents of the '1CU' – the technicians in the Ministry, as well as the AHC – labelling them 'sell-outs'. One particular phrase that was used quite openly throughout the discussions was that the proponents of '1CU' were the 'blue-eyed boys' of the World Bank – a term redolent with racial, 'othering' overtones. In this way, these intermediaries, who included ourselves, were portrayed as non-patriotic and more attuned to pleasing the white Washingtonians, rather than promoting the interests of their country. This is very similar to the attitudes and practices that developed in colonial Zambia, when the police and other civil servants were 'foreignised' and treated as belonging with the colonial masters (see, for instance, Luchembe 1992).

The opponents of '1CU' also brought to the fore the fundamental question of who has the right to make decisions, not only for the Copperbelt water sector, but also for Zambia in general. By focusing on othering, they managed to divert attention from a discussion of the technical to a focus on the emotive. In this way, they effectively took control of the unequal power relation between themselves and the World Bank, and used it to their own advantage. Ironically, the World Bank's main touted strength – being an organisation with wide international and foreign experience – became the stumbling block to building on the success of the AHC and indeed to the pursuance of the single utility model.

If the reaction of the local stakeholders was overt, it was also subtle. In this regard, after initially agreeing to what looked like '1CU', the final decision taken by the Minister in 2007 to do exactly what the World Bank did not want – namely to break up and share out the assets of the AHC amongst the three commercial utilities – is instructive. This action points to the fact that subalterns – be they 'common people', or national governments – can sometimes acquiesce with outside agencies just to 'keep the peace', but without surrendering their own long-term agenda. It is worth noting here that finding a short-term compromise with the Bank was critical, as the follow-on Bank operation in Lusaka was dependent on the Bank being satisfied with the outcome in the Copperbelt. The government therefore took the decision to merge AHC into Nkana to at least partially satisfy the requirements of the World Bank. Similarly, for the World Bank, the compromise position was necessary to safeguard its relationship with the government. It is possible to speculate, though, that the Bank may have taken this compromise position as a way of not giving in completely to government demands, but rather maintaining some semblance of having had an impact on a policy reform process. Part of the reason that the Bank and the technicians in the Ministry were comfortable with this compromise was that it ensured the mainte- nance of the integrity of the assets and systems installed through the MTSP. In the end, furthermore, the merger offered some hope that the single utility proposal could still become a reality, as an enlarged Nkana would come to show the logic of such a larger unit through economies of scale. It was also hoped that a suc- cessful, enlarged Nkana, without 'foreigners', would help remove some of the mistrust generated by the earlier involvement of the World Bank and Saur, both of which ceased to have a role in the Copperbelt water sector from December 2005.

However, two years later, with the new Bank operation effective in Lusaka,[10] the government, under pressure from the other two utilities, went against this agreement and did the very thing that had been so unpalatable to the Bank. This re-emphasises the point that the decision to merge AHC into Nkana had not necessarily dealt with the real concerns of the commercial utilities, but rather had been taken to satisfy the Bank. From a postcolonial point of view, the Minister's ultimate decision points to the kind of strategy described by James Scott (1985) in terms of 'onstage and offstage'. The 'onstage show' maximised symbolic com- pliance, orchestrated 'precisely in order to minimise compliance at the level of actual behaviour', that is, offstage (Scott 1985: 26; see also Wolputte 2004). It seems apparent that those who had the right to determine the future arrange- ments for the Copperbelt, that is, the local stakeholders, had actually decided in 2005 to keep the three utilities and split the assets of the AHC amongst them. The Bank, however, 'was not listening' and indeed coerced the government into taking an unpopular decision (the merger with Nkana). This raises an important question about who prescribes the objectives of foreign-funded projects. Who is responsible for setting the development agenda, and does the fact that a donor brings in finance entitle it to make policy prescriptions? This indeed is the practice in most donor-funded projects, but, as the case of the Copperbelt shows, it is neither necessarily welcome nor helpful. Those financing development programs in former colonial countries may wish to learn from this case of the World Bank.

Although the foregoing discussions have focused on highlighting the subaltern speaking, it is also worth commenting on the technicians in the ministry, the AHC and the local World Bank staff, who were in support of the single utility. This group tried unsuccessfully to push for the '1CU'. Their knowledge and argumentation were very much in line with those of the World Bank. These players speak to the postcolonial concept of 'hybridisation' because, by their adopted position, they were neither local nor foreign but both (Hoogvelt 2001; Abrahamsen 2003). Their role highlights the ambivalence of the dichotomy of 'the local' versus 'the foreign' expert. These are not objective categories, but rather are social constructs, through which the West continues to dominate the less developed parts of the world. The fact that we, the local proponents of the '1CU', were branded as sellouts and effectively 'foreign' was not reflective of the fact that we did not know or appreciate the value of the single utility model, or of private sector participation, before the arrival of the World Bank. This was knowledge that was available in the sector at the time and was known by all, including those who were against it. In other words, although it may have been an issue for political contention between the ideological left and right, there was nothing inherently 'local' or 'international' about the idea of private sector participation, or indeed a single utility. This is important for our current discussion, as it questions the validity and insistence of Western donors on bringing in technical assistance every time they bring some funding to a country.

Clearly, the focus of this chapter on the recent postcolonial history of the water sector in Zambia's Copperbelt has thrown light on a different way of looking at donor-engendered knowledge. It has, on the one hand, re-emphasised that policy-making is a highly political activity, which cannot rely on one single form of knowledge and is not necessarily dependent on one rationality. Rather, it involves a wide range of actors with multiple rationalities, interacting with, impacting upon and being impacted upon by others. There is no local or international knowledge that can be apolitical or purely objective. Whatever the policy reforms that are being proposed for places such as Zambia, those in the driving seat ought to be reminded that their actions are as much about what rationality to prioritise as they are about the shaping of society. Whether the aim is to get leaders to manage their utilities better, or to get more people served, the final outcome has a bearing on societal organisation and individual survival. Thus, key within reform debates must be a focus on substantive and procedural inputs that not only show evidence of positive societal improvements, but also have the political backing of the affected communities. Most importantly, reforms must seek ways of giving power back to the communities and countries being served. Surely the social shaping of any society cannot be left to outsiders. Rather, the start and end points must be the affected community, be it at local, regional or national level. Those who come to help should remember that they come to do exactly that – to help and not to take over.

## NOTES

1  The concept of 'transformative capacity' is borrowed from the work of Anthony Giddens (1987) on the nation-state and violence.
2  This idea of strategic conduct is borrowed from Anthony Giddens (1984), who defines it as the strategies of control within defined contextual boundaries. It implies a degree of choice and intentionality, and gives primacy to the practical and discursive consciousness of the human agent, although this does not mean that strategies develop outside of an institutional context containing structural constraints.
3  See Burdette (1988: 7–10); Hall (1965: 1–53); Hanna (1960: 23–40); Gelfand (1961); and Gann (1964) for discussions on the human geography of Zambia before and leading up to colonial rule.
4  The idea of forming one regional utility for the Copperbelt was also unsuccessfully attempted in the colonial era. Between February 1957 and April 1961, the then Ndola Municipal Council, together with the colonial administration, failed to get other local authorities in the region to form one regional utility (see Kazimbaya-Senkwe 2005 for more detailed discussion of this first attempt).
5  See Kazimbaya-Senkwe (2005) and Kazimbaya-Senkwe and Guy (2007) for more detailed exposition on the formation and operation of this dual system for water provision.
6  This view was expressed in interviews with officials from the local authorities, the new water utility companies, the Water and Sanitation Program, and the AHC-MMS. It must be noted that water services were not free but, rather, the miners had become used to not paying for the services as bills were generally deducted at source from their salaries.
7  In this section of the chapter we use quotations marked '. . .', which are not interview texts, but rather come from a recollection of the main arguments, based on our involvement with the case. We found this an effective way of relaying some of the key discussions without quoting people directly, as this would be a breach of confidentiality.
8  From mid-2000, new copper mines have sprung up in the North-Western Province bordering the Copperbelt, which are the main focus of new industrial growth in the country.
9  A country manager is the most senior officer of any local office of the World Bank, managing the affairs of the Bank in the country including staff and relations with the client government.
10  The World Bank is still engaged through the new Water Sector Improvement Project in Lusaka, whereas Saur left the country in 2006.

## REFERENCES

Abrahamsen, R. (2003) 'African Studies and the Postcolonial Challenge', *African Affairs* **102**, 189–210.

AHC-MMS (2005) *Mine Township Services Project IDA Credit N. 3386-ZA: Project Final Evaluation Report*. Lusaka, GRZ.

BCHOD (Brian Colqhuon, Hugh O' Donnell and Partners) with Ernst and Young (2003a) *Development of an Exit Strategy for the Mine Township Services Project (MTSP) Current Situation Analysis and Initial Analysis of Options Report (Vol. 1)*. Lusaka, GRZ.

BCHOD (Brian Colqhuon, Hugh O' Donnell and Partners) with Ernst and Young (2003b) *Development of an Exit Strategy for the Mine Township Services Project (MTSP) Stakeholders Workshop Report*. Lusaka, GRZ.

Burdette, M. M. (1988) *Zambia: Between Two Worlds*. Boulder, CO, Westview.

Chipungu, Samuel (1992) 'African Leadership under Indirect Rule in Colonial Zambia' in Chipungu, Samuel (Ed.) *Guardians in Their Time: Experiences of Zambians under Colonial Rule, 1890–1964*. London, Macmillan. pp. 50–73.

Crewe, E. and Harrison, E. (1998) *Whose Development?* London, Zed.

Escobar, A. (1995) *Encountering Development: The Making and Unmaking of the Third World*. Princeton, NJ, Princeton University Press.

Ferguson, J. (1999) *Expectations of Modernity: Myths and Meanings of Urban Life on the Zambian Copperbelt*. Berkeley, University of California Press.

Gardner, T. (1993) *The Present Economic Situation in Zambia and the Role of Privatization in Improving its Economy*. UNCTAD Discussion Paper 54, United Nations Conference on Trade and Development, Geneva.

Gann, L. H. (1964) *A History of Northern Rhodesia: Early Days to 1953*. London, Chatto and Windus.

Gelfand, M. (1961) *Northern Rhodesia in the Days of the Charter: A Medical and Social Study, 1878–1924*. Oxford, Basil Blackwell.

Giddens, A. (1984) *The Constitution of Society: Outline of the Theory of Structuration*. Cambridge, Polity Press.

Giddens, A. (1987) *The Nation State and Violence, Volume Two of a Contemporary Critique of Historical Materialism*. Cambridge, Polity Press.

GKW with Grant Thornton Associates Ltd (2003) *Review of Options for Private Sector Participation in the Provision of Water Supply and Sewerage Services on the Copperbelt*. Lusaka, GRZ.

Hall, R. (1965) *Zambia*. London, Pall Mall Press.

Hanna, A. J. (1960) *The Story of the Rhodesias and Nyasaland*. London, Faber.

Hansen, K. T. (1989) *Distant Companions: Servants and Employers in Zambia, 1900–1985*. Ithaca, NY, Cornell University Press.

Hoogvelt, A. (2001) *Globalization and the Postcolonial World: The New Political Economy of Development*. Basingstoke, Palgrave.

JanMohamed, A. R. (1985) 'The Economy of Manichean Allegory: The Function of Racial Difference in Colonialist Literature', *Critical Inquiry* **12**, 59–87.

Kazimbaya-Senkwe, B. (2005) 'The Social Construction of Access to Water in Zambia's Copperbelt: Beyond the Managerial Explanation for Inadequate Access'. PhD thesis. School of Architecture, Planning and Landscape, University of Newcastle Upon Tyne.

Kazimbaya-Senkwe, B. and Guy, S. (2007) 'Back to the Future? Privatisation and the Domestication of Water in the Copperbelt Province of Zambia, 1900–2000'. *Geoforum* **38**, 869–85.

Kothari, U. (2005) 'Authority and Expertise: The Professionalisation of International Development and the Ordering of Dissent', *Antipode* **37** (3), 425–46.

Loomba, Ania (1998) *Colonialism and Postcolonialism: The New Critical Idiom*. London, Routledge.

Luchembe, Chipasha (1992) 'Ethnic Stereotypes, Violence and Labour in early Colonial Zambia, 1889–1924', in Chipungu, Samuel (Ed.) *Guardians in Their Time: Experiences of Zambians under Colonial Rule, 1890–1964*. London, Macmillan. pp. 30–41.

Marcos (2000) 'Do Not Forget Ideas are Also Weapons'. Available at *Le Monde Diplomatique*: http://mondediplo.com/2000/10/13marcos. Accessed 22 July 2009.

Menard, Claude and Clarke, George (2000) *Reforming the Water Supply in Abidjan Cote d'Ivoire. Policy Research Working Paper*. Washington DC, World Bank.

Menard, Claude, Clarke, George and Zuluaga, Ana Maria (2000) *The Welfare Effects of*

*Private Sector Participation in Guinea's Urban Water Supply. Policy Research Working Paper.* Washington DC, World Bank.

Mudimbe, V. Y. (1988) *The Invention of Africa.* Bloomington, IN, Indiana University Press.

Parpart, J. (1995) 'Deconstructing the Development Expert', in Marchand M. and Parpart J. (Eds.) *Feminism, Postmodernism and Development.* London, Routledge. pp. 221–43.

Qotole, M. (2001) 'Early African Urbanization in Cape Town: Windermere in the 1940s and 1950s', *African Studies* **60** (1), 107–17.

Rakodi, C. (1997) 'Global Forces, Urban Change and Urban Management in Africa', in Carole Rakodi (Ed.) *The Urban Challenge in Africa: Growth and Management of its Large Cities.* Tokyo, The United Nations University. pp. 17–73.

Said, E. (1979) *Orientalism.* New York, Vintage.

Said, E. (1994) *Culture and Imperialism.* London, Vintage.

Scott, J. C. (1985) *Weapons of the Weak: Everyday Forms of Peasant Resistance.* New Haven, Yale University Press.

Simon, D. (1997) 'Urbanization, Globalization and Economic Crisis in Africa', in Carole Rakodi (Ed.) *The Urban Challenge in Africa: Growth and Management of its Large Cities.* Tokyo, The United Nations University. pp. 74–108.

Spivak, G. C. (1985) 'Can the Subaltern Speak? Speculation on Widow-Sacrifice', *Wedge* **7/8** (Winter/Spring), 120–30.

WSP (Water and Sanitation Program) (2006) *Getting Africa on Track to Meet the MDGs on Water and Sanitation: A Status Overview of Sixteen African Countries.* Nairobi, AMCOW.

Wolputte, S. V. (2004) 'Subject Disobedience: The Colonial Narrative and Native Counterworks in Northwestern Namibia, c.1920–1975', *History and Anthropology* **15** (2), 151–73.

World Bank (1994) *Zambia Poverty Assessment: Vol. IV, Urban Sector Services.* Washington DC, Human Resources Division, Southern Africa Department, Africa Regional Office.

Yeoh, Brenda (1996) *Contesting Space: Power Relations and the Urban Built Environment in Colonial Singapore.* New York, Oxford University Press.

# CHAPTER 10

# WOMEN'S SAFETY AUDITS AND WALKING SCHOOL BUSES

## THE DIFFUSION/DE-FUSION OF TWO RADICAL PLANNING IDEAS[1]

### CAROLYN WHITZMAN AND JANA PERKOVIC

## INTRODUCTION

The purpose of this chapter is to look at how certain planning ideas become internationally recognized and utilized as institutional policies and practices in a rapid manner, often to the detriment of their original intent. We will be focusing on the history of two recent participatory planning tools. The Women's Safety Audit Guide was developed in 1989 by a feminist initiative funded by local government, the Metropolitan Toronto Women's Action Committee on Public Violence Against Women and Children (METRAC). The Walking School Bus developed out of a short passage in *Towards an Eco-City: Calming the Traffic*, a book written by David Engwicht, an Australian urban designer and ecological activist, in 1992. Both ideas were rapidly adopted by community organizations and governments around the world. Both were characterized by strong emancipatory potential, and driven by the wish to challenge the status quo by empowering a group of people, who were seen as being barred from fully enjoying their rights as citizens to equal access to public space. But at some point, and in some settings, the initial radicalism of these ideas got lost.

This chapter is a step backward from two separate pieces of research that we have undertaken over the past two years. The first is a study of where and how women's safety audits have been effective internationally, funded by UN-Habitat and carried out by a group of feminist researchers and activists gathering under the banner Women in Cities International (WICI 2008; Whitzman *et al.* 2009). The second looks at institutional barriers and enablers to children's independent mobility, the freedom of those under 18 years to move around in public space without adult accompaniment, in Victoria, Australia. As part of this research, funded by the Volvo Research and Education Foundation under the aegis of the Australasian Centre for the Governance and Management of Urban Transportation (GAMUT), we have investigated the Walking School Bus program as one potential policy tool (Whitzman and Pike 2007).

We seek to answer three questions in this comparative study of the diffusion of the two ideas. First, what was the original intent of these tools, what problem(s) were they addressing, and how can they be considered "radical"? Second, how, where, and why did these tools spread and become institutionally entrenched in cities and countries all over the world? Third, in what circumstances were these participatory planning tools effective in empowering women and children? Did they have any impacts on the built, social, or policy environments of the places where they were used, and did they increase use of these public spaces?

Ideas gain power as they are formalized into policy tools and used as guides or guidelines. They become practices through being implemented in similar ways over a period of time. They become policies through being taken up by governments and community organizations in a formalized manner, and they become programs when organizations are funded to provide certain services related to the idea. In this way, ideas become a weapon in the power game in which planners are deeply implicated, through their role as "experts" on the built environment (see Ananya Roy's chapter in the present book).

Several of the contributors to this book suggest ways in which ideas become transformed as they are formalized and internationalized. Roy (Chapter 2) points out the usual tendency for issues such as poverty to be seen as local, rather than societal, national, or global challenges. She also describes differences between consensus on a grassroots idea in its place of origin, and the globalized consensus of the more powerful actors who may disseminate – and enforce – the programs and policies that arise from these ideas. André Sorensen (Chapter 6) also calls attention to the policy entrepreneurs who deploy ideas politically, refining and reinterpreting ideas as they travel from one governance setting to another. Both of these authors, as well as Dominic Stead and colleagues (Chapter 8), describe how social and economic situations in "lending" and "borrowing" countries (or cities or regions) might be very different.

Transformation and adaptation are essential and may be beneficial. Having said that, the emphasis of this chapter is explicitly normative, focusing on the difficult question of whether the ideas described had the potential to empower and change social relations, and whether they lost these values as they became institutionalized planning practices.

## PLANNING PRACTICES AS POLICY DIFFUSION AND DE-FUSION

Policy diffusion has been defined as "any pattern of successive adoptions of a policy innovation" (Eyestone 1977, cited in Stone 2001: 4). Studies of diffusion often identify not only how ideas, practices, policies, and programs are adopted sequentially or successively, but also the patterns by which they spread, and why policy ideas are adopted in some places but not others. Such studies have been criticized for being fascinated by the process of diffusion rather the content of the policies, for providing apolitical and neutral depictions of the "hows" and "wheres" of policies, rather than exploring the "whys" (Stone 2001: 4). For this reason, Diane Stone, a policy studies scholar, prefers the term "policy transfer." This concept would cover two processes. The first is the voluntary process of "systemically pinching ideas" in the hope that an innovative policy in one place will work in a different spatial context. The second is its obverse, the compulsion of less powerful political actors to undertake a policy by a more powerful actor, such as the International Monetary Fund or the World Bank (Stone 1999: 52).

As Stone points out, "both agency and structural factors will condition the degree of transfer and the character of implementation" (1999: 54). Agents such as newly elected governments, powerful policy units and lobbyists, or community organizations can create opportunities or constraints for the adoption of a policy from elsewhere. Conversely, structural issues such as economic recessions, natural or human disasters, or the nature of governance or society in a particular place shape the direction and character of policy transfer. In particular, conditions of uncertainty – when political, economic, social, or environmental change becomes unavoidable – are times when policy paradigms shift rapidly (Stone 1999: 54–5).

A final point made by Stone is important for an understanding of the diffusion of planning policy. This is her emphasis on both the macro-level and the micro-level aspects of policy transfer. The study of policy transfer "problematises the division between the national and international" (Stone 1999: 54). We would argue that there is an equal scope to include the local in this equation, particularly when policies "jump scale" from the local to national or international governance, as opposed to the more common "top-down" conceptualization of policy development (see Whitzman 2008: 142–3 for a discussion in relation to violence prevention).

As Stephen Ward (2000) discusses, the study of international planning exchanges can be seen to have explored three major aspects of diffusion. First, the mechanisms of diffusion: key personalities, milieux, and intergovernmental actions. Second, the extent to which ideas and practices are changed through diffusion; that is, how and why the application of the same idea in different settings leads to differences in its implementation. Finally, the fundamental causation of diffusion can be analyzed, in particular the tension between structure and agency also discussed by Stone.

In this context, the origins of the planning profession have been seen as a reaction to a significant structural change in society: the rapid onset of urbanization in Europe and North America, and the social and environmental impacts of this urbanization, throughout the nineteenth century (Ward 2000; Hall 2002). The urban planning profession has always been characterized by the tensions between utopian visions and utilitarian pragmatism, and between thinking globally and acting locally. Because the nature of this change was global, virtually all early planning "works and the ideas they contained were also part of an emergent international discourse of planning" (Ward 2000: 41). Visionary ideas were rapidly disseminated through conferences, magazines, and particular individuals; in recent years the internet has increased the rapidity of this process. However, the intent of the pioneers of planning has often been lost in the process of dissemination and formalization. The thesis of Peter Hall's history of planning in the twentieth century is that the radical and communitarian ideas that informed Ebenezer Howard and Patrick Geddes, based in the local self-governance ideas of anarchists such as Bakunin and Kropotkin, became "thoroughly diluted, or, as the faithful would say, traduced" as they spread globally (Hall 2002: 116).

A recent case study of the diffusion of Ecologically Sustainable Design guidelines into the regeneration area of Hulme in Manchester found a wide variability in the adoption of innovations. Barriers that resulted in a watering down of guidelines included conflicts with current bureaucratic standards, perceptions of market acceptability, and the previous education and work practices of principal actors (Symes and Pauwels 1999). Sorensen, in this book, describes how "during the processes of translating, disseminating, and adopting urban sustainability ideas into policy in Japan, the issues of intergenerational, transfrontier, and social equity that are such a central part of sustainability debates elsewhere have been almost entirely lost" (Chapter 6: p. 135). Recent critiques of the application of Creative City concepts in the Netherlands (Kooijman and Romein 2007) and in Darwin, Australia (Luckman et al. 2007) suggest that "the more neoliberalised version of creative city thinking, which emphasizes competing with large international cities for 'glamour industries' and mobile transnational professionals" has triumphed over a more inclusive approach that would "present alternative ways of imagining the cultural and economic futures of cities" (Luckman et al. 2007, unpaginated). Unidirectional dissemination of ideas from rich to poor nations, the loss of social justice goals from the focus of environmental and economic planning ideas, and the influence both of agents such as "policy entrepreneurs" and of the structural forces of societal norms are common themes in this literature on the diffusion of planning ideas and practices. So how have the ideas about women's safety audits and walking buses been generated? How and why have they been transferred, and how far have they retained their radical edge?

## WOMEN'S SAFETY AUDITS

The Women's Safety Audit Guide, developed in 1989, is a simple set of questions intended to support local activists in identifying safe and unsafe places, and to suggest how unsafe places can be improved (METRAC 1989; Kallus and Churchman 2004; WICI 2008). It is intended to support the prevention of violence against women in public and semi-public (e.g. university campus) space, through drawing on the expertise of those women who use the space in order to formulate recommendations that can then influence environmental change.

A public attitude survey in 1986 commissioned by the Toronto Transit Commission (TTC) found that 45 percent of women, compared with 13 percent of men, felt uncomfortable using TTC vehicles after dark (Whitzman 2002a: 101–2). The TTC worked with METRAC and the Toronto police force to improve the transit system's 60 subway stations in terms of safety and security. METRAC also consulted with the City of Toronto in developing recommendations to make High Park, the largest park in central Toronto, safer, after a survey in 1987 found that twice as many men as women used the park during the day, rising to three times as many men in the evening. To accomplish these two projects, METRAC developed a checklist, based on workshops with women's organizations and the literature on sexual assault in public and semi-public places. Although Crime Prevention Through Environmental Design (CPTED) principles were cited, the authors were critical of the "top-down" and gender-neutral perspective of these experts in their focus on "designing out crime." As the Women's Design Service, who later adapted the Women's Safety Audit Guide in the UK, summarized, designing out crime recommendations "often meant losing a vital ingredient for developing pleasant surroundings, namely an understanding of local needs and contexts" (Berglund 2007: 42). Traditional CPTED emphasis on the expertise of police officers and planners often meant a standardized and risk-averse approach to public spaces that "created soulless expanses of concrete," over-reliance on closed circuit television, and a reinforcement of women as helpless and dependent victims instead of citizens with both rights to influence public space and local expertise to suggest the right solutions (Berglund 2007: 42; see also Wekerle and Whitzman 1995: 12–13). METRAC emphasized that preventing violence against women also involved other aspects of social change, including judicial reform, media portrayals, the provision of services such as rape crisis centers and shelters, and attitudes of individuals. However, safety audits were seen as "wonderfully concrete and practical" ways to change the world in a small but significant localized manner (METRAC 1989).

The diffusion of the Women's Safety Audit Guide was assisted by an efflorescence of women in local government initiatives, within Canada and internationally, in the early 1990s. The Canadian government, and particularly the French-speaking government of Quebec, wished to emulate the perceived successes of European countries in establishing crime prevention initiatives in urban policy. By the mid-1990s, there were women's safety initiatives in several Canadian mid-sized cities, as well as one rural and one regional initiative (in British Columbia and Quebec respectively), and urban safety initiatives with at least some feminist input in the majority of Canada's ten largest cities (Andrew 1995; Whitzman 2002a: 100–1). Less than five years after its development, the Ottawa Women's Action Centre Against Violence was able to identify 69 organizations across Canada that had carried out safety audits, predominantly tertiary educational institutions, community organizations ranging from women's groups to residents' associations, and local governments (WACAV 1995: 6).

The international lines of diffusion were also influenced by the Canadian National Crime Prevention Council, which was committed to international linkages (NCPC 1995: 6). By 1994, there was an International Centre for the Prevention of Crime in Montreal, with support from six national governments (Whitzman 2008: 139). Women's Safety Audits were publicized at an Organization for Economic Cooperation and Development (OECD) conference on Women and Cities in Paris in 1994, and also at a conference on women's safety in Montreal in 2002 (Whitzman 2008: 141). The European Forum for Urban Safety organized a conference on women's safety in 2001, and the UN-Habitat Safer Cities Programme explicitly supported safety audits and gender mainstreaming in its work after its establishment in 2001 (Shaw and Andrew 2005: 299).

In England, several local governments began to use women's safety audits by the early 1990s. Urban regeneration programs, with a formal requirement of community consultation, became fertile ground for safety audits. The Women's Design Service, a London-based feminist planning consultancy, published *Making Safer Places: A Resource Book for Neighbourhood Safety Audits* in 1998, and received grants to work with women on safety audit projects in urban regeneration areas (Cavanagh 1998; Berglund 2007). Meanwhile, from 1991, the Australian state government of Victoria supported local government-led safety audits through its Victorian Community Council Against Violence, directly inspired by METRAC (VCCAV 1995), and from 1993 the New Zealand government supported local government safety audits in 60 councils through funding tied to coordinated community-based action (Whitzman 2008: 132).

According to Anne Michaud, the former coordinator of Montreal's Women and the City Committee, the Safety Audit Guide dissemination "followed different routes according to . . . language" (15 May 2008, personal communication). The French version of the METRAC guide, adapted and translated by the City of Montreal in 1993, was distributed in Europe (particularly France and Belgium) and French-speaking African countries. This was the version translated into various European languages by the European Forum on Urban Safety, and into Spanish for use in Latin American countries through a project sponsored by UNIFEM (United Nations Fund for Women). Anne attended several conferences and training sessions in Europe, Africa, and Latin America, which further disseminated the Women's Safety Audit Guide. By the time of our recent research in 2008, 69 articles and reports had been identified, and 43 organizations, from every continent, had engaged in women's safety audits (WICI 2008).

This rapid dissemination of the tool raises three questions. First, were safety audits effective in organizing women (and other disempowered groups) to improve the built environment and gain more of a say in decision-making around planning? Second, is there any evidence that changes, if they occurred, led to more equitable use of public space? And, finally, did the emphasis on women as both a vulnerable group and "experts of experience" remain as the safety audit was disseminated?

Certainly, a number of the early women's safety audits in Toronto led to immediate changes. The TTC's report on improving its subway system led to increased lighting and use of convex mirrors in passageways, designated waiting areas in all stations with emergency contact systems, appropriate staff training, and a poster campaign, while TTC continued their consulting with women's planning advocates for planning new subway stations (Whitzman 2002a: 103). As a result of the DisAbled Women's Network safety audit, a particularly inaccessible paratransit pickup stop near Toronto City Hall was eventually relocated to a safer spot with an emergency telephone adjacent (Whitzman 2002a: 109). In 1992, a group of women living in the Blake-Boultbee public housing project organized a safety audit (reproduced in Wekerle and Whitzman 1995, Appendix 2), which led to improvements to the entrances and common spaces of the buildings (Whitzman 2002a: 109). METRAC recently estimated that over 100 neighbourhoods in Toronto have been audited since 2000, and hundreds of people have been trained to lead audits, including "women from various ethno-racial communities, newcomers, disability communities, LGBTQ [lesbian, gay, bisexual, transgendered, or queer] communities, street-involved communities and youth" (Narina Nagra, METRAC Safety Director, 15 May 2008, personal communication). The audit guide has also been adapted for use on tertiary education campuses, for primary school children (including translation into five languages spoken by new migrants to Canada), and for young people in secondary schools.

The Women's Design Service has reported many specific improvements as a result of safety audits in London, Manchester, and Bristol, ranging from improved lighting and signage in parks and streets to the redesign of pedestrian under-passes and housing projects. In places as diverse at Petrovadosk in Russia, Dar es Salaam in Tanzania, and Mumbai in India, women's safety audits have led to concrete improvements both to the physical environment and to the management of public and semi-private (housing project) spaces (Whitzman et al. 2009). In several Canadian cities, work with particular groups of women under-represented in political decision-making – aboriginal, new migrant, and/or disabled – has been supported by the Canadian government (Shaw and Andrew 2005) and, in the UK, the Women's Design Service also focused on low-income and black women in their audits (Berglund 2007). In these diverse settings, the original METRAC Safety Audit Guide has been adapted for local use, but its origins are acknowl-edged and its feminist analysis remains.

The recent evaluation (WICI 2008) as well as two other meta-evaluations of safety audits (WACAV 1995; VCCAV 1995) came to similar conclusions. At their best, safety audits can involve a variety of people in a variety of settings, although an emphasis on diverse women as leaders remains. Audits can help develop good relationships between community organizations and local government, and they can help to bring about tangible changes to the built environment. However, there were often difficulties in involving the most vulnerable groups of women (home-less and low-income women, young women, "visible" minorities, people with disabilities); changes are difficult to implement unless there is a local government program with specific dollars earmarked for improvement; and audits sometimes are not grounded in a bigger picture of longer-term violence prevention. Perhaps most importantly, it is rare to document or evaluate physical environment changes made as a result of audits, and not one evaluation has shown increased use of or comfort in public space as a result of a women's safety audit or audit campaign. Given that the original intent was to contribute, in a small but specific manner, to the reduction of violence against women and insecurity in public space, this is highly troublesome.

One of the equivocal results of the dissemination of women's safety audits is how quickly they lost their gender focus, including in their city of origin. The initial 1989 safety audit of Toronto's High Park was ignored, and it took five years, a "professional" consultant's report, and an erasure of gender-specific language to effect improved lighting, signage, and activity-generation measures (Whitz-man 2002b). This loss of a gendered voice was mirrored around the world. Increasing responsibilities and decreasing funding streams in local government, disagreements among campaigners against violence against women over the gap between levels of violence in public and private space, and the short-term nature of community activism all led to the decline of municipal women's safety initiatives by the early 2000s (Shaw and Andrew 2005). Anne Michaud recalls that in communities without strong women's groups it became easy for police or gender-neutral crime prevention organizations to "act in a traditional 'protector' paternalistic pattern," wherein safety audits became "opportunities for the police to show women dangerous places to avoid" (15 May 2008, personal communication).

The European Forum for Urban Safety published *Guidance on Local Safety Audits: A Compendium of International Practice* in 2007. Despite years of gender mainstreaming efforts in Europe, the 135-page report does not mention the origin of the safety audit tool, ignores any women's safety audits in its 20 international case studies, and makes exactly one mention of gender in the entire document, including "women" along with "ethnic minorities, young people, homeless people, and businesses" amongst "particular perspectives" that might be involved. Despite the need for community "input," the guide adds that "Communities are not unfailingly correct in their assessment of problems or identification of responses. It is therefore always desirable to integrate community-based perspectives with 'external' technical analysis" (Husain 2007: 35).

In this transformed (and traduced) vision, safety audits become an agent of tokenistic consultation, rather than taking local expertise and leadership seriously. The autonomy, empowerment, and gender-specific intent of the original Women's Safety Audit are entirely abandoned.

In summary, the Women's Safety Audit provides an example of rapid international diffusion of a participatory planning tool. In a number of examples, the emancipatory intent was maintained and even enhanced through adaptation of the safety audit to particular groups, locations, and circumstances. However, in many other examples, the gender focus of the safety audit was lost, as was the emphasis on empowering and listening to the voices of the people most affected by violence and insecurity. It is impossible to say, given the limited evidence, whether safety audits have made women safer or more secure in the places where they have been used.

## THE WALKING SCHOOL BUS

The development of the Walking School Bus (WSB) provides a more extreme example of a simple idea for radical change that quickly became diluted, in this case by bureaucratic hurdles and risk management concerns. Originating as a holistic measure to tackle public health issues, strengthen local communities, reduce car use, and create positive patterns of independent mobility among children, stressing their rights as citizens to public space, the WSB quickly devolved into a top-down, inflexible program, thoroughly stripped of its emancipatory potential. Like the Women's Safety Audit, the purported goals of encouraging independent exploration and empowerment of a subject group in public space have all too often been forgotten.

The WSB began as a modest proposal put forward towards the end of urban designer David Engwicht's *Towards an Eco-City: Calming the Traffic* (1992):

> Parents, police, teachers and authorities map where each child lives in relation to the school and the safest routes for these children to go to and from school. Through local papers and other media outlets, volunteers (including senior citizens) are asked to become Walking Bus Drivers. These "drivers" walk a set route, much like a school bus, collecting children along the route and delivering them safely to school ... A coloured line can be painted on the side of the road to indicate where it runs and murals painted on the footpath at the various stops. A trolley can be pulled that would hold raincoats or school ports in the case of rain ... I am sure this scheme would do more than simply see children to school safely and allow parents to stop driving them. If senior citizens were encouraged to take part it would promote a wonderful sense of neighbourhood, especially when so many children today do not have grandparents living close by. It could be the start of a growing sense of place and some invaluable exchanges.
>
> (ibid.: 143–4)

Although there has been growing concern in many countries over the correlation between child obesity, exercise, neighbourhood walkability, and a sense of community, Engwicht was also responding to more general concerns about children's independent mobility. Hillman *et al.* (1990: 42) found that the proportion of seven- and eight-year-olds in the UK allowed to travel to school on their own had fallen from 80 percent in 1971 to 9 percent in 1990. In the United States the percentage of children and adolescents living within one mile of their school who used active modes of transport (walking, cycling, public transport) dropped from 87 percent to below 15 percent between 1969 and 2005 (Martin and Carlson 2005: 2161). This decline in children's autonomy was particularly acute in English-speaking developed countries. Whereas 80 percent of German 10-year-olds were allowed to travel alone to places other than school in 1990, only 38 percent of 10-year-olds in the UK and 34 percent of 10-year-olds in Sydney, Australia were allowed the same freedom (Tranter and Pawson 2001: 41).

As was the case with the Women's Safety Audit, several countries became interested in locally based initiatives to improve a vulnerable group's access to public space in the early 1990s. The Safe Routes to School Program, pioneered by the national government in Denmark as part of an ambitious road safety program in the 1980s stressing traffic calming and road engineering improvements, was soon adapted for use in North America, the UK, and Australia. According to King-ham and Ussher (2005: 502), the first WSB program was established in Canada in 1996. David Engwicht mentioned the idea to "a group of 'radical bureaucrats' and activists at a late night session in a Toronto pub" after a conference (15 May 2008, personal communication). After some research, WSB were independently piloted in three Toronto schools, growing into a comprehensive, community-based initiative, the Active & Safe Routes to School program (Jacky Kennedy, 29 September 2008, personal communication). In other countries, the WSB quickly emerged as one of the most popular elements of a Safe Routes to School program (McMillan 2005: 443), sometimes being promoted as a stand-alone solution to the complex issues of neighbourhood walkability, social interaction, and children's autonomous exploration.

In the UK, the WSB was pioneered in 1998 in Hertfordshire (Kearns and Col-lins 2003: 199). By 2001, in a survey by the Department for Transport, half of the surveyed 102 local authorities had set up WSB, and a further 31 planned to do so. By January 2002, there were 68 WSB in 41 schools in the county, although the numbers dropped to 26 programs in 22 schools the year after (Mackett *et al.* 2005: 4). Diffusion in Australia has varied greatly by state. The WSB program was piloted in 2001 by the Victorian Health Promotion Foundation (VicHealth) in four local governments with promising results, and, between 2001 and 2007, 58 of the 79 local councils in Victoria received funds to implement the program (VicHealth 2007a, unpaginated). In Western Australia, there were 23 schools participating in the WSB in 2007, with 37 routes involving 540 participants and 131 volunteers (DPI 2007, unpaginated). Every other state and territory is encouraging WSB initiatives at the time of writing, and the federal government has recently published a guide to WSB (YWCA 2007; DTEI 2007; DET 2007; Hobart City Council 2007; Queensland Transport 2007). In New Zealand, WSB were pioneered in Christchurch in 1999, after a local government officer heard about them at an Australian conference (Kearns and Collins 2003). By 2001, there was national funding for schools participating in the program, and, in June 2006, Land Trans-port NZ recorded approximately 330 WSB in about 120 schools, with over 4,000 registered users (Land Transport NZ 2008, unpaginated).

Although evaluations of the program are rare in North America, a number of studies in the UK, Australia, and New Zealand report equivocal findings in terms of impacts on the built and social environments. Engwicht sees some positive examples of the WSB as an "intermediate step" in Brisbane, reducing car traf-fic and leading to traffic improvements in areas where children previously had little independent mobility (2003, unpaginated). In a suburb of Melbourne, Aus-tralia, the parents running a WSB worked with their local council to successfully advocate for an improved pedestrian crossing at a busy road after children were timed taking 30 seconds to cross the road, whereas the "green man" showed for only 20 seconds (VicHealth 2007b).

Mackett *et al.* (2003: 6) have found that, in England, children are twice as likely to report positive social aspects of WSB as their parents, although both report greater knowledge of and friendships within neighbourhoods as a result of WSB implementation. English evaluations show no decrease in local car traffic: parents may walk their children to school, then return to use their cars (Mackett *et al.* 2003: 180). Two New Zealand evaluation studies have found both parents and children agreeing on the social and community benefits of WSB schemes, with children saying they want to walk to other places as a result of improved fitness or knowledge of their neighbourhood (Kearns and Collins 2003; Kingham and Ussher 2005). However, the Kearns and Collins (2003) evaluation points out that adult-dependent mobility is reinforced in WSB initiatives through the imposition of adult rules, which are inimical to children's independent exploration.

Bureaucratic formalization of the WSB, necessary for rapid diffusion through program funding, led to the pragmatic abandonment of many creative and unstructured aspects of the original idea. In the words of Canadian WSB activist Jacky Kennedy:

> [Soon after the pilot project] we discovered that parents today have become disconnected from their communities, that they don't trust their neighbours and, unless we dealt with safety issues and started walking programs in small steps, a Walking School Bus was a mistake.
>
> (29 September 2008, personal communication)

As a result, examples of extreme risk-mitigation rules abound in WSB implementation guides. Children are often required to hold hands or walk in twos, or are not allowed to distance themselves from the Bus. The UK Department for Transport (DT 2006) suggests that all children sign a "pupil promise" in which they agree to behave appropriately and follow the supervisors' instructions; in Australia it is called a "passenger pledge" (VicHealth 2003). Fluorescent vests or sashes for all children are required in the UK (DT 2006) and are commonplace in New Zealand (Christchurch City Council 2008; Kingham and Ussher 2005). WSB "drivers" have to wear ID, a whistle, and a vest in Canada (Informa Market Research 2001). Drivers in the UK, Canada, and Australia are required to pass police checks, and undergo training in road safety, duty of care, and emergency procedures (DT 2006; Hobart City Council 2004; Informa Market Research 2001). Routes often need to be safety audited by adults beforehand, taking away the freedom for children to choose where to walk. WSB schemes often require approvals from school boards, city councils, and police divisions before they can begin (ASRTS 2006), and local governments sometimes require public liability insurance in case of an accident (DT 2006; DET 2008). Drivers in Tasmania, Australia need to carry an Emergency Response Plan, the contents of which they need to be familiar with (Hobart City Council 2007).

WSB were intended to cut down on children's dependence on parents driving them to school, thus promoting positive environmental benefits for the community and health benefits for the children. However, several vital elements of Engwicht's original formulation were lost in the translation from idea to funded program. First, the community development notion of involving senior citizens and other people unrelated to the children quickly faded away, partly because of safety concerns about "stranger danger." Engwicht himself attacks the increasing formalization of WSB as an "evolutionary cul de sac" on his website in 2003:

> The moment the Walking Bus turns into an official program, it creates some significant difficulties, particularly in litigious and risk-averse cultures. One organizer told me that when she launched the Walking Bus Program she had over 100 people volunteer as drivers. But by the time they had completed their compulsory training and submitted to exhaustive background checks she only had 3 drivers left.
>
> (2003, unpaginated)

Second, the creative "reclaiming the street" aspect of painting murals and lines along footpaths largely disappeared. Perhaps the most damaging loss was the emphasis on children's independent mobility, the right of children to use public space as autonomous citizens. In the 1992 book in which Engwicht discussed the WSB – one among 'many zany ideas I threw up as seeds' (2003, unpaginated) – he talked about the value of streets as places, rather than as movement corridors:

> This freedom to explore the local neighborhood is probably the key ingredient in children developing a feeling that they belong to a neighborhood, a place. It not only gives them an opportunity to develop relationships with people of all ages who live in their neighborhood, it gives them an opportunity to develop a relationship with the placeness of their physical environment. Robbing children of a sense of place robs them of the very essence of life.
>
> (Engwicht 1992: 40)

VicHealth, the health promotion funder of the Victorian Walking School Bus program in Victoria, Australia, recently decided not to invest any further funds in the WSB as a stand-alone program, because it is too structured and inflexible, there is too high a turnover of parents and project officers, and, most importantly, there is little evidence that the WSB leads to increased children's independent mobility or physical activity in the majority of sites (unpublished "Walking School Bus Review," December 2007).

The WSB provides a stark case study of rapid international diffusion of an idea, accompanied by loss of the original idea's radical intent. Engwicht intended for the WSB to be one of many mechanisms by which children "reclaimed the street" and the neighborhood as a place for independent exploration. The ways in which the WSB became institutionalized as a program led to no change, or perhaps even a negative change, in children's autonomy over their movement in public space.

## CONCLUSION

In this chapter, we have described two recent examples of ideas that were rapidly disseminated internationally. In many ways, the stories of their dissemination fit in with the theoretical model described in the beginning of the paper. Like Garden Cities, Ecologically Sustainable Design, and Creative Cities, Women's Safety Audits and the Walking School Bus spread rapidly, in part because they were simple ideas that promised readily transferable answers to problems experienced internationally. Policy transfer of the Women's Safety Audit took place unidirectionally among rich countries and from rich to poor nations, although there was considerable transformation of the tool as it spread internationally. The WSB is still largely a rich, Anglo-nation program, although it is being piloted in South Africa (Roger Behrens, 18 May 2008, personal communication).

Both ideas attempt localized responses to societal problems, in this case increasing insecurity and avoidance of public space. Both ideas were intended to promote autonomy and empowerment of a subject group (women in one case, children in the other) over dependence and reliance on authority. Yet, as the literature suggests, these social justice goals have sometimes (although not always) been lost in the process of dissemination. The iterative nature of the dissemination – people learning about ideas second- and third-hand – may have had a negative impact on the original intent, as did the nature of its early institutionalization into governmental and quasi-governmental policies and programs. This was particularly true of the WSB, for which institutionalization was accompanied by extremely rigid risk-prevention mechanisms that emphasized children's dependence over their autonomy as citizens and users of public space.

"Jumping scale" from local to international programs was not necessarily the problem: UN-Habitat's Safer Cities Programme maintained a focus on gender as it incorporated the Women's Safety Audit Guide as a tool, although the European

Forum on Urban Safety eventually abandoned this. However, the agency of particular individuals as policy entrepreneurs – trainers or disseminators – appears to have been key, constituting the difference between Anne Michaud providing "train the trainer" workshops on women's safety audits in African cities, and David Engwicht suggesting an idea, then watching as the implementation ran off in a completely different direction.

Again, transferring an idea across contexts was not necessarily a bad thing: in many cases the Women's Safety Audit Guide was improved by adaptation to local circumstances in English regeneration areas or Dar es Salaam slums. But not acknowledging the origin of an idea, as appears to have happened in many cases, is a good indicator that its inventors' original intent was about to be transformed. The notion of policy transfer as compulsion can be applied to these case studies: several schools may have agreed to adopt the WSB program in order to get funding, but then have been bound by the arcane rules that proliferated over its implementation. Similarly, the Women's Safety Audit (or, in some cases, a more generic community safety audit) quickly became an approved tool, supported by funding from national governments in England and New Zealand, state governments in Australia, and UN-Habitat as an international governance body. Certainly, the processes of institutionalization and bureaucratization made it more difficult for these programs to support autonomy, which was the intent of these two tools. Independent evaluations of WSB initiatives have shown that, although they may increase children's and adults' friendships with other people in their communities, they have by and large failed to increase children's independent use of, and comfort in, public space. Given national and international funding and training support for the Women's Safety Audit, there needs to be similar scrutiny in discovering whether its implementation leads to increased women's use of, and comfort in, public space.

The Women's Safety Audit Guide and the WSB concept were both intended by their original authors as grassroots tools to educate individuals and communities about "reclaiming the street." In a larger sense, they were intended to support active participation in local governance and citizenship by providing particular subject groups – women and children – with a means to promote their greater access to public space and to the decisions surrounding the use of public space. They were intended to promote mobility, autonomy, and self-determination. Although there is nothing sacred about the original intent of an idea, the constant theme of the communitarian origins of planning practices being lost or transformed into authoritarian practices deserves continuing scrutiny from scholars, as planning ideas continue to circle the globe.

## NOTE

1 The authors would like to thank David Engwicht, Anne Michaud, Jacky Kennedy, Roger Behrens, and Narina Nagra for generously sharing their information on the Walking School Bus and Women's Safety Audit Guide. The Volvo Research and Education Foundation, through GAMUT (the Australasian Centre for the Governance and Management of Urban Transport), provided funding for Jana's research assistance in relation to the dissemination of the Walking School Bus. A group of people associated with Women in Cities International (http://www.womenincities.org) provided the authors with further information on women's safety audits: Margaret Shaw, Caroline Andrew, Fran Klodawsky, Marisa Canuto, and Kathryn Travers. Research on the dissemination of women's safety audits has been supported by a grant to Women in Cities International from UN-Habitat.

## REFERENCES

Andrew, C. 1995. "Getting Women's Issues on the Municipal Agenda: Violence against Women." In Garber, J. A. and Turner, R. S. (Eds.), *Gender in Urban Research*. Thousand Oaks, CA: Sage, pp. 99–118.

ASRTS (Active & Safe Routes to School). 2006. "Westvale's Trailblazers: How to Organize a Student Led Walking School Bus Program." Available: http://www.saferoutestoschool. ca/downloads/guide/wsb_westvale_trailblazers.pdf (accessed 1 June 2008).

Berglund, E. 2007. *Doing Things Differently: Women's Design Service at 20.* London: Women's Design Service.

Cavanagh, S. 1998. *Making Safer Places: A Resource Book for Neighbourhood Safety Audits.* London: Women's Design Service.

Christchurch City Council. 2008. "Safe Routes to School – Walking School Bus." Available: http://www.ccc.govt.nz/saferoutes/wsb/ (accessed 28 May 2008).

DET [Department of Education and Training (New South Wales, Australia)]. 2008. "Walking School Bus." Available: http://www.curriculumsupport.education.nsw.gov.au/policies/ road/travel/walkingbus1.htm (accessed 28 May 2008)

DPI [Department of Planning and Infrastructure (Western Australia)]. 2007. "Walking School Bus – Routes and Results – Trip Data." Available: http://www.dpi.wa.gov.au/ mediaFiles/ts_tripdata07.pdf (accessed 28 May 2008)

DT [Department for Transport (UK)]. 2006. "How to Set up a 'Walking Bus'." Available: http://www.dft.gov.uk/pgr/sustainable/schooltravel/grantsforwalkingbuses/howtoset-upawalkingbus (accessed 28 May 2008).

DTEI [Department for Transport, Energy and Infrastructure (South Australia)]. 2007. "Walking in Adelaide." Available: http://www.transport.sa.gov.au/personal_transport/walking/ index.asp (accessed 8 May 2008).

Engwicht, D. 1992. *Towards an Eco-City: Calming the Traffic.* Sydney: Envirobook.

—— 2003. "Is Walking School Bus Stalled in an Evolutionary Cul-de-Sac?" Available: http://www.lesstraffic.com/Articles/Traffic/wbstalled.htm (accessed 28 May 2008).

Eyestone, R. 1977. "Confusion, Diffusion, and Innovation." *The American Political Science Review,* **71** (2), 441–7.

Hall, P. 2002. *Cities of Tomorrow: An Intellectual History of Urban Planning in the Twentieth Century.* Cambridge, MA: Blackwell.

Hillman, M., Adams, J., and Whitelegg, J. 1990. *One False Move . . . A Study of Children's Independent Mobility*. London: Policy Studies Institute.

Hobart City Council (Tasmania, Australia). 2004. "Walking School Bus Guide." Available: http://www.hobartcity.com.au/hccwr/_assets/main/lib60037/walking%20bus%20guide.pdf (accessed 28 May 2008).

—— 2007. "Walking School Bus Program." Available: http://www.hobartcity.com.au/HCC/STANDARD/WALKING_SCHOOL_BUS.html (accessed 28 May 2008).

Husain, S. 2007. *Guidance on Local Safety Audits: A Compendium of International Practice*. Paris: European Forum on Urban Safety.

Informa Market Research. 2001. "Small Steps/Large Rewards: A Community Based Social Marketing Research Project." Greenest City, Ontario.

Kallus, R. and Churchman, A. 2004. "Women's Struggle for Urban Safety: The Canadian Experience and its Applicability to the Israeli Context." *Planning Theory & Practice*, **5** (2), 197–215.

Kearns, R. A. and Collins, C. A. 2003. "Crossing Roads, Crossing Boundaries: Empowerment and Participation in a Child Pedestrian Safety Initiative." *Space and Polity*, **7** (2), 193–212.

Kingham, S. and Ussher, S. 2005. "Ticket to a Sustainable Future: An Evaluation of the Long-Term Durability of the Walking School Bus Programme in Christchurch, New Zealand." *Transport Policy*, **12** (4), 314–23.

Kooijman, D. and Romein, A. 2007. *The Limited Potential of the Creative City Concept: Policy Practices in Four Dutch Cities* (draft). Based on paper presented at Regions in Focus, Lisbon, April 2007.

Land Transport New Zealand. 2008. "Walking School Buses." Available: http://www.landtransport.govt.nz/travel/school/walking-school-buses/index.html (accessed 28 May 2008).

Luckman, S., Gibson, C., Lea, T., and Brennan-Horley, C. 2007. "Darwin as "Creative Tropical City": Just How Transferable is Creative City Thinking?" Paper presented at 3rd State of Australian Cities National Conference, Adelaide, 28–30 November 2007.

Mackett, R.G., Lucas, L., Paskins, J., and Turbin, J. 2003. "A Methodology for Evaluating Walking Buses as an Instrument of Urban Transport Policy." *Urban Transport Policy Instruments*, **10** (3), 179–86.

—— 2005. *Walking Buses in Hertfordshire: Impacts and Lessons*. London: Centre for Transport Studies, University College London.

Martin, S. and Carlson, S. 2005. "Barriers to Children Walking to or from School: United States, 2004." *Journal of the American Medical Association*, **294** (17), 2160–1.

McMillan, T. E. 2005. "Urban Form and a Child's Trip to School: The Current Literature and a Framework for Future Research." *Journal of Planning Literature*, **19**, 440–56.

METRAC (Metropolitan Toronto Action Committee on Public Violence Against Women and Children). 1989. *Women's Safety Audit Guide*. Toronto: METRAC.

NCPC (National Crime Prevention Council of Canada). 1995. *First Annual Report of the National Crime Prevention Council*. Ottawa: Government of Canada.

Queensland Transport. 2007. "Kids Walking." Available: http://www.transport.qld.gov.au/Home/Safety/Road/Pedestrians/Pedestrian_guide/Kids_walking/ (accessed 28 May 2008).

Shaw, M. and Andrew, C. 2005. "Engendering Crime Prevention: International Developments and the Canadian Experience." *Canadian Journal of Criminology and Criminal Justice* (CJCCJ), **47** (2), 293–316.

Stone, D. 1999. "Learning Lessons and Transferring Policy across Time, Space and Disciplines." *Politics*, **19** (1), 51–9.

—— 2001. *Learning Lessons, Policy Transfer and the International Diffusion of Policy Ideas*. Working Paper No. 69/01. Warwick: Centre for the Study of Globalisation and Regionalisation.

Symes, M. and Pauwels, S. 1999. "The Diffusion of Innovations in Urban Design: The Case of Sustainability in the Hulme Development Guide." *Journal of Urban Design*, **4** (1), 97–117.

Tranter, P. and Pawson, E. 2001. «Children's Access to Local Environments: A Case Study of Christchurch, New Zealand.» *Local Environment*, **6**, 27–48.

VCCAV (Victorian Community Council Against Violence). 1995. *Safety Audits: Past Experience and Future Strategies, Notes from a March 1995 Forum*. Melbourne: VCCAV.

VicHealth (Victorian Health Promotion Foundation). 2003. "Walking School Bus: A Guide for Parents and Teachers." Available: http://www.vichealth.vic.gov.au/assets/contentFiles/WSB_InteractivePrint.pdf (accessed 1 June 2008).

—— 2007a. "Walking the Walk. Evaluation of Phases 1 and 2 of the Walking School Bus Program." Available: http://www.vichealth.vic.gov.au/assets/contentFiles/Walking%20the%20Walk.pdf (accessed 28 May 2008).

—— 2007b. *It's More than Just Walking! The Value-Adding Impact of the Walking School Bus Program on Local Environments and Communities*. J. A. Grant and Associates for VicHealth (Victorian Division), August 2007.

WACAV (Women's Action Centre Against Violence Ottawa-Carleton). 1995. *Safety Audit Tools and Housing: The State of the Art and Implications for CMHC*. Ottawa: Canada Mortgage and Housing Association.

Ward, S. V. 2000. "Re-examining the International Diffusion of Planning." In Freestone, R. (Ed.) *Urban Planning in a Changing World*. London: Taylor and Francis, pp. 40–60.

Wekerle, G. and Whitzman, C. 1995. *Safe Cities: Guidelines for Planning, Design, and Management*. New York: Van Nostrand Reinhold.

Whitzman, C. 2002a. "The Voice of Women in Canadian Local Government." In Andrew, C., Graham, K., and Rankin, S. (Eds.) *Urban Affairs: Back on the Policy Agenda*. Montreal: Queens University Press, pp. 93–118.

—— 2002b. "Feminist Activism for Safer Social Space in High Park, Toronto: How Women Got Lost in the Woods." *Canadian Journal of Urban Research*, **11** (2), 299–321.

—— 2008. *The Handbook of Community Safety, Gender and Violence Prevention*. London: Earthscan.

Whitzman, C. and Pike, L. 2007. *From Battery-Reared to Free-Range Children: Institutional Barriers and Enablers to Children's Independent Mobility in Victoria, Australia*. Melbourne: Australian Centre for the Governance and Management of Urban Transportation.

Whitzman, C., Andrew, C., and Shaw, M. 2009. "The Effectiveness of Women's Safety Audits." *Security Journal* (special issue on women's safety), **22** (3), 205–18.

WICI (Women in Cities International). 2008. *Women's Safety Audits: What Works and Where?* Montreal: WICI.

YWCA. 2007. "Walking School Bus." Available: http://www.ywca-canberra.org.au/children_community_services/walking_school_bus#downloads (accessed 9 July 2009).

# CHAPTER 11

# INSTITUTIONAL BIASES IN THE INTERNATIONAL DIFFUSION OF PLANNING CONCEPTS

SUKUMAR GANAPATI AND NIRAJ VERMA

## INTRODUCTION

Planners and policy-makers often borrow concepts from other countries to address common urban problems. There are numerous instances of the international flow of planning ideas from one context to another: business improvement districts (Hoyt 2006; Peel and Lloyd 2008), urban villages (Tait and Jensen 2007), enterprise zones (Mossberger 2000), coastal zone management (Leitmann 1998), and water-front redevelopment (Breen and Rigby 1996). While this kind of policy diffusion has been facilitated by globalization, it is also motivated by international organizations (e.g. the World Bank), planners with international exposure and networks, and rapid growth in international communications (Dolowitz and Marsh 1996, 2000; Healey and Williams 1993; Sanyal 2005).

Policy diffusion is tricky; several studies have documented how policy lessons from one context succeed or fail in other contexts (Allen *et al.* 1999; Braun and Gilardi 2006; Dogan and Pelassy 1990; Dolowitz and Marsh 2000; Lloyd *et al.* 2003; Mossberger and Wolman 2003; Weyland 2005). Yet the theoretical basis underlying a policy concept in such diffusion is often inadequately conceptualized (Braun and Gilardi 2006; James and Lodge 2003). A particularly knotty issue arises when the contextual evidence (i.e. "facts" on the ground) does not conform to the policy concept. In this chapter, we explore the application of "housing filtering," a policy concept that is well recognized in the American planning literature, in another context: that of Rome, Italy. The concept is defined as the passing of housing stock from more to less affluent segments in a housing market. The expectation embedded in the concept is that the "downward" filtering happens when the quality and value of old housing stock decline because of obsolescence, deterioration, and changes in style. The policy implication is that increasing the supply of low-cost housing can be achieved by any intervention that increases the overall housing stock.

A thick literature on filtering has spawned over the past hundred years, both as a positive description of decline of older inner cities and as a normative basis for low-income housing policies (Baer and Williamson 1988). In Rome, there is a surplus of housing units over the number of households. This should have been conducive to a similar downward filtering process, according to the housing filtering concept, as well as a general reduction in house prices in the market overall. Paradoxically, such filtering did not happen in Rome. Unlike the old, inner areas of American cities, the historical core of Rome bustles with activities, with housing prices high and rising.

This raises a theoretical dilemma for the diffusion of a policy concept. If contextual evidence contradicts the concept, does it negate the application of the concept? Karl Popper authoritatively argued that "it must be possible for an empirical scientific system to be refuted by experience" (1959: 18). In other words, Popper's objective in examining the generalization of a concept is its falsification − not its confirmation. From a policy diffusion viewpoint, Popper's falsification approach would suggest that the filtering concept is indeed not applicable to Rome, as the concept is falsified in the Roman context. However, we propose that this dichotomy of the concept and evidence − theory and data − may not be as oppositional as it appears. The application of a policy concept in another context is more complex than placing a bias on the side of theory or of data (evidence). Rather, there is also an institutional bias in the diffusion of a policy concept. The institutional context of Italy in general and Rome in particular precluded downward filtering. Instead, the conditions led to "reverse" filtering in Rome, where older housing stock is valuable and sought after by higher-income groups. Housing policies related to rent control, finance, and conservation facilitated reverse filtering. These broader institutional conditions limited the diffusion of the filtering concept in Rome.

Our argument is organized into four parts. First, we review the filtering concept in the American planning literature. Second, we explain the diffusion of the concept in the international context and provide a background of Rome. Third, we examine the filtering process in Rome. Fourth, we consider the institutional biases in the diffusion of the filtering concept in Rome. Finally, we conclude with some observations on the study's theoretical implications for policy diffusion.

## HOUSING FILTERING IN THE UNITED STATES

Housing filtering is a significant concept that originated in Great Britain and has persisted in the American planning literature for over 100 years (Baer and Williamson 1988). The filtering process and its policy implications had attracted considerable attention by World War II. Hoyt, for example, observed that low-income renters move out in bands from the city center to occupy houses left by higher-income groups (1939). Richard Ratcliff expounded on the filtering process in the 1940s and provided the classical definition of filtering. According to him, "housing tends to move downward in the quality and value scales as it ages." Consequently, there is a process of housing filtering, which is "the changing of occupancy as the housing that is occupied by one income group becomes available to the next lower income group as a result of the decline in market price, i.e. in sales price or rent value" (Ratcliff 1949: 321–2). The process is referred to as "downward filtering" as the existing housing stock "trickles down" the social hierarchy as the wealthier members of society move into newly constructed housing.

Since then the filtering concept has had significant policy implications for housing low-income households. Filtering, for example, was used as a rationale for legitimizing *used* housing as a solution for supplying low-income housing during the early twentieth century. In the housing policy debates following the Great Depression, the American real estate lobby maintained that a natural filtering process could be used to house the poor. Suburbanization following World War II aided spatial filtering, with the middle- and upper-income groups moving to newly constructed suburbs (Bier 1995). Federal housing programs (encouraging single family homes in the suburbs) and transportation policies (e.g. the National Highway Act 1956 that financed freeway construction) reinforced the filtering process (Berry 1980). Bier (2001) shows that filtering has begun to occur recently in older suburbs as well. Of course, the policy implications of filtering are not uncontested. Whereas supporters highlight the beneficial aspects of new construction, and consequent welfare filtering for low-income households (Howe and DeRidder 1993; Malpezzi and Green 1996; Ohls 1975; Olsen 1969; White 1971), critics argue that filtering has had limited usefulness for low-income groups and that it increases income inequality (Aaron 1972; Berry 1985; Boddy and Gray 1979; Needleman 1965). Ideologically, filtering has been criticized as an ineffective trickle-down mechanism resulting from market-oriented urban policies (Ha 2004; Lucy and Phillips 2006).

Housing economists have greatly enriched the filtering concept with various sophisticated formulations of models for filtering, with different perspectives. Fisher and Winnick defined filtering as "a change over time in the position of a given dwelling unit within the distribution of housing rents and prices in the community as a whole" (1951: 52). Lowry linked filtering to general price changes in the market, and proposed that filtering is "simply a change in the real value (price in constant dollars) of an existing dwelling unit" (1960: 363, original parentheses). These studies focused on the characteristics of the physical dwelling (value, quality), but not on the household characteristics. It was Grigsby (1963) who presented a seminal discussion on filtering by incorporating households into the social formulation of the concept (Baer and Williamson 1988; Galster 1996). Outlining a welfare model of filtering, he argued that "filtering occurs only when value declines more rapidly than quality so that families can obtain either higher quality and more space at the same price, or the same quality and space at a lower price than formerly" (Grigsby 1963: 97). He pioneered the matrix approach to filtering analysis, whereby the housing market is segmented into an array of linked sub-markets defined by characteristic groupings of substitutable dwellings (e.g. single family and multi-family housing units are distinctive sub-markets). He proposed that household mobility led to shifts in market values and filtering. His matrix related the characteristics of recent home purchasers to the characteristics of the housing sub-markets. Indeed, Grigsby's conceptualization has since been followed up in a number of empirical studies (Braid 1981; Schall 1981; Sweeney 1974).

Subsequently, researchers have taken multiple approaches towards filtering (Gibb 2003; Grigsby et al. 1987). Three strands of filtering analysis could be identified in the American planning literature. The first strand focuses on the housing units. It deals with the turnover process through vacancy chain analysis (Kristof 1965; Lansing et al. 1969; Sands and Bower 1976; White 1971), or through price changes (Arnott and Braid 1997; Coulson and McMillen 2007; Sweeney 1974), based on housing characteristics. The second strand takes a demographic approach, in which households filter through the housing stock (Myers 1975, 1981, 1983; Nourse 1973). The third strand focuses on the neighborhood level, examining the decline or gentrification of neighborhoods due to filtering (Bates 2003; Bond and Coulson 1989; Glaeser and Gyourko 2005; Hoyt 1939; Somerville and Holmes 2001; Stegman 1977; Temkin and Rohe 1996; Varady 1986). Gentrification is indicative of "reverse filtering," which implies that higher-income households replace longer-term, low-income residents in the area (Keating et al. 1996).

These three strands highlight three dimensions of filtering: housing units, households, and neighborhoods. Baer and Williamson (1988) also identified three dimensions of housing filtering: (1) housing unit and household characteristics, (2) households' command over resources, and (3) their locations in physical and social space. Galster and Rothenberg (1991) followed Baer and Williamson to propose a formal model that incorporates the characteristics of individual market participants, dwelling quality and price, and location. However, although we broadly concur with Baer and Williamson, we argue that the characteristics of housing units and households should be clearly separated for analytical purposes. The occupation of the same dwelling unit by households of different classes (the filtering of housing units) is distinct from the movement of a household between different types of dwelling units (household filtering). Moreover,

Baer and Williamson's second aspect of "command over resources" is clearly a household characteristic, referring to their economic ability to pay for housing. Hence, in our framework, we adopt the following three dimensions for analysis:

1   Housing unit filtering: This is linked to the unit's physical condition, style, age, availability of public services, and other characteristics of the built structure. In this, different sub-markets of single versus multi-family housing can be identified.
2   Household filtering: In contrast, this is linked to demographic and related economic characteristics, and includes household mobility.
3   Neighborhood filtering: Neighborhood filtering is linked to the broader geographical characteristics of the area where the housing units and households are located.

## THE INTERNATIONAL DIFFUSION OF THE HOUSING FILTERING CONCEPT

Karl Popper famously argued that empirical falsification is the genuine test of a concept (1959). Empirical confirmation does not, by itself, establish the veracity of a concept. In other words, a theoretical concept that internalizes other attendant concerns is harder to shoot down, but, if shot down, the stakes are higher. It is in this context that we examine the application of the filtering concept, which has been well established in the American planning literature, to Rome. Empirical studies on the policy diffusion of the filtering concept to other international contexts are still emerging (Baer 1991; Baer and Koo 1994; Ha 2004; Skaburskis 2006). Our study adds to this emerging literature.

The few studies that exist on filtering in the international context are critical of the concept. Research on developing countries indicates the manifestation of "reverse filtering," as "income and demand rise faster than the rate of new construction of dwellings of a corresponding value" (Johnson 1987: 175). Slum tenements, for example, are occupied by richer sections of the society when their status is legalized, and are upgraded through an improvement in the quality of the slum environment (Johnson 1987; Strassman 1982). Ferchiou claims that dwellings in the middle range of values initiate the longest chains of moves in developing countries, although these chains end before reaching the poorest families (1982). Applying the concept to Seoul, Ha criticizes filtering as a neo-liberal approach of the South Korean government's housing renewal projects that does not aid low-income households (2004). Studies on Canadian cities refute the incidence of filtering and its usefulness as a strategy for housing low-income households (Harris 1990; Skaburskis 2006). White (1984) observes that filtering is weak in European cities because there is no "social *cachet*" for new housing, the middle class does not shun the city center, and there are constraints on urban expansion that result in an overall excess of demand over supply.

Although the above studies generally lean towards Popper's theme of falsifying the filtering concept in the international context, they have paid much less attention to why there is limited diffusion of the concept. In particular, the institutional biases that affect the diffusion of the filtering process have not been given much attention. Our study fills this gap in the emerging international literature on filtering. A consideration of institutional conditions is important. Whereas the trickle-down concept may be applicable in the United States, where housing is largely provided by the competitive private sector, the institutional conditions of housing markets in other contexts could be distinctive, thus affecting the filtering of housing differently (see, for example, Hegedus and Tosics 1991 for a discussion of filtering in a socialist context). By institutions, we refer to the laws, regulations, and norms that shape human behavior (North 1990; Verma 2007). In the context of housing filtering, institutions could affect all three dimensions of filtering identified above (housing units, households, and neighborhood). For example, rent control reduces the incentives for housing maintenance; housing finance policies could enable or restrain households' ability to pay for housing. In a place such as Rome, the rich historical legacy in the city's core and the value that elites place on city-center living are also important for understanding neighborhood filtering.

To analyze housing filtering, we follow a largely traditional division of Rome (*Commune di Roma*) into the following four areas:

1  The *Rioni*, which is the central historical core within the 19-kilometre Aurelian walls constructed in 275 AD, and encompassing the legendary seven hills of Rome.
2  The *quartieri*, the semi-central area of Rome developed within the *Grande Raccordo Annulare* (GRA), a ring road concentric with the Aurelian wall and constructed after the master plan prepared in 1962.
3  The *suburbi*, also a semi-central area, which forms an outer band of the *quartieri* on the west side of Rome within the GRA. According to Bagnasco, there is no substantive geographical difference between the *quartieri* and the *suburbi* – the distinction is largely administrative and historic (1987: 21).
4  The *Zone Agro Romano*, which is the largely peripheral agricultural outskirts of Rome, parts of which have been invaded by urban growth.

Each of the above areas is subdivided into several neighborhood districts (*suddivisioni toponomastiche*), totaling 122 for Rome overall (22 in the *Rioni*, 35 in the *quartieri*, 6 in the *suburbi*, and 59 in the *Zone Agro Romano*). These neigh-borhood districts form the unit of analysis for filtering at the neighborhood level.

Rome grew historically as a monocentric city with peripheral developments around the historical core of the *Rioni*. Major historical roads such as Via Appia, Via Aurelia, and Via Flaminia emanate out of the city in a radial pattern. After Rome became the capital of a unified Italy in 1870, many of the existing buildings in the *Rioni* were expropriated by a law that secularized and abolished ownership privileges for religious groups (Agnew 1995: 44). Housing in the *Rioni* has had to compete with other functions of the capital city. The growing population was accommodated in the *quartieri* or the *suburbi*. The peripheral growth of Rome, however, has not been contiguous; it has been variously described as an "oil stain" (*macchia d'olio*) or as "leap-frog" development because of speculative rounds of non-contiguous peripheral development (Agnew 1995; Fried 1973). Despite the similarity of this leap-frog development with American cities, a key difference is that land consumption for housing is low. According to Fried, "84 percent of the city's population lives concentrated in only 12 percent of the city's territory — some 70 square miles in and around the old city" (1973: 77). The urbanized area of Rome grew from 19 percent in 1971 to 26 percent in 1981 (Bellicini and Toso 1995), while the population grew marginally by 2 percent (see Figure 11.4).

The division of Rome into center–periphery does not, however, capture the complexity of its contemporary growth. Unlike other Italian cities such as Milan, Turin, or neighboring Naples, Rome is not an industrial city. Rather, its growth has been motivated by its status as the seat of Italian national government, the Papal site, a tourist center, and a location for commercial trade (Mocine 1969: 376). It has also become an important center for higher education in Italy. The three mas-ter plans of 1931, 1962, and 2000 envisaged growth of other centers besides the historical core to accommodate these growing functions. For example, the *Espozione Universale di Roma* (EUR), an exposition to celebrate the achieve-ments of Mussolini's Fascist regime, conceived after the 1931 plan, was planned in the south of the *Rioni*. The 1962 master plan called for the *Sistema Direzionale Orientale* (SDO), a roadway axis to the east for relocating public administrative offices, decongesting the city center, and rejuvenating that part of the city. The 2000 master plan proposed a system of nearly 70 metropolitan, urban, and local nodes to decentralize administrative and commercial activities (Figure 11.1). The decentralization of activities with newer developments outside the city center is reminiscent of the suburbanization process in American cities, and could reason-ably be expected to stimulate downward filtering. However, filtering in Rome has been distinctive from American cities, as explained below.

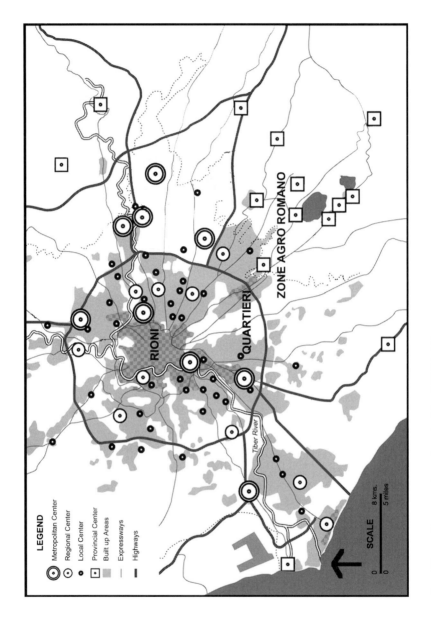

**Figure 11.1** Master plan of Rome. Source: redrawn from Archibugi (2001: 23).

## HOUSING FILTERING IN ROME

The process of housing filtering in Rome is examined here with respect to the three dimensions outlined earlier: housing unit filtering, household filtering, and neighborhood filtering. We argue that Rome presents a deviation from American cities in which the process of downward filtering is not observed. From a Popperian perspective, Rome is emblematic of the international literature that lends support to falsifying the filtering concept. We suggest that Rome provides a case of "reverse filtering," wherein older housing units have maintained their value and did not filter down to low-income households. Unlike the inner-city areas of American cities, which are generally characterized by blight and poor economic conditions, the *Rioni* remains a sought-after area by the elite class.

### HOUSING UNIT FILTERING IN ROME

The predominance of old housing and the peculiar nature of the new housing developments in the peripheral zones in Rome have contributed to the phenomenon of reverse housing unit filtering. Housing growth in Rome happened in distinctive geographical waves over time. Figure 11.2 shows the number of residential buildings by the period of their construction, and the geographical zones in which they were constructed, until 2001. As this shows, building activity in Rome grew with the post-World War II real estate boom until 1971, and reduced

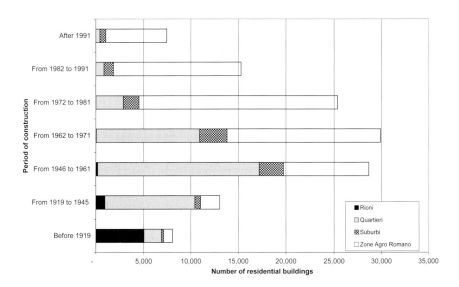

**Figure 11.2** Spatial distribution of residential buildings by period of construction in Rome, 2001.
Source: based on Istituto Nazionale di Statistica (2006: 125–6).

after that. Residential construction was at its lowest in the 1990s. The figure also shows the predominance of old housing stock: nearly 96 percent of residential construction in the *Rioni* took place before 1945. Indeed, building activity in the *Rioni* has been mainly limited to the renovation, rehabilitation, and subdivision of existing units. A substantial majority of the buildings in the *quartieri* (90 percent) and the *suburbi* (66 percent) are also old, built before 1971. Newer residential construction is mainly in the *Zone Agro Romano*, where nearly 60 percent has been built after 1971.

Overall, the lion's share of residential buildings is in the *quartieri* (34 percent) and the peripheral *Zone Agro Romano* (54 percent); the *Rioni* and the *suburbi* account for only 5 percent and 7 percent respectively. Multi-family housing (two or more units in a building) is the norm in Rome, accounting for 74 percent of residential buildings (Istituto Nazionale di Statistica 2006). Luxury homes in Rome are mainly villas or *villinis*, which are two- or three-storied apartment buildings, mostly evident in Parioli and other neighborhoods to the north of the *Rioni,* and in Trionfale, Aurelio, and Portuense in the *suburbi*. *Palazzines* are three- to five-story apartments in certain neighborhoods of the *Rioni* (e.g. Prati, Trastavere, Testaccio), and in the older neighborhoods of the *quartieri*. Such older housing in Rome did not lose its quality with age. Figure 11.3 shows the quality of residential buildings by period of construction. As the figure shows, in 2001, over two-thirds of the buildings constructed until 1961 were in "excellent" or "good" condition;

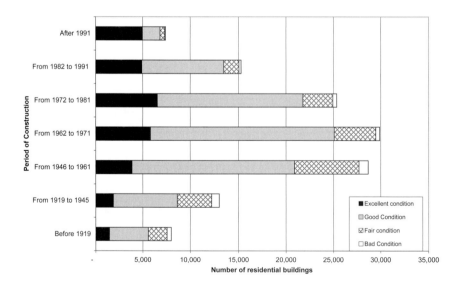

**Figure 11.3** Quality of residential buildings by period of construction in Rome, 2001. Source: based on Istituto Nazionale di Statistica (2006: 77).

for buildings constructed after 1961, the proportion of buildings in such condition was even higher (four-fifths or more). The obsolescence of older housing is not a common trait in Rome, thus precluding the push factor of the filtering process otherwise observed in American cities (Baer 1991).

Although the peripheral developments in the *Zone Agro Romano* are newer and seem to be similar to the suburbanization observed in American cities, the similarity is superficial. Unlike the better-quality single family homes in the suburbs of US cities, the newer housing in the *Zone Agro Romano* has not been necessarily of a desirable quality for upper-income households to move into. The zone has had a history of illegal construction (*abusivismo*), which did not conform with the master plan. Such housing arose in the context of the post-war real estate boom (Guttenberg 1988). According to Adler (1988: 382), there were over 120 illegal developments, housing over 800,000 people in the periphery. Peripheral developments in Rome were also characterized by spontaneous developments such as *barraches* (shacks) in *borgates* (slums). This self-constructed (*auto-produzzione*) housing had relatively less access to public infrastructure, and was predominantly occupied by low-income households (Donne 1992). In recent times, however, many *barraches* have disappeared and the *borgates* have been integrated with the city's fabric through the provision of services. The Istituto Autonomo per le Case Popolari (IACP), a public sector agency for low-cost housing, built dense *palazzi* or *intensivi*, which are high-rise buildings of 10 to 12 stories. These low-quality, peripheral developments have hardly provided a pull factor attracting higher-income households to move, unlike American suburban housing.

Data on housing prices indicate that the older housing units in the central city have maintained their value in Rome. Table 11.1 provides a snapshot of the prices of housing units in central (the *Rioni*), semi-central (the *quartieri* and the *suburbi*),

**Table 11.1** Median value of housing units in Rome, 1988–94 (million lire per square meter)

|             | 1988 | 1989 | 1990 | 1991 | 1992  | 1993 | 1994 |
|-------------|------|------|------|------|-------|------|------|
| *Center*    |      |      |      |      |       |      |      |
| Luxury      | 6.68 | 8.78 | 11.6 | 12.1 | 11.84 | 8.95 | 8.32 |
| Economy     | 2.81 | 3.34 | 4.5  | 4.74 | 4.75  | 4.34 | 4.14 |
| *Semi-center* |    |      |      |      |       |      |      |
| Luxury      | 3.41 | 4.35 | 4.87 | 5.36 | 5.52  | 5.1  | 4.65 |
| Economy     | 1.77 | 2.06 | 2.63 | 2.95 | 3.04  | 2.84 | 2.67 |
| *Periphery* |      |      |      |      |       |      |      |
| Luxury      | 3.26 | 3.92 | 4.79 | 5.15 | 5.04  | 4.5  | 4.32 |
| Economy     | 1.51 | 1.89 | 2.3  | 2.49 | 2.6   | 2.44 | 2.23 |

Source: obtained in person by authors from Centro Ricerche Economiche Sociali di Mercato per l'Edilizia e il Territorio (CRESME), June 1995.

and peripheral (the *Zone Agro Romano*) areas between 1988 and 1994. As the
table shows, housing prices in the central areas have been significantly higher
than those in the semi-central and peripheral areas. The difference between
prices in the semi-central and peripheral areas has not been as significant over
the years. More recent housing price data also indicate that the older housing in
the central areas of the city is valued significantly higher than that in the semi-
central and peripheral areas (Nomisma 2005, 2007; Scenari Immobiliari 2008).

## HOUSEHOLD FILTERING IN ROME

Demographically, Rome experienced a high rate of population growth through
both natural increase and migration after becoming the national capital. Migration was particularly high between 1870 and 1930 and peaked in 1936, when
Rome became the largest city in Italy. The Fascist regime tried unsuccessfully to
curb the growth through anti-urbanization laws, which remained in place from
1936 until 1961. Figure 11.4 shows the population growth in Rome between
1951 and 2001. As the figure shows, Rome's population grew dramatically in the
post-war period from 1951 to 1971. Population peaked in 1981 and then began
to decrease. The population in the historical core of the *Rioni*, which accommodated over 96 percent of Rome's population in 1870, began to reduce with
the residential growth in the *quartieri* (its share was 69 percent in 1921). In the
post-war years, the *Rioni's* population further dwindled rapidly, from 25 percent

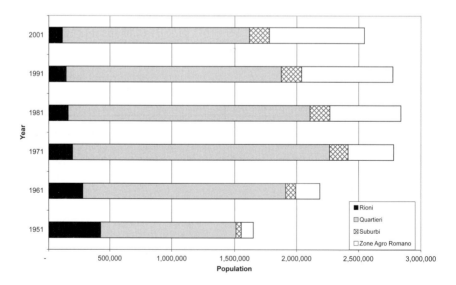

**Figure 11.4** Rome's population growth, 1951–2001. Sources: compiled from Table 5.1 in
Agnew (1995: 75) and Istituto Nazionale di Statistica (1995, 2006).

in 1951 to 4 percent in 2001. The *quartieri*, which had begun to gain population before World War II (its share increased from 23 percent in 1921 to 51 percent in 1936), continued to grow steadily until its share of the population peaked at 75 percent in 1961. The semi-central area of the *quartieri* and the *suburbi* together still accommodated the largest share of Rome's population in 2001 (65 percent). Suburbanization is evident in the growth of the share of the population in the *Zone Agro Romano,* from 6 percent in 1951 to 30 percent in 2001.

The population decline in Rome did not imply that there was reduction in housing demand. It was quite the opposite as the number of households increased despite the population decrease. As Table 11.2 shows, the increase of households continued until 2001, although the rate of increase slowed after 1971. This increase in households despite a decrease in population can be attributed to the growing popularity of "nuclear" family arrangements and higher numbers of single-person households: the average number of people per household in Rome has come down steadily from 3.9 in 1951 to 2.5 in 2001. Yet the historical relationship between household formation and housing production should have been conducive to "downward" household filtering, as the growth in households has been slower than the increase in housing units over each decade. That is, since 1971, the supply of housing units has exceeded the number of households. At this aggregate level of surplus housing supply, it is reasonable to expect that overall housing demand would decrease. The over-supply should have been conducive to the downward filtering process, as households had a greater variety of housing choices. Paradoxically, however, despite this surplus, the reverse filtering of households has occurred: richer households have not moved from the older housing in central areas. In central Rome, an average family required 3.6 years of family savings to own a home in 1965; but in 1993, this required 10.1 years

**Table 11.2** Household formation and housing units in Rome, 1951–2001

|  | Households | | Housing units | |
|--|--|--|--|--|
| *Year* | *Number* | *Decadal increase (%)* | *Number* | *Decadal increase (%)* |
| 1951 | 425,797 | – | 319,230 | – |
| 1961 | 591,850 | 39 | 572,246 | 79 |
| 1971 | 826,990 | 40 | 873,802 | 53 |
| 1981 | 939,045 | 14 | 1,015,769 | 16 |
| 1991 | 1,018,692 | 9 | 1,132,934 | 12 |
| 2001 | 1,039,152 | 2 | 1,151,736 | 2 |

Sources: compiled from Table 5.1 in Agnew (1995: 75) and Istituto Nazionale di Statistica (1995, 2006).

of savings. In contrast, four years of savings were required to buy a house in the peripheral belt in 1965; in 1993, this took just 5.7 years' savings, a much smaller increase. Households need to have a higher socio-economic status to afford the older housing in central neighborhood districts. This paradox is not limited to Rome. Since the 1960s, the national housing stock in Italy grew at a rate faster than that of household formation, and has consistently been above the number of households (Padovani 1996; Padovani and Vettoretto 2003). Yet there is sustained pressure on the housing market, as is indicated by rising house prices and building costs, which have increased at a faster pace than the cost of living (van Hees 1991; Scenari Immobilari 2008).

Four reasons could be attributed to this paradoxical situation. First, as indicated in the previous section, new housing in the peripheral *Zone Agro Romano* has not necessarily been attractive, because of the low quality of housing developments. Richer households have had little incentive to move, in the context of poor quality of housing stock in poor locations. Second, there is a high incidence of vacant dwelling units in Rome. Vacant dwelling units have constituted nearly 11 percent of total stock since 1981 (see Figure 11.6), effectively obliterating the effect of the increased supply of housing units. Third, partly related to the issue of specu-lative construction and vacant homes, is the phenomenon of "second homes," whereby affluent households own a second house in tourist or peripheral areas, thus skewing the ownership pattern. Although the extent of this phenomenon in Rome is not known, Padovani and Vettoretto (2003: 92) estimate that about 10 percent of households in Italy have a second home. Fourth, institutional con-straints such as rent control and housing finance availability adversely affected residential mobility in Rome (as will be explained later on). These factors are seen nationally, so that the filtering process is also applicable beyond Rome to Italy in general (Padovani 1996).

## NEIGHBORHOOD FILTERING IN ROME

Similar to reverse filtering at the housing unit and household level, reverse filter-ing is evident at the neighborhood level too. The older, central neighborhoods are among the more prestigious and sought-after areas in Rome. Figure 11.5 shows residential population density based on neighborhood districts (*suddivi-sioni toponomastiche*) of Rome in 2001. As the figure shows, population density was highest in the *Rioni* (although it accommodated only 4 percent of Rome's population). The *quartieri* also depicts high density in the eastern and western neighborhood districts adjoining the *Rioni*. Density falls off sharply in the *Zone Agro Romano*, although the neighborhood districts in the south-west and east of the zone reflect relatively higher density. This density pattern shows that Rome's growth is not strictly concentric around the *Rioni*. Rather, density follows a secto-ral pattern in the *quartieri* and the *Zone Agro Romano*. Agnew and Bolling (1993) also argue that the city's development follows more of a sectoral pattern than a concentric one. In contrast, Aureli and Baldazzi (1998: 44) suggest that the city has developed in "concentric bands, in which the originally differentiated house-holds have tended over time to assume homogenous characteristics." According to Aureli and Baldazzi (1998), these bands emerged as the interstitial spaces of the original "oil stain" development filled up. These different narratives follow the earlier dichotomy between the concentric urban development depicted by Bur-gess (1925) and the sectoral pattern identified by Hoyt (1939). We propose that both views are partially right in their depictions of the city. As McElrath suggested early on, "urbanization and social rank are clearly both concentric and zonal phe-nomena" in Rome (1962: 390).

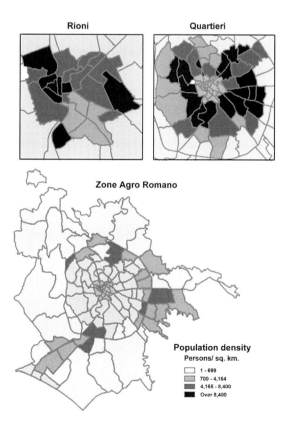

**Figure 11.5** Population distribution in Rome, 2001. Source: based on Istituto Nazionale di Statistica (2006), Cartogramma 7.

The socio-economic geography of Rome indicates that reverse household filtering has occurred, with older housing in the central neighborhoods of the *Rioni* or the semi-central *quartieri* and *suburbi* being actively sought by the upper and middle classes. The historical center of Rome did not lose its significance, in spite of the contemporary development of nodes surrounding the center; if anything, the peripheral developments reinforced its importance. Unlike American inner-city areas, the highest class/status areas from a socio-economic viewpoint have historically been clustered in the center of Rome. In his analysis of social rank in Rome (as measured by occupation and education), based on the 1951 census, McElrath observed that social rank is "highest in the central zone, then declines slightly in the second zone, and declines sharply in the third or outer zone" (1962: 389).

Later analyses affirm McElrath's observations. Agnew and Bolling's (1993) analysis based on the 1981 census reveals five types of socio-economic area in Rome:

1   the upper-class districts, which are distributed throughout the northern *quartieri*, and to a lesser extent in the southern *Rioni* and to the south near EUR;
2   middle-class, tertiary districts, housing higher-rank white-collar employees, located in the north and south of the central city;
3   socially and occupationally diversified districts, with a mix of both blue- and white-collar employees, located mostly in the *Rioni*, some inner western and southern *quartieri,* and northern *quartieri/suburbi*;
4   employee and worker neighborhoods, with low-paid workers in industry or services, located in a wedge extending from the eastern side of the central city and along the western *quartieri*;
5   homogeneous worker neighborhoods, with the highest proportion of industrial workers and a high degree of unemployment, located mostly in the *Zone Agro Romano* and scattered in some *quartieri* neighborhoods to the north-east, south-west, and east.

Evidently, in Agnew's analysis, the *Rioni* and older neighborhoods of the *quartieri* are more attractive to the affluent and the middle class. He argues that the "old" historic center of Rome has "not only maintained its historic, symbolic and functional centrality, but recent years have seen its centrality reinforced by the accretion of new functions and activities" (Agnew 1995: 91). *Rioni* neighborhood districts, such as Castro Pretorio, Esquilino, Ludovisi, Prati, Ripa, Sallustiano, and San Saba, have been populated predominantly by white-collar employees belonging to the middle and upper classes. Many sections of the traditional working-class districts became gentrified with the immigration of affluent new-comers to the city. Foreign immigrants have also been concentrated in the *Rioni* (about 60 persons per 1,000 residents), compared with the *quartieri* (16 per 1,000) and the *Zone Agro Romano* (12 per 1,000) (Istituto Nazionale di Statistica 1995). Cristaldi (2002) argues that there is socio-spatial segregation of immigrant residents in Rome.

Two subsequent studies by Aureli and Baldazzi (1998) and Pacione (1998) using the 1991 census also provide evidence of the attractiveness of the older, central neighborhoods, although these studies reveal that upper-income neighborhoods also began to arise in the peripheral districts of the *Zone Agro Romano*. Aureli and Baldazzi (1998) identified five clusters of socio-economic groups in Rome:

1   The city of new household regimes, which comprises 21 districts, located mainly in the *Rioni*. These are predominantly younger, single-person households, belonging to a higher economic and professional category, who have gradually replaced the traditionally older population of small-scale retailers and artisans.
2   The ageing city, which comprises 11 districts distributed in the northern *quartieri* (Trionfale and Nomentano) and the EUR, with a very high social and occupational status.
3   The post baby-boom city, which is made up of 33 districts spread around the semi-peripheral regions, consisting of lower-middle-class, white-collar workers, mostly employed in the public sector.
4   The city of social hardship, which comprises 21 districts in the *Zone Agro Romano* outside the GRA, with modest housing quality occupied by people of lower economic strata.
5   Prestige in the periphery, again in the *Zone Agro Romano* region predominantly to the north, but consisting of high-quality housing owned by self-employed professionals.

Pacione (1998) used a broader set of variables to analyze Rome's social geography. He identified seven socio-spatial clusters:

1   middle-class family households (11 districts), located to the north-east (e.g. Castel Giubileo) and south-west (e.g. Torrino);
2   upper-class households (21 districts), located in the *Rioni* (e.g. Monti and Esquilino), and in contiguous districts to the north (e.g. Tor di Quinto and Pinciano) and south (e.g. Appio-Latino and Ostiense);
3   working-class households in amenity-deficient housing (18 districts), located in the *Zone Agro Romano* (e.g. San Vittorino, Borghesiana, and Casalotti);

4   working-class households in state housing (20 districts), located on the suburban edge of the city (e.g. Torre Spaccata, Torrenova, and Suburbio Aurelio);

5   mixed social class households (20 districts), located within the GRA in areas such as Tomba di Nerone, Pietralata, and Ardeatino;

6   upper-class households occupying the old city core (10 districts), in areas such as Ponte, Parione, and Trevi;

7   rural periphery, with districts such as Fregere, Santa Maria di Galeria, and Torrimpietra, where many units are "second homes."

A more recent study by Montanari *et al.* (2007) also reveals that the historic core has maintained its high value, and the central locations are still favored by information technology firms and front-office functions in the tertiary sector. They argue that the "peripheries constitute the second best" (ibid.: 145). All of the above-mentioned studies undertaken over the past six decades indicate that neighborhood filtering in Rome has proceeded spatially in a way quite unlike that experienced in American cities. The older neighborhoods in the central areas have undergone reverse filtering rather than downward filtering.

## FALSIFICATION OR CONFIRMATION BIAS? INSTITUTIONAL FACTORS IN THE FILTERING PROCESS

Undoubtedly, the spatial pattern of housing filtering at each of the housing unit, household, and neighborhood levels has been distinctively different from that of American cities. From a Popperian perspective, the experience of Rome (and other non-American cities where empirical studies have tested the housing filtering concept) would suggest falsification of the filtering concept. Neither falsification nor confirmation, however, explains *why* the diffusion of the filtering concept did not occur in Rome. To explore this question, institutional biases need to be examined. We argue that the broader institutional conditions in Italy in general and Rome in particular were not conducive to the downward filtering observed in American cities. Rather, they supported a reverse filtering process. We highlight three such institutional factors: rent control policies, housing finance policies, and conservation policies.

### RENT CONTROL POLICIES

Rent control has been in effect in Italian cities in various forms since World War II. Rents were initially frozen at a level based on when a structure was constructed, with standard allowance for rent increases. Consequently, sitting tenants who predated the war paid only a nominal rent compared with market rates. Fabrizio and Poggio (2004: 193) indicate that rent control led to a collapse of the housing market in urban areas in the 1960s. Subsequently, the Fair Rent Act (*Equo Canone*) was enacted in 1978 to protect both landlords and tenants. It required rent to be conditional on the quality of the house. However, the Act also turned out to be problematic, as landlords were not allowed to re-evaluate rents for sitting tenants, allowing them to evict tenants only at the end of their lease (Fabrizio and Poggio 2004: 193; van Hees 1991: 21). Rent control had undesirable consequences on the private rental housing market: poor maintenance and management of existing housing units by landlords, reduced incentives for the private sector to produce new rental units, and a withdrawal of existing housing units from the rental market. This has contributed to the low level of new rental housing in Italy in general, and in Rome in particular. As van Hees notes:

> When in the period from 1978 to 1981 the prices of houses nearly tripled and in addition the mortgage rate rose considerably (whereas the new rent act only allowed a partial inflation-correction), the rent . . . ended up below the levels of the costs of maintenance and management. In Italy this led to the increasing withdrawal of houses (especially) from the private rented market.
>
> (1991: 27, original parentheses)

The *Equo Canone* was repealed in 1998, allowing for mutually agreed-upon rental contracts between a landlord and tenant, with some stipulations on how a landlord can reclaim the property before a contract expires.

Over a longer time frame, in Italy as a whole, rental housing units decreased from 49 percent in 1951 to 19 percent of stock in 2002, while the scale of owner-occupied housing increased from 40 percent to 71 percent over the same period (Fabrizio and Poggio 2004: 189). Home ownership rates increased in Rome too, with the city boasting the highest percentage of owner-occupied units among Italian cities in the 1960s (Fried 1973: 268). Figure 11.6 shows housing tenure in Rome from 1971 to 2001, indicating an increase in the total number of housing units from nearly 870,000 units to over 1.1 million between 1971 and 2001. This increase was predominantly in owner-occupied units, which rose dramatically in number from nearly 272,000 to nearly 657,000 (a 141 percent increase); rental units decreased from nearly 488,000 to nearly 289,000 (a 58 percent decrease) over the same period. Much of the rental housing was located in the *Rioni*, principally because of the predominance of single-person households and the foreign tourist population. In 2001, rental housing units comprised 34 percent of housing stock in the *Rioni*, compared with 29 percent and 27 percent in the *quartieri* and the *Zone Agro Romano* respectively (Istituto Nazionale di Statistica 2006: 127).

The growth of illegal *abusivismos* in the peripheral *Zone Agro Romano* is also partly attributed to this lack of rental housing and increased demand for home ownership (Agnew 1995; van Hees 1991). Ave argues that rent control affected the housing market adversely and resulted in a reverse filtering process by setting an "access price" for home ownership:

> In such a property market, "filtering up" is only effective in rising housing standards for those who are already owners. In other words, the creation of new housing at the top end of the market may well "free" housing at the lower levels, but will not reduce its relative price. There is thus a structural hindrance to the formation of a "society of owners" that does not depend upon the number of available houses as much as it does on the "access price".

(1996: 32)

Lastly, rent control policies provided a disincentive for landlords to rent, so that vacant housing units remained unutilized. As Figure 11.6 shows, the number of unoccupied (i.e. vacant) units increased after 1971, but has held steady since then (unoccupied units have hovered at around 11 percent of the housing stock since 1981). Despite the high demand for rental housing in the *Rioni*, the vacancy rate was 20 percent in 2001, almost twice the rate in the *quartieri* and the *Zone Agro*

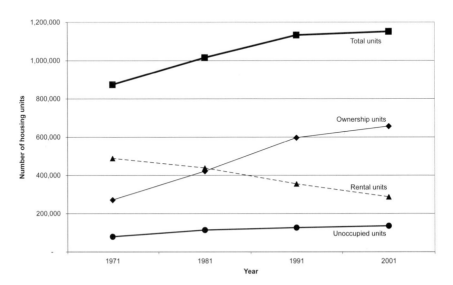

**Figure 11.6**  Housing units in Rome, 1971–2001. Source: based on Commune di Roma (2005: 15).

*Romano.* An overwhelming 73.6 percent of the vacant houses were intended neither for sale nor for rent in the early 1990s (Istituto Nazionale di Statistica 1995).
Local government attempted in vain to bring vacant houses into the rental market
by imposing the *Imposta Comunale sugli Immobili* in 1993, which purported to
increase the property tax on houses that have not been occupied by their owners
for over six months, but this had a limited effect (Ave 1996).

## HOUSING FINANCE POLICIES

Italy's mortgage finance market has traditionally been relatively undeveloped
compared with that of Organization for Economic Cooperation and Development
(OECD) countries in general (Aalbers 2007). The minimum down payment for
mortgage loans was 50 percent until 1980, when the payment was reduced to
25 percent; it was further reduced to 20 percent in 1993. Even after such formal policy adoption, banks continued to use the threshold of 50 percent to lend
because of the weak judicial system in recovering mortgage defaults (Fabrizio and
Poggio 2004). Moreover, the average maturity of mortgage instruments ranges
from 10 to 15 years, with high interest rates (Guiso *et al.* 1994; van Hees 1991).
The effect of the combination of high down payments, short maturity periods, and
high interest rates has been that there is less dependence on formal financing.
Over 70 percent of housing investments in Italy are based on personal sources
of income, so that home ownership is biased toward older age groups who have
built up substantial savings and can borrow from informal sources. The average
age of home ownership in Italy was 40 years compared with 30 years in other
OECD countries in the early 1990s (Guiso *et al.* 1994). Yet the rate of home
ownership also increased partly because of fiscal policies that provided a favorable environment for home ownership. There is no wealth tax; property and other
related taxes are based on an administrative value that is generally below market
prices; and rebates are given for a household's primary residence (Fabrizio and
Poggio 2004: 193). Housing finance policies were deregulated in the late 1990s,
when the limits on down payments were lifted, information on credit risks for lending improved, banks were restructured, and greater competition between banks
for mortgage finance has ensued with the establishment of the European Union
(Aalbers 2007).

Rent control and limited mortgage availability for housing have reduced housing mobility in Italy in general since the 1960s (Cannari *et al.* 2000). In the 1980s,
there was pressure on the ownership market because of the squeeze placed on
rental housing by *Equo Canone*; in the 1990s, new house sales were motivated
by a demand for better housing quality, which was "particularly intense for historic buildings located in prime urban areas (usually central areas)" (Ave 1996:

102). Padovani confirms that, in cases in which there was sufficient demand for high-income residential and commercial uses, "there was a natural tendency to intervene in the older urban fabric, which was usually centrally located" (1984: 266). The development strategy for these areas aimed at renovating older buildings, to make them appealing to people who could afford to pay for the locational preferences of the area. In sum, the dominant owner-occupied market proved to be "less and less capable of taking in the growing number of households, which resulted in a standstill of the [downward] filtering process" (van Hees 1991: 26). According to Ave (1996), the proportion of first-time homeowners fell from seven out of ten housing market transactions in 1980 to two out of ten transactions in 1990. That is, transactions were mainly confined to the existing housing stock.

## CONSERVATION POLICIES

Conservation policies towards older housing stock through rehabilitation and renovation began in the 1970s, partly because of the reduction in the supply of new housing stock (Figure 11.2). The *Piano di Recupero Urbano* (Urban Renewal Plan) was implemented as a part of the *Piano Decenale* (the 10-year development plan) in 1978, which provided state funds for restoration to both private owners and local administrations. In return for such state funds, a percentage of the renovated housing was to be allocated to households falling below certain income levels. Public and private investment in the rehabilitation of older housing increased not only in Rome, but also in Italy in general, because of the older age of housing stock. At the beginning of the 1960s, investment in rehabilitation accounted for only 15 percent of total housing investments; this rose to 42 percent by the late 1970s and to 61 percent in the late 1990s (Padovani 1996: 199; Padovani and Vettoretto 2003: 91).

Although the rehabilitation efforts were motivated by social equity goals of providing housing to low-income groups, "the restored units were usually targeted for sale to medium- and upper-income level households, because of their central location and the good historical character of the renovated buildings" (Ave 1996: 47). Rehabilitation of housing took on an especially significant meaning in the *Rioni*. The increased private interest in rehabilitation was instrumental in the gentrification of several neighborhood districts, including the traditionally working-class neighborhoods such as Testaccio. Conservation policy in Rome is, however, distinct from other Italian cities; it is much stricter, and strives to maintain the original ambiance of the city. Fried explains regulations thus:

> In Zone A1 which contains buildings of the highest historical or artistic importance, renovation will be allowed strictly for the purposes of health and safety; identical form, facade, color, volume and even internal structure have to be retained.

> Buildings in A2 zones, in themselves less important than those in A1 but forming a characteristic "ambiente", may be renovated, providing that their external color and appearance are not changed or their total floor space increased. In A3 districts, buildings may be renovated on a speculative basis, on condition that the characteristic architecture of the district is preserved ... In no building within Zone A can any alterations or additions be made without authorization of the superintendent of monuments.
>
> (1973: 59)

The 2000 master plan also lays out detailed guidelines for rehabilitation, demolition, and reconstruction of buildings in the historical core. These conservation efforts became effective in maintaining Rome's timeless image of the eternal city (Agnew 1995: 76), and enhanced the prestige of living in the center. All these efforts aided in enhancing the value of the old housing stock in most parts of the *Rioni*.

## CONCLUSION

Although housing filtering has attracted attention in the American planning literature, the literature on its diffusion in the international context is still emerging. We have argued that the filtering process observed in Rome is a deviation from that of American cities. A Popperian approach would hold that the filtering process, which has been broadly confirmed in American cities, is falsified in the Roman context. Indeed, the limited literature that exists on housing filtering in the international context is critical of the concept's applicability. This raises the dilemma of a bias toward falsification or confirmation: When the concept and evidence do not reinforce each other in an easily discoverable way, do we reject the concept as false? Or are we so vested in theory that we reject the facts as being inadequate or irrelevant?

We have suggested that this dichotomy of theory and facts may not be as oppositional as it first appears. Falsification and confirmation do not exhaust the universe of a discourse of inquiry. Rather, institutional biases could inhibit the diffusion of a concept. The institutional conditions in Rome facilitated reverse filtering, in contrast to the downward filtering observed in American cities. The social geography of Rome indicates that the central areas of the city have been more prestigious and attractive for people of higher socio-economic status. We identified three institutional factors facilitating reverse filtering: rent control policies, housing finance policies, and conservation policies. Although Rome provides a case for the falsification of filtering, we are able, in our view, to protect the value of the filtering concept in American cities by drawing institutional boundaries around the diffusion of the concept. That is, there are important institutional parameters that need to be made explicit when applying a planning concept in a different context.

## References

Aalbers, M. B. (2007). "Geographies of housing finance: The mortgage market in Milan, Italy." *Growth and Change*, **38** (2), 174–99.

Aaron, H. J. (1972). *Shelter and subsidies: Who benefits from federal housing policies?* Washington DC: Brookings Institution.

Adler, M. (1988). "The American dream and central city blight are American." *Journal of Economic Behavior & Organization*, **9** (4), 381–92.

Agnew, J. (1995). *Rome*. Chichester: John Wiley and Sons.

Agnew, J. and Bolling, K. (1993). "Two Romes or more? The use and abuse of the center–periphery metaphor." *Urban Geography*, **14** (2), 119–44.

Allen, C, Gallent, N., and Tewdwr-Jones, M. (1999). "The limits of policy diffusion: Comparative experiences of second-home ownership in Britain and Sweden." *Environment and Planning C: Government and Policy*, **17** (2), 227–44.

Archibugi, F. (2001). *The new master plan of Rome: A plan without strategy.* Accessed online at http://www.francoarchibugi.it/pdf/masterplan_rome.pdf (15 December 2008).

Arnott, R. J. and Braid, R. M. (1997). "A filtering model with steady-state housing." *Regional Science and Urban Economics*, **27** (4–5), 515–46.

Aureli, E. and Baldazzi, B. (1998). "Households and territory: The location of the population of Rome in relation to housing supply characteristics." *Social Indicators Research*, **44** (1), 97–118.

Ave, G. (1996). *Urban land and property markets in Italy*. London: UCL Press.

Baer, W. C. (1991). "Filtering and Third World housing policy." *Third World Planning Review*, **13** (1), 69–82.

Baer, W. C. and Koo, C. (1994). "Housing turnover in developing nations: The case of Seoul." *Journal of Planning Education and Research*, **13** (2), 104–18.

Baer, W. C. and Williamson, C. (1988). "The filtering of households and housing units." *Journal of Planning Literature*, **3** (2), 127–52.

Bagnasco, C. (1987). "Roman toponymy: Characteristics and historical development." In M. Bonnes (Ed.), *Urban ecology applied to the city of Rome* (pp. 19–22). UNESCO Programme on Man and Biosphere. Rome: Istituto di Psicologia Consiglio Nazionale delle Ricerche.

Bates, L. K. (2003). *Can housing filter without the neighborhood filtering? An empirical investigation.* Chapel Hill, NC: Dept. of City and Regional Planning, University of North Carolina-Chapel Hill.

Bellicini, L. and Toso, F. (1995). "Rome." In J. Berry and S. McGreal (Eds.), *European cities, planning systems and property markets* (pp. 235–47). London: E & FN Spon.

Berry, B. J. L. (1980). "Inner city futures: An American dilemma revisited." *Transactions of the Institute of British Geographers*, **5** (1), 1–28.

Berry, B. J. L. (1985). "Islands of renewal in seas of decay." In P. E. Peterson (Ed.), *The new urban reality* (pp. 69–96). Washington DC: Brookings.

Bier, T. (1995). "Housing dynamics of the Cleveland area." In W. D. Keating, N. Krumholz, and D. C. Perry (Eds.), *Cleveland: A metropolitan reader* (pp. 244–60). Kent, OH: Kent State University Press.

Bier, T. (2001). *Moving up, filtering down: Metropolitan housing dynamics and public policy* (Discussion paper). Washington DC: Brookings. Accessed online at http://www.brookings.edu/reports/2001/09metropolitanpolicy_bier.aspx (15 December 2008).

Boddy, M. and Gray, F. (1979). "Filtering theory, housing policy and the legitimation of inequality." *Policy and Politics*, **7** (1), 39–54.

Bond, E. and Coulson, E. (1989). "Externalities, filtering and neighborhood change." *Journal of Urban Economics*, **26** (2), 231–49.

Braid, R. (1981). "The short-run comparative statics of a rental housing market." *Journal of Urban Economics*, **10** (3), 286–310.

Braun, D. and Gilardi, F. (2006). "Taking "Galton's Problem" seriously: Towards a theory of policy diffusion." *Journal of Theoretical Politics*, **18** (3), 298–322.

Breen, A. and Rigby, D. (1996). *The new waterfront: A worldwide urban success story.* London: Thames & Hudson.

Burgess, E. W. (1925). "The growth of the city: An introduction to a research project." In R. E. Park, E. W. Burgess, R. D. McKenzie, and M. Janowitz (Eds.), *The city: Suggestions for investigation of human behavior in* the *urban environment* (pp. 47–62). Chicago: University of Chicago Press.

Cannari, L., Nucci, F., and Sestito, P. (2000). "Geographic labour mobility and the cost of housing: Evidence from Italy." *Applied Economics*, **32** (14), 1899–906.

Commune di Roma. (2005). *Roma: Mosaico Statistico No. 3.* Rome: Commune di Roma. Accessed online at http://cedoc.sirio.regione.lazio.it/DOCUMENTI/349643MosaicoStatistico3_2005.pdf (15 December 2008)

Coulson, N. E. and McMillen, D. P. (2007). "The dynamics of intraurban quantile house price indexes." *Urban Studies*, **44** (8), 1517–37.

Cristaldi, F. (2002). "Multiethnic Rome: Toward residential segregation?" *GeoJournal*, **58** (2–3), 81–90.

Dogan, M. and Pelassy, D. (1990). *How to compare nations: Strategies in comparative politics.* Chatham, NJ: Chatham House Publishers.

Dolowitz, D. P. and Marsh, D. (1996). "Who learns what from whom: A review of the policy transfer literature." *Political Studies*, **44** (2), 343–58.

Dolowitz, D. P. and Marsh, D. (2000). "Learning from abroad: The role of policy transfer in contemporary policy-making." *Governance: An International Journal of Policy and Administration*, **13** (1), 5–23.

Donne, M. D. (1992). "Rome the capital: The impending suburbs and strategies of integration-decentralization." *Journal of Architectural Education*, **46** (1), 21–7.

Fabrizio, B. and Poggio, T. (2004). "Home ownership and social inequality in Italy." In K. Kurz and H. P. Blossfeld (Eds.), *Home ownership and social inequality in comparative perspective* (pp. 187–232). Stanford, CA: Stanford University Press.

Ferchiou, R. (1982). "The indirect effects of new housing construction in developing countries." *Urban Studies*, **19** (2), 167–76.

Fisher, E. M. and Winnick, L. (1951). "A reformulation of the filtering concept." *Journal of Social Issues*, **7** (1–2), 47–85.

Fried, R. C. (1973). *Planning* the *eternal city: Roman politics and planning since World War II.* New Haven, CT: Yale University Press.

Galster, G. (1996). "William Grigsby and the analysis of housing sub-markets and filtering." *Urban Studies*, **33** (10), 1797–805.

Galster, G. and Rothenberg, J. (1991). "Filtering in urban housing: A graphical analysis of a quality-segmented market." *Journal of Planning Education and Research*, **11** (1), 37–50.

Gibb, K. (2003). "Urban housing models." In T. O'Sullivan and K. Gibb (Eds.), *Housing economics and public policy: Essays in honour of Duncan Maclennan* (pp. 22–37). Malden, MA: Blackwell Publishing.

Glaeser, E. L. and Gyourko, J. (2005). "Urban decline and durable housing." *Journal of Political Economy*, **113** (2), 345–75.

Grigsby, W. G. (1963). *Housing markets and public policy*. Philadelphia: University of Pennsylvania Press.

Grigsby, W., Baratz, M., Galster, G., and Maclennan, D. (1987). "The dynamics of neighborhood change and decline." *Progress in Planning*, **28** (1), 1–76.

Guiso, L., Jappelli, T., and Terlizzese, D. (1994). "Housing finance arrangements, intergenerational transfers and consumption: The Italian experience." *Economic Modelling*, **11** (2), 145–55.

Guttenberg, A. (1988). "*Abusivismo* and the *borgate* of Rome." In Carl V. Patton (Ed.), *Spontaneous shelter: International perspectives and prospects* (pp. 258–76). Philadelphia: Temple University Press.

Ha, S. (2004). "Housing renewal and neighborhood change as a gentrification process in Seoul." *Cities*, **21** (5), 381–9.

Harris, R. (1990). "Self-building and the social geography of Toronto, 1901–1913: A challenge for urban theory." *Transactions of the Institute of British Geographers*, **15** (4), 387–402.

Healey, P. and Williams, R. (1993). "European urban planning systems: Diversity and convergence." *Urban Studies*, **30** (4–5), 701–20.

van Hees, I. L. M. (1991). "The Italian housing market: Its failures and their causes." *Urban Studies*, **28** (1), 15–39.

Hegedus, J. and Tosics, I. (1991). "Filtering in socialist housing systems: Results of vacancy chain surveys in Hungary." *Urban Geography*, **12** (1), 19–34.

Howe, D. A. and DeRidder, T. (1993). "Targeting the elderly to meet the housing needs of very low and low income families." *Journal of Planning Education and Research*, **12** (3), 241–8.

Hoyt, H. (1939). *The structure and growth of residential neighborhoods in American cities*. Washington DC: Federal Housing Administration.

Hoyt, L. (2006). "Importing ideas: The transnational transfer of urban revitalization policy." *International Journal of Public Administration*, **29** (1–3), 221–43.

Istituto Nazionale di Statistica (ISTAT). (1995). *I Grandi Communi: Roma, 13 censimento generale della popolazione e delle abitazioni*. Rome: ISTAT.

Istituto Nazionale di Statistica (ISTAT). (2006). *Popolazione residente e abitazioni nei grandi comuni Italiani: Roma. 14 Censimento generale della popolazione e delle abitazioni*. Accessed online at http://www.istat.it/dati/catalogo/20071113_01/gc_roma.pdf (15 December 2008).

James, O. and Lodge, M. (2003). "The limitations of 'policy transfer' and 'lesson drawing' for public policy research." *Political Studies Review*, **1** (2), 179–93.

Johnson, T. E. (1987). "Upward filtering of housing stock." *Habitat International*, **11** (1), 173–90.

Keating, W. D., Krumholz, B., and Star, P. (Eds.). (1996). *Revitalizing urban neighborhoods*. Lawrence: University Press of Kansas.

Kristof, F. (1965). "Housing policy goals and the turnover of housing." *Journal of the American Institute of Planners*, **31** (3), 232–45.

Lansing, J. B., Clifton, C. W., and Morgan, J. N. (1969). *New homes for poor people: A study of chains of moves*. Ann Arbor, MI: Institute of Social Research.

Leitmann, J. (1998). "Policy and practice options for managing protected areas: Lessons from international experience." *Journal of Environmental Planning and Management*, **41** (1), 129–44.

Lloyd, M. G., McCarthy, J., McGreal, S., and Berry, J. (2003). "Business improvement districts, planning, and urban regeneration." *International Planning Studies*, **8** (4), 295–321.

Lowry, I. S. (1960). "Filtering and housing standards: A conceptual analysis." *Land Economics*, **36** (4), 362–70.

Lucy, W. H. and Phillips, D. L. (2006). *Tomorrow's cities, tomorrow's suburbs*. Chicago: American Planning Association.

Malpezzi, S. and Green, R. K. (1996). "What has happened to the bottom of the US housing market?" *Urban Studies*, **33** (10), 1807–20.

McElrath, D. C. (1962). "The social areas of Rome: A comparative analysis." *American Sociological Review*, **27** (3), 376–91.

Mocine, C. R. (1969). "The new plan for Rome." *AIP Journal*, **35** (6), 376–82.

Montanari, A., Staniscia, B., and Di Zio, S. (2007). "The Italian way to deconcentration: Rome: The appeal of the historic centre. Chieti-Pescara: The strength of the periphery." In E. Razin, M. J. Dijst, and C. I. Vazquez (Eds.), *Employment deconcentration in European metropolitan areas: Market forces versus planning regulations* (pp. 145–78). Dordecht, the Netherlands: Springer.

Mossberger, K. (2000). *The politics of ideas and the spread of enterprise zones*. Washington DC: Georgetown University Press.

Mossberger, K. and Wolman, H. (2003). "Policy transfer as a form of prospective policy evaluation: Challenges and recommendations." *Public Administration Review*, **63** (4), 428–40.

Myers, D. (1975). "Housing allowances, submarket relationships, and the filtering process." *Urban Affairs Quarterly*, **11** (2), 215–40.

Myers, D. (1981). "Housing progress in the seventies: New indicators." *Social Indicators Research*, **9** (1), 35–60.

Myers, D. (1983). "Upward mobility and the filtering process." *Journal of Planning Education and Research*, **2** (2), 101–12.

Needleman, L. (1965). *The economics of housing*. London: Staples.

Nomisma. (2005). *Il Rapporto 2005: Osservatorio sul mercato immobiliare*. Bologna: Nomisma Real Estate.

Nomisma. (2007). *III Rapporto 2007: Osservatorio sul mercato immobiliare*. Bologna: Nomisma Real Estate.

North, D. (1990). *Institutions, institutional change and economic performance*. New York: University of Cambridge.

Nourse, H. O. (1973). *The effect of public policy on housing markets*. Lexington, MA: Lexington Books.

Ohls, J. C. (1975). "Public policy toward low income housing and filtering in housing markets." *Journal of Urban Economics*, **2** (2), 144–71.

Olsen, E. O. (1969). "A competitive theory of the housing market." *The American Economic Review*, **59** (4), 612–22.

Pacione, M. (1998). "The social geography of Rome." *Tijdschrift voor Economische en Sociale Geografie*, **89** (4), 359–70.

Padovani, L. (1984). "Italy." In M. Wynn (Ed.), *Housing in Europe* (pp. 247–80). London: Croom Helm.

Padovani, L. (1996). "Italy." In P. Balchin (Ed.), *Housing policy in Europe* (pp. 188–209). London: Routledge.

Padovani, L. and Vettoretto, L. (2003). "Italy." In N. Gallent, M. Shucksmith, and M. Tewdwr-Jones (Eds.), *Housing in the European countryside: Rural pressure and policy in Western Europe* (pp. 91–115). London: Routledge.

Peel, D. and Lloyd, G. (2008). "Re-generating learning in the public realm: Evidence-based policy making and business improvement districts in the UK." *Public Policy and Administration*, **23** (2), 189–205.

Popper, K. R. (1959). *The logic of scientific discovery*. New York: Basic Books.

Ratcliff, R. U. (1949). *Urban land economics*. New York: McGraw-Hill.

Sands, G. and Bower, L. (1976). *Vacancy chains in the local housing market*. Ithaca, NY: Center for Urban Development Research, Cornell University.

Sanyal, B. (2005). "Hybrid planning cultures: The search for the global cultural commons." In B. Sanyal (Ed.), *Comparative planning cultures* (pp. 3–28). London: Routledge.

Scenari Immobiliari. (2008). "Rome in 2008." Rome: Scenari Immobiliari. Accessed online at http://www.scenari-immobiliari.it/ENPublic/fset0q.aspx?cat=M2&page=fset0q_M2.aspx (15 December 2008).

Schall, L. (1981). "Commodity chain systems and the housing market." *Journal of Urban Economics*, **10** (2), 141–63.

Skaburskis, A. (2006). "Filtering, city change and the supply of low-priced housing in Canada." *Urban Studies*, **43** (3), 533–58.

Somerville, C. T. and Holmes, C. (2001). "Dynamics of affordable housing stock: Microdata analysis of filtering." *Journal of Housing Research*, **12** (1), 115–40.

Stegman, M. A. (1977). "The neighborhood effects of filtering." *Real Estate Economics*, **5** (2), 227–41.

Strassman, P. (1982). *The transformation of urban housing: The experience of upgrading in Cartagena*. Baltimore: Johns Hopkins University Press.

Sweeney, J. L. (1974). "A commodity hierarchy model of the rental housing market." *Journal of Urban Economics*, **1** (3), 288–323.

Tait, M. and Jensen, O. B. (2007). "Travelling ideas, power and place: The cases of urban villages and business improvement districts." *International Planning Studies*, **12** (2), 107–28.

Temkin, K. and Rohe, W. (1996). "Neighborhood change and urban policy." *Journal of Planning Education and Research*, **15** (3), 159–70.

Varady, D. P. (1986). *Neighborhood upgrading*. Albany: State University of New York Press.

Verma, N. (2007). "Institutions and planning: An analogical inquiry." In N. Verma (Ed.), *Institutions and Planning* (pp. 1–14). Oxford: Elsevier.

Weyland, K. G. (2005). "Theories of policy diffusion: Lessons from Latin American pension reform." *World Politics*, **57** (2), 262–95.

White, H. C. (1971). "Multipliers, vacancy chains, and filtering in housing." *Journal of the American Planning Association*, **37** (2), 88–94.

White, P. (1984). *The West European city: A social geography*. London: Longman.

CHAPTER 12

# DEVELOPMENTAL PLANNING FOR SUSTAINABLE URBANIZATION IN ASIA

**JIEMING ZHU**

## INTRODUCTION

Turning ideas into action, urban planning is a mechanism expected to function in the transformation of society according to objectives pre-set collectively. Whether planning has achieved what is intended remains a task of historical stocktaking (Friedmann 1987), and such an evaluation could most likely yield mixed results. This chapter approaches planning from the perspective of its three forms: zoning, for the regulation of physical development; spatial land-use plans for the configuration of city structures, following ideas about human settlements; and processes of plan making, for the coordination of social stakeholders' interests. The nature of these three forms of urban planning is elaborated to probe how planning can turn ideas into action, and thus shape cities in line with planned goals.

I will focus on Asia, which is a late developer and one of the less developed regions in the world, with an urbanization level far below that of developed countries. Today, an urbanizing Asia is facing serious challenges of high population density and thus acute land scarcity. Prevalent informal developments coexist alongside flourishing private, gated housing estates. These twin phenomena result from the failure of planning in the public domain. A deterioration of urban quarters, and social segregation caused by the gated communities, aggravate a worsening social divide and environmental problems. As land and people are two essential concerns in urban planning, sustainable urbanization in the Asian context must lie in efficient land developments to accommodate people in decent housing. Inefficient economic development wastes resources unnecessarily, adding to tension in social relations and pressure on the environment.

The reality in Asian developing countries is that the legitimacy of regulatory planning authorities is significantly weakened by the incapacity of municipal governments to provide public and social goods. When public governance fails, private governance arises. In many Western countries, urban planning seems to have lost a developmental orientation, apparently no longer attempting to mold a sustainable mode of urbanization. Yet many Asian cities are now experiencing a process of rapid urban development much greater than that which gave momentum to the urban planning movement in Western Europe and the United States a century ago. Developing capacity for the mobilization of land resources and a response to market forces is crucial in high-density, developing Asia. This is essential to curb a vicious cycle that is causing locked-in urban decay, and private planning, which exacerbates social segregation and undermines attempts to build sustainable urban environments.

## THE NATURE OF URBAN PLANNING

There is a broad consensus that the general objectives of urban planning are to help achieve economic efficiency, social equity and environmental sustainability in shaping and reshaping the urban built environment (CSD 1999; UN-Habitat 2009). However, there is no consensus that urban planning is able to successfully achieve these noble aims. The nature of urban planning needs to be scrutinized further.

### PLANS: DEVELOPMENTAL INTENTIONS

According to a definition widely cited in the UK in the 1960s and 1970s, urban planning is "the art and the science of ordering the use of land and the character and siting of buildings and communication routes so as to secure the maximum practicable degree of economy, convenience and beauty" (Keeble 1969: 1). Clearly, this definition refers to the role of planning in city-making. An understanding of planning as a positive instrument for socio-economic change is demonstrated by efforts to build cities according to pre-prepared plans. Well-known urban design ideas such as the Garden City, the Radiant City, the City Beautiful, and the Neighborhood Unit (see Chapter 4) have been inspirational to urban planners for many generations. The preparation of plans, or plan-making, has always been at the core of the planning profession as well as a concern of the general public, as the implementation of plans can influence the character of urban physical structures and thus the lives of urban residents.

Regional planning in developed countries intends to coordinate a balanced regional development. This is done either by allocating designated marginal areas a greater share of public resources, or by restricting developments in prosperous localities, so that less favorable areas are more likely to receive investment (Wannop 1995).[1] Such measures are based on a normative concept of "growth poles," which gained currency in the mid-twentieth century to address unequal regional development, overtaking the positive theory of polarized development (Friedmann and Weaver 1979). However, the "growth poles" theory lacks supporting empirical evidence, and regional economic development mediated by the redistribution of market-driven economic development activities does not necessarily achieve a positive outcome.

Local economic development has become one of the top priorities for municipal governments in many Western industrial cities. In such cities, developmental approaches have shifted from promoting better overall conditions in rapidly expanding cities to a concern with reviving the economies of cities experiencing structural change of their economies and suffering job losses. In inner cities, where land and property costs are comparatively low but still fail to attract investment, it is obvious that markets have failed. Urban planning as a tool of public intervention is therefore tasked with formulating courses of action to create positive socio-economic change. To promote economic development, local governments must take on "an initiating rather than a passive role" (Blakely 1994: 52). Economic development and public/private partnerships have replaced welfare provision, and governments have become "enterprise states" (Cochrane 1991). Place marketing is actively promoted, aiming to develop economic confidence and to attract inward investment, especially mobile international capital. City governments have shifted their roles from conventional regulators to entrepreneurial developers (Jessop 1998).

The link between local economic development strategies and urban planning is that such strategies are often property-led, such as the "development of high-profile prestige property projects and investment in city place promotion or boosterist activities, geared at enhancing the economic position of a city in relation to other urban centres" (Loftman and Nevin 1998: 129).[2] Insofar as the firms behind such activities are either largely autonomous or privately owned, as growth engines they are not subject to government planning, but operate freely according to market principles. The capacity of local governments and communities to stimulate or to maintain economic activities in particular areas is thus limited, and often the most that city planning departments can do is to marshal the land-related resources that are one way or another under government control. However, urban renewal practices have not proved that property-led regeneration is a convincing model leading to sustainable local growth (Turok 1992). Local developmental planning remains an unproven solution.

In market economies, where development decisions are taken primarily by private developers, there are few resources within planning systems to stimulate market initiatives and thus to guarantee the implementation of plans. Planning departments can exercise a measure of control only when the development market is buoyant (by picking and choosing between proposals), or when developers are public agencies (such as in Singapore, or with the national capital New Town Development Corporations that built Brasilia and Canberra).[3] By the end of the twentieth century, urban planning in developed countries had increasingly become a tool for urban governments to mediate between various interests in a pluralist society, instead of being a statement of visions and missions.

## DEVELOPMENT CONTROL: REGULATORY

The regulation of physical development in cities has a long history and may be considered an archaic form of town planning. According to McLoughlin, with this approach "control was exercised by the full force of *the law* and was very largely negative in effect, i.e. the schemes and their implementation were concerned with what should not occur rather than what should come about" (1973: 15–16, original emphasis). Singapore's first-ever comprehensive land-use Master Plan was created only in 1958, but since 1856, over 100 years earlier, Singapore Municipal Commissioners had had the power to demand that private persons who wished to build structures submit notice of their intentions to the authorities. The purpose of such development control was to ensure adequate light, air, and services to buildings.

Perceived "as a set of activities which seek to maintain the existing order rather than to initiate and even sustain radical changes" (McLoughlin 1973: 32), development control is essential in maintaining order in shaping the built environment through internalizing externalities and preserving the status quo, based on the property rights of existing land owners. It is a somewhat passive tool of plan implementation.[4] In this model, planning acts as an effective means of maintaining the interests of property owners and establishing order for the land market, provided that the planning machinery has statutory power. Such mechanisms for regulating urban development were often transferred from developed to developing countries, notably through colonial channels.

In developed countries, minimal legal controls based on public health and private contracts seem to have managed dramatic urban changes reasonably well. Many old cities have become cultural assets through the merits of a combination of embedded bottom-up diversity in the built-up environment and spontaneous development. A plausible reason for such successful legal management in such cities is that the pace and scale of urbanization were much slower and smaller than many developing countries experienced in the twentieth century.

## THE PROCESS OF PLAN-MAKING: REGULATING COMPETITION AMONG STAKEHOLDERS

Riding on the wave of post-World War II economic booms and dynamic urbanization, an expansion of planning practices gave planners a chance to reflect on the procedural theory of planning (Faludi 1973). The essence of procedural theories of plan-making at that time rested with the rational procedure and scientific method for decision-making. Such a rationality demanded that "clear objectives . . . be identified and then achieved, either by large steps (comprehensive plans), small steps (incrementalism) or popular will (advocacy)" (Cooke 1983: 67). The assumption was that planners should improve the welfare of all members of society if plans were generated rationally.

However, rational planning theory overlooked the complex political nature of planning. As Davidoff comments, "the right course of action is always a matter of choice, never of fact" (1965: 331). Building consensus in the formulation of planning goals and objectives is practically illusive in pluralist societies. Yet the participation of communities and residents in the planning of their locale, instead of its being governed by planners' rational thinking, has nevertheless become the foundation of plan-making processes in Western conceptions of planning. Reflecting the political nature of town planning, the current focus on public participation is a focus on procedures to mediate conflict over what development should take place and where, rather than on translating policies into action.

A lack of consensus can stall planning actions. Therefore, consensus-building in pluralist democratic and fragmented societies emerges as a central issue if urban planning is to remain meaningful and effective. Consensus-building stimulates the development of communicative or collaborative planning, which is emerging as a new paradigm of procedural theory (Healey 1992, 1997; Innes 1995). Collaborative planning offers a way in which "political communities may organize to improve the quality of their places" (Healey 1997: xii). Since the 1970s, in the West there has been a clear shift of interest from substantive theories of planning (that is, plans) to procedural theory of planning (the process of plan-making), as by then most Western countries were fully urbanized with mature economies, and facing a slowing urban physical change, which meant that plans were not in great demand. The democratic management of urban change in societies with diverse social structures became an essential issue in planning.

## The nature of urban planning: more regulatory than developmental

So far, this investigation has shown that urban planning can be an effective tool for maintaining spatial order, coordinating economic development with orderly land use and sufficient public and merit goods, and managing the landed interests of diverse urban communities. But urban planning is not able to shape new physical landscapes according to pre-set goals and socio-economic policies without a capacity for mobilizing economic resources and social support. Urban planning in its conventional mode is passive, and tends to maintain the status quo. As a public instrument, urban planning in many Western contexts had become, by the end of the twentieth century, more regulatory than developmental.

In a diverse community with a pluralist polity and a market economy, planning consensus is hard to achieve and thus development actions have to remain on the shelf. Balancing and coordinating various stakeholders' interests makes participatory planning more conservative than visionary, and keeping existing relationships unchanged often ends up as the only default option if agreements cannot be reached. For example, sprawling suburbanization as witnessed in the growth of American cities resulted as a compromise between an expanding population seeking new residential districts, and the interests of residents of existing suburbs who resisted more intense development in their own areas (the "Nimby" – "Not In My Back Yard" – phenomenon). Although this is not considered a sustainable mode of development, the United States at least has enough land to accommodate urban sprawl. High-density Asian countries, in contrast, cannot afford low-density sprawl. Many current planning ideas and techniques for managing urban development are therefore not appropriate.

## ASIAN URBANIZATION AND ITS CHALLENGES

### RAPID URBANIZATION

The urbanization levels of most Asian developing countries are far below those of developed countries (Table 12.1). Social and economic developments are, to a great extent, equivalent to levels of industrialization and urbanization. Cities in Asian developing countries are still growing to accommodate large numbers of rural-to-urban migrants and urbanizing economies. An expansion of urban spatial structures is critical for these cities to provide rapidly growing urban economies with sufficient infrastructure and physical premises, while deteriorating old towns have to be refurnished and redeveloped.

According to Davis and Golden (1954) and Zelinsky (1971), the progress of urbanization proceeds through a phase of first accelerating, then decelerating urban growth, driven by rising and then falling rates of industrialization and immigration to cities. It took England and Wales 100 years (1801–1901) to increase urban residents as a percentage of the total population by 44 percentage points. In contrast, East Asia (excluding mainland China) took 50 years (1950–2000) to increase its urban population by 36 percentage points (Table 12.2), Venezuela 34 years (1936–70) to increase its urban population by 47 percentage points (Chaves 1975) and the former Soviet Union 44 years (1926–70) to increase its urban population by 38 percentage points (Lappo and Pivovarov 1975). It has been recognized that late developers tend to have faster urban growth rates than early developers. Rapid urbanization since the late twentieth century has been a

**Table 12.1** Urbanization levels in Asia (% of population living in cities, 2007)

| | |
|---|---|
| *World* | *50* |
| Developed countries | 75 |
| Asia | 41 |
| China | 42 |
| Japan | 66 |
| Mongolia | 57 |
| Cambodia | 21 |
| Indonesia | 50 |
| Laos | 21 |
| Malaysia | 69 |
| Myanmar | 32 |
| Philippines | 64 |
| Thailand | 33 |
| Vietnam | 27 |
| Bangladesh | 26 |
| India | 29 |
| Pakistan | 36 |
| Sri Lanka | 15 |

Source: United Nations Population Fund (2007).

**Table 12.2** Estimated urbanization level (urban population as % of the total) in China, East Asia, and West Europe (1950–2000), and in England and Wales (1650–1951)

| | 1950 | 1960 | 1970 | 1980 | 1990 | 2000 | 2004 |
|---|---|---|---|---|---|---|---|
| Mainland China[a] | 12.5 | 19.8 | 17.4 | 19.4 | 26.4 | 36.2 | 41.8 |
| East Asia[b] (excluding mainland China) | 33.1 | 41.0 | 51.6 | 59.6 | 66.0 | 69.1 | – |
| West Europe[c] | 65.3 | 69.7 | 74.3 | 76.6 | 78.6 | 80.5 | – |
| | 1650 | 1750 | 1800 | 1801 | 1901 | 1951 | |
| England and Wales[d] | 8.8 | 16.7 | 20.3 | 33.8 | 78.0 | 80.8 | |

Sources: compiled from: a. NBSC (2005); b. United Nations (2004); East Asia includes China (inclusive of Taiwan, Hong Kong, and Macao), North Korea, South Korea, Japan, and Mongolia; c. United Nations (2004); West Europe is composed of Austria, Belgium, France, Germany, Liechtenstein, Luxembourg, Monaco, the Netherlands, and Switzerland; d. de Vries (1984: 39) for data from 1650 to 1800, urban population of all cities with at least 10,000 inhabitants; Law (1967) for data from 1801 to 1901; and Champion (1975) for 1951 data.

significant characteristic of Asian development. For instance, within 18 years, 250 million additional people in China moved to cities (Table 12.3).

## CHALLENGES: HIGH POPULATION DENSITY AND ACUTE LAND SCARCITY

The high population density prevalent in Asia makes urban land resources very scarce, and generates intensive competition for access to land. This intensifies both the spatial and temporal processes of urbanization in terms of people and land. The efficient use of land to maximize building space and urban facilities becomes a critical issue on the urban planning agenda. Sustainability in Asian developing countries hinges on their economic sustainability first and foremost, which, in turn, relies much on the efficiency and productivity of their economies. In developing countries endowed with natural resources on a per capita basis far below the world average, social and environmental sustainability depends much more on efficient wealth creation in the first place. Inefficient economic development wastes resources unnecessarily, and the poor economy adds to tension in social relations and pressure on the environment.

Asia's population has accounted for about 60 percent of the world total, while its urban population as a percentage of the world total urban population increased from 32 percent in 1950 to 49 percent in 2005 (see http://esa.un.org/unpp/, accessed 19 October 2007). Asia has urbanized much faster than the rest of the world over the past 50 years. However, the land area of Asia is only about a quarter of the world total. Asia is thus the most densely populated region in the world. While South-East Asia's population was growing faster in the past 50 years than the world average, population density rose significantly because of the unfavorable endowment of land resources (Table 12.4). Moreover, population is unevenly distributed in these underdeveloped countries, making for even higher densities. For instance, Java is the most populated region of Indonesia. Its land area accounts for 6.9 percent of the national total; however, about 60 percent of Indonesians live in Java. Located in Java, the national capital city of Jakarta had a population of 1.8 million in 1952, and this figure hit 8.6 million in 2003 with a

**Table 12.3** Urbanization and increase of urban population, China

|                                                      | 1950 |      | 1980 | 1982 |       | 2000 |
| ---------------------------------------------------- | ---- | ---- | ---- | ---- | ----- | ---- |
| Urbanization level (urban population as % of total)  | 12.5 |      | 19.4 | 21.4 |       | 36.2 |
| Net increase of urban population (million)           |      | 93.4 |      |      | 253.9 |      |

Sources: compiled from NBSC (1999) and Shen (2005).

**Table 12.4** Population density in the world and in South-East Asian countries (persons per km²)

| Region/country | 1950 | % of world level | 2005 | % of world level |
|---|---|---|---|---|
| World | 19 | 100 | 48 | 100 |
| Asia | 44 | 232 | 124 | 258 |
| South-East Asia | 40 | 211 | 124 | 258 |
| Bangladesh | 305 | 1,605 | 1,064 | 2,217 |
| Philippines | 67 | 353 | 282 | 588 |
| Vietnam | 83 | 437 | 256 | 533 |
| Thailand | 40 | 211 | 123 | 256 |
| Indonesia | 42 | 221 | 119 | 248 |

Source: http://esa.un.org/unpp/, accessed on 12 October 2007.

**Table 12.5** Rising population density in Dhaka, Bangladesh

| Year | Approximate area (km²) | Population (thousands) | Density (person/km²) |
|---|---|---|---|
| 1947 | 31.1 | 250 | 8,000 |
| 1971 | 103.6 | 1,500 | 14,500 |
| 1998 | 300 | 7,000 | 23,300 |

Source: Mahtab-uz-Zaman and Lau (2000: 143).

city area of just 650 km² (Firman and Dharmapatni 1994). Dhaka, the capital of Bangladesh, is another example that has experienced the rapid intensification common among Asian cities (Table 12.5).

## FAILURE OF PLANNING AS A REGULATORY TOOL

Long before modern urban planning emerged, the early urbanization of the countries now recognized as developed was shaped primarily by traditional land-use regulation practices. For instance, Britain was significantly transformed from a largely rural economy to a city-centered society during the Industrial Revolution (1750–1830): "by 1900, four Britons out of five were town-dwellers, compared to one in four two centuries earlier" (Sutcliffe 1981: 3). The population census revealed that, by 1911, 80.1 percent of the population were urban residents (Ashworth 1954). It is evident that the dramatic changes in Britain brought about by urbanization over the two centuries before 1900 were not guided and controlled by a framework of modern urban planning. The very term in English "town planning" was not coined until 1905 (Sutcliffe 1981), and the first UK Housing and Town Planning Act came into force only in 1909.

The fact that the idea of comprehensive public intervention emerged so late in British urban development poses an interesting challenge for historians. A reasonable inference would be that previous development controls were largely effective in managing urban land development when the pace of urbanization was relatively slow. Before the emergence of formal urban planning, the construction of city buildings and roads was controlled by piecemeal, ad hoc mechanisms exercised by public health authorities through by-laws (public health and building legislation), and by private landowners through covenants that restricted development (McLoughlin 1973). However, such mechanisms have not been available to guide development in Asia's current rapid urbanization. Instead, weak state governance and weak urban land use regulations have allowed developers catering for high-income residents to build where they liked, while low-income residents have been forced to help themselves to space wherever possible.

## URBAN LAND DEVELOPMENT WITHOUT EFFECTIVE DEVELOPMENT CONTROL

Walking on the streets or looking at the maps of many cities in Asian countries, the lack of mechanisms for regulating development is very obvious. This lack of development control could be attributed to the fact that these countries are still more or less rural societies, and, thus, that development control over land use as an urban institution has not yet been firmly established. In Vietnam, Leaf (2002) estimated that the proportion of urban premises built in the 1990s without official approval could be as high as 90 percent of all buildings developed. During the period 1992–4 in Hanoi, only 2,700 permits were granted for housing construction, whereas over 13,000 houses were actually built or re-built (Trinh and Nguyen 2001). Two in-depth, small-scale investigations revealed that illegal construction was rampant. A survey carried out by the Hanoi People's Committee in 1992 showed that, of 170 new houses built in a neighborhood, 150 did not have building permits. Those with official approvals disregarded the maximum two-story height restriction (Gillespie 1995). In a precinct of 2.5 ha in Ho Chi Minh City, where 2,675 households and 11,096 residents lived, 103 construction and renovation projects were carried out in 1995, and only five of these had permits (Luan *et al.* 2000). In Indonesia, similarly, development controls are not strictly observed as rules for land development, with many informal developments ignoring planning guidelines. Two-thirds of the total developments (including those by developers) in the Jakarta metropolis do not comply with zoning (Table 12.6).

**Table 12.6** Land development in compliance and non-compliance with zoning in Botabek (Jakarta metropolis without Jakarta central city)

| Compliance with zoning | | Non-compliance with zoning | | % of non-compliance in terms of area |
|---|---|---|---|---|
| No. of sites | Size (ha) | No. of sites | Size (ha) | |
| 237 | 17,433.5 | 403 | 33,338.0 | 65.7 |

Source: Susantono (1998: 140).

## CORRELATION BETWEEN INFORMAL DEVELOPMENTS AND NON-OBSERVANCE OF DEVELOPMENT CONTROL

Effective demand for formal housing, and underdeveloped housing financial systems, are not enough to support a housing development industry. Therefore, at the early stage of urbanization in many developing countries, self-built urban housing was a ubiquitous mode of housing provision. In Indonesia, about 85 percent of the annual new housing supply in the 1980s was built by the occupants or residents themselves (Struyk *et al.* 1990: 69). Between 50 and 70 percent of newly built housing spaces in Hanoi were constructed by private households on their own small landholdings in the 1990s (General Statistics Office, Socialist Republic of Vietnam 2003). This correlates with the situation in other cities in the developing world: "informal housing is estimated to account for 84 percent of all housing units built in Cairo from 1970–1981" (Brennan 1993: 83).

Because most poor migrants cannot afford formal housing by the market, they either squeeze into existing housing quarters and make these places denser, or build makeshift shelters on whatever vacant land is available legally or illegally. In the context of high population density, problems of land scarcity have been exacerbated by this mode of self-development through the construction of low-rise buildings on the periphery of cities where there are few services. In contrast, land use is far less efficient in urban, built-up areas where infrastructure and amenities are already provided up to a certain extent. According to a survey of six major Vietnamese cities (Hanoi, Ho Chi Minh City, Hai Phong, Da Nang, Can Tho, and Nha Trang) in the 1980s, single-story buildings made up 75 percent of the total built-up residential area. If two-story buildings are added, the total comes to 90 percent. The average number of stories for housing stock in Hanoi in the same period was 1.86 (Trinh and Parenteau 1991). With such low-rise development, scarce urban resources are seriously underutilized.

Because of the scarce provision of public and social goods, local governments' legitimacy in regulating urban and land development is considerably weakened; urban residents rely mainly on their own initiative to solve housing problems. Self-built housing is a laudable self-help initiative when the market and the state do not perform. However, it becomes unsustainable in the setting of high population

density. Self-built housing tends to ignore planning control guidelines in order
to maximize individual benefits, which subsequently imposes negative externalities on the neighborhood. Development control is made irrelevant. Disorganized
constructions in defiance of zoning (if there is any) produce illegal buildings and
informal settlements. Sooner or later, the neighborhood slides into a slum.

### DETERIORATED URBAN QUARTERS AND PRIVATE SUBURBAN HOUSING ESTATES

Because of poor economies and poverty, urban slums and shanty towns are common scenes in developing countries. Weak economies also plague the state's
capacity to provide public and social goods. Affordable public housing is far from
adequate, and urban infrastructure is always deficient and not up to standard. In
1991, Dowall and Leaf estimated that about 78 percent of Jakarta households did
not have access to piped water and drew water from household wells instead.
The massive flooding in Jakarta in early 2007 revealed the crisis in public works
faced by the municipal government. "Jakarta still relies on flood canals and sluice
gates built by the Dutch 160 years ago" (Ghani 2007: 1). On one of the worst
days, three-quarters of the capital city was under water.

In spite of the obvious truism that urban poverty can be attributed to poor
national economic performance, it seems that urban deterioration is also exacerbated by the absence of planning control over informal developments. Increasingly
fragmented land parcels prevent land amalgamation for improvement and redevelopment. For example, the current land use structure of an urban district in
central Jakarta took shape as early as the 1860s (Figure 12.1a). Land lots along

**Figure 12.1** (a) Pecenongan, Jakarta, in the 1860s. Note: Darker areas refer to villages and
paddy fields. Source: Merrillees (2000: 94). Courtesy Archipelago Press. (b)
Pecenongan, Jakarta, in 2006. Source: Google Earth (2006).

the main roads were developed for urban use, whereas rural settlements lay away from the roads. Villages and paddy fields were shielded by urban buildings. One and a half centuries later, the city's spatial structure remains exactly the same with only two visible changes: the whole area has become much denser, and rural villages have degenerated into urban slums (Figure 12.1b). Large land parcels are few and open space scarce. The intensity of land use has been driven up by continuous urbanization and an increase in the urban population. However, uncontrolled land subdivision has trapped this district in a problematic mode of building development. Irreversible deterioration seems locked in.

Gated housing estates, planned and built by private developers, have now emerged in the suburbs of Jakarta (Figure 12.2). "By the mid-1990s there were

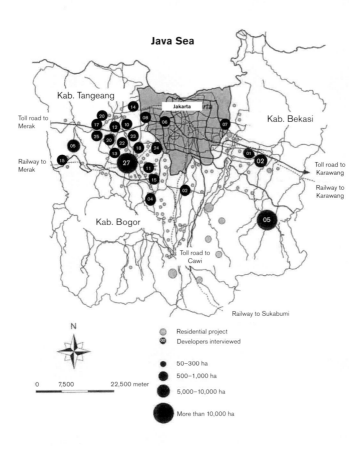

**Figure 12.2** Development of private housing estates in Jabotabek. Source: Winarso and Firman (2002: 498).

25 large subdivision projects in the Jakarta Metropolitan Area, ranging from 500 to 30,000 ha in size, and there were hundreds of small projects of under 500 ha" (Firman 2000: 14). Accordingly, private developers have to leapfrog into the suburbs in order to build large-scale, self-contained new towns, because the central area of the city is trapped in a vicious cycle of degeneration. Private new towns with economies of scale are the current viable mode for the private provision of public goods. Negative environmental externalities, existing in places where public planning controls are absent, are effectively internalized by the planning and development controls of private land developers. In contrast to the situation in Rome, Italy, described in Chapter 11, in Jakarta the rich are deserting old city cores.

The landed interest in the city is also trapped in situations that the stakeholders do not wish to see. Without effective collective action, environmental degradation will be irreversible. When the state fails to intervene by breaking vicious cycles, urban planning fails to perform a developmental role. As a result of not positively guiding urban development according to planning objectives, urban planning has also lost legitimacy in regulating the land development market and the containment of urban sprawl. The state's capacity for land-use planning is curtailed by the ever-expanding landed interests of wealthy groups. As a result, a social divide is created between the poor city and the rich suburbs, while other economic inefficiencies and environmental costs reduce the livability and sustainability of urban life.

## Making planning developmental for sustainable Asian urbanization

In the context of rapid urbanization in Asia, the regulatory form of urban planning is failing, with substantial informal development instead. At the same time, urban land is acutely scarce, whereas the economy is growing rapidly, generating yet further demand for urban land. Unless Asian countries can evolve a more developmental approach to urban expansion, underpinned by urban planning concepts that are well established internationally, there is a danger that rapid urbanization in Asian developing countries will proceed in ways that are tragically unsustainable. In facing up to this challenge, practices evolving in other Asian cities may be more useful than borrowing from Western experiences. In this section of the chapter, I review some useful practices that are emerging from Singapore and China.

## REDEVELOPMENT OF OLD TOWNS: OVERCOMING "NIMBY" IN THE INTERESTS OF THE FUTURE

### LAND ACQUISITION ACT: SINGAPORE'S SUCCESS

Because of uncontrolled land subdivision and resultant fragmented land owner-ship, it is often the case that landowners in high-density cities develop their plots as demand increases and land values rise. This aggravates the problem of land scarcity. Inefficient land utilization makes land artificially expensive, and increases living and business costs as a result, which is not in the best interests of the city. In this case, urban space becomes too expensive for new migrants, whereas existing landowners benefit from unearned land rents. For example, according to a report by McKinsey Global Institute (2001), Mumbai's land was 9.6 times more expensive than Singapore's, measured by a ratio of cost of m² of land to GDP per capita in 1999, and much of the urban land in Mumbai is not available to the market.

The redevelopment of the Niucheshui district in Singapore from 1960 to 2000 shows how this problem can be overcome, and the potential impact of plan-ning with effective implementation mechanisms. The redevelopment process was facilitated very effectively by compulsory land acquisition and the state sale of sites. In the 1950s, most street blocks in Niucheshui were divided by individual landowners into long strips with a narrow frontage (Figure 12.3). A so-called "shophouse" was built on each strip. Shophouses were mostly two or three sto-ries high, with a shop on the ground floor and a residence above the shop. It was evident that the assembly of small land pieces into a large plot for comprehensive urban renewal would not be easy.

The Land Acquisition Act was enacted in 1966 to facilitate land amalgamation at a low transaction cost. To a nation built on the foundations of private own-ership and free-market economics, an unconventional and controversial clause contained in the Act dictates that the state can acquire land "for any residential, commercial or industrial purposes"; and "[t]he suggestion of adding a qualifying phrase 'of public benefit' was dismissed" (Yeung 1973: 38–9). Section 5(1) of the Act states that,

> whenever any particular land is needed: (a) for any public purpose; (b) by any person, corporation or statutory board, for any work or an undertaking which, in the opinion of the Minister, is of public benefit or of public utility or in the public interest; or (c) for any residential, commercial or industrial purposes, the President may, by notification published in the Gazette, declare the land to be required for the purpose specified in the notification.

> (Land Acquisition Act 1966)

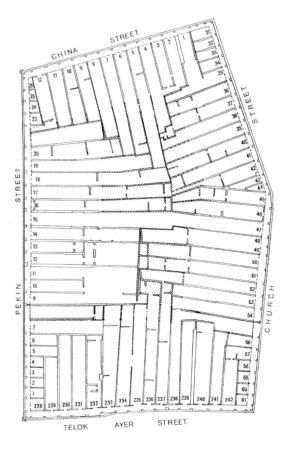

**Figure 12.3** Fragmented land holdings in Niucheshui. Source: author.

This gives the government power to acquire land and make it available for redevelopment. The Act has enabled the acquisition of many fragmented parcels of land occupied by old shophouses in Niucheshui, for both road widening and the development of offices, hotels, shopping centers, and public housing. Niucheshui has been transformed significantly, with land uses upgraded and street blocks refurbished to accommodate economic activities that produce jobs with decent pay (Figure 12.4).

Singapore, a small city-state, has successfully built a compact city where public transport dominates and citizens live in decent housing estates with ample public spaces. Fifty years ago in the 1950s, as many as about 90 percent of Singaporeans lived in dilapidated and temporary dwellings (Weldon and Tan 1969). By 1990, 87 percent of the population lived in public housing apartments (HDB 2003). The Land Acquisition Act played an indisputable role in achieving

**Figure 12.4**  Niucheshui, 2000. Source: author.

this. In 1949, state land accounted for only 31 percent of the total land stock. With the compulsory land acquisition, however, the government has become the largest landowner, holding 76.2 percent of land in 1985 (Motha 1989). From 1985 to 1994, a further 16.8 km² of land was compulsorily purchased from the private owners (*The Straits Times*, 9 October 1995). Land rents captured during development and redevelopment have been made available for the government to provide affordable social housing and public facilities that benefit the whole populace.

UNLOCKING LAND RESOURCES DURING TRANSITION: CHINA'S STORY

In China, economic reforms introduced since 1980 have set up the development of a market orientation as the goal for systemic change of the economy. Rigidity in land resource allocation, however, has constituted an immediate obstacle to the initiation of urban land markets. Although land leasing was invented as a new institution in 1988, initially it only led to a development market primarily of greenfield sites, involving the conversion of land from agricultural uses to urban occupation (Yeh and Wu 1996). Potential redevelopment of brownfield sites remained hampered. Driven by a formidable pent-up demand for premises in central city locations, institutional change was called for to eliminate supply-side constraints that were upheld by the old institution of socialist land-use rights, and thus to unlock the land redevelopment process. A new institution of land development rights has since been created to make land available for redevelopment while the existing land users' socialist land-use rights are compensated for (Zhu 2004).

In the 1990s, sensational media reports claimed that Shanghai was the world's largest construction site (*The Straits Times*, 15 January 1998). This was probably not an exaggeration. Between 1993 and 2000, building construction and refurbishment across the whole of Shanghai were undertaken at an unprecedented scale: 131.2 million m² of new spaces constructed. During the same period, in the city's Jing'an District, 2.32 million m² of additional building floor area were constructed, which accounted for 53 percent of the building stock in 1993 (SMBS 1994–2001). A survey reveals that, during the period 1992–2000, land redevelopment carried out amounted to a total area of 135.7 ha, accounting for 17.8 percent (762 ha) of the total area of the district (Figure 12.5). A substantial amount of the land area has been made available to be redeveloped for higher and better uses, which has transformed the district significantly. Existing residents may have to quit their apartments, which are of very poor quality after being neglected for many decades, but there are compensations of new housing either on site or somewhere else from the government or the developer.

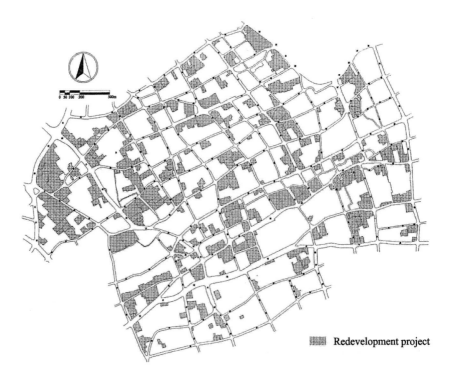

**Figure 12.5** Land redevelopment projects in Jing'an District, Shanghai, 1992–2000. Source: author.

## Development of new towns: China's state-led strategic development plans

Rapid urbanization and the influx of migrants to China's cities constitute tremendous challenges to an urban planning system molded on the centrally controlled economy. Blueprint plans based on top-down economic projections were unable to cope with market-oriented urban development. Capricious market conditions made plans irrelevant and useless, often within a few years of their adoption. The plans neither show positive guidance towards the achievement of planning objectives, nor have the flexibility to accommodate unexpected socio-economic change.

On the one hand, city governments have now realized that rapid urbanization is driven by the two engines of industrialization and real estate development. Interrelated economic growth and physical expansion need to be spatially coordinated, instead of cities being allowed to expand in an unplanned, incremental and often concentric manner. Rapidly growing cities such as Shanghai and Guangzhou have seized the opportunity to build a new town beside the existing old town, creating a dual-city structure. On the other hand, city governments have to rely increasingly on local funding because of decentralization. Decentralization has also phased out regional cooperation in the planning of individual cities, which results in competition among cities in the region. In this context, city governments need "corporate" plans that provide the city with visions and growth strategies. Physical master plans, as the product of the central planning regime and a passive blueprint, are clearly not able to undertake this task.

The Strategic Development Plan (SDP), a non-statutorily required plan, initially emerged spontaneously from the cities' rapid urbanization. It is a spatial configuration of a city's economic potential, with a vision of rapid development driven by inward investment and large-scale land development. Its main priority is to set up a coordinating mechanism between spatial structures and economic expansion, which is expected to enhance urban competitiveness and to set the city on a trajectory of virtuous physical–economic development cycles. On the one hand, the dynamic growth of urban economies requires spatial structures to coordinate the numerous private housing estates, industrial zones, shopping centers, and other land development activities initiated by the developers, whose number has mushroomed since the 1990s. At the same time, the SDP enables the municipal government to appropriate land resources to finance infrastructure construction and thus to lead urban expansion.

SDPs provide a vision that enables the local developmental state to marshal social support. The gist of an SDP is often represented by a succinct slogan that is easily understood by the general public. Guangzhou simply puts the aim of its future as "Small change in a year, moderate change in three years, and great change in five years." Zhuhai proposes that the city should have "large ports, great industries and grand development." Shenyang declares "Shenyang in the north as Guangzhou in the south," with connotations that Shenyang should be as dynamic and prosperous as Guangzhou. The Shanghai Urban Planning Exhibition Hall, the first in the country, has attracted many citizens to view its exhibits of achievements and visionary developments of the future. It has aroused civic pride and inspiration among local residents. Although not every resident benefits from substantial urban change, the majority and newcomers should have their welfare linked with the growth and expansion. The government earns its legitimacy by garnering social support. Taking this to be a good city marketing project, many other cities have followed suit.

## CONCLUSION

The examination of the nature of urban planning from the perspective of its three forms (development regulation, plans, and the process of plan-making) has shown that urban planning became, in the later twentieth century, more regulatory than developmental, unless such activity could mobilize resources. Zoning or development control is fundamentally regulatory, and processes of plan-making are meant to regulate competition among stakeholders. Regulations over land uses are no doubt essential for social organization, economic development, and environmental protection. Embedded with visionary goals, land-use plans are probably the only instrument of planning capable of turning ideas into action, although the perfect implementation of plans remains a massive challenge.

In much of Asia, because of weak economies and thus inadequate state capacity to provide public and social goods, the regulatory authority of municipal governments is weakened by a lack of legitimacy for planning control over residents' self-development initiatives. Informal and haphazard developments are rampant in the cities of Asian developing countries. Because of primitive building technologies and basic building materials, informal developments are dominated by the mode of low-rise buildings, associated with high site coverage. Hence, land utilization is inefficient, exacerbating the serious problem of land scarcity. Land subdivision becomes uncontrollable under the pressure of the influx of new migrants to cities, and land amalgamation for redevelopment for efficient uses becomes extremely difficult. New migrants have to find their urban shelters elsewhere, and often end up erecting makeshift structures. The legitimacy of planning systems' regulatory power in poor developing countries lies, to a large extent, in planning's capacity to solve challenging urban problems. For the rapidly urbanizing countries of Asia, a new paradigm of urban planning has to be progressive, building up the capacity of land resource mobilization in the best interests of the future. Experiences in countries with strong states, such as Singapore and China, might be useful in this regard.

## NOTES

1  For example, in Britain, the 1947 Town and Country Planning Act introduced Industrial Development Certificates (IDCs) for which industrialists wishing to build new factories of 5,000 ft² or more in size were required to apply (Hall 1999). IDCs were intended to divert industrial expansion to designated "development areas." Turok (1989) claims that the shortage of factory space in London in the 1950s and 1960s was one of the reasons for the rapid growth of surrounding new towns. From late 1964, Office Development Permits were also introduced to control the construction of new offices of the same size, requiring evidence of the necessity of new developments in certain restricted areas. Office decentralization was also facilitated through rigid planning controls and conducive financial subsidies. By 1977, a total of at least 170,000 and possibly as many as 250,000 office jobs were relocated from central London (Alexander 1979: 65), although as many as 44.5 percent of these moved a distance of less than 15 miles (Daniels 1975).

2  Birmingham, UK provides an example of a transition in local government's role from providing city residents with services and welfare to managing city affairs with entrepreneurial approaches. Over the years, the physical fabric of the city has been substantially transformed by the construction of the International Convention Centre, a National Indoor Arena, the Hyatt Hotel, Brindleyplace and a Centenary Square (Loftman and Nevin 1998). Besides business development, community-based improvement schemes, and training in labor skills, Blakely (1994) suggested various land-related programs to regenerate cities: land banking, physical infrastructure development on industrial and commercial land, speculative building, flexible zoning, regulatory improvements through simplification, the development of a detailed physical improvement plan for tourism, and townscaping.

3  Or when private developers are philanthropists committed to social reform (such as Robert Owen, who built New Lanark, Scotland), and are concerned with social welfare (such as James W. Rouse, who built Columbia, Maryland, United States).

4  There can be a cultural foundation for strict development control. For example, in Britain, when this model was prevalent in the eighteenth to nineteenth centuries, social evils (slums, pollution, poor public health, congestion) were believed to derive from disorders associated with the *laissez-faire* market. Public intervention to root out these disorders was therefore justified (McLoughlin 1973).

## REFERENCES

Alexander, I. (1979) *Office Location and Public Policy*, London: Longman.

Ashworth, W. (1954) *The Genesis of Modern British Town Planning: A Study in Economic and Social History of the Nineteenth and Twentieth Centuries*, London: Routledge & Kegan Paul.

Blakely, E. J. (1994) *Planning Local Economic Development: Theory and Practice*, second edition, Thousand Oaks, CA: SAGE.

Brennan, E. M. (1993) "Urban Land and Housing Issues Facing the Third World," in Kasarda, J. D. and A. M. Parnell (Eds.), *Third World Cities: Problems, Policies and Prospects*, Newbury Park, CA: SAGE, pp. 74–91.

Champion, A. G. (1975) "The United Kingdom," in Jones, R. (Ed.), *Essays on World Urbanization*, London: George Philip and Son, pp. 47–66.

Chaves, L. F. (1975) "Venezuela," in Jones, R. (Ed.), *Essays on World Urbanization*, London: George Philip and Son, pp. 186–94.

Cochrane, A. (1991) "The Changing State of Local Government in the UK," *Public Administration*, **69**, 281–302.

Committee for Spatial Development (CSD) (1999) *The European Spatial Development Perspective*, Luxembourg: European Commission.

Cooke, P. (1983) *Theories of Planning and Spatial Development*, London: Hutchinson.

Daniels, P. W. (1975) *Office Location: An Urban and Regional Study*, London: G. Bell and Sons.

Davidoff, P. (1965) "Advocacy and Pluralism in Planning," *Journal of the American Institute of Planners*, **36** (4), 331–8.

Davis, K. and H. Golden (1954) "Urbanization and the Development of Pre-Industrial Areas," *Economic Development and Cultural Change*, **3**, 6–26.

Dowall, D. E. and M. Leaf (1991) "The Price of Land for Housing in Jakarta," *Urban Studies*, **28** (5), 707–22

Faludi, A. (1973) *Planning Theory*, Oxford: Pergamon.

Firman, T. (2000) "Rural to Urban Land Conversion in Indonesia during Boom and Bust Periods," *Land Use Policy*, **17**, 13–20

Firman, T. and I. A. I. Dharmapatni (1994) "The Challenges to Sustainable Development in Jakarta Metropolitan Region," *Habitat International*, **18** (3), 79–94.

Friedmann, J. (1987) *Planning in the Public Domain*, Princeton, NJ: Princeton University Press.

Friedmann, J. and C. Weaver (1979) *Territory and Function: The Evolution of Regional Planning*, Berkeley: University of California Press.

General Statistics Office, Socialist Republic of Vietnam (2003) *Statistical Yearbook 2002*, Hanoi: Statistical Publishing House.

Ghani, A. (2007) "Floods Cripple Much of Jakarta," *The Straits Times*, 6 February, p. 1.

Gillespie, J. (1995) "The Role of the Bureaucracy in Managing Urban Land in Vietnam," *Pacific Rim Law & Policy Journal*, **5** (1), 59–124.

Google Earth (2006) Available: http://earth.google.com.

Hall, P. (1999) "The Regional Dimension," in Cullingworth, B. (Ed.), *British Planning: 50 Years of Urban and Regional Policy*, London: Athlone Press, pp. 76–90.

Healey, P. (1992) "Planning through Debate: The Communicative Turn in Planning Theory," *Town Planning Review*, **62** (2), 143–62.

Healey, P. (1997) *Collaborative Planning: Shaping Places in Fragmented Societies*, Basingstoke: Macmillan.

Housing and Development Board (HDB) (2003) *HDB Annual Report 2002/2003*, Singapore: HDB.

Innes, J. (1995) "Planning Theory's Emerging Paradigm: Communicative Action and Interactive Practice," *Journal of Planning Education and Research*, **14** (3), 183–90.

Jessop, B. (1998) "The Narrative of Enterprise and the Enterprise of Narrative: Place Marketing and the Entrepreneurial City," in Hall, T. and P. Hubbard (Eds.), *The Entrepreneurial City: Geographies of Politics, Regime and Representation*, Chichester: John Wiley & Sons, pp. 77–99.

Keeble, L. (1969) *Principles and Practice of Town and Country Planning*, London: Estates Gazette.

Land Acquisition Act (1966) Available: http://statutes.agc.gov.sg/non_version/cgi-bin/cgi_retrieve.pl?&actno=Reved-152&date=latest&method=part.

Lappo, G. M. and Y. L. Pivovarov (1975) "The Soviet Union," in Jones, R. (Ed.), *Essays on World Urbanization*, London: George Philip and Son, pp. 223–35.

Law, C. M. (1967) "The Growth of the Urban Population in England and Wales, 1801–1911," *Transactions of the Institute of British Geographers*, **41**, 125–43.

Leaf, M. (2002) "A Tale of Two Villages: Globalization and Peri-Urban Change in China and Vietnam," *Cities*, **19** (1), 23–31.

Loftman, P. and B. Nevin (1998) "Pro-growth Local Economic Development Strategies: Civic Promotion and Local Needs in Britain's Second City, 1981–1996," in Hall, T. and P. Hubbard (Eds.), *The Entrepreneurial City: Geographies of Politics, Regime and Representation*, Chichester: John Wiley & Sons, pp. 129–48.

Luan, T. D., N. Q. Vinh, with B. Wiesman and M. Leaf (2000) "Urban Housing," in Boothroyd, P. and P. X. Nam (Eds.), *Socioeconomic Renovation in Viet Nam: The Origin, Evolution, and Impact of Doi Moi*, Singapore: Institute of Southeast Asian Studies, pp. 51–100.

Mahtab-uz-Zaman, Q. M. and S. S. Y. Lau (2000) "City Expansion Policy versus Compact City Demand: The Case of Dhaka," in Jenks, M. and R. Burgess (Eds.) *Compact Cities: Sustainable Urban Forms for Developing Countries*, London: Spon Press, pp. 141–52.

McKinsey Global Institute (2001) "India: From Emerging to Surging," *The McKinsey Quarterly*, No. 4, Emerging Markets. Available: http://www.mckinsey.com.

McLoughlin, J. B. (1973) *Control and Urban Planning*, London: Faber and Faber.

Merrillees, S. (2000) *Batavia in Nineteenth Century Photographs*, Singapore: Archipelago Press.

Motha, P. (1989) *Singapore Real Property Guide*, third edition, Singapore: Singapore University Press.

National Bureau of Statistics of China (NBSC) (1999) *Comprehensive Statistical Data and Materials on 50 Years of New China*, Beijing: China Statistics Press.

National Bureau of Statistics of China (NBSC) (2005) *China Statistical Yearbook, 2005*, Beijing: China Statistics Press.

Shen, J. (2005) "Counting Urban Population in Chinese Censuses 1953–2000: Changing Definitions, Problems and Solutions," *Population, Space and Place*, **11** (5), 381–400.

Shanghai Municipal Bureau of Statistics (SMBS) (1994–2001) *Shanghai Statistical Yearbook*, Beijing: China Statistics Publishing (in Chinese).

Struyk, R. J., M. L. Hoffman and H. M. Katsura (1990) *The Market for Shelter in Indonesian Cities*, Washington DC: Urban Institute Press.

Susantono, B. (1998) "Transportation and Land Use Dynamics in Metropolitan Jakarta," *Berkeley Planning Journal*, **12**, 126–44.

Sutcliffe, A. (1981) "Introduction: British Town Planning and the Historian," in Sutcliffe, A. (Ed.), *British Town Planning: The Formative Years*, Leicester: Leicester University Press, pp. 2–14.

*The Straits Times* (1995). Available at http://www.straitstimes.com.

*The Straits Times* (1998). Available at http://www.straitstimes.com.

Trinh, D. L. and Q. V. Nguyen (2001) *Socio-economic Impacts of "Doi Moi" on Urban Housing in Vietnam*, Hanoi: Social Sciences Publishing House.

Trinh, P. V. and R. Parenteau (1991) "Housing and Urban Development Policies in Vietnam," *Habitat International*, **15** (4), 153–69.

Turok, I. (1989) "Development Planning and Local Economic Growth: A Study of Process and Policy in Bracknell New Town," *Progress in Planning*, **31**, 59–150.

Turok, I. (1992) "Property-Led Urban Regeneration: Panacea or Placebo," *Environment and Planning A*, **24** (3), 361–79.

United Nations (2004) *World Urbanization Prospects: The 2003 Revision*, New York: United Nations.

United Nations Population Fund (2007) "State of World Population 2007: Demographic, Social and Economic Indicators." Available: http://www.unfpa.org/swp/2007/english/notes/indicators/e_indicator2.pdf. Accessed 27 April 2008.

UN-Habitat (2009) *Planning Sustainable Cities: Global Report on Human Settlements*, London: Earthscan.

de Vries, J. (1984) *European Urbanization 1500–1800*, London: Methuen and Co.

Wannop, U. A. (1995) *The Regional Imperative: Regional Planning and Governance in Britain, Europe and the United States*, London: Jessica Kingsley Publishers.

Weldon, P. and T. H. Tan (1969) *The Socio-Economic Characteristics of Singapore Population 1969,* State and City Planning Project, Technical Paper No. 40, Singapore: Department of Statistics.

Winarso, H. and T. Firman (2002) "Residential Land Development in Jabotabek, Indonesia: Triggering Economic Crisis?" *Habitat International*, **26**, 487–506.

Yeh, A. G. O. and F. L. Wu (1996) "The New Land Development Process and Urban Development in Chinese Cities," *International Journal of Urban and Regional Research*, **20** (2), 330–53.

Yeung, Y. M. (1973) *National Development Policy and Urban Transformation in Singapore: A Study of Public Housing and the Marketing System*, Chicago: Department of Geography, University of Chicago.

Zelinsky, W. (1971) "The Hypothesis of the Mobility Transition," *Geographical Review*, **61**, 219–49.

Zhu, J. M. (2004) "From Land Use Right to Land Development Right: Institutional Change in China's Urban Development," *Urban Studies*, **41** (7), 1249–67.

CHAPTER 13

# A TRANS-PACIFIC PLANNING EDUCATION IN REVERSE

## Reflections of an American with a Chinese Doctorate in Urban Planning and Design

### Daniel Benjamin Abramson

## Introduction: traveling in time

In this chapter, I present my own experience as a graduate of the masters program in Architecture and City Planning at the Massachusetts Institute of Technology, who attended Tsinghua University in Beijing to became the first American to earn a Chinese doctorate in urban planning, and who has continued to remain engaged in Chinese urban planning from bases both in Canada and in the United States. The aspect of my experience that is "in reverse" is that the usual transnational educational path for planning students seeking higher degrees is from "South" to "North" (which includes Europe and Japan, as well as North America), or from "East" to "West." Here, I try to apply my reversed perspective to the understanding of how and why ideas and practices of planning do or do not "travel," and in particular to how a moment in history affects the reception of foreign ideas. More personally, I reflect on how my education at MIT prepared me (or how it didn't) for further learning and action in China, and, inversely, how experiencing Chinese planning provided a frame for appreciating my American education.

Of course, I cannot speak with authority to the full range of planning expertise in China or anywhere else. My own subfields are urban and housing design, site planning, community planning, and historic preservation. In China, however, I have participated in various types of exchanges between Chinese planners and counterparts (governmental, professional, and academic) from Hong Kong, Taiwan, Japan, India, Indonesia, Australia, the United States, Canada, the UK, France, Germany, and Scandinavia, on a broad range of topics ranging in scale from neighborhoods to regions, and from disciplines as varied as architectural history and aesthetics, land management, and real estate economics. Indeed, during China's dynamic opening to exchanges of all kinds in the 1990s, after decades of isolation, faculty and students in well-connected schools were extremely eager to engage experts from abroad in different disciplines. Much of that "engagement" was superficial, however, and ran afoul of barriers to internal cross-disciplinary collaboration. The narrative that follows is an effort to understand some of the obstacles to substantive disciplinary exchange between Chinese planners and their counterparts from abroad.

The starting point of this essay is the quite limited disciplinary range of the earliest exchanges between non-Chinese planners and designers, and their counterparts at Tsinghua,[1] which is generally considered one of China's top two or three schools of urban planning and design. The focus of these early exchanges was *design*, a limitation that originated partly in the particular characters of the partner institutions – what they each brought to the table, and what they had in common. More importantly, though, the focus on design reflected a broad range of political, societal, and technological conditions that were specific to the historical moment.

Conditions in China in the late 1980s and 1990s that elevated design within the planning profession included an urgent demand for physical development, of both buildings and infrastructure, after a long period during which China's leader, Mao Zedong, emphasized rural development and attacked most technical professions, including planning and architecture, as classist. After Mao's death in 1976, his successor, Deng Xiaoping, undertook a redefinition of development itself, and sought to re-professionalize development planning. Where Mao had been nicknamed "The Great Helmsman," Deng was dubbed "The Chief Designer." These factors were combined with the continuation of a broader, mid-twentieth-century culture of planning-as-engineering. Other conditions for educational exchange in planning contributed to the prominence of design, including language barriers, and the attendant convenience of graphic communication; the continued political sensitivity of socio-economic information; and the opacity and inaccessibility of decision-making processes – all of which hampered non-design modes of planning such as socio-economic analysis, or advocacy (Abramson 2005).

Many of these conditions are typical of planning exchanges in developmentally asymmetrical contexts. The direction of exchange of planning expertise over the past century or more has been mostly from West to East. Historically, modern planning has largely originated in the experience of urbanization in Europe and North America – and in the colonial/imperial expansion by which Europeans and North Americans extracted the resources necessary to urbanize (Wright 2002). Even when China borrowed (and then later was forced to accept) forms of modernization from another Asian power, Japan, these forms were in turn largely derived from European and North American models (Lu 2006). Nationalist and socialist anti-colonial/imperial movements of liberation and independence subsequently begat their own modern approaches to planning, but these typically perpetuated the treatment of planning-as-engineering, with its emphasis on globally transferable infrastructure and its neglect of social and cultural dimensions of the public realm (Sorensen 2005). This was as true of the period of Soviet influence in China's planning in the 1950s as it had been of earlier periods of Japanese, Western European, and North American influence.

The broadly perceived global "standard" of planning remains associated with the economic dominance of the most urbanized societies: those of North America, Western Europe, and Japan, followed by the "East Asian Tigers" Singapore, Hong Kong, Taiwan, and South Korea. This, at least, became the case in China after Mao's collectivist rural industrialization gradually gave way to city-based market-oriented economic reforms in the 1980s and early 1990s. Rejecting Mao's drive to redefine modernity in Chinese terms on the basis of mass movements, Deng Xiaoping projected an essentially Western definition to serve as a guide for development, and encouraged its realization through participation in global trade regimes, and the professionalization and legalization of government, including urban planning.[2] As David Bray has put it, "a Marxian teleology of revolution has been replaced by a Weberian teleology of modernity" (2005: 159). Development remains the "absolute principle" (*fazhan cai shi ying daoli*) of government policy, even as the official definition of "development" itself has undergone subtle shifts over the past 30 years (Fan 2006).

Despite the truth that "universal standards are never really placeless" (Wright 2002: 127) – that is, unique local physical, cultural and political conditions necessarily demand unique planning responses whatever the stated norm might be – the teleology of modernity puts relentless emphasis on the adoption of global norms. This is especially true in China, where, in the 1980s, the adoption of global professional standards and the emulation of foreign models seemed to be the only alternative to the paralyzing imperative of class struggle that had infused nearly all pursuits during the Cultural Revolution.

Most of the leading planning scholars who write in both Chinese and English (see, for example, Mee-Kam Ng, Wu Fulong, and Zhang Tingwei) have grappled directly with the question of which "Western" planning theories are most relevant to the planning of China's cities (Ng and Wu 1997; Tang 2000). An awareness of a developmental time lag between China's current urban reality and the non-Chinese "sources" of urban theory informs this work (see also Zhu's discussion in Chapter 12). For those with direct experience of planning China's cities, there is an even keener desire to understand the current transformation through the lens of Western history (Zhang and Fang 2004).

In my own experience, for example, although my teachers and fellow students at Tsinghua University fundamentally understood that American planning was probably just *American* planning, and not necessarily *good* planning in any absolute sense, I was often at a loss to explain to people in the street or the village why an American such as I would study planning in China. They would assure me that

America's planning is better – and they did not mean just "better for America." A sense of lost time gave special urgency to the assumption that, in order to achieve a Japanese, European, or North American standard of living, it is necessary to adopt or approximate the planning approaches of those countries.

On a practical level, this sense of "lost time" implies an urgent need to solve problems. Certainly this need is what drives the bulk of Chinese interest in foreign practices. On a more conceptual level, however, the sense of lost time is another aspect of a teleological world view. It carries with it also a sense of historical relativism and determinism, perhaps strengthened by official Marxist ideology: the path of development is more or less linear. One "stage" must be passed through before the next can be reached; difficulties encountered today are the price for a better tomorrow. And of course the cities of the affluent West are "ahead" of Chinese cities, according to the small but persistent academic industry that exists in China to estimate the level of development of Chinese cities by comparing them to Western ones, often with a high degree of precision using specific indicators of such qualities as their "internationalization," the relative strength of their service sectors, their quality of life, etc. One such study cited by a senior planner in Beijing in 1996 estimated that Beijing was approximately 30 years "behind" Paris in its development (Dong 1996).

A parallel implication of falling behind is the possibility of "doing it right this time." It was with this view in mind that one of my Tsinghua classmates once asked me, "Don't you feel that being here is like living in the film *Back to the Future*?" She was not thinking in ironic, postmodern terms. She meant that, like Marty McFly, I might be experiencing something akin to time travel: being both immersed in the past, and also presented with an opportunity to create a better "present." In contrast to her positive and transformative aspiration, the most common refrain I heard among North American and European planners visiting China in the 1990s was their desire to help their Chinese counterparts to "avoid the mistakes of the West" and to "appreciate the good things that Chinese culture and environment already has." This contrast between the heroic optimism of Chinese planners in the 1990s and the modesty, tentativeness, and sense of limits of most Western counterparts was the product of a peculiar set of historical circumstances.

In China, the 1990s ushered in an unprecedented opportunity to advance the physical improvement of cities through large-scale, state-sponsored redevelopment, after decades of urban neglect. At this time, North America and most of Western Europe, by contrast, were already in the second decade of a marketist reaction to the state-led urban renewal and Third World development approaches that had earlier dominated planning into the 1970s. For its part, Japanese influence was muted by the contraction its economy experienced after the 1980s. Although marketism was a global movement – Deng Xiaoping and Margaret Thatcher came to power at the same time – the Chinese version maintained, indeed renewed, its faith in the ability of state-backed planners to draw up complete, detailed, and utterly new visions of the city of the future that could be implemented successfully in a very short time. Meanwhile, planners in the West, and especially the Anglophone West, adopted an incrementalist attitude that sharply questioned the feasibility and desirability of grand visions (Hall 2002: Chapters 10 and 11). The contrast was manifested in the different perspectives of planners at Tsinghua and at MIT, who undertook the series of exchanges that began in the 1980s, and in which I took part in the 1990s.

## NEGOTIATING PLANNING CULTURES: THE MIT–TSINGHUA URBAN DESIGN STUDIOS

I became familiar with China's world of planning by participating in a joint urban design studio between MIT and Tsinghua University in the summer of 1992. It was the third joint studio in a series inspired by Kevin Lynch's visit to China with Tunney Lee in 1980, and made possible by a gift from an anonymous donor to create the Paul Sun fund at MIT. In the Lynchian tradition, the studios explored cultural dimensions of development by focusing on the physical environment, and by providing students with the task of designing physical interventions in the city at the neighborhood scale.

The studio was in many ways a natural extension of my education and experience up to that point. Before the studio, I had traveled in China as a shoestring tourist in 1987–8, and spent four years studying for the Master of Architecture and Master in City Planning at MIT.[3] After the studio, I stayed in Beijing to pursue a doctorate in the Department of Urban Planning and Design at Tsinghua University. Upon completing my dissertation for Tsinghua in late 1997, I took a postdoctoral fellowship at the University of British Columbia's Centre for Human Settlements, and in 2001 began teaching in a tenure-track position in Urban Design and Planning at the University of Washington (UW) in Seattle. At UW, I have also been an active member of the China Studies program.

This personal chronology embraces a crucial period in China's urbanization and its planning, even as attention in the United States to planning issues in China remained minimal. In 1992, when I joined the MIT–Tsinghua studio, the global relevance of China's urbanization and planning was not at all clear. In the eyes of the Americans participating in the studio (as well as most other North Americans and Europeans I knew at the time), the suppression of the 1989 democracy movement still cast a dark shadow over China. The previous MIT–Tsinghua studio had been cancelled because of the violence of 4 June. A number of the MIT students, including me, felt this even more keenly, because they had been involved in a

series of MIT initiatives in Eastern Europe that responded to opportunities result-
ing from the more successful democracy movements that had taken place there.
These included a course on property rights by Karen Polenske; an investigation of
Krakow's real estate market by the Center for Real Estate; an exchange with Russian community-based planners; and, perhaps most extensively, a United States
Agency for International Development (USAID)-funded collaboration between
Warsaw Technical University and the Special Interest Group in Urban Settlements (SIGUS 1991a–d). The SIGUS Poland Initiative formed the frame for my
masters thesis, *Participation in Post-Socialist Housing*. In the light of the overt
"political reconstruction" that drove the new planning initiatives in Eastern Europe,
China appeared to have frozen itself in time.

In fact, a quieter "political rehabilitation" was taking place in China's party-
state that would have tremendous consequences for urban planning and
economic development. Municipalities and sub-municipal districts were given
greater latitude to raise funds for local industrial and urban development, and to
retain the resulting revenues. As early as the mid-1980s, municipal governments
throughout China had considered market-leveraged approaches to urban housing redevelopment (He 1993). In the months following June 1989, however, as
a direct response to the discontent of urban workers who bore the brunt of the
government's crackdown, the municipality of Beijing in particular accelerated its
plans for a massive housing improvement program. The city had already approved
a number of small but innovative pilot projects that were undertaken on a simple
cost-recovery basis. They minimized the off-site resettlement of residents, and
were designed to be compatible with the city's low-rise fabric (Abramson 1994).
Nevertheless, these projects were seen as inadequate models for large-scale
improvement.

When the program was approved in April 1990 for widespread implementation, it involved three new elements (or "three combines," as they were called by
the government) intended to help scale up the improvements (Lü 1994). Redevelopment would be combined with (1) the relocation of inner-city residents to new
suburban districts, (2) housing reforms that favored ownership over rental tenure,
and that shifted housing from a form of in-kind wage paid by employers to a cash
expense paid by residents, and (3) the transfer of responsibility for real estate
management from government agencies and other employers over to professional
companies. (As an afterthought, and without any particular strategy for it, the
government later added a "fourth combine": redevelopment should be combined
with historical preservation.)

At the time, few officials or scholars acknowledged the political-economic
implications of the program. In practice, it allowed developers to capitalize on
nascent differences in land value between locations, and created a widespread

speculative investment market in housing. The reforms also fueled a massive expansion of urban infrastructure, and reshaped the city into a collection
of housing and commercial enclaves, distinctly associated with particular levels
of resident income and consumption. Likewise, when the MIT–Tsinghua urban
design studio series resumed in summer 1992, none of the participants, including
the Tsinghua hosts, quite realized the amount of development pressure that would
be brought to bear on the sites for which they produced schemes. Some ten
housing redevelopment projects throughout the city were completed by the end
of 1991, but scholars at Tsinghua who were familiar with the program had not yet
analyzed these for a clear sense of the trend they represented. Instead, the studio
participants studied the most well-known of the initial pilot projects, Ju'er Hutong,
a small and context-sensitive development designed under the direction of Tsinghua Professor Wu Liangyong, one of the host faculty for the studio (Wu 1999).

The MIT students in particular tended to view the programs for the studio
sites as inappropriately ambitious and disconnected from their immediate context.
Given the government's lack of significant investment in the city center during the
decades up to that point, the studio's programs appeared to have a somewhat
utopian quality. It was very unclear how or when they might be implemented,
although, during a preparation seminar at MIT, Professor Gary Hack told the students that, in China, plans can take a very long time to develop but, when the
government decides to implement them, it can do so very quickly. The very first
joint studio in 1985 included a scheme for the redevelopment of the university
district of Haidian, which was planned as a large high-technology center alongside an expansion of one of Beijing's major ring roads; yet by 1992 no such
development had yet taken place. In the 1992 studio, the team that I joined
worked on a scheme for Desheng Men Wai ("Outside-the-Desheng-Gate," or
De-Wai for short), an old *faubourg*-like neighborhood outside one of Beijing's last
remaining fortified gates, which was slated for drastic redevelopment, including
bisection by a new expressway. In both cases, the MIT–Tsinghua student teams
proposed more modest changes to the existing environment than the programs
implied. Despite the time it took for these programs eventually to become reality,
I believe that all of the studio participants would have been shocked to see the
actual development, whose monumentality contrasts remarkably with their own
visions (Figures 13.1 and 13.2).

In all the MIT–Tsinghua studios of the 1980s and 1990s, the student schemes
favored the preservation of existing communities, activities, and key elements of
the urban fabric, including street alignments and the low-rise, intimate scale of
housing and public spaces. In the case of the scheme for De-Wai in 1992, the
students opposed the highway program, and instead proposed a design for a
modest roadway and a more intimate relationship between the tower and the

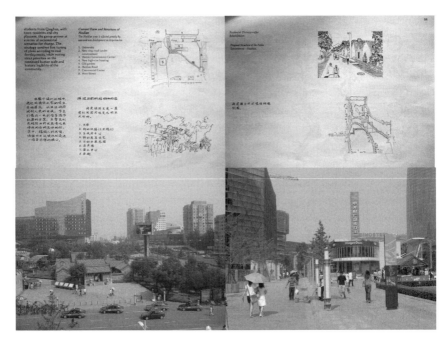

**Figure 13.1** Haidian, 1985 studio vision and actual development. Top left: in the local government
brief, widened perimeter roads appear around a block bisected by an intimate
diagonal lane. Top right: plans show the development as envisioned by the studio
group [Qing hua da xue (Beijing China) and Massachusetts Institute of Technology
School of Architecture and Planning 1985: 26, 28]. The actual development, shown
bottom left and right, reveals the preservation of just one historic courtyard (photos
by author, 2007). For a description of the actual design of the completed project,
see Marshall (2003: Chapter 6).

neighborhood than the program specified. The studio participants certainly shared
the general societal inability to foresee the dynamic development unleashed by
the renewal policies of the early 1990s. More to the point, however, the planning
values and epistemology of the students and faculty themselves explain why their
schemes were so different from what ultimately emerged on the ground. What
follows are some generalizations based on my recollections of the studios I joined
or later observed, conversations with faculty and students at Tsinghua, and interviews with MIT faculty who have been active in the studios over the decades.[4]

Certainly, there were differences between the MIT and Tsinghua partners in
the ways that they approached planning and design problems in general. The MIT
students tended to work more inductively. Although they drew on examples of
design with which they were familiar, they believed strongly that designs should
emerge from the unique qualities of each place and the self-expressed priorities
of the local population. They considered existing conditions to be reflective of

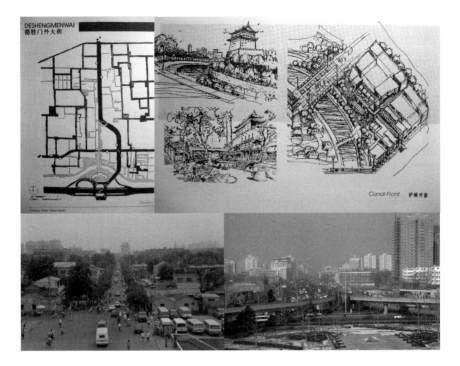

**Figure 13.2** De-Wai project, 1992 studio vision and actual development. Top left and right: the studio vision of the development [Qing hua da xue (Beijing China) and Massachusetts Institute of Technology 1992: 10, 12]. De-Wai as it appears from the Desheng Gate arrow tower is shown in the bottom left image in 1992, and in the bottom right image in 2002 (photos by author). For description, see Abramson (2007) and Lü (1993).

complex and deeply rooted social and cultural realities that would be ignored at the peril of the plan or design, and defined problems and opportunities according to what they saw and what local stakeholders told them (if they were free to do so). Perhaps the students' lack of familiarity with China's environment and society tended to strengthen the modesty and even tentativeness that the inductive approach inherently encouraged, but this tentativeness was also informed by attitudes generally current in the Master of Architecture and Master in City Planning (MCP) programs at MIT at that time. (Even the title of the degree, Master *in* City Planning, expresses an attitude of particular modesty toward the discipline.)

Perhaps the single most influential book for MCP students then was *Planning, Rethinking Ciudad Guayana* (Peattie 1987), Lisa Peattie's cautionary tale about large-scale, internationally conceived, urban design-driven development projects in the Third World that lack consideration for the existing life of local residents. Peattie's book was recommended reading for all incoming MCP students in 1990. Her influence was strong also in the SIGUS program, based in the

Department of Architecture. In the Urban Design program, which straddled both the Departments of Architecture and of Urban Studies and Planning, perhaps an even greater influence was Kevin Lynch's legacy. Lynch's inductive and empirical approach to understanding city form, and his interest in local cultures, the particularities of place, and the agency of the city's inhabitants, suffused most of the Urban Design curriculum. His influence was felt in courses such as Julian Beinart's Theory of City Form (which began as a course taught by Lynch until 1979),[5] Gary Hack's Site Planning (based on the book he edited with Lynch), and studios taught by Jack Myer and Tunney Lee. Indeed, I believe that the great majority of my instructors in both Architecture and City Planning shared both Peattie's and Lynch's values in various fundamental ways.

It would probably be fair to say that the Tsinghua students and faculty operated more deductively than their MIT counterparts. As Gary Hack has put it to me, and as I observed myself as a doctoral student at Tsinghua, the Chinese students and faculty strove to understand each place in the context of other such places; to categorize situations as belonging to this or that type, and then to apply the appropriate design response according to a catalog of existing models. The Beaux Arts pedagogical model was still very much in place, especially in the junior-level architectural design studios at Tsinghua. Instructors would provide students with a program for which they had to draw a nearly predetermined plan *parti*, only leaving them free to improvise on the façade. Planning studios, of course, dealt with larger scales and more varied sets of considerations than the architectural studios, but their approach typically involved a similarly standard series of problem-solving steps that fundamentally reduced the solution to a limited set of models. Nearly all planning students had to pass courses in architectural design. They focused their creative energies mainly on developing new design standards or new prototypical models for broad application.[6]

Although I perceived a lack of sensitivity to locality and community in Tsinghua's pedagogy, and students themselves chafed under what they felt was a restriction on their creativity, I also saw that the reliance on standardization and deductive design provided an effective education for students who were to join a tiny profession responsible for meeting enormous demands for physical construction. In the early 1990s, Beijing's inner-city neighborhoods typically accommodated between 500 and 1,000 residents per hectare – an astounding density, considering that housing was almost universally only one story high. It was not unusual for individuals to have less than four square meters of indoor living space each, and most households shared a single running water tap with many others and had no private toilet. Under a regime whose legitimacy depended on improving living standards, physical construction was an obvious priority. At this time, however, the number of architects per capita in China was less than one-tenth of that in the United States. Most undergraduate architecture and planning students began work on actual construction projects before their final year, and had to be able to take on major project responsibilities as soon as possible after graduating (Abramson 1997a).

Apart from these differences in how the two schools taught their students to think about planning and design problems, the particular Tsinghua faculty who participated in the studio shared many essential values with their MIT counterparts. The two most central faculty, Professors Zhu Zixuan and Wu Liangyong, were specialists in historic architecture and urban design; were active in preservation planning; and had a keen interest in the particularity of place. Wu Liangyong had been especially close to Liang Sicheng, China's first modern historian of architecture and the founder of the Tsinghua School of Architecture. In many ways, Liang's legacy and Wu's influence were to Tsinghua what Kevin Lynch's was to MIT. Indeed, both Zhu and Wu met Lynch when he first visited China in 1980 with Tunney Lee (see "Nanjing (1980)" in Lynch *et al.* 1990: 226–32). In 1983, Zhu participated in a symposium at MIT that Lynch organized to discuss urban design collaborations in China, Japan, and Korea. On a subsequent visit, Zhu was one of the last people to speak with Lynch before he died in 1984 (Lynch *et al.* 1990: 23).

Gary Hack, along with James (Ric) Richardson and Peter Droege, went on to lead what was to be the first studio group from any country outside China to Tsinghua in 1985. In 1987, the MIT group was led by John de Monchaux, Dennis Frenchman, and Ric Richardson again, and Gary Hack returned in 1992 with Jan Wampler of MIT's Department of Architecture. Jan Wampler and Dennis Frenchman then led each MIT group thereafter. On the Tsinghua side, the participation of faculty who worked closely either with Zhu or with Wu – in particular Professors Mao Qizhi and Zhang Jie – helped to maintain some basic continuity in approach, but there was greater turnover among the Tsinghua faculty than among MIT leaders throughout the studio series.

The turnover in Tsinghua faculty's participation was due, in part, simply to their unvarying role in the relationship as hosts rather than visitors, but it was related also to the rapid increase in actual development projects for which they and their students provided design services in the 1990s. They became very busy – for example, the *siesta*-like custom of resting for one or two hours after lunch every day disappeared from the routine of Tsinghua architecture and planning students in the mid-1990s. They were remunerated according to the total floor area of the projects they designed and the speed with which they completed the designs, and therefore they found the small-scale, preservation- and community-oriented focus of the studio to be less and less relevant to the tasks and incentives they typically faced. Indeed, long-term planning and academic design-related research in general became more difficult to pursue in the 1990s than before, despite increased funding and improved facilities. The lure of design commissions for rapid, large-scale development projects was too great.

## BECOMING A CHINESE PLANNING STUDENT

With the help of a travel grant from the MIT East Asian Architecture and Planning Program, I was able to remain at Tsinghua after the 1992 studio ended. Professor Lü Junhua, the faculty member who was undertaking the actual planning for the redevelopment of De-Wai, invited me to join her research group. Lü's group was unusually committed to pursuing research, especially resident social surveys, as a component of its neighborhood redevelopment planning projects. At that time her group was planning three such projects at the edge of Beijing's old city, each of which involved about 40 hectares of land and about 20,000 residents. Soon after I joined the group, we began work on a smaller, fourth project at the very heart of the city, alongside the moat around the Forbidden City, and within a year the group had also added a series of redevelopment projects in another historic city center, Quanzhou, in Fujian Province on the south-east coast.

Although my Chinese language ability was very rudimentary at this point, and I was not proficient with Chinese design standards, Lü saw my participation in her group's work as worthwhile in a number of ways. Most of her students were studying English as a formal part of their professional education, and were eager for a chance to use it with a native-speaking colleague (I later taught the School of Architecture's Professional English course for graduate students for two years). I was also valuable to the group's literature searches, as much of the methodological and historical material relevant to our work was in English. My background in housing design and development, and work in historic contexts, seemed to suit the nature of the group's projects. More generally, Lü recognized the historic importance of China's current wave of urban redevelopment, and appreciated the perspective of a student whose home society had already experienced large-scale redevelopment. Finally, I served as a kind of "ambassador" for the group in its collaborations with faculty and students from abroad. These included architecture and planning groups from the Paris-Villemin School of Architecture, France; the Norwegian Institute of Science and Technology in Trondheim; the University of Technology, Sydney, Australia; and McGill University and the University of British Columbia (UBC) in Canada. Lü also collaborated with Peter Rowe at Harvard, although this was late into my time at Tsinghua and I was too deeply involved with my doctoral thesis to participate (see their book, Lü et al. 2001). To a lesser extent, I also helped other Tsinghua faculty in their collaborations with foreign partners, especially the next MIT studio group in 1995.

For my part, I wanted to improve my Chinese, to become knowledgeable about Chinese planning practices, and to be involved in the historic changes that were taking place in Chinese cities. I had left the United States during a deep economic recession that was especially hard on the design and development professions, and that seemed reflected in a particularly dark mood in American popular culture. By contrast, the profound sense of optimism among the students in China was intoxicating. They were learning skills whose potential utility appeared boundless, and developers and government officials craved their ideas. I had not intended to pursue a further degree when I left MIT, but in China I was excited by the prospect of conducting research that was grounded in so much actual development, and of serving such an obvious and immediate need. China's rapid urban development was truly tantalizing. It begged for new planning ideas and approaches, and yet the very speed and scale of projects essentially precluded any application of research, or experimentation with decision-making processes. I was soon reminded of a sign hanging in the office of a housing developer for whom I had worked before studying at MIT: "The Opportunities are Insurmountable."

Tsinghua granted me "visiting scholar" status for up to a year, but had to bend its rules to do so, because I did not yet have a doctoral degree. Within a few months, it became clear that enrolling as a doctoral student at Tsinghua was my best, and perhaps only, means to participate in the planning of Chinese cities.[7] The private professional sector was too embryonic to offer much opportunity. I quickly became acquainted with the handful of private or quasi-private firms doing design work, and nearly all of their projects were limited to individual buildings or even interiors. Government agencies and official planning institutes at that time would not hire a foreign planner. Even after I became a student at Tsinghua, I was barred from one or two local government planning meetings simply because I was a foreign national. At most other meetings or visits to government agencies, or during surveys of residents, one of the Chinese members of the group typically had to accompany me. Professor Lü nevertheless treated me fully as a member of the group, and gave me as much access to information and as much responsibility for contributing to the group's work as any other student.

The camaraderie and cohesion I felt with Professor Lü's other students surpassed anything I had experienced in American schools. Her group was a tight-knit unit that frequently met at her small apartment, shared meals, debated issues, and carefully divided the tasks of research and design among the different levels of students. I was one of three doctoral students. (We were later joined by a fourth, Johan Nilsson, a Swedish masters graduate of the Chalmers Institute of Technology who was the only other Western doctoral student in planning at Tsinghua during my time there.) There were also various numbers of masters and bachelors students, and one postdoctoral researcher in the group, and I always felt I had a closer relationship with them and with our advisor, Professor Lü, than with the other doctoral students or faculty at Tsinghua.

Bonds of loyalty between students and their advisors are typically strong in Chinese universities, and are to be expected in a society in which many forms of specialized information are available primarily through personal channels. Although my knowledge of how other faculty and students related to each other at Tsinghua is limited, I have a strong impression that relations within Lü Junhua's group were exceptional in a number of ways. Professor Lü's acceptance of Johan and me into her group was unique at the time, and I believe no other Western European or North American has since enrolled in Tsinghua's doctoral planning program. Given our lack of fluency with Chinese language and design practices, and the bureaucratic inconveniences of having foreigners engaged in government work, Lü's decision reflected a willingness to sacrifice short-term efficiency for an unpredictable kind of creativity. Discussions among our group were highly critical of current planning policy and practices, but were always tempered by the need to propose workable solutions based in an empirical knowledge of urban conditions, and an ideal of improving the lives of average citizens.

Lü's motivation for social research and urban design in neighborhood redevelopment projects had different roots from those of the other faculty with whom I was most familiar at Tsinghua. Her expertise was in housing rather than architectural history. Although she shared, for example, Wu Liangyong's and Zhu Zixuan's preferences for low-rise urban environments and for new construction that was compatible with historic urban fabric, her values derived more from a tradition of observing and defining residents' needs than from an appreciation for historic forms as such. Her own mentor, Professor Hua Lanhong, was famous in Beijing's twentieth-century planning history for having opposed Wu Liangyong's mentor, Liang Sicheng, in debates about the fate of Beijing's historic city center in the early 1950s. Hua was an unabashed modernist, whereas Liang was a preservationist at heart (Abramson 2007: 133). In much more subtle ways, Lü and Wu carried this debate down to the end of the twentieth century.

Based on Lü Junhua's values, her group seemed more likely than most others at Tsinghua to undertake the kind of socially informed, community-based physical planning that my American education had taught me to pursue. Some young faculty at Tsinghua also shared these values – particularly those who had returned from studying abroad – but they did not have Lü's independence and seniority. As it turned out, although we were able to conduct surveys, write theses, and publish research on what a more community-sensitive neighborhood planning approach in China might look like, we were largely unable to test this approach in the actual projects for which we were commissioned to produce analyses and designs. We operated in a system that relied on extremely rigid standards to guarantee a basic environmental quality for residents, even as it gave planning officials and developers great freedom to negotiate the terms of development that concerned them most: municipal infrastructure improvement, increased density, and leeway to relocate existing populations and industries. The decision-making process itself was never a subject of the plan, let alone the participation of residents.

Under these circumstances, I still hoped that Tsinghua's collaborations with various foreign counterparts might provide opportunities to influence local policymakers, test new planning approaches, and transform the way that planners defined and learned their profession. By far the most ambitious and extensive collaboration in the School of Architecture was with the University of British Columbia's Centre for Human Settlements (CHS).[8] The Canadian International Development Agency had funded CHS from the very beginning of the 1990s to organize the Asian Urban Research Network (AURN), a consortium of planning and geography scholars at universities and research institutes in Indonesia, Thailand, Vietnam, and China. Tsinghua was one of three Chinese universities that participated (along with Tongji University in Shanghai and Zhongshan University in Guangzhou). The AURN intended both to obtain research findings on planning practices and urban development realities (ranging from the neighborhood level to municipalities and metropolitan regions) as well as to use the act of collaborative research to strengthen Asian planning institutions and education. In particular, the AURN sought to promote the use of socio-economic and political research in urban planning.

Although Lü Junhua was not central to Tsinghua's participation in the AURN, the faculty at the University of British Columbia were interested in her group's surveys of neighborhood residents and her efforts to draw from those surveys a set of recommended policies and design improvements for neighborhood redevelopment. When the city of Quanzhou, in Fujian Province, commissioned her group and that of Tsinghua Professor Sun Fengqi to undertake a series of city-center neighborhood redevelopment plans, Professor Michael Leaf led a group from UBC to conduct a joint summer research studio with Lü and Sun (Leaf *et al.* 1995). That collaboration became the basis for my own postdoctoral work with Leaf at UBC between 1998 and 2001, which involved a number of additional studios and efforts to promote direct community participation in neighborhood planning in Quanzhou (Abramson *et al.* 2000, 2001; Abramson 2005).

In most of the AURN projects, as well as in the initial collaboration in Quanzhou, the Canadian planning faculty were frustrated in their attempts to draw research data from projects, and to integrate policy concerns and social science with planning research. For their part, the Chinese partners were impatient with the AURN's research-oriented mission, given the greater urgency of solving physical design problems. The continuing political sensitivity and inaccessibility of much socio-economic data in China, and Chinese academics' inability to deal directly with decision-making processes, were also a problem. In China, prevailing systems of bureaucratic control and rewards still generally inhibited lateral collaboration and data sharing between different areas of expertise at the same level in government or academia.

Similar difficulties bedeviled efforts to expand the scope of MIT's relationship with Tsinghua. After 1992, three years passed before another MIT–Tsinghua urban design studio took place, and another three years passed before the following one. There were some discussions of considering a larger spatial scale in the studio briefs, adding transportation and economic real estate components, and trying to understand more of the decision-making process in which each topic was embedded. However, the studios of 1995 and 1998, and indeed those of 2000 and 2002, all retained the small scale and the focus on historic preservation that characterized the earlier studios. To do more than that required too much interdisciplinary and governmental coordination than was possible for the Tsinghua faculty who participated in the studio. In the mid-1990s, too, MIT's Center for Real Estate launched a major initiative to collaborate with Tsinghua on real estate-related research, which ultimately foundered. The initiative was probably ahead of its time, but also perhaps inappropriate for the partners concerned. The interest and capacity of Tsinghua's faculty, as well as available local governmental support, were insufficient both to gather the data that the research required, and to undertake its analysis.

Underlying all of these disappointments and frustrations was a discomfort with the fundamental asymmetry of research resources and freedom enjoyed by the Chinese partners on one hand, and the Western partners on the other. Certainly the Chinese partners felt the asymmetry more acutely, but I believe their North American and European counterparts felt it too, to varying extents. Money and analytical capacity flowed from the West. Data flowed from the East. I was never able to escape my non-Chinese status as a student at Tsinghua. Language remained something of a barrier, but, more importantly, my Westerner's perspective was essential to my role and identity as a student, and ultimately to the topic of my dissertation on neighborhood redevelopment in Beijing (Abramson 1997b).

## AN AMERICAN SEA TURTLE[9]

Upon completing graduation requirements for my doctoral degree, I had a choice to pursue postdoctoral work either at the Chinese University of Hong Kong's Department of Architecture or at UBC's Centre for Human Settlements. Although the former position would have given me an opportunity to remain more closely engaged with Chinese planning and design, I chose to go to UBC, primarily because I felt a need to see what my experience in China might mean back in North America. Of course, through my active connection with AURN, I knew that UBC would also offer a hospitable environment in which to continue research on Chinese planning. It turned out to be a very unusual base in this regard, as China still was not a particular interest among most North American planning academies. As recently as 2000, when I attended my first annual conference of the Association of Collegiate Schools of Planning, there were only six China-focused presentations at the entire meeting. (There were more than 20 such presentations at the ACSP's 2008 conference.) Until 2006 (Abramson 2006), the *Journal of the American Planning Association* had published no refereed overview of China's urban planning profession, and during the previous 20 years it had published only three articles on China, most recently in 1999 (Wu and Yeh 1999). Most planning scholars in North America with a knowledge of China, who were largely Chinese themselves, were teaching or researching primarily non-China-related topics. I, too, upon taking a tenure-track teaching position in Seattle in 2001, had quickly to establish a research program focused on North America, although I was able to continue my China-focused resear ch and some teaching as well.

By now, the demands that China's urbanization is making on the planning profession and on academia worldwide have become more pressing and obvious. Engagements that were not possible or considered in the 1990s have become very popular. Not only has MIT reduced the gap between its regular Beijing studios to two years, but Professors Jan Wampler in Architecture and Tunney Lee in Urban Studies and Planning have also independently organized additional field studios in between.[10] At the University of California, Berkeley, where no faculty in the College of Environmental Design were interested in China when I inquired in 1993, there are now at least five faculty independently conducting urban design-related studios, teaching and research in China, and more who are conducting social and economic research related to China's urban development. After relocating from MIT to become Dean of the University of Pennsylvania's Graduate School of Fine Arts in 1996, Gary Hack oversaw the development of semester-long studios with both Tsinghua and Tongji University, in which students in China and the US work on the same problem, communicating both by internet and by spending part of the semester at each university.[11] Indeed, there have been far too many new planning-related interactions between Chinese and non-Chinese institutions over the past decade for me to monitor. From those that I have observed, however, it appears that design and physical planning is the sub-area of planning that involves the most foreign expertise, and that remains the most dynamic aspect of planning in China at the present. Perhaps nowhere else are architects more frequently called upon to undertake urban-scale projects.

As a former student in China who has returned to the United States, I see this as presenting a problem, and I am ambivalent about what disciplinary mode is most appropriate for my own involvement with Chinese planning. The skills that I learned at MIT in urban design, site planning, and community engagement are perhaps my most globally "portable" technical planning skills. While teaching at the University of Washington, I have employed these skills not only in China, but also locally, in Seattle, and in Kobe, Japan, through an extensive exchange relationship between UW and Kobe University (Tanaka *et al.* 2009). But I have been compelled also to develop and disseminate my knowledge of China's specific cultural context for planning. To generalize, it seems that any student or professional who has devoted a significant portion of his/her life to practice in a cultural context other than his/her own must develop two identities: a strictly disciplinary one, and one that is based in a broader cultural literacy. It seems that there could be a more explicitly recognized professional role for this combination of skills.

China's demands on global planning expertise raise another question relevant to current ideas about the field of planning: what exactly should be the role of design? During rapid urbanization, the undeniable centrality of physical construction requires a fundamental re-examination of the relation between design and the other modes of planning: analytical, policy-making, advocacy, and action. In the West, during recent decades, planners have tended to view design as the most primitive, or "orthogonal," mode of planning, particularly susceptible to monopolization by the powerful, and necessarily subsidiary to analysis, policy, and social action or mobilization (Friedmann 1987). When Langley Keyes taught the core Masters in City Planning course to my class at MIT, Planning and Institutional Processes, he described the discipline of planning as a historical layering of modes or "paradigms," with design being the earliest mode, dominant up through the late nineteenth century, but later augmented by progressivist social reform, rationalist governmental reform, explicit power-broking, and communitarian political action. According to this view, Chinese planning still follows an essentially nineteenth-century paradigm.

Yet when major infrastructural changes are required, whether to respond to critical environmental demands or to accommodate vast population movements, design constraints and opportunities need to be considered at all stages of a planning process. As the chairman of one of China's largest private planning and design firms put it to me, planners in China perform a service similar to that of lawyers in the United States. They help clients navigate a complex and opaque forest of regulatory and environmental constraints. Designs, though they may appear to represent a finished idea of what will be built, are often just tools in a multi-staged negotiation over the control of land, the attraction of investment, or some other part of the development process. It is frustrating for foreign designers who do not realize this, and are commissioned to design a potentially cutting-edge project (such as an eco-city or a new university campus, for example), to discover that their designs only served to gain approval to develop a piece of land that otherwise would have been off-limits to development. Kris Olds has produced a particularly sophisticated study of these relationships as they are manifested in Shanghai and Vancouver (Olds 2001), but their implications for global planning practice in China have not been adequately discussed within the planning profession.

Another challenge that the Chinese urbanization and planning experience presents to the global profession, and that is closely related to the nature of design as a mode of planning, is the question of how and when to undertake "big plans" and rapid implementation, without sacrificing identity and democracy. With this question, we return to the modesty, tentativeness, and sense of limits expressed in the work of the MIT participants in the early Beijing studios. Gary Hack, in his presentation to my cohort of MCP students taking Planning and Institutional Processes, remarked that Daniel Burnham's credo, "Make no little plans," seems to have been replaced by its opposite, "Make no big plans." He was simply stating a historical fact. From Patrick Geddes to Jane Jacobs and beyond, reformers of planning throughout the twentieth century attacked the profession for its "surgical" approaches and its grand narratives and gestures, and advocated careful modification instead.

Chinese planners have noted the trend. One planning official, who had recently visited neighborhood planners at a community development association in Chicago, remarked wistfully a couple of years ago, "It seems that Chinese planning has adopted the principles of Western medicine, while Western planning appears increasingly to follow those of Chinese medicine."[12] By this he meant that planning in the West has come to treat the environment holistically and gingerly, best cured by small, careful, and non-invasive measures. Planning in China, by contrast, is reductionist, and embraces radical surgery, much in the mode of earlier eras of planning in the West (Zhang and Fang 2004).

In the early 1990s, a number of factors in the experience and attitude of Western planners led to their over-riding desire to help China avoid the mistakes of the West. First, Western planning scholars, students and professionals had by this time thoroughly absorbed the notion that their discipline was indeed guilty of many mistakes. The emergence of postcolonial criticism made their sense of guilt that much stronger. Second, they shared with their Chinese counterparts the sense of a developmental time lag in China. The drive to "Reform and Open" under Deng Xiaoping, coming on the heels of deep isolation during the last decade of Mao's rule, only made this sense more acute, despite a wistful regret on the part of some who had hoped Mao's experiment might have succeeded in establishing a different path of development. Third, the ensuing rapidity of growth, which was just now becoming perceptible at a time when the globalization of culture and economy became an explicit concern of planners and designers, enabled outsiders to imagine that China was on the brink of making Western mistakes, but at an unprecedented scale, with severe consequences for all.

At the same time, some Western observers, mainly designers, have found China's radical physical transformation to be an exhilaratingly new world. It allows them to use the Chinese experience as a club with which to beat a Euro-dominated discourse of urbanism that emphasizes history, identity, participation, and the human scale (Koolhaas *et al.* 2000: 309ff). Others invoke the sustainability imperative to support China's apparently top-down planning processes; quick, coordinated action to save the planet appears to demand the bypassing of cumbersome democratic decision-making processes.

Such hopes and usages are as uncritical and unobservant of actual Chinese development as they are despairing and critical of Western practices and norms. For all its apparent hierarchy and top-down decision-making, Chinese urbanization is as uncoordinated, inefficient, and fraught with conflict as is/was the urbanization of any large, complex and rapidly transforming society. The sometimes vaunted, often maligned, dictatorial powers of Chinese central government in fact depend on a complex web of local and highly personalistic relations, which can contribute to a surprising diversity of local planning practices (Leaf and Hou 2006). Because the myth of central control is key to the legitimacy of the state, however, the diversity of practice is usually at best unheralded, and frequently masked. Truly effective (i.e. locally responsive) solutions to urban problems in China are therefore especially difficult to promote and adapt, even when they are successfully implemented in one place.

Thus, the difficulty of learning from others' mistakes remains. Part of "becoming a Chinese planning student" was learning to feel frustration at the mere mention of this possibility by Western planners. Chinese planners must operate in a unique experiential universe. Despite the apparent transborder fluidity of planning ideas and values, each context for implementation is unique, and dependent on historical and institutional precedents and circumstances. Ironically, in a period of such rapid change and historical compression, this "path dependency" is that much more keenly felt by those who are caught in it, even as the drama of transformation makes path dependency invisible to those who view it from the outside. Path dependency should not be used as an excuse to ignore good ideas of any origin, domestic or foreign. Rather, it requires that we acknowledge and appreciate the unpredictable, dialectical (or reflexive) nature of innovating in order to solve current problems based on fundamental principles of social justice and empirical truth. If we do this, we will feel, as Kevin Lynch did in Nanjing, "right at home," regardless of where we practice and whence we come (Lynch *et al.* 1990: 230).

## NOTES

1 Also spelled "Qinghua," according to the standard *hanyu pinyin* romanization system used in the People's Republic of China since the 1950s. "Tsinghua" is a relatively recent revival of the pre-standard romanized name dating back to the early twentieth century.

2 Despite the important practical role of Hong Kong, Singapore, Taiwan, Korea, and Japan in actually facilitating China's entry into the global export market, norms of urban planning and development during the era of Reform and Opening were at least as dependent on perceived models in Europe and especially North America. Both architectural and planning licensing standards, for example, ultimately followed the US model rather than the British, even though Hong Kong had been working under British standards for decades.

3 I also met my wife, then a graduate student in Materials Science at MIT, who is a native of Beijing. Later, in Beijing, we lived in her parents' apartment not far from the Tsinghua campus.

4 I am grateful specifically for the time and insights that John de Monchaux, Dennis French-man, Daphne Gondhalekar, Gary Hack, Yang Jiang, and Jan Wampler shared with me.

5 In his lectures for this subject, Beinart enjoyed showing a slide of the Russian avant garde architect Konstantin Melnikov in his old age, depicting him "looking humbled by the mistakes he has made," but nonetheless wise and observant (see Russian Avantgarde Foundation 2008). It seemed to me as a student that Beinart's characterization of this portrait summed up a contemporary, chastened, postmodern attitude towards the bold Modernism of the earlier twentieth century.

6 Tsinghua was, of course, not the only planning school in China, and there were others that required less of an architectural orientation in their students. Among the strong design and engineering schools, Tongji University in Shanghai is known for having a more multi-disciplinary planning program, for example. Moreover, there is a whole branch of planning in China that is based in geography, which is strong at Beijing University, Nanjing University, and Zhongshan University in Guangzhou. The geography programs, however, generally confine themselves to regional planning or municipal comprehensive/master planning. The design schools, whether architectural or engineering, tend to dominate the discipline at a wider range of scales, from the municipality down to the development site, and these are the scales at which plans are most commonly implemented.

7 Before I could enroll at Tsinghua I had to overcome a number of financial and institutional barriers. The Tsinghua administration and the Department of Urban Planning and Design were very supportive of my enrollment, and they helped me obtain a Chinese Ministry of Education scholarship, but I still needed to be able to defer payments on my earlier student loans from the United States while I was studying in China. As a rule, any student who pursues further education at a foreign university "comparable to an institution of higher education in the United States" is able to defer such payments, but, because no American had yet studied for a graduate degree in China, no Chinese university was listed as comparable (United States Code 2002). I had to personally arrange for Tsinghua's application to the US Department of Education for this status so that I could defer loan payments while studying there.

8 It is interesting to note that the most extensive exchanges were with institutions in North America and Europe, not with other Asian countries. Lü Junhua's group did have an exchange with faculty and students from Tsukuba, Japan, soon after I left Tsinghua in 1997, but that was the group's only Asian exchange of which I am aware. I believe the situation was similar for other faculty at Tsinghua as well.

9 "Sea turtles" is slang for Chinese people who return to China after studying or working abroad.

10 In the mid-1990s, Jan Wampler unsuccessfully sought partners at Tsinghua to conduct a studio on village housing design. In 2007 he was able finally to carry one out (see Wampler 2007). Beijing's expansion to double its size, which put development pressure on many of its suburban villages during this time interval, was surely a factor in making the studio topic relevant to Chinese planners.

11 Laurie Olin and Tony Atkin led several of these studios. As Gary Hack informs me, Laurie also became a faculty member at Tsinghua and oversaw the development of their MLA program, and during the early to mid-2000s was commuting regularly and there was a regular flow of students and faculty back and forth. And for the past five or six years UPenn has had a formal joint venture with Tsinghua in the area of energy and building simulation, working jointly on dozens of projects around the world, under the umbrella of the T.C. Chan Center, which has offices both in Beijing and in Philadelphia.

12 I cannot provide the exact date of his statement, but Mr. Huang Shiqing, Vice Director of the Quanzhou Municipal Bureau of Urban and Rural Planning, made this observation in a meeting on a community-based urban environmental management project supported by the Ford Foundation from 1999 through 2004.

## REFERENCES

Abramson, D. (1994) "New Housing in Old Beijing: A Comparative Survey of Projects Completed to Date – Beijing's Old and Dilapidated Housing Renewal (Part V)," *China City Planning Review*, **10** (3), 42–56.

Abramson, D. (1997a) " 'Marketization' and Institutions in Chinese Inner-City Neighborhood Redevelopment: A Commentary on 'Beijing's Old and Dilapidated Housing Renewal' by Lü Junhua," *Cities*, **14** (2), 71–5.

Abramson, D. (1997b) "Neighborhood Redevelopment as a Cultural Problem: A Western Perspective on Current Plans for the Old City of Beijing." Doctoral dissertation, Tsinghua University.

Abramson, D. B. (2005) "The 'Studio Abroad' as a Mode of Trans-Cultural Engagement in Urban Planning: A Reflection on Ten Years of Sino-Canadian Educational Exchange," *Journal of Planning Education and Research*, **25** (1), 89–102.

Abramson, D. B. (2006) "Urban Planning in China: Continuity and Change," *Journal of the American Planning Association*, **72** (2), 197–215.

Abramson, D. B. (2007) "The Aesthetics of City-Scale Preservation Policy in Beijing," *Planning Perspectives*, **22** (2), 129–66.

Abramson, D., Leaf, M., and the students of UBC Plan 545B (2000) *Urban Development and Redevelopment in Quanzhou, China: A Field Studio Report* (Vancouver, University of British Columbia, Centre for Human Settlements).

Abramson, D., Leaf, M., Anderson, S., and the students of UBC Plan 545B (2001) *Governance and Design: Participatory Planning, Residential Design Guidelines and Historic Preservation in Quanzhou, Fujian, China: A Year 2000 Studio Report* (Vancouver, University of British Columbia, Centre for Human Settlements).

Bray, D. (2005) *Social Space and Governance in Urban China: The Danwei System from Origins to Reform* (Stanford, CA, Stanford University Press).

Dong, G. (1996) Conversation with Dong Guangqi, Vice Director, at the Beijing Municipal Institute of Urban Planning and Design, 26 April.

Fan, C. C. (2006) "China's Eleventh Five-Year Plan (2006–2010): From 'Getting Rich First' to 'Common Prosperity'," *Eurasian Geography and Economics*, **47** (6), 708–23.

Friedmann, J. (1987) *Planning in the Public Domain: From Knowledge to Action* (Princeton, NJ, Princeton University Press).

Hall, P. G. (2002) *Cities of Tomorrow: An Intellectual History of Urban Planning and Design in the Twentieth Century*, 3rd edition (Oxford, UK: Blackwell Publishers).

He, H. (1993) "Social and Economic Aspects of Beijing Old-City Redevelopment Programs," *Building in China*, **6** (3–4), 16–24.

Koolhaas, R., Boeri, S., Kwinter, S., Tazi, N., and Obrist, H. U. (2000) *Mutations: Rem Koolhaas, Harvard Project on the City, Stefano Boeri, Multiplicity, Sanford Kwinter, Nadia Tazi, Hans Ulrich Obrist* (Bordeaux, France, ACTAR; arc en rêve centre d'architecture).

Leaf, M. and Hou, L. (2006) "The 'Third Spring' of Urban Planning in China: The Resurrection of Professional Planning in the Post-Mao Era," *China Information*, **20** (3), 553–85.

Leaf, M. L., students of UBC course Plan 545B, Cairns, M., Halliday, D., Harrington, M., Izuhara, M., Martinson, L., Oyhenart, G., Poppelwell, T., and Tuerah, N. (1995) *Planning for Urban Redevelopment in Quanzhou, Fujian, China* (Vancouver, University of British Columbia, Centre for Human Settlements).

Lu, D. (2006) "Travelling Urban Form: The Neighbourhood Unit in China," *Planning Perspectives*, **21** (4), 369–92.

Lü, J. (1993) "Beijing's Old and Dilapidated Housing Renewal (Part I)," *China City Planning Review*, **9** (3), 27–35.

Lü, J. (1994) "Beijing's Old and Dilapidated Housing Renewal (Part IV)," *China City Planning Review*, **10** (2), 34–46.

Lü, J., Rowe, P. G., and Zhang, J. (Eds.) (2001) *Modern Urban Housing in China, 1840–2000* (Munich, Prestel).

Lynch, K., Banerjee, T., and Southworth, M. (1990) *City Sense and City Design: Writings and Projects of Kevin Lynch* (Cambridge, MA, MIT Press).

Marshall, R. (2003) *Emerging Urbanity: Gloabl Urban Projects in the Asia Pacific Rim* (London, Spon Press).

Ng, M.-K. and Wu, F. (1997) "Challenges and Opportunities – Can Western Planning Theories Inform Changing Chinese Urban Planning Practices?," in A. G. O. Yeh, X. Xu, and X. Yan (Eds.) *Urban Planning and Planning Education under Economic Reform in China* (Hong Kong, Centre of Urban Planning and Environmental Management, University of Hong Kong), pp. 147–70.

Olds, K. (2001) *Globalization and Urban Change: Capital, Culture, and Pacific Rim Mega-Projects* (Oxford, Oxford University Press).

Peattie, L. R. (1987) *Planning, Rethinking Ciudad Guayana* (Ann Arbor, University of Michigan Press).

Qing hua da xue (Beijing China) and Massachusetts Institute of Technology School of Architecture and Planning (1985) "Beijing Urban Design Studio," Summer 1985, MIT East Asian Architecture and Planning Program.

Qing hua da xue (Beijing China) and Massachusetts Institute of Technology (1992) "Beijing Urban Design Studio: Longfusi Market, Deshengmenwai, Xiangshan" ["Beijing Cheng Shi She Ji Yan Jiu Ban: Long Fu Si Jie, De Shen Men Wai Dai Jie, Xiang Shan"] (n.p., Tsinghua University; Massachusetts Institute of Technology).

Russian Avantgarde Foundation (2008) "About Melnikov." Russian Avantgarde Foundation, available http://www.melnikovhouse.org/about-melnikov.php (archived by WebCite® at http://www.webcitation.org/5css0CJ3w) (accessed 8 December 2008)

SIGUS (Special Interest Group in Urban Settlements) (1991a) *Assessment of the Development Process: Lublin, Poland* (Cambridge, MA, MIT School of Architecture and Planning).

SIGUS (Special Interest Group in Urban Settlements) (1991b) *Preliminary Construction Sector Inventory and Assessment, Lublin Region, Poland* (Cambridge, MA, MIT School of Architecture and Planning).

SIGUS (Special Interest Group in Urban Settlements) (1991c) *SIGUS Reports: The Poland Housing Initiatives Preparatory Field Work in Lublin, Poland: Summary* (Cambridge, MA, MIT School of Architecture and Planning).

SIGUS (Special Interest Group in Urban Settlements) (1991d) *Summary of the Participatory Planning Exercise: Lublin, Poland* (Cambridge, MA, MIT School of Architecture and Planning).

Sorensen, A. (2005) "The Developmental State and the Extreme Narrowness of the Public Realm: The Twentieth Century Evolution of Japanese Planning Culture," in B. Sanyal (Ed.) *Comparative Planning Cultures* (New York, Routledge), pp. 223–58.

Tanaka, T., Abramson, D. B., and Yamazaki, Y. (2009) "Using GIS in Community Design Charrettes: Lessons from a Japan–U.S. Collaboration in Earthquake Recovery and Mitigation Planning for Kobe," *Habitat International*, **33** (4), 310–18

Tang, W.-S. (2000) "Chinese Urban Planning at Fifty: An Assessment of the Planning Theory Literature," *Journal of Planning Literature*, **14** (3), 347–66.

United States Code (2002) "Title 20, Chapter 28, Subchapter I, Section 1002, Definition of Institution of Higher Education for Purposes of Student Assistance Programs," available http://law.justia.com/us/codes/title20/20usc1002.html (accessed 27 July 2009).

Wampler, J. (2007) *Beijing Housing Studio: Liangxiang & Changyang Villages* (Cambridge, MA, Jan Wampler, Department of Architecture, MIT).

Wright, G. (2002) "Building Global Modernisms," *Grey Room*, **7**, 125–34.

Wu, F. and Yeh, A. G.-O. (1999) "Urban Spatial Structure in a Transitional Economy: The Case of Guangzhou, China," *Journal of the American Planning Association*, **65** (4), 377–94.

Wu, L. (1999) *Rehabilitating the Old City of Beijing: A Project in the Ju'er Hutong Neighbourhood* (Vancouver, UBC Press).

Zhang, Y. and Fang, K. (2004) "Is History Repeating Itself? From Urban Renewal in the United States to Inner-City Redevelopment in China," *Journal of Planning Education and Research*, **23** (3), 286–98.

# CHAPTER 14

## CROSSING BORDERS

DO PLANNING IDEAS TRAVEL?

**JOHN FRIEDMANN**

## CAUTIONARY TALES

One of the main themes of this volume is the transfer of planning ideas from one country to another, and the questions of what happens to the ideas in the course of this transfer, with what results. Interesting as these stories are in themselves, each a unique tale from the past, what I miss from most of the accounts is what anthropologists call a thick description of the process of the transfer itself.[1] I would like to fill this gap with a story from my own practice when, in the latter part of the 1960s, I worked for the Ford Foundation in Chile, in charge of a large-scale, multi-year technical assistance program to the national government concerned with regional development planning and a variety of other issues regarding housing, urban policy, and social programming. Although unable to adopt the anthropologist's method of "thick description," I hope at least to evoke some of the things that happened when an overseas technical mission worked in close collaboration with a reform-minded, democratic government on a range of planning issues.[2]

I will follow this with a second story that calls attention to some of the difficulties of inserting what appear to be desirable planning practices from one country into the political and cultural context of another. The general tenor of the essays in this volume is, one could argue, fairly optimistic about transferring planning practices around the globe, especially from presumptively more developed countries to those still undergoing a process of "development."[3] On the whole, Western planners tend to be an optimistic lot, yearning for improvements in the lives of humankind. I am one of them, and have staked a large part of my life on the hope that modernization, as I used to understand this concept, is a global aspiration, desired by most. Naturally, I thought that as an unquestionably modern man, and as a planner to boot, I had an obligation to help others to become modern in turn. My long experience has taught me, however, that modernity doesn't come in a single cut, *prêt-à-porter*, as it were; and that the modernity I wanted to help others attain might for various reasons be resisted or, as in Sanjeev Vidyarthi's chapter, be re-imagined by indigenous modernizing elites.

My second story begins in 2007 when I was appointed (honorary) adviser to the China Academy of Urban Planning and Design (CAUPD), an autonomous agency within the Ministry of Construction (today the Ministry of Housing and Urban–Rural Development). It concerns my admittedly limited efforts to persuade the Academy to follow up on what to me seemed two attractive ideas: first, to undertake a series of experiments with development planning at the neighborhood level, and, second, to promote the idea of neighborhood planning in a revision of the planning curricula taught at leading universities, such as Tsinghua and Tongji (located in Beijing and Shanghai respectively). To date, my efforts have failed to win visible support. I will therefore try to identify what I perceive to be some of the reasons why the idea of neighborhood (also called "community") planning, involving a high degree of civic participation, which so appeals to us in North America, meets with profound skepticism from the Chinese planning bureaucracy. My analysis of these reasons is meant as a cautionary tale for those who advocate the universalism of planning ideas and for whom, in Tom Friedman's words, the world is flat (Friedman 2007).

## TRANSFORMING AN AID PROGRAM IN CHILE

In the deep winter of the cold war during the 1960s and 1970s, Chile, a long, thin strip of a country along the western edge of South America, became one of a number of battle fronts in the ideological confrontation that structured cold war geo-politics. The American aid program (USAID) was spending millions of dollars in direct economic assistance to Chile for the construction of social housing, and was getting worried about the lack of community facilities, which, they hoped, would help calm the rising swell of popular discontent in the country. Accordingly, the Ford Foundation was approached to fund a program that would design and put in place a few pilot projects of so-called *equipamiento comunitario* (community facilities), as well as instruct Chilean architects and planners in how to link these facilities with large-scale social housing programs. In 1963, Ford approved the idea, and invented what turned out to be a Byzantine arrangement of collaborators to undertake it. This involved five institutions: a firm of architectural and planning consultants, Rice University in Houston, an ad hoc group of academics from Harvard and MIT, Harvard University's Graduate School of Design, and the International Institute of Education. The Chilean government under President Arturo Alessandri, an arch-conservative and scion of a large land-owning family who was notorious for refusing to shake hands with his peons, signed the agreement, but soon afterwards lost the elections. The winning Christian Democrats were led by Eduardo Frei, a moderate liberal who stood for social reforms ranging from housing to land redistribution. Chile was about to reach the halfway point in its urban transition and was ready to trounce the feudal oligarchy that had traditionally ruled the country, but was determined to do so within a democratic framework.

Aware of the in-country criticisms of its community facilities program, and in light of the new political situation, the Foundation approached me to assess the program and make appropriate recommendations. After a flying visit to Chile, my report suggested a complete restructuring of the existing program involving a broadening of its objectives and the relocation of advisory services in Santiago. The Foundation liked what I had written, and asked me to head up the newly named Urban and Regional Development Advisory Program in Chile (URDAPIC). I left MIT, where I had been teaching for four years, arriving in Santiago in June 1965.[4]

The new mission included four areas of activity: planning community facilities in the context of urban development; the social integration of "marginalized" households, by acknowledging their claims to housing and other citizen rights; regional development planning as a way to guide the location of public investment; and a program for graduate education and applied research in planning. The counterpart agencies for this effort, to which advisors would be attached, were to be the Ministry of Housing (then being formed), the Office of Popular Promotion (a new agency directly accountable to the President of the Republic), the newly established National Planning Office (ODEPLAN), and the Pontifical Catholic University of Santiago. At the last of these, the Ford Foundation aimed to help establish a new Interdisciplinary Center for Urban Development (CIDU) to provide the training and research aspects of the program. My own role as coordinator of the Foundation's efforts stood outside this institutional framework, and my name had not even been submitted to the government for clearance. Quite simply, I represented the Foundation's interest in the program as a whole.

The situation in which we found ourselves was extremely tenuous. The young lions who spearheaded the reforms of the new regime were suspicious of the Foundation's motives, yet were themselves uncertain about how to proceed with the new initiatives. Moreover, there were tensions concerning power relations, particularly with regard to ODEPLAN, where we had hoped to provide assistance in regional development planning. The Ministry of Finance was loath to relinquish its power over the budget, regarding ODEPLAN as an interloper whose job, they thought, should be focused more on drawing up a national plan that could serve as bait for foreign financial assistance – rather than it actually having the executive power to steer development through budgetary allocations. In the end, the Ministry of Finance retained de facto planning powers through a program budget, while ODEPLAN divided into three sections: one concerned with the preparation of a long-range national development plan; another with managing foreign assistance; and a third to draw up plans for the regional decentralization of national administrative offices that would include the appointment of regional governors responsible for the coordination of development projects. Regional decentralization was fortunate in having the support of the President and his closest advisors. It was also of direct interest to URDAPIC. Decentralizing government was seen as a way of putting a halt to the further expansion of Santiago by identifying development projects at strategic locations throughout the country.[5]

The Foundation had deep pockets, and we could fund up to ten technical advisors who would work with these new institutions. But how legitimate was our presence, given the negative history of the earlier Foundation program in *equipamiento comunitario,* and the unproven abilities of the advisory staff being recruited? None of us had extensive experience in advising a national government on the specifics of housing, urban development, regionalization, and so forth. Moreover, our assistance had not actually been requested by the present government, but was inherited from the defeated Alessandri government. It would only take a letter from President Frei to send us packing.

The very fluidity of the situation, however, allowed us to make our case. Over time, trust was established through personal relations and dialogue, advisors were recruited, and we were able to move ahead, working closely with Chilean colleagues. The account of what we jointly accomplished would take too long to relate here. What I would like to do instead is to lay out some of the things we learned over the course of the next four years. As I think back on this period of my life, I am astonished at how little we, as government advisers, actually knew that was directly relevant to Chile and could somehow be "transferred." We had no "bundles" of planning knowledge into which we could dip for solutions that could then be confidently applied to the Chilean situation. The very concept of a national policy for regional development, for example, was no more than a range of ideas I had put together in three years of study in Venezuela, none of which had ever been tested in practice (see Friedmann 1966). Together with our Chilean counterparts, we had to learn by doing, putting into practice this most pragmatic of planning epistemologies. Below, I will briefly comment on four things that I took away with me from this experience.

First, as advisors, we were engaged in what I came to call innovative planning. This was a term I coined to distinguish the process in which we were engaged from the traditional forms of "allocative" planning. Budgets and land use plans both allocate scarce resources. In contrast, what we were doing in Chile was to help devise new institutions and try to make them work, all of this in real time. As planners, we were not engaged in drawing up paper plans, but improvised solutions in accord with the accelerated timeline of the reform government (Friedmann 1973).

Second, the URDAPIC team was engaged in a form of mutual learning, which I subsequently proposed as a new approach I called transactive planning.[6] Formally defined, mutual learning is a process by which, in given situations, the abstract theoretical knowledge of planning experts is conjoined with the practical knowledge of ordinary people. It is a process through which theory and practice are brought together, each complementing and strengthening the other in generating new knowledge. In our situation, the "ordinary people" were our Chilean counterparts who were professionals themselves. Still, we came together, working side by side as we jointly considered the problems at hand, exchanging ideas through dialogue. The idea was that neither expert nor local bureaucrat had sufficient knowledge of their own, but that together they might be able to come up with workable solutions to the problems they faced.

There were certain preconditions, however, which had to be in place before mutual learning could occur. We were an advisory group that was composed (with two exceptions) of experts from abroad. Initially only a few of us spoke Spanish, although this was the country's language of everyday communication, and we had to master it quickly or become irrelevant. In addition, each of us had to acquire a modicum of knowledge about the country itself, its history, geography, economics, culture, and politics, so that what technical knowledge we possessed could be transformed into strategic advice. We, the so-called experts, also had to learn something about the dynamic institutional and interpersonal fields in which we had to work. In addition to language, history, politics, and geography, we were obliged to become familiar with the bureaucratic sub-culture within which we worked and, more generally, how to get things done. All of this proved to be a challenging assignment. It also made it clear to me that one of the most important (if elusive) qualities of a good planning advisor is to be a quick learner. To be effective in a situation such as ours, a planner would need to learn all these things during the first few months of what was typically a two- or three-year employment contract.

Third, in innovative planning (and probably in every sort of planning), politics is inevitably in command. As advisers, we had to "go with the flow." The political direction and the priorities of our Chilean colleagues had to be respected if we wanted to be heard. In the case of the Office of Popular Promotion, for example, where URDAPIC had initially placed a senior adviser, we decided to withdraw our participation once it became evident that the Office was being used chiefly for partisan politics. This was an extreme case, but there were many instances in which advisers were unable to prevail because of the government's priorities, or in which a solution that might have seemed "obvious" to the adviser would necessitate a prolonged process of persuasion, testing his patience.[7] It was a constant challenge to remind ourselves that, whereas our counterparts would presumably remain in Chile forever and would have to live with the consequences of their actions, the foreign advisers would depart within a few years for lives elsewhere.

Fourth, political dynamics can wipe out most if not all achievements of innovative planning. In Chile's case, this happened, first, when the socialist Popular Unity government of Salvador Allende was elected to office in 1970 with a new mandate, and definitively in 1973, when the military coup, sanctioned by the American government and supported by the CIA, invested General Augusto Pinochet with dictatorial powers.[8] The coup annulled Chilean democracy for 17 years, a victim of cold war paranoia. As an advisory group we had been allies of the Christian Democratic regime, and, as a result, most of what we had achieved was almost instantly dismantled. The Interdisciplinary Center for Urban Development at the Catholic University was shut down and restarted under new leadership in the Faculty of Architecture, where it remains to this day, principally focused on urban design and physical planning. The National Planning Office remains as well, as does the Ministry of Housing and Urban Development, but only as bureaucratic entities, with new priorities. In short, the two regime changes (of which the second was imposed at the point of a gun) created a series of discontinuities, and, instead of permitting normal democratic processes to do the slow work of social reconstruction, the highly ideological temper of the times (and foreign subversion) sought to incorporate Chile into the expanding American empire. Under the neoliberal order decreed by General Pinochet, unemployment soared, reaching 40 percent at one point, while a small minority became rich. Democracy did not return to Chile until 1990, 21 years after I had returned to the United States to head up a new Urban Planning Program at the University of California in Los Angeles. But my Chilean experience had left me with a wealth of ideas about planning that I could transfer back into my work as an academic. I made social learning central to my writing, seeing planning as a form of praxis, that is, as the constant alternation of knowledge and action, theory and practice in the dynamic, rapidly changing situations of our time. For innovative, progressive planners, the past is not a reliable guide to the future, and what we think we know because we have read it somewhere, or have had an experience that has taught us a lesson, needs to be constantly revisited and critically re-examined.[9]

## NEIGHBORHOOD PLANNING IN CHINA?

My second story reflects on why an idea such as neighborhood or community planning, which has been popular in North America since at least the 1960s if not earlier (see Vidyarthi's chapter in this volume for a particular version of this idea), fails to find a responsive audience in contemporary China. In the United States, neighborhood planning with the direct involvement of the local community can be traced back to Lyndon B. Johnson's "war on poverty," which, among other things, gave the impetus to the invention of community development corporations and other community-based organizations. The turbulent 1960s also gave rise to the idea of democratizing planning through the direct participation of those likely to be affected by proposed interventions.

Now more often referred to as community planning, it was reinforced in the United States by the rise of neoliberal policies during the 1970s, when the federal government devolved responsibility for welfare and pro-poor development to local areas. These changes in national policy in turn spurred the active participation of what we now refer to as civil society, that is, the self-organization of social groups for public causes.[10] This tradition of democratizing planning all the way down to the grassroots continued in the new millennium, as political philosophers turned their attention increasingly to what they called a deliberative politics. Although most of these discussions turned on the politics of the nation-state, a few, such as Archon Fung's, saw the future for a deliberative politics chiefly at the local level.[11]

With this as background, it is perhaps not surprising that I should wonder whether Chinese planners, given their country's accelerated march to become modern, might not be prepared to think about a form of local planning that would enable the hundreds of millions of people now living in cities to register their neighborhood concerns through a participatory process of self-study and priority setting. A word is perhaps in order here about Chinese city planning. Physical planning and design are taught at many universities throughout the country, typically in schools of architecture (see Abramson's chapter in the present book). Young planners are trained to draw up 20-year master plans for cities, which are then detailed at successively diminishing scales down to specific site plans. But Chinese cities are now not only expanding in population at exceptionally high rates, they are also being restructured as a result of rapidly rising incomes and auto-mobility. Commercial centers are soaring skyward at key intersections throughout the metropolitan area, and dozens of new towns are built seemingly overnight on the periphery, where city joins countryside in so-called peri-urban zones. Along the seaboard, cities such as Shanghai, Ningbo, Hangzhou, and Nanjing (to mention only the Yangzi delta urban cluster) report a population of multiple millions, without counting the extensive rural areas for which the central municipality is now administratively responsible. Given this massive scale of city building, it is not surprising that planners should focus primarily on mega-projects of elevated roadways, bridges, undergrounds, shopping malls, office towers, sports arenas, and the like, instead of, say, local neighborhood parks and playgrounds, which in the urgent rush to modernity are easily forgotten.

In the 1990s, the immense dislocation of people from their accustomed habitats became a major concern of the central government. Between 100 and 150 million young rural people from all over China were surging into coastal cities. Most of them found work but were denied the right to take up permanent residence in the city. At the same time, urban redevelopment was razing inner-city neighborhoods, whose inhabitants had to find alternative places to live in distant suburbs. The peri-urban fringe of the new metropolis was becoming a fragmented life space for people who had little to say to one another. Recently arrived migrant workers from beyond the region might constitute a majority of the population of a peri-urban village, speaking dialects that to indigenous ears sound unintelligible and rude. At the same time, the original villagers were now enjoying rental incomes from these same migrants, while middle-income urbanites were buying into nearby high-rise apartment buildings, and the wealthy were living in housing estates surrounded by walls spiked with broken glass and razor wire. For the authorities in Beijing, this new mobility bordered on chaos, and they began seriously to study ways that might restore a sense of order.

The Ministry of Civil Affairs (MCA) was charged with responsibility for resolving this problem. After a number of experiments in different parts of the country, what they came up with was an ingenious adaptation of an existing institution, the Residents' Committee (*jumin weiyuanhui*). Its existence was already enshrined in China's constitution as a people's organization, and thus as a realm of (theoretical) autonomy from the state. In imitation of village elections, Residents' Committees were supposed to be freely elected, but in practice were mostly headed by a member of the Communist Party. The neighborhood areas that these committees controlled were quite small, their responsibilities were limited, and their leadership was often short on education and commitment.

MCA's basic idea was to enlarge and strengthen these committees, together with the neighborhood area for which they were responsible, which would now encompass from 1,000 to 4,000 households; to create a central facility for each newly designated neighborhood area, called *shequ* (pronounced shĕ-chü); and to assign a small number of trained professional staff to each committee. These were referred to as social workers, and would be paid by the relevant Street Office – the lowest level of public administration in an urban administrative District. The new responsibilities of these enlarged *shequ* Residents' Committees were left somewhat vague and in practice they varied a great deal. They were supposed to deliver welfare checks to retired workers, provide care for the elderly and retraining for unemployed workers, develop youth programs, mediate local conflicts, and ensure public order. With the official blessing of the State Council, MCA initiated a massive community construction (*shequ jianshe*) effort throughout the country. Large coastal cities now have hundreds of these new neighborhood areas with their respective staff of social workers and Residents' Committees. The Communist Party has a leading presence in each, and all *shequ* are able to draw upon large numbers of volunteers to accomplish their work.[12]

In an attempt to answer my question about the feasibility of a neighborhood planning approach that might be articulated through these *shequ* Residents' Committees, I conducted a research project in Ningbo, a large industrial city located across Hangzhou Bay south of Shanghai.[13] What could neighborhood planning accomplish in this city? We came up with three sets of questions that a neighborhood planning process involving self-study might want to answer:

1 *Social inclusion*: What is needed to make significant progress towards equalizing access to the city across the new class divides? Are existing schools and health, transportation, and recreation services in the neighborhood sufficient to avoid a deepening of class divisions, with, on the one hand, an educated, well-fed, and well-housed middle class, and, on the other, a poorly educated, poorly fed, and poorly housed underclass of manual workers? Some steps are already being taken in Ningbo and in Zhejiang Province to relieve present housing shortages. But unresolved questions remain: How should the new housing be allocated, and does the example of Libang Village – an exemplary village for migrant workers – provide a viable model for this? Or should mixed housing projects be furthered? What are the possibilities of public/private partnerships in housing provision?

2 *Ecologically sustainable development*: How much is being done to create greater awareness among the local population of environmental issues as they affect life in the neighborhood? What practical issues arise from an environmental perspective at the neighborhood scale, such as pedestrian access (sidewalks), noise abatement, tree planting, solid waste recycling, low-energy lighting, mixed land use, or working with local businesses and work units to reduce or eliminate air and water pollution? What possibilities exist, working in collaboration with the Street Office, for inter-*shequ* collaboration in job creation, to place more jobs within walking or bicycling distance from homes? Should the use of the 10-minute service circle pioneered in Ningbo be encouraged as a means for creating more walkable neighborhoods in peri-urban *shequ,* in order to reduce the need for long-distance commuting?

3 *Livability or quality of life*: What can be done to create a neighborhood that is friendly and inviting to live in? Are there sufficient "places of encounter" such as parks, playgrounds, and sport facilities, where class barriers can be surmounted? Are there tea rooms or other places where retired people can spend time socializing? What can be done to promote street festivals? What possibilities exist for neighborhood beautification? Can schools provide space for public use when they are not in session? What can be

done to strengthen the collective memory of important neighborhood events and personalities? How can cultural activities be promoted, such as drama, storytelling, dancing, poetry contests, and musical performances? How can local creative talent be encouraged?

As our paper pointed out, a neighborhood planning process could lead, as the next step, to the identification of possible projects, together with a listing of priorities according to whether a project should be (1) urgently addressed, (2) implemented in the intermediate future, or (3) safely postponed for a later time. The list of priority projects could then be presented at the Street Office level (or above) for approval and implementation. To engage the neighborhood in such a process, however, would require outside help, and here we saw an opportunity for a new type of planner who does not yet exist in China, but whose mission as a professional would be to guide *shequ* neighborhoods towards a sustainable development.

This was the essential message. I presented it at a planning conference in the fall of 2008 in Xiamen and also a few days later at the China Academy for Urban Planning and Design in Beijing. But my audience showed only mild interest. This does not mean that the idea of neighborhood planning was dead on arrival, but it did force me to think about some of the difficulties that would have to be overcome before something like this idea could begin to take root. What are these obstacles?[14]

An obvious but nevertheless significant difficulty is that the conditions for a participatory approach to planning are not present in today's China, where hierarchy continues to be relied upon in decision-making. It is true that there have been occasional attempts to draw on academic and professional expertise from outside the government in making important decisions, but this is a far cry from what is at issue here, the participation of ordinary people in neighborhood development. Another way to put this is to say that China has yet to develop a culture of participation, and such a culture would presumably require an unfettered media and a permissive public sphere, where opinions could be freely expressed without fear of being publicly reprimanded or worse. Even in university classrooms, there is a good deal of self-censorship, and professors have on occasion been asked to explain themselves to agents of Public Security when a student would denounce them for harboring "dissident" views. It could, of course, be argued that allowing neighborhoods to have their say in drawing up the master plan of the city, or even to embark on projects of neighborhood improvement on their own or in collaboration with District government, would not run afoul of the principle of hierarchy, since District planners would retain the final say over what to permit or refuse. One could then imagine that experiments of this sort might be run here and there, and, if they were successful, perhaps the idea of participatory planning might spread. But, at present, there is no more than an outside chance of this, given that the central government sees no pressing reason why such experiments should be undertaken in the first place.

Another difficulty is that neighborhood planning in the sense used here is not a government priority at this time. In my Chilean story, I mentioned how expert advice was frequently taken when it accorded with broad policy directions but was dismissed when this was not the case. The same holds true for China. The formation of *shequ* Residents' Committees was taken seriously by the State Council when it feared chaos resulting from uncontrolled rapid urban change, and the revival of this old institution along the lines explained above is indeed progressing rapidly. But no one has seriously considered linking *shequ* neighborhoods into the formal planning process of the city. Physical planning stops at the District level. And in the District's perspective, to improve neighborhood facilities, a top-down approach using nationwide standards for community facilities could easily be accomplished in a matter of weeks, instead of the laborious process of involving a whole community in a neighborhood planning process that would eventually lead to the identification of priority projects from below.

As we envisaged it, neighborhood planning would require expert help from outside, and our proposal suggested creating a special training program for neighborhood planners at the university level. Some elite institutions already teach something like urban sociology, but these courses are not part of the required curriculum and generally do not involve hands-on experience in specific neighborhoods. To create a new curriculum in neighborhood planning would of course require additional resources that might or might not be found, but that would be forthcoming only if there were a significant demand for such a specialization within the standard planning curriculum. So long as demand cannot be demonstrated, it is unlikely that any university administration would fund a request for expanding the curriculum in this direction.

Finally, there is a question of which Ministry would have to promote the idea of neighborhood planning. My colleague and I had no choice in the matter, and presented our ideas to CAUPD, part of the Ministry of Housing and Urban and Rural Development. But the revival of the *shequ* Residents' Committees is the responsibility of the Ministry of Civil Affairs, just as "city planning" is seen in China today as intrinsically about city building, whereas "regional planning" (where it exists) is identified with geography as a discipline. It is therefore entirely possible that our paper will never be read beyond city planning circles, just as most planning professors rely chiefly on the specialized literature in their own field. Unless it is internalized within professional education, cross-disciplinary work is the exception even in North America.

I don't want to sound too pessimistic. But I believe that the odds are against neighborhood planning in China at this time. Change may come, but it may take years before the country is ready to consider an approach such as the one that we suggested.

## TRAVELING AND TAKING ROOT

This comment began with a question: Do planning ideas travel? There is obviously a range of possible responses, although the short answer is that some ideas travel whereas others do not. The Walking School Buses described by Whitzman and Perkovic were abandoned on arrival. Roy's microcredit finance mechanism for poor women, invented in Bangladesh, appealed to the World Bank, which stripped the financial mechanism from its Bangladeshi institutional and cultural context, and sent it around the globe as a "best practice," one planning idea among many in the continuing struggle against poverty. From Vidyarthi's account of how the American idea of the neighborhood unit was received in Nehru's India, we learn how it was re-imagined as a quasi-magical design that (some hoped) would turn devout, caste-conscious Hindus into secular neighbors living peacefully side by side in bungalow-style housing.

In the first of my own case studies, I question whether I had anything to transfer at all, even though our advisory team worked alongside Chilean counterparts for four years. On the other hand, I succeeded in learning a great many things that I subsequently could put to use in my own educational practice and would write about so that others might benefit from my experience. These tended to be intangible planning ideas, such as "social learning," or the fact that planning consultants need to be closely attuned to their clients if they expect their ideas to be taken seriously.

My second example is about a planning idea that will probably not travel successfully to China, because it is not tailored to current policy priorities. Chief among the reasons given above for this is the fact that China's planning culture, unlike America's, has no tradition of grassroots democracy, preferring the top-down model that has served it so well over thousands of years.[15] By the same reasoning, Americans would reject a hierarchical model of decision-making, should someone ever be foolish enough to seriously propose it, say, to the federal Department of Housing and Urban Development (HUD).

Is there a grand conclusion, then, that can be drawn from both my own experiences and the several essays in this volume that address the question of traveling planning ideas? Perhaps not. As a profession we are increasingly in touch with colleagues globally, and ideas do flow across borders. They flow, but do not necessarily take root. Most of us continue to work locally, within cultural frameworks that are given, and through institutional channels that remain largely invariant over long periods of time.

## EPILOGUE

As I was putting the finishing touches to this chapter, I read André Sorensen's account in Chapter 6 of "compact city" ideas and how they have fared in the Japanese policy environment. Sorensen is deeply informed about his subject, and his conclusions supplement my own, but in a much more nuanced way. "Compact cities" is a currently fashionable, although strenuously debated, idea in Western policy discourse. It was initially ignored by Tokyo bureaucrats, because, as they quite rightly observed, their own national capital was already in conformity with most of the criteria: a walkable city with the best public transit system in the world, extensive use of solar hot water panels, and so forth. What had not been high on their agenda, however, was the problem faced by small and medium cities in the rest of the country, which were struggling as declines in population, business activity, and municipal revenues started to present a serious policy challenge for municipal governments as well as for the Ministries in charge of planning policies. The new rhetoric of compact cities allowed municipalities to frame and legitimize policies that would strengthen and revitalize their flagging core areas, while restraining suburban and ex-urban growth.

Sorensen's conclusion is at least partially worth repeating here. Though phrased with respect to Japan, his words have a more general applicability.

> The Japanese case suggests that ideas can be important, but that they do not always have the impacts that their originators intended, and they are particularly unlikely to mean the same thing when they have been translated into a different cultural setting, political system, and policy context. The ways in which urban sustainability issues are perceived and the solutions that make sense in different contexts are strongly influenced by the available and effective policy levers, and by past patterns of institutional development. These factors create both capacities and preferences among relevant actors. As sustainable cities ideas are so varied, and possible policy approaches so diverse, it is not surprising to find that different actors will interpret the imperative to promote sustainability differently, and will adopt those aspects of the idea that best fit their own situation . . .
>
> Finally, it is significant that key elements of ideas can be lost in the process of translation. For example, during the processes of translating, disseminating, and adopting urban sustainability ideas into policy in Japan, the issues of intergenerational, transfrontier, and social equity that are such a central part of sustainability debates elsewhere have been almost entirely lost. The most influential

elements of the sustainable cities and compact cities ideas in the Japanese context have been those that promise to solve major Japanese spatial and economic problems, and that can be implemented within the frameworks of existing policy tools and programs (pp. 133, 135 above).

## NOTES

1   Among the contributions addressing the traveling of planning ideas are those by Bing Wang (planning Chinese cities "scientifically" during the Republican and early Maoist eras); Ananya Roy (who describes Bangladeshi microfinance programs traveling to the World Bank where, once stripped of their original context and meaning, they were re-circulated to poor countries around the world as "best practice," losing much in the process); Sanjeev Vidyarthi (whose account relates how the neighborhood unit, an early American planning idea inspired by a noble purpose, re-emerges in India after Independence, where it is re-imagined as an appropriate design for "producing" modern citizen-neighbors secular in orientation and freed of caste identities); Dominic Stead and his collaborators (relating how sustainable transport policies are exported to Central and Eastern Europe, where enthusiasm for cars after decades of communist austerity trumps earnest Western planners' advocacy of investments in public transit); and Carolyn Whitzman and Jana Perkovic [recounting how progressive planners' inventions of Women's Safety Audits (Toronto) and the "Walking School Bus" (Australia) meet with often unexpected receptions when inserted in local contexts around the world]. The chapters by Nihal Perera, on his experiences of settlement planning in Sri Lanka, and by Dan Abramson, on an early career involving doctoral study and urban design advice in China, come closest to my suggestions for an account of the actual process of learning through and from the transfer of experience from one country to another.

2   For the method of "thick description," see Yanow and Schwartz-Shea (2006).

3   Various authors use a number of different words to talk about traveling planning ideas, among them transfer, copy, emulate, and re-imagine. Resistance, or, more strongly, dismissal, is scarcely mentioned, although it is often encountered in practice (see, for example, Chapter 9).

4   I draw here on my detailed account of URDAPIC's activities, *Urban and Regional Development in Chile* (1969). A copy of this 251-page report can be accessed at the library of the University of California, Los Angeles.

5   A key program of the Frei government, a radical land reform, was all but aborted by a recalcitrant Congress, which limited its impact to only a small number of model reform settlements. The rural exodus to Santiago therefore continued and even accelerated during the Christian Democrat administration, despite its efforts.

6   See Friedmann (1973). Decades later, transactive planning based on dialogue would morph into the communicative planning paradigm formulated by John Forester (1989).

7   URDAPIC had an entirely male staff, hence the gendered pronoun.

8   President Allende died of a gunshot wound defending La Moneda, the Chilean Presidential Palace.

9   My book *Planning in the Public Domain: From Knowledge to Action* describes the social learning tradition of planning as one of four traditions that include, in addition, social reform, systems analysis, and social mobilization (Friedmann 1987).

10   See Douglass and Friedmann (1998).

11  See Fung (2004), and also Forester (1999). In a more recent contribution to the literature on the democratization of planning, deliberative politics, and communicative action, Xavier de Souza Briggs focuses on the ability of communities to give policy direction and to carry out specific projects, which he calls "civic capacity." See Briggs (2008).

12  For details, see Bray (2006) and Ren (2006). There are various models of *shequ* organization. Shanghai, for example, has opted for an administrative approach, in which Residents' Committees are somehow conflated with the Street Office level of administration.

13  See Friedmann and Fang (2009). A Chinese version is in press.

14  In Kolkata (Calcutta), neighborhood or ward planning is officially the lowest of three planning levels, and has been for some time. But according to a detailed study, in the highly politicized environment of the city, the absence of non-partisan civil society actors and the lack of political opposition to the ruling party have rendered ward-level planning moot. See Pal (2008).

15  The American "grassroots" tradition can be dated back to the draft US Constitution of 1776. China's planning culture is briefly discussed in Friedmann (2005). For a fuller account, see Abramson (2006).

## REFERENCES

Abramson, D. (2006) "Urban Planning in China: Continuity and Change," *Journal of the American Planning Association,* **72** (2), 197–215.

Bray, David (2006) "Building 'Community': New Strategies of Governance in Urban China," *Economy and Society,* **35** (4), 530–49.

Briggs, X. d. S. (2008) *Democracy as Problem-Solving,* MIT Press, Boston, MA.

Douglass, M. and Friedmann, J. (Eds.) (1998) *Cities for Citizens,* John Wiley, London.

Forester, J. (1989) *Planning in the Face of Power,* University of California Press, Berkeley.

Forester, J. (1999) *The Deliberative Practitioner: Encouraging Participatory Planning Processes,* MIT Press, London.

Friedman, T. L. (2007) *The World is Flat: A Brief History of the Twenty-First Century,* Picador, New York.

Friedmann, J. (1966) *Regional Development Policy: A Case Study of Venezuela,* MIT Press, Cambridge, MA.

Friedmann, J (1969) *Urban and Regional Development in Chile: A Case Study of Innovative Planning.* Available at the UCLA Library.

Friedmann, J. (1973) *Retracking America: A Theory of Transactive Planning,* Anchor Press, New York.

Friedmann, J. (1987) *Planning in the Public Domain: From Knowledge to Action,* Princeton University Press, Princeton, NJ.

Friedmann, J. (2005) "Globalization and the Emerging Culture of Planning," *Progress in Planning,* **64** (3), 183–234.

Friedmann, J. and Fang, C. (2009) "Toward Sustainable Neighborhoods: The Role of Social Planning in China – A Case Study of Ningbo, Zhejiang Province" [in Chinese]. *Urban Planning International* (Beijing), **24** (1), 16–24.

Fung, A. (2004) *Empowered Participation*, Princeton University Press, Princeton, NJ.

Pal, A. (2008) *Planning from the Bottom Up: Democratic Decentralisation in Action*, IOS Press under the imprint of Delft University, Delft.

Ren Y. (2006) "Globalization and Grassroots Practices: Community Development in

Contemporary Urban China," in Fulong Wu (Ed.), *Globalization and the Chinese City*, Routledge, London, pp. 292–309.

Yanow, D. and Schwartz-Shea, P. (Eds.) (2006) *Interpretation and Method: Empirical Research Methods and the Interpretive Turn,* M. E. Sharpe, New York.

CHAPTER 15

## SIMILARITY OR DIFFERENCES?
WHAT TO EMPHASIZE NOW FOR EFFECTIVE
PLANNING PRACTICE[1]

**BISHWAPRIYA SANYAL**

In the first decade of the twenty-first century, it is conventional wisdom that the
newly industrializing nations in the "global South" are very different from the post-
industrialized nations in the "global North" in terms of culture, economy, and
planning institutions. The dominant sentiment in the planning community is that
such differences should be acknowledged explicitly in any effort to international-
ize planning practice and education. This view, held by development scholars as
well as practitioners, does acknowledge the intensification of global linkages, as
is evident from a burgeoning literature on globalization, but prefers to focus on
the differences between nations and peoples in various stages of economic and
political modernization. In part, this is a reaction to the harm done by the rigid
models of development – both economic and political – imposed in the past on
newly modernizing nations by scholars and practitioners who did not appreciate
such differences. As Albert Hirschmann (1987) wrote, international development
experts treated these nations as if they were wooden toys that could be wound
up to go through the same motions of progress as modernized nations did in the
late eighteenth and early nineteenth centuries. But, if one accepts that neither
the developmental priorities nor the institutional settings – which include planning – could be the same in the two types of nations, then the implication is that
the appreciation of such differences is a prerequisite for a realistic, postcolonial
view of how the global South can chart its destiny independently, free of Northern
notions of development.

The argument for stressing differences over similarities is convincing at first
hearing. However, it calls for more scrutiny because it is being used to discourage
the cultivation of universalist moral sentiments that are necessary for effective
planning practice now. For example, Samuel Huntington (1997) has emphasized
inherent differences between civilizations to justify armed conflict. On the other
side of the ideological spectrum, Clifford Geertz (1983), Arturo Escobar (1992),
and others have also emphasized cultural differences among social formations
and warned against the perils of hegemonic forces of modernization. In between,
business advocates, such as Michael Porter (2000), have urged managers to

appreciate cultural differences among global trading partners to reduce the "transaction costs" of international operations and promote transnational expansion. Although these three sets of views vary widely in their ultimate concerns, they all focus on the differences between social settings, and thereby underestimate the pressing current need that motivated me in writing this paper, namely that, to address current planning problems in both the North and the South, planners need a new mindset – a new planning imagination – which looks beyond apparent differences between two social contexts and articulates overlapping concerns, similar aspirations, and conventional principles, such as social justice, to enhance the quality of life in both settings. Borrowing a term from Richard Shweder (2003), I am eager to see planners articulate the conceptual boundaries of "a global social commons." This is more necessary now than ever before; and I am concerned that the current emphasis on differences over similarities among the peoples of the world hinders the cultivation of such universalist planning sentiments.

The search for the global social commons goes back as far as the creation of the League of Nations after World War I (Glover 1999). Although this initial effort was not successful, a new wave of initiatives motivated by similar sentiments was introduced after World War II (Bauer *et al.* 1984). One that stands out is the United Nation's Universal Declaration of Human Rights in 1948 (Hunt 2007). This was followed by a string of other declarations by multilateral agencies, such as the International Labor Organization (ILO), all stressing shared ideas and values to guide post-war development in both industrialized and newly industrialized countries. The cold war, which started in the late 1940s, somewhat dampened this spirit of universalism, but modernization efforts by both camps emphasized inherent human similarities over differences.[2]

This manner of thinking was challenged in the early 1970s, as described above, and, even though the Brandt Commission made an effort in 1983 (Independent Commission on International Development Issues and Brandt 1983) to emphasize interconnections over differences among the peoples and nations of the world, the universalist approach that had led to the Declaration of Human Rights never regained its original importance. In the following decade, the collapse of the former Soviet Union created the illusion that capitalism and Western-style democracy had proven to be universal principles for organizing the political economies of both industrialized and still-industrializing nations (Fukuyama 1989), but the apparent triumph of capitalism did not last long, and the disillusionment that ensued created the moment for Huntington (1997) to propose an impending clash of civilizations.

Huntington is not alone, however, in emphasizing inherent differences among the peoples of the world. Development scholars with dramatically opposite ideologies from Huntington's have also emphasized differences over similarities, albeit for very different reasons. And there now exists a new group of scholars, such as Michael Porter (2000), who worry about the differences among the peoples of the world as impediments to the global integration of business activities. Hence, they argue that a new group of business managers who understand such differences is necessary for business to flourish in a global economy.

I review all three modes of thinking in the second part of the paper and scrutinize their validity and their implications for planning practice. In Huntington's view, there is no choice but war between contending civilizations. At the other extreme are post-developmentalists who are essentially multiculturalists and communitarian in orientation. They prefer differences, specificity, and relative autonomy from global interconnections. In between, the business approach calls for more business transactions between globally competing nations, but has nothing to say about human needs, rights, and responsibilities. Drawing on the review of these three modes of thinking that emphasize differences over similarities, I conclude that contemporary planning challenges in both the North and the South require a reversal of this emphasis. Instead of emphasizing differences among the peoples of the world, more attention must be given to human similarities of the kind that Hannah Arendt espoused in her book *The Human Condition* (1959). This sensibility is more necessary now than ever before, to make globalization work for the benefit of humankind (Stiglitz 2006).

## FROM SIMILARITIES TO DIFFERENCES

Soon after World War II, the decolonization of Asia and Africa and the creation of the United Nations changed the way that development planners thought about the peoples of the world. The language of colonialism, which had justified the dominance of one group of people over others, was replaced by a very different language that emphasized the equality of all human beings and the free exchange of ideas and trade among the sovereign nations of the world. The United States had played a key role in structuring this new language after World War II. As President Harry S. Truman described in his inaugural address in 1949 (Truman 1967), the world was no longer to be governed by exploitative relationships between colonial and colonized nations. Instead, the free exchange of goods among independent nations would be the norm, and new relationships would be protected and supervised by a new set of international institutions, such as the International Monetary Fund (IMF), which would prevent developed nations from sliding back to the protectionist trade policies of the past (ibid.).

The creation of the United Nations in 1945 was a bold statement of the equality of the peoples of the world, even though the United Nations Security Council's structure gave some nations – the victors of World War II – more influence in critical international affairs. The language of the documents proclaiming the creation of the United Nations and other international organizations, such as the ILO, is striking in its portrayal of people as equal and similar in terms of their potentials and aspirations (Jolly *et al.* 2005). Although not all colonies had become independent by the end of the 1940s, the tone of discussion regarding colonialism had changed drastically, delegitimizing previously held notions that some peoples of the world were inferior to others and were not able to self-govern. One factor that led to the erosion of the idea of the moral authority of "civilized nations" was the conduct of some developed nations during the war. In particular, the slaughter of the Jewish people in Germany, which until then had boasted of being the center of a great civilization, was a major factor in reshaping global conversations about racial differences and human rights (Nussbaum 1997).

The Holocaust became a symbol of what should not be experienced by any human being anywhere in the world. The United Nations' Universal Declaration of Human Rights emerged from the collective acknowledgement that all individuals, irrespective of their economic and political status, have certain inalienable rights. Led by Eleanor Roosevelt, this declaration of equality among peoples received support from across the world. One notable exception was the objection of the Association of American Anthropologists (AAA) on the grounds that such "universal principles" were at odds with the varying cultural practices of indigenous people around the world. The AAA argued that the preservation of cultural diversity was more important than the proclamation of universal principles, even though one could say that the protection of such diversity might itself be viewed as a sort of universal principle (Glover 1999).

The newly independent nations – now called "developing nations" – would mature, it was thought, the same way as the developed nations had in the nineteenth and early twentieth centuries, through industrialization, urbanization, and agricultural modernization, which would require an expansion of market relationships and the transformation of subsistence farmers and peasants into a competitive urban labor force (Lewis 1955). Their political systems would undergo major transformations as well: from traditional kinship-based systems of governance by tribal leaders in villages, to large-scale, nationally based and electorally managed governments. New political systems would comprise competing political parties that would represent the interests of newly emerging groups tied together not by old tribal alliances, but by shared interests based on their new stakes in the evolving capitalist economy (Huntington 1968). In other words, capitalism and Western-style democracy were expected to evolve together, each reinforcing the other, as in the already developed nations. Notable aberrations from this model – such as

Germany and Spain in the 1930s – were disregarded as anomalies, exceptions to universally applicable golden rules (Packenham 1973).

The cold war, whose beginning some historians trace back to Winston Churchill's famous "Iron Curtain" speech, was both a source of inspiration and a challenge to the universal principles of human rights, capitalism, and democracy. Even though communism was portrayed as the opposite of capitalism and democracy, the arguments of the time never portrayed the people living in countries dominated by the two systems as being inherently different. Ideological differences were explained by differences in political and economic systems. In fact, both sides argued that human beings are similar. The West argued that all people love freedom, whereas the Communists stressed that all people naturally long for human solidarity and equality. Each group blamed the other's political system for not meeting the needs of the people, and assumed that eventually its own system would be proven right. To put it another way, each side framed its identity vis-à-vis an enemy who was blocking the way to the universalization of its cherished principles regarding human behavior (Nye 2002).

Despite the sharply different ideological views, the two camps were in agreement that accelerated industrialization was the only way to modernize the economies of the newly decolonized nations. The only dissent in this celebration of industrialization and modernization was that of Gandhi and a few anarchists (Toye 1987). On the whole, both the West and the Communists strongly believed that the low standard of living in developing countries could be improved only by increasing their productivity. This required industrialization, accompanied by changes in physical and social infrastructure to facilitate the transformation from isolated, self-contained communities of subsistence farmers toward the emergence of interconnected cities that would house industrial workers (Todaro 1981).

By the 1970s, however, the scenario had changed significantly and there was a total reversal in how planning scholars and practitioners viewed the processes and challenges of development (Sanyal 1994). Two factors contributed to this reversal. First, a worldwide economic downturn had slowed the growth rates of most developing nations, including those, such as Brazil, that had performed reasonably well during the previous two decades. The sharp economic decline had created large-scale unemployment and underemployment, and it forced governments to reduce various subsidies they had been offering to urban working-class families. Yet migration from the countryside to the cities continued, and, together with the natural growth of the urban population, this influx of impoverished rural peasants created increasing gaps between the demands for employment and shelter and the ability of cities to provide them. As a result, by the 1970s, most cities in developing nations were marked by growing slums and squatter areas, informal, illegal, and low-productivity economic activities, and inadequate, badly maintained physical infrastructure, all of which raised questions about the efficacy of the development model. Dudley Seers's famous article (1969) captured the sentiment of the time quite well. Seers was among a growing number of development scholars who had begun to argue that the developmental model needed complete rethinking because the economies of developed and developing nations were diametrically opposite in nature, and that a model based on the experience of developed countries was totally inappropriate for the transformation of developing countries facing very different constraints from those that developed nations had had to deal with at comparable stages of industrialization (Singer 1981).

A second factor that contributed to the sentiment that developing nations were very different from the developed nations is the fact that by the mid-1970s many developing nations had changed from democracies into authoritarian regimes (O'Donnell 1973). In Latin America, for example, only three nations still had democratically elected governments by 1975. In Asia and Africa there was a similar trend from democracies to dictatorships. This disillusioned both development scholars and practitioners who had earlier assumed that there was a direct relationship between economic and political systems, that capitalism and democracy went hand in hand, and that a nation could not have a market economy without a multiparty democracy, and vice versa. By the mid-1970s it had become apparent that relationships between economic and political systems were more complex, with multiple possible permutations and combinations. What is more, tribalism of the old kind had not transformed into enlightened nationalism despite many efforts at nation-building. On the contrary, elections, which are a central mechanism of democracy, encouraged tribalism as the political candidates appealed to such affinities of the voters (Eisenstadt and Roniger 1984).

These two trends, economic and political, created the conditions for a serious questioning of the old paradigm of development and democracy. Such questioning emerged from many quarters but was most vividly articulated by several development anthropologists who had returned to their own countries after living in developing countries for as long as 10 or 15 years. These anthropologists argued that people in developing countries were very different from people in developed countries, and that foreign aid policies guided by the hegemonic Western developmental paradigm had failed to change the cultural, social, economic, and political practices of the people on the ground because such policies were alien to them (Robertson 1984).

The term "Third World" was coined around this time as part of a model to describe the differences among nations: the First World of developed and democratic nations who constituted the core of the global capitalist system; the Second World of Communist and somewhat undeveloped nations who traded mostly among themselves; and the Third World of poor, underdeveloped nations with autocratic regimes that governed by force a growing number of unruly, uneducated, undisciplined people who were very different from the wealthy democratic citizens of the First World. Not even the Marxists spoke of the similarities among the peoples of the world by the mid-1970s. Although the Marxists had predicted that there would be a global uprising against capitalism as it suffocated from its own contradictions, the urban poor of the Third World were different from "the proletariat" they had expected to emerge (Santos 1979). None of the Western theories of development fitted the reality on the ground in the so-called Third World. That is why the dominant sentiment changed from "we are the same" to "we are different" in a matter of 30 years after World War II (Packenham 1973).

## THE IDEOLOGIES OF DIFFERENCE

It would be inaccurate to argue that no one had emphasized differences among the peoples of the world before the 1970s when the conceptual link between capitalism and democracy was broken. Starting with Max Weber's classic book, *The Protestant Ethic and the Spirit of Capitalism* (1904–5), there had been a strand of argument that certain cultures are more likely to prosper because they value qualities such as hard work, thrift, investment, and innovation, which are essential for wealth accumulation. Conversely, some cultures cling to old values and primordial ties that hinder change and are not conducive to rapid economic development (Pye and Verba 1965). This argument had lost its persuasive power by the early 1970s, however, as economic growth had declined in previously prosperous nations, while other nations that had lagged behind generated significant economic growth despite the general downturn in the global economy. The steady growth of Japan, South Korea, Taiwan, and Hong Kong in the 1960s raised questions regarding the validity of arguments that had earlier portrayed these nations as lacking the entrepreneurial spirit necessary for modern capitalism to flourish. As the global economic problems deepened, the United States unilaterally disbanded the old system based on the gold reserve in 1971 (Helleiner 1980). Cultural explanations of prosperity were replaced by various political–economic explanations, led by the neo-Marxists on the left and the neo-classical economists on the right.[3] This ideological divide lost its potency as Soviet communism collapsed, inspiring Francis Fukuyama to declare that capitalism and democracy had triumphed and would spread to every corner of the world (Fukuyama 1989).

The apparent triumph of capitalism did not lead to a convergence of ideologies, however. The ideological harmony Fukuyama had anticipated never materialized. On the contrary, ethnic violence erupted across the world, following the creation of multiple new states based on ethnicity. And the old struggles in the Middle East intensified as the United States defended Kuwait against Iraq and faced hostile regimes in Iran and Afghanistan (Nye 2002). This was the setting in which Samuel Huntington revived the "cultural argument" in a new form in his now famous book, *The Clash of Civilizations* (1997). Huntington argued that the notions of progress, rationality, democracy, and capitalism, which emerged out of the Enlightenment in the West, are distinctively different from the notions underlying other civilizations. He proposed that, despite the end of the cold war, the world would not experience "perpetual peace" as envisioned by Immanuel Kant (1795). In contrast, the Western nations would be confronted by other civilizations – in particular Islamic and Chinese – whose cultural values, social priorities, and political institutions were diametrically opposed to those of the West. The attack on the United States on 11 September 2001 provided buoyancy to Huntington's argument, and soon many others joined his camp by proposing that Islamic people in particular were fundamentally different from people of other faiths (Lewis 2003).

As the post-9/11 events unfolded and the United States engaged in wars in Afghanistan and Iraq, the discussion of similarities versus differences took yet another turn. The American political commentator Robert Kagan published a book, *Of Paradise and Power: America and Europe in the New World Order* (2003), arguing that many European nations – particularly France – did not support the war in Iraq because Europeans, except for the British, were fundamentally different from North Americans in that they believed in Kant's notion of perpetual peace, whereas the Americans and British believed in Hobbes' approach to political conflict.[4] In other words, those who did not volunteer to join the "coalition of the willing" were portrayed as not sharing the values underlying the American notion of freedom.

Meanwhile, Samuel Huntington published a new book criticizing the American immigration policy that allowed the proportion of Latinos in the country to increase sharply (2004). Huntington argued that Latinos are fundamentally different from Anglo-Saxons or Jewish Americans, and that, by letting them in, the United States was diluting its original Judeo-Christian identity. This argument about how identities are threatened is, of course, not new. It had emerged in England in the 1960s (Gilroy 2005), and more recently it has influenced civil discourse even in Amsterdam, a city known for social diversity and peaceful coexistence. Thanks to the ideology of difference that is pervasive in discussions of development, this attack on immigrants as contaminating the pure identity of the "original population" has now become a common agenda item – along with criticisms of income-tax rates and "bloated bureaucracies" – on right-wing political platforms in both rich and poor nations.[5] This is why it is so important to critically assess the rationale underlying Huntington's position. Let me quote Huntington to elaborate his position:

> In the post-Cold War world, the most important distinctions among people are not ideological, political or economic. They are cultural. People and nations are attempting to answer the most basic question humans can face: Who are we? And they are answering that question in the traditional way humans have answered it, by reference to things that mean the most to them. People define themselves in terms of ancestry, religion, language, history, values, customs and institutions. They identify with cultural groups: tribes, ethnic groups, religious communities, nations, and, at the broadest level, civilizations. People use politics not just to advance their interest but also to define their identity. We know who we are only when we know who we are not and often only when we know who we are against.
>
> (1997: 21)

Huntington's emphasis on cultural differences was built on a key assumption that Western culture is the product of the Enlightenment, which emerged from the convergence of a set of factors: scientific thinking in contrast to superstitions; analytical thinking in contrast to emotional outbursts; the separation of governance from the practice of personal faith; preference of reason over belief; and so on. Huntington argued that the elements which led to the Enlightenment are all Western in origin and are somewhat alien to non-Western cultures, which oppose the intrusion of such Western values propagated by Western media and Western nations.

When one looks below the surface, however, many elements associated with the Enlightenment were practiced by non-Western societies long before the eighteenth-century Enlightenment. Amartya Sen's research (2000) on Islamic rulers in India in the fifteenth and sixteenth centuries is particularly useful in this regard. As Sen documents well, some Islamic rulers, such as the emperor Akbar, governed by relying on qualities that Huntington had attributed to the Enlightenment. The tolerance of multiple religions – in fact, the celebration of multiple religious faiths – is exemplified by inscriptions regarding Jesus at the entrance to famous Mughal buildings![6] Sen also documents that some Mughal emperors encouraged open deliberations regarding many aspects of social life. Such deliberations in their daily court drew on a long tradition of analytical thinking and reasoning, which had led to the discovery of many scientific principles before the Western Enlightenment (Teresi 2002). For example, Sen reminds us that the principles of algebra, a core idea in scientific analysis, were first formulated in what is now Iraq. Similarly, the concept of "zero" was formulated in India, which has a long tradition of mathematical and statistical analysis. None of these inventions reduce the importance and contribution of the Enlightenment. They simply demonstrate that ideas and innovations traveled across political boundaries long before what we now call "globalization." That is why, instead of boasting about the virtues of

Western civilization, and declaring wars to protect it from "the others," it may be more fruitful to better understand the multiple and growing connections among the cultures of the world.

This is not to say that all forms of past and present connections are to be cherished without critical assessment of their impact on the quality of ordinary people's lives. It is only to say that what on the surface appear to be very different civilizations may prove, after careful historical analysis, to have old connections through trade, travel, or the professional exchange of ideas and experiences. This has been acknowledged by the relatively recent effort to document what is called "global history," which promises to cultivate a new sensibility appropriate for planning practice in a world deeply influenced by increasing interconnections among people whose destinies are more intertwined than ever before (Mazlish 2006).

## THE IDENTITY TRAP

One objective of global history is to transcend old-style historiography confined to the current territorial boundaries of nation-states. Its other objective is to transcend historical analyses of the kind that emerged in the early 1970s, under such titles as "women's history," "queer history," or "labor history." Although the proponents of global history explicitly acknowledge the historical oppression of minorities and relatively powerless groups, they argue that stories of such injustices cannot be portrayed accurately by confining scholarly work to one particular group of people whose lives must have been intertwined with many other actors and social institutions (Finley 1975).

The proponents of multicultural history, who are usually left-leaning ideologically, reject this notion of one history, arguing that there are multiple ways of understanding the world, and that differences in interpretations of historical events result from the diverse experiences of historical actors whose social and political powers varied widely (Sandercock 1998). Some have pushed this line of argument to the extreme by proposing that there is no truth to be revealed by any one set of neutral historical evidence. Instead, there should be multiple interpretations of "reality," each valid in its own way (Kelly 1984). The multicultural historians demand that histories of individual groups, recorded preferably by their own members, be respected equally, and valorized as historical documents that portray more accurately the suffering and oppression of the specific groups concerned. Despite such conceptual differences between the proponents of global history and those of multicultural history, they both agree that the nation-state cannot be the central point of reference of historical analysis. Whereas the world-history proponents urge an expansion of scale in understanding social change, the multiculturalists prefer to focus at the local level, where the everyday experiences of the oppressed are most tangible, vivid, and personally meaningful (Edwards 2004).

This preference to emphasize the local over either the national or global context was interjected in developmental thinking at around the same time as it was beginning to influence the discussion of urban policies in post-industrialized nations – particularly in the US and the UK. The argument for localism in developmental planning was articulated most persuasively by Clifford Geertz and a group of scholars who called themselves "post-developmentalists" (Sachs 1992). Implicit in their title was a critique of the old developmental paradigm, which they argued had failed because of a top-down approach to developmental efforts that homogenized local variations in culture, economy, and even politics in the name of nation-building, economic efficiency, and Western-style political order. The impact of top-down developmental efforts had been counter-productive, these critics argued. Instead of enhancing their quality of life, such efforts had stifled the creative energy of social groups at the bottom, and further strengthened the oppressive institutions at the top of the social hierarchy.

Many of the post-developmentalists were anthropologists with considerable research experience in developing countries. By the 1970s they had become disillusioned by both economic and political events, and they blamed past developmental efforts for virtually every adverse outcome (Robertson 1984). For example, some argued that the developmental efforts were a form of neo-colonialism in that they were not intended to create broad-based economic development, whereas the national governments could continue these developmental programs only by relying on authoritarian regimes (Thomas 1984). Others argued that the developmental approach imposed a set of Western ideas and aspirations on people whose preferences were never taken into account when the policies and programs were designed (Peattie 1981). Still others argued that the real goal of developmentalism was to change local cultures to fit the needs of Western markets (Esteva 1992). These arguments rested on the assumption that the local cultures had been self-reliant, self-governing, and relatively egalitarian before modernization efforts, and that the indigenous institutions that had held the local culture together were being destroyed by expanding markets with an a-religious morality imposed from the top.

Underlying all such criticism of development practices was a deep concern that the authentic identity of indigenous peoples was under attack from a homogenizing, Western-influenced, and ultimately profit-driven approach (Eisenstadt 1966). Large projects that required relocation of people were heavily criticized as destroying both the livelihoods and collective identities of local communities. Arguments based on the importance of cultural identity over all other priorities were used in discussions of both industrializing and industrialized nations. As research on multiculturalism evolved in the US and the UK, its central concern about disrespect of alternative identities – particularly those of minority groups – also influenced developmental discourse. More intriguingly, some elite groups in developing nations joined the chorus that their national identities were being threatened by the spread of Western ideas of economic and political modernization (Berger and Huntington 2002). By this time the term "globalization" had been popularized in both developed and developing nations, generating a growing body of articles and books that warned against its evil effects on tranquil, harmonious, and civil communities that were being decimated by externally induced economic changes and alien social practices. Some argued that globalization had created a crisis of identities, disrupting traditional and indigenous social relationships, undermining solidarities that had ensured social reciprocity in the past (Roy and Srivastava 1986).

The book that first counteracted the populist celebration of communities, at both local and national levels, was Benedict Anderson's *Imagined Communities* (1983). Along with Anderson, Eric Hobsbawm (see, for example, 1997) had long expressed serious reservations about this new trend in historical analysis that emphasized identity issues over political–economic explanations; but Anderson's critique was more pointed. He demonstrated that nation-states, which are proclaimed to be "natural communities," had been socially crafted for political and economic purposes. Anderson coined the term "imagined communities" to challenge the claim that nations evolve organically, naturally, without state or market interventions. He demonstrated that popular conceptual boundaries by which communities are demarcated as homogeneous entities are historically incorrect. By drawing attention to this myth about the homogeneity of communities, Anderson was not undermining the values commonly associated with communities; he was merely highlighting historical processes of change, flux, intermixing, and "contamination" – to borrow a term from Appiah (2006) – which are usually not discussed by communitarians, who instead emphasize the innate qualities of communities that are impervious to external influences.

Much has been written already regarding the notion of identity and its use and misuse for framing planning problems, so I will not reiterate those arguments (Finley 1975). For our purpose, what is important to highlight is how the notion of identity emphasizes inherent differences over similarities and interconnections. Appiah's research (2005) is particularly relevant with regards to this point. By drawing on the experience of the Ashanti community in Ghana, he demonstrates convincingly that, because of external influences in the form of technological and other changes, the identity of the Ashanti people is evolving continuously. More importantly, Appiah and also Sen (2006) document how one individual may ascribe to multiple identities. An individual can be from a certain tribe but also identify with a community of musicians, for example, or other groups who share skills that he or she may have or aspire to have. Individuals' identities may also evolve as a result of travel or migration, as they internalize values or social practices very different from the ones they were born into. Such a mix of values and practices may make them more resilient than someone who remains cloistered within his/her primordial community. If one considers Anderson's argument that what is considered to be a primordial community itself is to be questioned on empirical grounds, one begins to appreciate that change and intermixing are prevalent, and multiplicity of identities is more real and perhaps more meaningful than single identities based on kinship groups or nationalities.

Amin Maalouf's (2000) research on the dangers of mono-identities is useful in this regard. As he documents well, individuals with single identities are more vulnerable to mental stress when subjected to change, and they are more likely to turn violent when their singular identity is threatened, because they rely on only one identity to construct meaning for their lives. In other words, if we are to consider Appiah and Maalouf's argument seriously, we would conclude that not only are singular identities rare in a rapidly changing and integrating world, but also adherence to mono-identities may deter the peaceful coexistence of a diverse population.

Let me focus this argument on the particular case of planners. As I mentioned earlier, starting in the 1970s, it became customary to accentuate the differences in planning cultures among different nations, or even among various localities within nations. The appreciation of differences and specificities rested on the assumption that external influences in general had a homogenizing effect because they disregarded local practices, thereby also disregarding local culture and customs, and hence lacked a fine-grained understanding of people and places. We tested this assumption in a book project that drew on case studies of planning cultures in 12 different nations, developing as well as developed (Sanyal 2005). Our study indicated that, when subjected to historical analysis, all planning cultures reveal themselves to be in constant flux, sometimes resisting but at other times facilitating social change in response to both internal and external pressures. The study concluded that, if planning cultures are viewed in this dynamic way, in contrast to traditional notions of culture that are used to evoke a sense of immutability and inheritance, it becomes possible to go beyond "cultural essentialism," which is not only exclusionary and parochial, but also an inaccurate representation of history.

In arriving at this conclusion, our study drew on the wisdom of Richard Shweder, a cultural anthropologist, whose research I referred to earlier in this paper. The following quote from Richard Shweder summarizes the status of contemporary knowledge regarding the relevance of culture and identity in shaping social practices:

Cultural elements are too hard to define, too easily copied and too long detached from their points of original creation [for it to be possible to delimit their boundaries]. Contacts between cultures and processes such as borrowing, appropriation, migration and diffusion have been ubiquitous for so long that little remains of the authentically indigenous.

(2003: 13)

Shweder and Appiah do not mourn the loss of "the authentic." On the contrary, they applaud the intermixing of cultures even if they do not endorse all outcomes. And by valorizing intermixing over accentuating innate differences, these authors open up a range of human possibilities for transfer of knowledge, questioning of conventional norms, and transfer of planning practices. This, in turn, renews the appreciation of what sociologists commonly refer to as the power of agency over structure,[7] and thereby opens up unlimited possibilities for planning in a globally interconnected world.

## THE MIDDLE GROUND OF GLOBAL BUSINESS

In contrast to the views from the right and the left of the ideological spectrum, both of which emphasize differences among people, there is now a growing voice – particularly within Western academic institutions – that all students must have an understanding of cultures beyond their national boundaries (Widdig 2003). The argument for international exposure of students can be summarized as follows. The globalization of trade, finance, culture, and flows of people has created an interconnected world. Because of this, to perform well in this world as a professional, one needs to transcend parochialism and cultural isolationism and understand how other cultures function (Olson *et al.* 2005). This argument does not have the moral undertone of the Peace Corps program started by President John F. Kennedy in the United States. It does not advocate in the old way that Western planners travel to poor nations to help them. Rather, it is directed by self-interest in the sense that it calls for knowledge of others so one can do good business in an interconnected world. Michael Porter (2000) was one of the original spokespersons of this utilitarian point of view, which now is so widespread that it has become part of the mission statement of most universities (Biddle 2002). The argument, if any, is no longer about the validity of this approach, but how to implement it at least cost and within a system that does not create either legal or financial problems for universities.

This view of the world, which acknowledges differences among national cultures and advocates that such differences be appreciated, does not have much to say about similarities, however. The focus is on the global economy and how it is creating incredible opportunities for businesses with global reach. The primary concern is that, if cultural differences in the way business is conducted are not understood, the costs of business transactions will increase, thereby reducing profitability. To give Michael Porter his due credit, this line of thinking does not glorify cultural essentialism of the kind communitarians propagate. In fact, it accepts that cross-national business ventures may ultimately create cultural convergences – and it encourages such convergences, again, to reduce transaction costs.

Should the construction of what Shweder (2003) calls the global social commons rest on the logic of international business practices? True, business practices in general have played a positive role in connecting people by the exchange process, and will continue to seek new territories in the unending search for higher profits, as Marx rightly predicted. But will this process inevitably lead to a better world – a world of free exchange of planning ideas, as the editors of this volume hope? It may be useful to learn from history once again as we seek to answer this question. For one, the record of the impact of transnational business has not been uniformly positive, contrary to the prevailing messages propagated by business schools (Burbules and Torres 2000). In the past, many wars were fought precisely because of clashing business interests. Colonialism was, after all, a type of business venture with the "noble goal" of civilizing the natives (Mamdani 1996). In other words, business cannot be relied upon as a mechanism for the social construction of common concerns, because it is ultimately based on business interests, and not on universalistic moral principles – such as human rights (Stoer and Cortesão 2000). This is not to say that the business practices between trading partners cannot have huge beneficial social effects. As is well documented, both international trade and external investments in productive activities can serve as mechanisms for technology transfer and can lead to change in regulations, which is a central focus of planning activities (Amsden 2001). But all business transactions are ultimately dictated by profitability – and this central driving force may not always match well with other social concerns of interest to planners who are trying to improve the quality of life in cities, regions, and nations.

The search for profitability can also create conflicts, in both growing and sluggish markets. This is acknowledged by business proponents, and, as a result, some of the best business schools in the United States and elsewhere now offer courses on negotiating strategies to avoid conflicts (Khurana 2007). Such courses usually recommend that students understand the business rituals and related social practices of "the others" to create a sense of trust. But, in practicing the art of business negotiations, one learns to understand "the other" mainly as a prospective business client, and that is often where the cultivation of similarities ends. Usually, the parties try to familiarize themselves with one another's social customs, especially regarding food, formal greetings, and so on, but the business deal remains, of course, their main focus. Learning to negotiate and avoid dis-agreements are important business skills, but such skills are not sufficient for addressing global planning challenges, some of which have resulted from global business ventures (World Social Forum 2004).

The problem with the Porter-inspired approach to international understanding is that it views the world only as one integrated marketplace. In this view, the industrializing and industrialized nations are engaged in similar activities related to production, consumption, investment, and export. What binds the peoples of the world together is global competition for investment, export, and growth. But, as the growing literature on anti-globalization and counter-globalization reminds us, the cities, regions, and nations around the world do not want to be considered as market players only (International Forum on Globalization 2004). Many issues that the Porter model does not take into account, such as increasing inequality, environmental degradation, or ill effects of trade, require a somewhat different understanding of the world from that of the global business model.

The Seattle riots in 1999 during a meeting of the World Trade Organization were the first sign that the conventional understanding of the world as composed of trading partners was limited (Stiglitz 2006). Since then, as the global financial crisis expanded and deepened, reducing the global economic growth rate to below zero, the power of the Porter model as an organizing principle for global understanding has dwindled. One could, of course, argue that Porter's ideas are more relevant now than ever before; that this is precisely the time to educate a new and large cadre of business managers who can help reinvigorate the global economy. But there are many other tasks that must be addressed before the global economy flourishes again: new rules and regulations have to be formulated to discourage financial speculation; growing income inequalities between social classes and regions have to be reduced; trade relationships have to be equalized; and new global institutions have to be created for rescuing poor nations caught in poverty traps. The list goes on and on. What is important for our purpose is to ask what kind of an understanding of the world will be conducive to finding alternative solutions. Will it be the Huntingtonian fear of clashing civilizations, or the multiculturalist demands for identity politics, or Porter's business ideas of optimizing the competitive advantages of cities, regions, and nations? All three approaches emphasize differences over similarities among the peoples of the world, and fall short of what is needed to address the current crises of economy, ecology and ideas: a new sense of human solidarity, empathy for "the other," and political cooperation among the peoples of the world.

## CONCLUSION

I began this paper by describing how development planning had changed its emphasis from similarities to differences between developed and developing nations. I then critiqued three positions on differences, arguing that none of the three points of view is adequate for addressing the planning challenges of our times. These critiques led me to conclude that it may be worthwhile to return to understanding similarities among the peoples of the world, not in the way that development economists had conceptualized the world immediately after World War II, but instead by focusing on human solidarity, empathy, and the possibilities for progressive social change, induced not only from within specific social formations, but also from outside (Singer 2002).

What would be the key features of the new planning imagination and how would it come about, one may ask. To provide an adequate answer to these legitimate questions will require at least another full-length paper, if not a book. Hence, the best I can do in these brief concluding comments is to provide only a few remarks as to why it may be worthwhile now to emphasize similarities over differences between the peoples of the world.

As planners we need to acknowledge that we live in one world, not three or four, and that our lives across this fragile globe are more interconnected than ever before. There are huge overlaps in the concerns, aspirations, and expectations of people around the world, and it is important to appreciate such overlaps without ignoring the specificities of each setting. An image comes to my mind as I think about the fragile globe. It is the earliest image of the globe from space that was transmitted around the world in the news media. That was the moment when people around the world saw, for the first time, that we live in one world, and a new sensibility emerged that it is now time for us to cultivate more fully.

Global interconnections – in particular, the flow of ideas – are not a new phenomenon. If one traces the origins of ideas in mathematics, sciences, arts, and literature, one would be surprised to find multiple flows originating in many places and traveling in many directions. Thus, modernization is not a purely Western idea that the rest of the world should resist in the name of multiculturalism, to preserve the cultural identities of non-Western societies. On the contrary, what is necessary is that we address the challenges of globally linked problems by identifying the common ground – a global social commons – which would emphasize commonality over differences, and valorize linkages and "contamination" over purity of cultures. Most importantly, this would redefine a central notion in planning: that of public interest, whereby the "public" is not confined to those belonging to one community, city, region, or even nation. This is not a call to ignore the specificity of places, but a call to understand how the specifics are shaped by global trends, and why global concerns can ultimately benefit local communities.

And, finally, the purpose of refocusing on similarities over differences is not to strengthen the current structure of ideological domination of the West – just the opposite. In the same way as colonialism was rejected by emphasizing that people everywhere are equally capable of charting their own destinies, we need to reject both Orientalism, which Edward Said (1978) warned against, *and* Occidentalism, which is the reverse way of stereotyping Western people as "others" (Buruma and Margalit 2004). But this cannot be achieved by labeling every person on the globe as a consumer in the world's marketplace. The vocabulary of the market is not appropriate to meet the conceptual challenges we face in finding a way out of the "common crisis" created, in part, by the market. Sooner or later, we as planners have to grapple with an old ideal in planning – namely, social justice – but we will grapple with it at a very different time from when John Rawls examined the concept (1971). In Rawls's analysis, "the original condition" referred to a population within any one national territory, but now the notion has to be expanded to cover the world; and, to do so, we need to go beyond apparent differences among the peoples of the world and search for their similarities as human beings.

## NOTES

1  I am grateful for the research assistance provided by Ninad Pandit, one of my best Masters students, who is now heading for Princeton University to study History.

2  In the Western nations, the idea of human freedom and choice was central to capitalism and democracy; the communist block argued that economically and socially oppressed peoples of the world would eventually unite to end capitalist exploitation.

3  On the ideological right, see Bhagwati (1982). On the ideology of the left, see Cockcroft *et al.* (1972).

4  Kagan argues that, although the Europeans favor a Kantian approach of pacification, North Americans tend to align themselves with a Hobbesian position of *realpolitik*, willing to use force against their adversaries if necessary (2003).

5  For example, in India there is a growing opposition to immigration from Bangladesh, which used to be part of India before 1947!

6  See the inaugural address made by Professor Akbar S. Ahmed at the Mahatma Gandhi Memorial Center in Washington DC: "The Mughal emperor Akbar, who inspired my father to name me after him, provides us [with an example which] would certainly challenge those today who think of Islam as fanatical and extremist. If you go to Fatehpur Sikri, and I recommend you doing it when you are next in India, enter the grand Baland Darwaza and on the right hand side you will see a quotation. There is a line which reads: 'This world is a bridge, build not your house upon it but pass lightly over it – thus sayeth our Lord Jesus, peace be upon Him'" (Ahmed 2004, unpaginated).

7  On the agency versus structure argument, see Alford and Friedland (1985).

# REFERENCES

Ahmed, A. (2004). "The Search for a Muslim Ideal in South Asia: The Path to Inclusion. Inaugural Address at the Mahatma Gandhi Memorial Center, Washington, DC." Available: http://www.pakistanlink.com/Letters/2004/Jan04/16/02.html. Accessed 9 July 2009.

Alford, R. R. and R. Friedland (1985). *Powers of Theory: Capitalism, the State, and Democracy*. Cambridge, Cambridge University Press.

Amsden, A. H. (2001). *The Rise of "the Rest": Challenges to the West from Late-Industrializing Economies*. Oxford, Oxford University Press.

Anderson, B. R. (1983). *Imagined Communities: Reflections on the Origin and Spread of Nationalism*. London, Verso.

Appiah, A. (2005). *The Ethics of Identity*. Princeton, NJ, Princeton University Press.

Appiah, A. (2006). "The Case for Contamination." *The New York Times*, 1 January, 1–11.

Arendt, H. (1959). *The Human Condition*. Garden City, NY, Doubleday.

Bauer, P. T., G. M. Meier, *et al.* (1984). *Pioneers in Development*. New York, Published for the World Bank, Oxford University Press.

Berger, P. L. and S. P. Huntington (2002). *Many Globalizations: Cultural Diversity in the Contemporary World*. Oxford, Oxford University Press.

Bhagwati, J. N. (1982). "Directly Unproductive Profit-Seeking (DUP) Activities." *Journal of Political Economy* **90**, 988–1002.

Biddle, S. (2002). "Internationalization: Rhetoric or Reality?" American Council of Learned Societies, Occasional Paper No. 56. New York, American Council of Learned Societies.

Burbules, N. C. and C. A. Torres (Eds.) (2000). *Globalization and Education: Critical Perspectives*. New York, Routledge.

Buruma, I. and A. Margalit (2004). *Occidentalism: The West in the Eyes of its Enemies*. New York, Penguin Press.

Cockcroft, J. D., A. G. Frank, *et al.* (1972). *Dependence and Underdevelopment: Latin America's Political Economy*. Garden City, NY, Anchor Books.

Edwards, M. (2004). *Civil Society*. Cambridge, Polity Press.

Eisenstadt, S. N. (1966). *Modernization: Protest and Change*. Englewood Cliffs, NJ, Prentice-Hall.

Eisenstadt, S. N. and L. Roniger (1984). *Patrons, Clients, and Friends: Interpersonal Relations and the Structure of Trust in Society*. Cambridge, Cambridge University Press.

Escobar, A. (1992). "Planning," in W. Sachs (Ed.) *The Development Dictionary: A Guide to Knowledge as Power*. London, Zed Books. pp. 132–45.

Esteva, G. (1992). "Development," in W. Sachs (Ed.) *The Development Dictionary: A Guide to Knowledge as Power*. London, Zed Books. pp. 6–25.

Finley, M. I. (1975). *The Use and Abuse of History*. London, Chatto and Windus.

Fukuyama, F. (1989). "The End of History?" *The National Interest* **16**, 3–18.

Geertz, C. (1983). *Local Knowledge: Further Essays in Interpretive Anthropology*. New York, Basic Books.

Gilroy, P. (2005). *Postcolonial Melancholia*. New York, Columbia University Press.

Glover, J. (1999). *Humanity: A Moral History of the Twentieth Century*. London, Jonathan Cape.

Helleiner, G. K. (1980). *International Economic Disorder: Essays in North–South Relations*. London, Macmillan.

Hirschmann, A. O. (1987). "The Political Economy of Latin American Development: Seven Exercises in Retrospective." *Latin American Research Review* **21** (3), 7–36.

Hobsbawm, E. J. (1997). *On History*. London, Weidenfeld & Nicolson.

Hunt, L. A. (2007). *Inventing Human Rights: A History*. New York, W. W. Norton & Co.

Huntington, S. P. (1968). *Political Order in Changing Societies*. New Haven, CT, Yale University Press.

Huntington, S. P. (1997). *The Clash of Civilizations and the Remaking of World Order*. New York, Touchstone.

Huntington, S. P. (2004). *Who are We? The Challenges to America's National Identity*. New York, Simon & Schuster.

Independent Commission on International Development Issues and W. Brandt (1983). *Common Crisis North–South: Cooperation for World Recovery*. Cambridge, MA, MIT Press.

International Forum on Globalization (2004). "A Better World is Possible (Report Summary)," in F. Lechner and J. Boli (Eds.) *The Globalization Reader*. Malden, MA, Blackwell Publishers. pp. 438–48.

Jolly, R., L. Emmerij, *et al.* (2005). *The Power of UN Ideas: Lessons from the First 60 Years*. New York, United Nations Intellectual History Project.

Kagan, R. (2003). *Of Paradise and Power: America and Europe in the New World Order*. New York, Alfred A. Knopf.

Kant, I. (1795). *Zum ewigen Frieden: Ein philosophischer Entwurf*, trans. Ted Humphrey (1983) in *Perpetual Peace, and Other Essays on Politics, History, and Morals*. Indianapolis, Hackett Publishing Co. pp. 107–39.

Kelly, J. (1984). *Women, History, and Theory: The Essays of Joan Kelly*. Chicago, University of Chicago Press.

Khurana, R. (2007). *From Higher Aims to Hired Hands: The Social Transformation of American Business Schools and the Unfulfilled Promise of Management as a Profession*. Princeton, NJ, Princeton University Press.

Lewis, B. (2003). *What went Wrong? The Clash between Islam and Modernity in the Middle East*. New York, Perennial.

Lewis, W. A. (1955). "Economic Development with Unlimited Supplies of Labour," in A. N. Agarwala and S. P. Singh (Eds.) *The Economics of Underdevelopment*. London, Oxford University Press. p. 510.

Maalouf, A. (2000). *In the Name of Identity: Violence and the Need to Belong*. New York, Penguin Books.

Mamdani, M. (1996). *Citizen and Subject: Contemporary Africa and the Legacy of Late Colonialism*. Princeton, NJ, Princeton University Press.

Mazlish, B. (2006). *The New Global History*. New York, Routledge.

Nussbaum, M. C. (1997). *Cultivating Humanity: A Classical Defense of Reform in Liberal Education*. Cambridge, MA, Harvard University Press.

Nye, J. S. (2002). *The Paradox of American Power: Why the World's Only Superpower Can't Go it Alone*. Oxford, Oxford University Press.

O'Donnell, G. A. (1973). *Modernization and Bureaucratic-Authoritarianism: Studies in South American Politics*. Berkeley, Institute of International Studies, University of California.

Olson, C. L., M. F. Green, *et al.* (2005). *Building a Strategic Framework for Comprehensive Internationalization*. Washington DC, American Council on Education.

Packenham, R. A. (1973). *Liberal America and the Third World: Political Development Ideas in Foreign Aid and Social Science*. Princeton, NJ, Princeton University Press.

Peattie, L. R. (1981). *Thinking about Development*. New York, Plenum Press.

Porter, M. (2000). "Attitudes, Values and Beliefs, and Microeconomics of Poverty," in L. E. Harrison and S. P. Huntington (Eds.) *Culture Matters: How Values Shape Human Progress*. New York, Basic Books. pp. 14–28.

Pye, L. W. and S. Verba (1965). *Political Culture and Political Development*. Princeton, NJ, Princeton University Press.

Rawls, J. (1971). *A Theory of Justice*. Cambridge, MA, Belknap Press of Harvard University Press.

Robertson, A. F. (1984). *People and the State: An Anthropology of Planned Development*. Cambridge, Cambridge University Press.

Roy, R. and R. K. Srivastava (1986). *Dialogues on Development: The Individual, Society and Political Order*. New Delhi, Sage Publications.

Sachs, W. (Ed.) (1992). *The Development Dictionary: A Guide to Knowledge as Power*. London, Zed Books.

Said, E. W. (1978). *Orientalism*. New York, Pantheon Books.

Sandercock, L. (1998). *Making the Invisible Visible: A Multicultural Planning History*. Berkeley, University of California Press.

Santos, M. (1979). *The Shared Space: Two Circuits of the Urban Economy in Underdeveloped Countries*. London, Methuen.

Sanyal, B. (1994). *Cooperative Autonomy: The Dialectic of State–NGOs Relationship In Developing Countries*. Geneva, International Institute for Labour Studies.

Sanyal, B. (2005). *Comparative Planning Cultures*. New York, Routledge.

Seers, D. (1969). "The Meaning of Development." *International Development Review* **11** (4), 2–6.

Sen, A. K. (2000). "East and West: The Reach of Reason." *New York Review of Books* **47** (12).

Sen, A. K. (2006). *Identity and Violence: The Illusion of Destiny*. London, Allen Lane.

Shweder, R. A. (2003). "'Who Owns Native Culture?': The Gatekeepers." *The New York Times*, 14 September, 13.

Singer, H. W. (1981). "Thirty Years of Changing Thought on Development Problems," in R. P. Misra and M. Honjo (Eds.) *Changing Perception of Development Problems*. Singapore, Maruzen Asia for United Nations Centre for Regional Development, Nagoya, Japan. pp. 69–76.

Singer, P. (2002). *One World: The Ethics of Globalization*. New Haven, CT, Yale University Press.

Stiglitz, J. E. (2006). *Making Globalization Work*. New York, W. W. Norton & Co.

Stoer, S. R. and L. Cortesão (2000). "Multiculturalism and Education Policy in a Global Context," in N. C. Burbules and C. A. Torres (Eds.) *Globalization and Education: Critical Perspectives*. New York, Routledge. pp. 253–74.

Teresi, D. (2002). *Lost Discoveries: The Ancient Roots of Modern Science – From the Babylonians to the Maya*. New York, Simon & Schuster.

Thomas, C. Y. (1984). *The Rise of the Authoritarian State in Peripheral Societies*. New York, Monthly Review Press.

Todaro, M. P. (1981). "Development Planning: Theory and Practice," in *Economic Development in the Third World*. London, Longman. pp. 429–66.

Toye, J. F. J. (1987). *Dilemmas of Development: Reflections on the Counter-revolution in Development Theory and Policy*. Oxford, Blackwell.

Truman, H. S. (1967). "Inaugural Address, January 20, 1949," in *Documents on American Foreign Relations*. Princeton, NJ, Princeton University Press.

Weber, M. (1904–5) *Die protestantische Ethik und der Geist des Kapitalismus*, trans. Talcott Parsons (1930) *The Protestant Ethic and the Spirit of Capitalism*. London: Allen & Unwin.

Widdig, B. (2003). "Intellectual Education at MIT." *MIT Faculty Newsletter* **15**, 14–15. Cambridge, MA, Massachusetts Institute of Technology.

World Social Forum (2004). "Porto Alegre Call for Mobilization," in F. Lechner and J. Boli (Eds.) *The Globalization Reader*. Malden, MA, Blackwell Publishers. pp. 435–7.

# INDEX

AAA (Association of American Anthropologists) 332
Aalbers, M.B. 257
Aaron, H.J. 239
Abed, F. and Matin, I. 36
Abed, Fazle 36, 38
Abercrombie, Sir Patrick 53, 61
Abolina, K. and Zilans, A. 185
Abrahamsen, Rita 191, 192, 193, 194, 196, 211, 215
Abramson, D. et al. 303
Abramson, Daniel B. 3, 5, 9, 12, 13, 17, 18, 289–310, 290, 294, 297, 302, 303, 304, 305, 319, 326n1, 327n15, xi
Abu-Dayyeh, N. 59, 61
academics, contribution of 7, 12–13, 16, 17–18, 19, 21n8, 97, 118, 314
Academy for Urban Planning and Design (CAUPD), Beijing 314, 322
Active and Safe Routes to School (ASRTS) 231
Adams, Frederick 56–7
Addams, Jane 74
Adler, M. 247
Afghanistan 41
Africa 14; American planning involvement in 57; authoritarianism in 334; East Africa, Italian empire in 50; 'Primitive Africa,' invention of 191–2; see also Zambia
agency: dynamics of local agency 13; factors, effect on implementation of women's safety audits 221; individual agency, adaptation of planning ideas and 6, 233; knowledge and indigenous agency 48–9; opposition between structural and agency perspectives 20, 221–2, 342, 347n7; planning ideas and work of 16–17, 145; settlement and lack of 146
Agnew, J. 243, 252, 256, 259
Agnew, J. and Bolling, K. 251, 252
Ahmed, Akbar S. 337, 346n6
aid agencies 4, 5, 7, 11, 12, 16, 144–5, 146
Aldhous, W. et al. 91n5
Aldrich, D.P. 128
Alessandri, Arturo 314

Alexander, I. 285n1
Alford, R.R. and Friedland, R. 346n7
Allen, C. et al. 237
Allende, Salvador 318, 326n8
Almandoz, A. 55
Alterman, R. 21n10
Åman, A. 58
American Institute for Indian Studies (AIIS) 90n1
Amsden, A.H. 343
Amunugama, Sarath 155
Anderson, Benedict 107, 340
Andrew, Caroline 224
Aoki, Y. 122–3
Appadurai, Arjun 143, 146, 148
Appiah, A. 340, 341
Arendt, Hannah 331
Argyris, C. and Schon, D. 18
Armstrong, A.M. 54, 61
Ashcroft, B. et al. 143
Ashworth, W. 273
Asia 14, 15–16; American planning involvement in 57; Asian Urban Research Network (AURN) 303–4, 305; authoritarianism in 334; Civil Lines in 82–3; see also Mahaweli Development Project; sustainable urbanisation in Asia
Association for Social Advancement (ASA) 36
Aureli, E. and Baldazzi, B. 251, 253
Australia: Australian Centre for the Governance and Management of Urban Transportation (GAMUT): women's safety audits, walking school buses and 219–20, 234n1; Canberra 267; Creative City concept in Darwin 222; Victorian Community Council Against Violence (VCCAV) 224, 226; Victorian Health Promotion Foundation (VicHealth) 229, 231–2; Walking School Bus concept 229–30, 231–2
authoritarianism 48, 148; effect on planning practices 334, 339
Ave, G. 257, 258

Baer, W.C. 241, 247
Baer, W.C. and Koo, C. 241

Baer, W.C. and Williamson, C. 238, 240, 241
Bagnasco, C. 242
Bahrain 57
Bakunin, Mikhail 222
Balducci, Alessandro 22n14
Banerjee, T. 5, 6, 56, 57, 63
Banerjee, T. and Baer, W.C. 74, 78
Bangladesh 12, 324; alternative consensus
    in, effects of 39; *Challenging the Frontiers
    of Poverty Reduction/Targeting the Ultra
    Poor* (BRAC) 37; civil society organisations
    in 36–7; counter-hegemonic consensus
    in 37, 39–40; Grameen Bank 29, 30, 36,
    37, 39, 40, 42n2; institutions and systems
    in 37–8; knowledge, politics of 38–9;
    political and social empowerment 37–8;
    poverty alleviation, consensus on 37; Rural
    Advancement Committee (BRAC) 36, 37–9;
    sustainability, idea of 38
Barrett, B. and Usui, M. 118
Bates, L.K. 240
Bauer, Catherine 76
Bauer, P.T. *et al.* 330
Bawa, Geoffrey 159
Beasley, Larry 22n14
Behrens, Roger 232, 234n1
Beinart, Julian 298, 309n5
Bellicini, L. and Toso, F. 243
Bennett, C.J. 188n3, 188n4
Berger, P.L. and Huntington, S.P. 340
Bergeron, S. 40
Berglund, E. 223, 224, 226
Berry, B.J.L. 239
Berry, W. 156
best practice guidance 6, 22n29, 30, 35, 37, 38,
    41, 42, 179, 324, 326n1
Bhagwati, J.N. 346n3
Bianca, S. *et al.* 62
Biddle, S. 342
Bier, T. 239
Bijlani, H.U. 91n8
Birch, E.L. and Silver, C. 2
Birch, Eugenie 149
Blair, Tony 34
Blakely, E.J. 267, 285n2
Blau, E. and Platzer, M. 53
Blyth, M. 119
Boddy, M. and Gray, F. 239
Bond, E. and Coulson, E. 240
Booth, P. 21n10
Bourne, L.S. 127
Braid, R. 240
Brandt Commission (1983) 330
Braun, D. and Gilardi, F. 237
Bray, David 291, 327n12
Brazil 55; Brasilia 267
Breen, A. and Rigby, D. 237
Breheny, M. 127
Brennan, E.M. 275
Briggs, X. da S. 12, 326n11

Bromley, R. 60
Bruntland Report (1987) 123, 126
Bruton, M.J. 62
Buchanan, Colin 62
Build Sri Lanka.com 61
Burbules, N.C. and Torres, C.A. 343
Burdette, M.M. 216n4
bureaucracy 9, 30, 34, 121, 145, 146, 150–51,
    182; bid rigging and corruption in 124;
    of building inspections 100; bureaucratic
    formalisation of WSBs 230–31; bureaucratic
    sub-cultures 317; risk management and
    bureaucratic hurdles 227–8; standards of,
    conflict with Sustainable Design 222
Burgess, E.W. 251
Burgess, R. 127
Burnham, Daniel 50, 103, 307
Buruma, I. and Margalit, A. 346
Bush, George W. 31
business: interests of, social commons and clash
    with 343–4; land scarcity and costs of 279;
    middle ground of global business 342–4;
    MITI in Japan and responsiveness to 131–2;
    suburban locations for, traffic patterns and
    178–9
Butcher, K. 21n2

Calder, K.E. 122
Callon, M. 8, 21n13
Calthorpe, P. 127
Cammack, P. 30
Campbell, J.L. 119, 120
Canada 128; Canadian National Crime
    Prevention Council (NCPC) 224;
    International Centre for the Prevention of
    Crime, Montreal 224; Maduru Oya Dam
    construction, Sri Lanka 145; METRAC
    (metro Toronto Women's Action Committee
    on Public Violence Against Women and
    Children) 219, 223–4, 225, 226; Montreal
    Women and the City Committee 224–5;
    New Urbanism in 148–9; Ottawa Women's
    Action Centre Against Violence (WACAV)
    224; Toronto Transit Commission (TTC) 223,
    225
Cannari, L. *et al.* 257
Canuto, Marisa 234n1
Cavanagh, S. 224
Çelik, Z. 49
Central and Eastern Europe (CEE) 10;
    Budapest 176; change in, rapidity of
    186; German-style transport authorities
    (*Verkehrsverbünde*), establishment of 173,
    181; Prague 176, 181; Soviet planning in
    58, 59; urban transport, West–East policy
    transfer 174, 175–9; Warsaw 176, 178–9;
    *see also* Latvia; Poland
centralised planning: master plans as product
    of 283; socialist planning principles and
    107–10

Cervero, R. 127
Chakraberty, Dipesh 80, 90–91n4
Chatterjee, Partha 80, 81, 148–9
Chenery, H. *et al.* 42n1
Cherry, G.E. 52
Chicago, Burnham plan of 75
children, independent mobility of 228
Chile 324; *equipamiento comunitario*
    (community facilities) 314, 316; Ford
    Foundation in 313, 314, 315–17;
    Interdisciplinary Center for Urban
    Development (CIDU) 315; mutual
    learning 316–17; National Planning Office
    (ODEPLAN) 315, 318; political direction
    and priorities 317–18; political dynamics,
    dangers of 318; transforming aid program in
    314–18; Urban and Regional Development
    Advisory Program in Chile (URDAPIC) 315,
    316, 317, 326n4
China 2, 5, 9, 10, 11, 15–16, 67, 125, 324;
    Academy for Urban Planning and Design
    (CAUPD), Beijing 314, 322; centralised
    planning system and socialist planning
    principles 107–10; cities in transition
    95–114; commercial centres, growth of 319;
    Confucian education in 101–2; Construction
    Bank 109–10; cultural assimilation, premises
    of 96–7; decentralisation in 283; Desheng
    Men Awi ('Outside-the-Desheng-Gate')
    295; diffusion of spatial planning 96–7;
    dislocation of people, major concern 319–
    20; ecologically sustainable development
    321; feasibility of neighborhood planning
    approach 321–2; First Five-Year Plan 108;
    formal representation in spatial planning
    102–7; German planning at Qingdao
    49; Greater Shanghai Plan (1930) 103,
    104, 105; Guangzhou 98, 283, 284;
    ideological link with Soviet Union 108–9;
    industrialisation 283; industrialisation, Soviet
    experience of 109; institutional fragmentation
    112; institutional infrastructure, creation of
    97–102; land resources, unlocking during
    transition in 281–2; Lilong housing 98–9,
    114n2; livability 321–2; market orientation
    in 281–2, 294; Master Plan for Shanghai
    (1953) 109; Ministry of Civil Affairs (MCA)
    320; modernisation in, accelerated march
    towards 319; Nanking, Treaty of (1842)
    98; Nanking (Nanjin) 102–3, 105, 106,
    113; National Government Enabling
    Act for Municipal Planning and Zoning
    105; Nationalist Central Committee 103;
    nationalisation strategies, implementation of
    109–10; neighborhood planning in 318–24;
    participatory planning 322–3; physical
    improvement opportunities in 1990s 292–3,
    293–57; political chaos 112; political
    rehabilitation in 294; pragmatism of recent
    reforms 113; prioritisation of neighborhood

planning 323; Qing dynasty 112–13; quality
    of life 321–2; real estate development 283;
    Residents' Committees 320–21, 323;
    Shanghai 97, 98–9, 100–105, 107, 109, 111,
    113, 114n2, 283; Shanghai, world's largest
    construction site 282; Shanghai Urban
    Planning Exhibition Hall 284; Shenyang 284;
    Sino-Japan War 105, 107; social inclusion
    321; social infrastructure, creation of 97–
    102; socialist planning principles, centralised
    planning system and 107–10; Soviet
    planning influence in 58; spatial planning
    95–114; spatial planning, diffusion of
    96–7; spatial planning, formal representation
    in 102–7; spatial planning, practice of
    borrowing in 110–13; spatial planning,
    redistribution of urban growth and 110;
    standardisation and hierarchical organisation
    of neighborhoods 108–9; state-led strategic
    development plans 283–4, 292–3; State
    Planning Commission 108; Strategic
    Development Plan (SDP) 283–4; Taiping
    Rebellion 98; Tianjin 98; urbanisation,
    modernisation and 95–114; urbanisation,
    rapid growth of 283; urbanisation, Soviet
    experience of 109; *see also* Shanghai
Chipungu, Samuel 191
Chowdhury, Shafiq 36
Chowdhury, Zafrullah 36
Christaller, Walter 22n17
Christchurch City Council 230
Churchill, Henry 79, 88
CIAM (Congrès Internationale pour Architecture
    et Urbanisme) 2, 21n7
Ciborowski, Adolf 53, 59
City Form, Beibart's Theory of 298; *see also*
    urbanisation
*City Planning Review,* and *Annals* (City Planning
    Association of Japan) 128–9
Clarke, George 207
*The Clash of Civilizations* (Huntington, S.) 336
Clinard, M. and Chatterjee, B. 91n8
Clinton, Bill 30, 34–5
CNU (Congress for the New Urbanism) 91n8
Cochrane, A. 267
Cockroft, J.D. *et al.* 346n3
Cody, J.W. 56, 57, 105
cold war, effect on planning practices 333
collaboration 159, 209, 290, 294, 299, 304,
    313, 321, 322; with faculty and students
    from abroad 300, 303; Perry with like-
    minded individuals 75–6
Colombia 55
colonialism: Dutch colonial planning in Indonesia
    52; independence from, maturation in 332–
    3; independence from, maturation in planning
    practice and 332–3; moral principles and
    343; replacement of language of 331–2; *see
    also* postcolonial transnational planning
Columbian Exposition (1893) 75

commercial centres: growth in China of 319;
   policies in support of 131
communities: Ashanti community in Ghana 340–
   41; client-communities, lack of sensitivity
   in China to 298; community participation in
   neighborhood planning, promotion of 303–4;
   *equipamiento comunitario* (community
   facilities) in Chile 314, 316; existing
   communities, preference for preservation
   of 295–6; Greenbrook planned community
   in US 88; identity and framing of planning
   problems 340–41
communities of practice 5, 7, 11, 21n6
compact cities 126–35, 325–6
Comprehansive Assessment System for Building
   Environmental Efficiency (CASBEE) 124,
   135n3
Confucian education in China 101–2
consensus: counter-hegemonic consensus in
   Bangladesh 37, 39–40; planning action and
   269; Washington consensus 12, 33, 35–6,
   37, 38, 40
conservation policies 254; institutional biases,
   international diffusion and 258–9
Constantinos and Emma Doxiadis Foundation 60
Construction Bank of China 109–10
Consultative Group to Assist the Poor (CGAP)
   30–32, 33, 35, 37, 38–9, 40
Cooke, B. and Kothari, U. 6, 22n28
Cooke, P. 269
Cooley, Charles 75
Le Corbusier 53, 56, 63
Côte d'Ivoire 207
Coulson, N.E. and McMillen, D.P. 240
Crewe, E. and Harrison, E. 194
Crime Prevention Through Environmental Design
   (CPTED) 223
Crooks, Joe 53
CSD (Committee for Spatial Development) 3,
   266
Cuba 55
cultures: bureaucratic sub-cultures 317; cultural
   assimilation in China, premises of 96–7;
   cultural diversity and differences 16–18, 187,
   332, 336–7; cultural essentialism, parochial
   nature of 341; disciplinary cultures 9; identity
   and, social practice and 341–2; intermixing
   of, potential for 342; multiculturalism 331,
   338–9, 340, 344, 345; planning cultures,
   constant flux in 341; planning cultures,
   negotiation of 293–300
Cyprus, British planning influence in 61
Czech Republic 177

Daniels, P.W. 285n1
Daniels, T. 22n16
Das, Bhagwan 90n2
Davidoff, P. 269
Davie, M. 49
Davies, H.W.E. *et al.* 21n10

Davies, Richard Llewelyn 62
Davis, K. and Golden, H. 270
de Jong, M. 188n3
de Jong, M. *et al.* 175, 188n3
de Monchaux, John 299, 309n4
de Ventós, M.R. 55
decentralisation 243, 283, 285n1; regional
   decentralisation of national offices 316
decolonisation 331, 333; *see also* colonialism;
   postcolonial transnational planning
Denison, E. and Ren, G.Y. 98
Denmark 163
Desheng Men Awi ('Outside-the-Desheng-
   Gate') 295
design: Ecologically Sustainable Design for
   Hulme, Manchester 222; elevation within
   planning profession 290; MIT-Tsinghua
   Urban Design Studios 289, 293–300;
   problems in, differences between MIT and
   Tsinghua approaches to 296–7; Urban
   Design 293, 297–8; urban design ideas,
   inspiration from 266; *see also* urban design
DET (Department of Education and Training,
   NSW, Australia) 229, 231
development: 'absolute principle' of government
   policy 291; democracy and, challenges
   to old paradigm of 333–5; developmental
   control, correlation of informal development
   with non-observance of 275–6; informal
   development, correlation with non-
   observance of developmental control
   275–6; making planning developmental for
   sustainable urbanisation in Asia 265–85;
   minority needs, influence on developmental
   discourse 340; models for, dangers of
   rigidities in 329; of new towns 283–4; of old
   towns 279–82
Development Planning Unit, UCL 65
developmental planning: practices in, criticisms
   of 339–40; sustainable urbanisation in Asia
   278–84
Dewey, John 22n33, 74
Dierwechter, Y. 132
difference: emphasis over similarities 329–31;
   ethnic violence, difference and 335–6;
   ideologies of 335–8; institutional differences
   in planning practices 16–18
DisAbled Women's Network 225
Dix, G. 61
Dogan, M. and Pelassy, D. 237
Dolowitz, D. 188n3
Dolowitz, D. and Marsh, D. 173–4, 188n3,
   188n4, 237
Dong, G. 292
Dong Dayou 103–4
Donne, M.D. 247
Douglass, M. and Friedman, J. 326n10
Dowall, D.E. and Leaf, M. 276
Downs, A. 132
Doxiadis, Constantinos 60–61

Drew, Jane 56
Droege, Peter 299
DT (Department for Transport, UK) 230, 231
DTEI (Department for Transport, Energy and
    Infrastructure, South Australia) 229
Dudley, G. and Richardson, J. 188n5
Dunnill, Frank 146–7, 156, 160
Dutt, Ashok K. 89

Easterly, William 34
ECMT (European Conference of Ministers of
    Transport) 184
Ecochard, Michel 51, 62
ecological sustainability 222, 232, 321; see
    also sustainability; sustainable urbanisation
    in Asia
economic competitiveness 3
Edwards, M. 338
Egypt 52; French planning influence in 62; urban
    development in 275
Eisenstadt, S.N. 117, 339
Eisenstadt, S.N. and Roniger, L. 334
elites 1, 113, 144, 313, 340; city-centre living,
    value placed on by 242, 245; colonial
    elites 50, 151; elite institutions 323; Indian
    indigenous elites 80, 82, 87, 88–9, 90;
    intellectual elites 74, 112; interests of 6,
    37–8, 85; local elites 11, 99; nationalism of
    84, 105; neighbourhood units, attraction for
    9; power of 13; professional elites 64, 102
Elkin, T. et al. 127
Emmett, R.C. 56, 57
endogenous development: exogenous and
    endogenous forces, interplay between 13,
    16; policy transfer, endogenously driven 174
Engwicht, David 228, 229, 231, 232, 234n1
Enlightenment, transnational contributions 336,
    337–8
environmental conditions 3, 126, 303;
    environmental crisis of 1960s, effects of
    124–5; safety audits and improvements in
    built environment, role in 225–6; walking
    school buses and improvements in built
    environment 229–30
Ernst & Young 201, 204
Erthiopian Telecommunications Corporation 61
Escobar, Arturo 143, 147, 148, 155, 156, 193,
    330
Esteva, G. 339
ethical issues see moral; moral compass
Ethiopia 59, 68n3; British planning influence
    in 61
Euronatur 182
European Commission 127, 178
European Union (EU) 3, 11–12, 133; Forum
    for Urban Safety 224, 225, 227, 232–3;
    Guidance on Local Safety Audits: A
    Compendium of International Practice
    (Forum for Urban Safety) 227; transnational
    aid network 160, 165

Evans, M. 188n3
Evans, M. and Davies, J. 188n3
Evenson, N. 51, 56
Ewing, R. 127
exogenous planning ideas: external imposition,
    imperial experience of 48, 49–50; planning
    practices and 9–10
Eyestone, R. 221

Fabrizio, B. and Poggio, T. 255, 257
Fainstein, S. 3
Faludi, A. 21n5, 269
Faludi, A. and Waterhout, B. 3
Fan, C.C. 291
Feldhoff, T. 123
Fengqi, Professor Sun 303
Ferchiou, R. 241
Ferguson, F. 206
Fine, B. 33
Fine, B. et al. 31
Finley, M.I. 338, 340
Finnemore, M. 28
Firman, T. 278
Firman, T. and Dharmapatni, I.A.I. 273
Fisher, E.M. and Winnick, L. 239
Flyvbjerg, Bent 147
Forbes 'Top Microfinance Institutions' 32
Ford Foundation 54, 57, 60, 310n11, 313, 314,
    315
Forester, John 17, 22n30, 326n6, 326n11
The Fortune at the Bottom of the Pyramid
    (Prahalad, C.K.) 34
Foucault, Michel 41, 114n5
France 125; empire of 49; planning influence
    of 62
Frei, Eduardo 314, 316
Frenchman, Dennis 299, 309n4
Fried, R.C. 243
Friedman, Tom 314
Friedmann, J. and Fang, C. 327n13
Friedmann, J. and Weaver, C. 266
Friedmann, John 3, 9, 13, 17, 18, 265, 306,
    313–27, xi
Fry, Maxwell 56
Fujita, K. and Hill, R.C. 125
Fukuda, Yasuo 117, 129
Fukuyama, Francis 330, 335
Fuller, M. 50
Fung, Archon 319, 326n11

Galster, G. 240
Galster, G. and Rothenberg, J. 240
Ganapati, Sukumar 3, 8, 237–60, xi–xii
Gandhi, Mohandas K. 63, 333
Gann, L.H. 216n4
Gans, Herbert 78
Garces, Wilson 53
Gardner, T. 206
gated housing estates 277–8
Geddes, Patrick 22n18, 64, 222, 307

Geertz, Clifford 330, 339
Gelfand, M. 216n4
gentrification 240, 258
geo-politics 6, 314
Germany 8, 52, 125, 332, 333; empire of
    49; Federal Environment Agency - UBA
    (Umweltbundesamt) 179–80, 181, 182,
    184, 186; German planning at Qingdao,
    China 49; Institute for Transport Ecology
    184; Randenigala and Rantabbe Dam
    construction, Sri Lanka 145; Soviet
    planning in East Germany 58; Technische
    Hochschule, Berlin 83; Weimar Republic 83
Ghana 54; Ashanti community in 340–41;
    Doxiadis Foundation in 60; Ghana
    Construction Company 59
Ghani, A. 276
Ghorayeb, M. 62
Gibb, K. 240
Giddens, Anthony 216n2
Giebels, L.J. 61
Gillespie, J. 274
Gillette Jr., Howard 74, 75, 78, 79
Gilroy, P. 336
Glaeser, E.L. and Gyourko, J. 240
Glenn, H.P. 18
globalisation 28, 29, 30, 35, 38, 40, 113, 128,
    220, 237, 307–8, 331, 337–8, 340, 342;
    alternative solutions for global economy 344;
    global interconnectedness 20–21, 329–30,
    345–6; global planning expertise, China's
    demands on 306; global social commons
    343; ideas, global flow of 345–6; planning
    practices, development of global community
    in 19–21
Glover, J. 330, 332
Glover, William 90n1
Goh, Beng-Lan 148
Gondhalekar, Daphne 309n4
Goonatilaka, Susantha 155
Goonewardena, K. 35
Gordon, P. and Richardson, H. 127
governance 2, 9, 11, 21n7, 337; corporate
    governance 109–10; extra-territorial
    governance 98; global economic and
    governance systems 28, 220–21; imperial
    governance 50; international governance
    233; kinship-based systems of 332; local
    self-governance 222; municipal governance
    134; public governance, failure of 265–6;
    state governance, failure of 274; 'top-down'
    governance 64
Grant, Jill 7, 148
Greeley, Roland 56–7
Greener, I. 188n3
Grenell, Peter 86
Grigsby, W. et al 240
Grigsby, W.G. 239, 240
Grunsky, Carl E. 104
Guangzhou, China 98, 283, 284

The Guardian 63
Guinea 207
Guiso, L. et al. 257
Güller, Peter 177, 179
Gunewardene, K.A. 155
Gunn, Zann 21n1, 22n26
Guttenberg, A. 247
Gutton, André 62

Ha, S. 239, 241
Haas, P.M. 21n6
Hack, Gary 295, 298, 299, 307, 309n4
Hajer, M. 22n20
Hall, Peter 68, 119, 222, 285n1
Hall, P.G. 293
Hall, Richard 216n4
Hancock, Macklin 61
Hanna, A.J. 216n4
Hansen, K.T. 191
Harris, R. 64, 242
Harris, R. and Arku, G. 65
Harris, R. and Giles, C. 53, 67
Hashemi, S. 37
Hashemi, S. and Rosenberg, R. 37
Healey, P. and Williams, R. 237
Healey, Patsy 1–22, 147, 159, 269, xii
Heath, Kingston W. 159
Hegedus, J. and Tosics, I. 242
Hein, C. 4, 21n11, 49
Helleiner, G.K. 335
Henriot, C. 99
Henry, Murphy 105
Héritier, A. et al. 188n3
Hillier, J. 21n11
Hillier, J. and Healey, P. 22n19
Hillman, M. et al. 228
Hines, T.S. 50
Hirschmann, Albert 329
Hobart City Council 229, 230, 231
Hobbes, Thomas 346n4
Hobsbawm, Eric J. 340
Hoch, Charles 17, 22n30
Holm-Hansen, J. 174, 188n3
Holocaust 332
Holston, James 143
Home, R. 49, 64
Hoogvelt, A. 191, 215
Hoover, Herbert 78
Hori, Y. et al. 129
Hosagrahar, Jyoti 82
Hossain, N. and Matin, I. 37
housing: economics of 239–40; filtering 237–8;
    filtering in Rome 242–4, 245–54, 259;
    filtering in US 238–41, 242, 259; finance
    policies 257–8; focus on households 240,
    241, 248–50; focus on neighborhoods
    240, 241, 250–54; focus on units 240,
    241, 245–8; institutional factors in filtering
    process 254–9; international diffusion
    of housing filtering concept 241–4,

259–60; low-income housing supply 239; *Participation in Post-Socialist Housing* (Abramson, D.B.) 294; reverse housing filtering 241
*Housing for the Machine Age* (Perry, C.) 79
Howard, Ebenezer 222
Howard, John 56–7
Howe, D.A. and DeRidder, T. 239
Hoyt, H. 237, 238, 240
Hoyt, L. 251
Hsu, C.Y. 108
Huang Yu 105, 106
Hulme, D. and Mosley, P. 37
*The Human Condition* (Arendt, H.) 331
Human Settlements, University of British Columbia Centre for (CHS) 303
Hungary 59
Hunt, L.A. 330
Hunting Technical Services 155, 157, 158
Huntington, Samuel 330, 332, 336, 337, 344
Hutchinson, B. 148

IAURIF (Institut d'Aménagement et d'Urbanisme Ile de France) 62
ICLEI (International Council for Local Environmental Initiatives) 118
ideas: compact cities ideas, sustainability and 126–35; exogenous planning ideas 9–10; global flow of 65–6, 345–6; individual agency, adaptation of planning ideas and 6, 233; internationalisation of power of 220; millennial development, battle of ideas within 34, 36; momentum for and channels of diffusion of 11; planning ideas, circulation of 4–5, 7–13; planning ideas and work of agency 16–17, 145; role in city planning 119–22; transfer of policy ideas 173–4; translation and adaptation of diffused ideas 10; urban design ideas, inspiration from 266; as weapons 27
identity: identity trap, planning practices and 338–42; immigration and perception of threats to 336–7; individuals, multiple identities of 340–41; mono-identities, dangers of 341
ideology: link between Soviet Union and China 108–9; Marxist ideology 113, 114n4
*Imagined Communities* (Anderson, B.) 340
Imura, H. 124
Inam, Aseem 90n1
Independent Commission on International Development Issues (1983) 330
India 12, 52, 67, 324; Albert Mayer's work in 88–9, 90; American neighborhood units, reimaging for 73–91; bazaar's and shopping centres 88; caste and religious traditions 85; collaborations of Perry with like-minded individuals 75–6; Delhi, General Plan for (Town Planning Organisation) 84–5; development, modernisation and 80–81;

Doxiadis Foundation in 60; homogenisation, benefits of 79–80; HUDCO (Housing and Urban Development Corporation) 85; iconic projects in 89; indigenous elites and national planning agenda 80–83; Institute of Architects 51; introduction of neighborhood unit to 79–80; ITPI (Institute of Town Planners, India) 81, 83, 90n2; land acquisition 81–2; national planning agenda 80–83; neighborhood chains, 'band-towns' 86–7; neighborhood units, acceptance of 82; neighborhood units, criticisms of concept 78; Otto Koenigsberger's adaption of neighborhood units for 83–8, 89–90; partition of 55; Perry and the neighborhood unit 74–9; planning, definition of concept for 81; postcolonial planning in 56–7, 61, 63; reimaging the neighborhood unit 83–9; social welfare, neighborhood institutions and 75; spatial planning, discipline of neighborhood units in 85–6; spatial planning, social concerns and 76–8; state, urban development and 81–2; *Supplementary Notes to the Architectural Study of Superblock L-37* (Mayer, A. and Nowicki, M.) 88; town planning in British India 49
Indonesia 50, 51, 67; Dutch colonial planning in 52; leadership interest in planning matters 63; postcolonial planning in 61; urban development in 274–5, 276–8
industrialisation: Asian urbanisation and 270–72; in China 108–9, 110–11, 283, 291; in newly independent nations 332–4; in Sri Lanka 145–6; *see also* urbanisation
Informa Market Research 230
infrastructure 29, 161, 176–7, 179, 185–6, 247, 270, 275–6, 283–4; globally transferable infrastructure 291; infrastructural change in China, need for 306–7; irrigation infrastructure 141, 150, 152; Japanese investment in 123–4, 127–30, 132–3, 135n2; physical infrastructure 50, 57, 152, 158, 285n2, 290, 334; planning for 61, 104–5; social and institutional infrastructure, creation of 97–102, 112–13; social infrastructure 333
innovation 10, 12, 14, 37, 41, 49–50, 64; capacity for 64; export of thought and 113; interchange of plans, ideas and 110; policy innovation, adoption of 221, 222; test beds for 50; transnational diffision of 337–8; value of 335
insider practice 17–18
institutional biases, international diffusion and 237–60; conservation policies 258–9; falsification of filtering concept in international context 241–2, 254–9; gentrification 240; households, focus on 240, 241, 248–50; housing economics 239–40; housing filtering 237–8; housing

filtering in Rome 242–4, 245–54, 259;
housing filtering in US 238–41, 242,
259; housing finance policies 257–8;
housing units, focus on 240, 241, 245–8;
institutional factors in filtering process
254–9; international diffusion of housing
filtering concept 241–4, 259–60; low-
income housing supply 239; neighborhoods,
focus on 240, 241, 250–54; policy diffusion,
trickiness of 237–8; rent control policies
254–7; reverse housing filtering 241
institutional fragmentation in China 112
institutional frameworks 28, 96, 97–8, 101, 173,
315
institutional infrastructure in China, creation of
97–102
institutional structures and policy ideas 175
Inter-American Development Bank 60
interactions: between active agency and
structural forces 20; cultural differences and
interactions among partners 187; forcing of
78; ideas, tensions and contestations arising
from diffusion of 10; negotiated imposition,
interactions as 67; Perry's collaborations and
interactions with like-minded individuals 75–
6; social interactions 34, 229; transnational
interaction 1–7
international aid 6, 7
International Bank for Reconstruction and
Development (IBRD) 53–4, 60
International Centre for the Prevention of Crime,
Montreal 224
The International Development of China (Sun
Yat Sen) 105
International Forum on Globalization 344
International Labor Organization (ILO) 330, 332
International Monetary Fund (IMF) 30–31, 221,
331; Structural Adjustment Programme
(SAP) 206
international planning exchanges 221–2,
289–90
international understanding, counter-
globalisation and 344
Iraq: British planning influence in 61, 62;
Doxiadis Foundation in 60; Polservice in 59
Iriye, A. 53
Irving, R.G. 49
Isaacs, Reginald 79
Israel 51, 57, 163
Italy: empire of 50; see also Rome, Italy

Jacobs, Jane 78, 147, 158, 307
Jacoby, W. 188n3
James, O. and Lodge, M. 188n3, 237
JanMohamed, A.R. 192
Jansen, Hermann 104–5
Japan 2, 7–8, 10; agenda-setting processes in
120–22; compact cities ideas, sustainability
and 126–35; construction state 123–4;
developmental state 123–4; Dokken Kokka

('construction state') 123; empire of 49–50;
Highways Public Corporation 123; ideas,
role in city planning 119–22; Jizoku Kanou
na Toshi ('sustainability and equilibrium in the
city') 122; Large-Scale Retail Stores Law
(LRSL) 130, 131, 132; Liberal Democratic
Party (LDP) 121–2, 131; Local Agenda 21,
implementation of 118; Ministry of Economy
132; Ministry of Foreign Affairs 131; Ministry
of Internal Affairs and Communications
126; Ministry of International Trade and
Industry (MITI) 130–32; Ministry of Land,
Infrastructure and Transport 123, 128;
National Land Sustainability Planning Act
(2005) 117, 127, 134; Plaza Accords
(1986) 131; population decline 125–6;
Sustainable Building Consortium (JSBC)
135n3; sustainable cities, concept of 122–
6; technocratic orientation 124–5; Town
Planning Laws (Machizukuri Sanpo) 132;
translation of sustainability concept 122–3;
urban sustainability 117–36
Jeanneret, Pierre 56
Jenks, M. et al. 22n16, 127
Jessop, B. 267
Jiang, Yang 309n4
Joglekar, M.N. 85
Johnson, K.M. 51
Johnson, Lyndon B. 319
Johnson, T.E. 241
Jolly, R. et al. 332
De Jong, Martin 8, 10, 173–88, xii
Jordan: British planning influence in 61; Doxiadis
Foundation in 60; postcolonial planning in 61
Journal of the American Planning Association
305
Journal of the Institute of Town Planners, India
89
Judge, E. 177

Kabeer, N. and Matin, I. 39
Kagan, R. 346n4
Kaidô, K. 129
Kajander, Tommi 169n2
Kalia, Ravi 52, 56, 61, 63, 88, 89
Kallus, R. and Churchman, A. 223
Kamstra, Allen 88
Kant, Immanuel 336
Karunaratna, H.N.S. 145
Kazakhstan 59
Kazimbaya-Senkwe, B. and Guy, S. 196, 216n6
Kazimbaya-Senkwe, Barbara Mwila 3, 4, 10, 11,
14, 15, 17, 191–216, xii
Kearns, R.A. and Collins, C.A. 229, 230
Keating, W.D. et al. 240
Keeble, L. 266
Kelly, J. 338
Kennedy, Jacky 229, 230, 234n1
Kennedy, John F. 342
Keyes, Langley 306

Khan, Masood 82
Khandker, S. 39
Khilnani, Sunil 81
Khurana, R. 343
King, A.D. 48, 82
Kingdon, J.W. 11, 120–21
Kingham, S. and Ussher, S. 229, 230
Kisby, B. 119
Kitahara, K. 129
Klodawsky, Fran 234n1
Knill, C. 188n3
knowledge: circuits of knowledge 5–6, 10, 27; contesting forms of 204–11; diffusing and contesting forms of 211–15; donor-engendered knowledge 191–216; indigenous agency and 48–9; networks and flows 67; participative accumulation of 8; planning knowledge, distinctiveness of 65–6; planning knowledge, emerging dynamics in postcolonial flows of 62–5, 65–6; politics of 38–9, 41; space of 41–2
Koenigsberger, Otto 15, 52, 56, 57, 64–5, 83–5, 86–7, 88, 89–90, 91n5, 91n7, 141, 168
Koizumi, Junichiro 123
Kooijman, D. and Romein, A. 222
Koolhaas, R. et al. 308
Kothari, U. 191, 194
Krishna Swamy, M.C. 89
Kristof, F. 240
Kropotkin, Peter 222
Kuwait, British planning influence in 61–2
Kyoto Protocol 118, 128

Ladi, S. 188n3
land scarcity 272–3
Land Transport NZ 229
Lanhong, Hua 302
Lansing, J.B. et al. 240
Laos, French planning influence in 62
Lappo, G.M. and Pivovarov, Y.L. 270
Latin America 12, 14, 55, 334; US influence in 55
Latvia 178; Central Statistical Bureau 183–4; Ministry of Transport 184; see also Riga
Laurie, Nina 212
law 8, 9, 80, 149, 210, 242, 243, 268; anti-urbanisation laws 248; implementation of regulation and 99, 101; Large-Scale Retail Stores Law (LRSL) 130, 131, 132; legal systems 52; municipal law in China 105; national city planning laws 130; planning law 49; Town Planning Laws (Machizukuri Sanpo) 132
Le Galès, P. 21n7
Leaf, M. 274
Leaf, M. and Hou, L. 308
Leaf, M. et al. 303
League of Nations 330
learning processes 182

Lebanon 55; Doxiadis Foundation in 60; French planning influence in 62
Lee, Tunney 293, 298, 299, 305
Legro, J.W. 119
Leitman, J. 237
Lesbirel, S.H. 128
de Leuw Cather 57
Lewis, B. 336
Lewis, W.A. 332
Libya 50
Lijewski, T. 175, 178
Lilong housing in China 98–9, 114n2
Lindblom, Charles 147
Liscombe, Rhodri Windsor 84, 91n6
Littlefield, Elizabeth 31
Liu Thai Ker 67–8
Liyanage, J. 53
Lloyd, M.G. et al. 237
locality: inhabitants and, importance of 146; lack of sensitivity to 298; local economic development 267; preference for emphasis on local 339; translocality 160
Lock, Max 61, 64
Loftman, P. and Nevin, B. 267, 285n2
Logan, J.R. and Molotch, H.L. 169n3
Logan, W.S. 58–9, 63
Loomba, Ania 191
Lortie, A. 62
Low, N. et al. 126
Lowry, I.S. 239
Lu, D. 290
Lü, J. 294, 297, 300, 301, 302, 303, 309n8
Lü, J. et al. 300
Luan, T.D. et al. 274
Lubambo, Peter 3, 4, 10, 11, 14, 15, 17, 191–216, xii
Luchembe, Chipasha 213
Luckman, S. et al 222
Lucy, W.H. and Phillips, D.L. 239
Lutyens, Sir Edwin 49
Lynch, K. et al. 299, 308
Lynch, Kevin 293, 298, 299, 308

Mabogunje, A.L. 57, 61
McCormack, G. 123, 128
McCulloch, A. 62
McElrath, D.C. 251, 252
McFarlane, C. 67
Macfarlane, Peter 61–2
Mackett, R.G. et al 229, 230
McKinsey Global Institute 279
Mackintosh-Smith, T. 21n2
McLoughlin, J.B. 268, 274, 285n4
McMillan, T.E. 229
McNamara, Robert 28, 42n1
MacPherson, K. 105
Mahaweli Development Project, Sri Lanka 141–69; accelerated Mahaweli project 144–5; action planning 141, 158–66, 168; construction 145–53; inside-out planning

effort 141, 158–66, 168; irrigation projects 143–4; landscapes of uncertainty 157–8; Mahaweli Architectural Unit (MAU), 141–3, 153, 157–8, 159–61, 163–4, 167–8, 169n13; Mahaweli area and towns 142; Mahaweli Authority 144, 149, 151, 160, 161, 162, 169n1; Mahaweli Engineering and Construction Agency 151, 152, 153, 159; neglected settlers 153–8; negotiation 145, 147, 149; people-centred process 167–9; reflective learning 158–66; representation 151, 153
Majone, G. 22n20, 188n4
*Making Safer Places: A Resource Book for Neighbourhood Safety Audits* (Women's Design Service) 224
Malaysia 49, 51, 67
Mallaby, S. 28
Malpezzi, S. and Green, R.K. 239
Malta, British planning influence in 61
Mamdani, M. 343
Manchuria 49
Mao Tse Tung 290, 291, 307
Marcos, Ferdinand 211
Marcos (Subcomandante, Zapatista ANL) 27
Marefat, M. 62
market economics: failure of 33; market fundamentalism 33; market importance 34–5; market orientation in China 281–2, 294; market practices, ascendance of 67; profitability, conflicts in search for planning practices 343–4; sustainable urbanisation in Asia 267–8; workings of markets 33–5
market societies 34
Marshall, T. 12
Martin,S. and Carlson, S. 228
Marx, Karl 292, 335
Marxist ideology 113, 114n4
Masser, I. and Williams, R. 19
Master of City Planning (MCP) programs 297–8
Matin, I. and Begum, S.A. 38
Matsuhashi, K. 129
Matsunaga, Y. 129
May, Ernst 83
Mayer, Albert 56–7, 63, 83, 84, 87, 88–90
Mazlish, B. 338
MDB (Mahaweli Development Board) and Sogreah 153, 155
Meller, H. 64
Melnikov, Konstantin 309n5
Menard, C. *et al.* 207
Menard, Claude 207
Mendis, Willie 155, 169n10
METRAC (Metro Toronto Women's Action Committee on Public Violence Against Women and Children) 219, 223–4, 225, 226
Michaud, Anne 227, 234n1
microfinance 29, 31–2, 38, 41–2
Microfinance Gateway (2008) 38

Microfinance Information Exchange (MIX) 32
Miller, D. *et al.* 127
Miller, Herbert 75
Minoprio, Anthony 61–2
MIT (Massachussetts Institute of Technology) 12, 55; MIT East Asian Architecture and Planning Program 300; MIT–Tsinghua Urban Design Studios 289, 293–300
Mitchell, Timothy 41, 145
Mjøs, O.D. 29
MLCERG (Max Lock Centre Exhibition Research Group) 61, 64
Mocine, C.R. 243
Modak, N.V. 56
modernisation: in China, accelerated march towards 97–8, 102, 113, 319; facilitation in China of 110–11; global aspiration 313; in Japan 117, 290–91; national development and 73, 79, 80; in newly independent nations 332–3; political modernisation 329, 340; theorems of 28; urbanisation and 95
Montanari, A. *et al.* 254
Montreal Women and the City Committee 224–5
Moore, Mick 144
moral attitudes (and moral compass) 2–3, 13, 16, 17–18, 20, 339, 342, 343
moral authority 101, 118, 135, 332
moral dilemma 112
moral sentiment 329
Morimoto, A. and Koike, H. 129
Morocco 49, 51; French planning influence in 62
Moser, Werner 61
Mossberger, K. 237
Mossberger, K. and Wolman, H. 237
Mosse, D. 15
Motha, P. 281
Mudimbe, V.Y. 191
Muller, H.P. and Hettige, S.T. 143–4, 149, 151, 152
multiculturalism 331, 338–9, 340, 344, 345
Mumford, E. 53, 55
Mumford, Lewis 76
Muramatsu, M. 122
Mussolini, Benito 243
Myanmar (Burma) 67
Myer, Jack 298
Myers, D. 240
Myers, G.A. 60

Nagra, Narina 225, 234n1
Nakamichi, K. *et al.* 129
Nanking (Nanjin) 102–3, 105, 106, 113; Treaty of (1842) 98
Nasr, J. and Volait, M. 6, 9, 13, 48
Needleman, L. 239
Nehru, Jawahar Lal 56, 80–82, 83, 85–6, 87–8, 90n3
neighbourhood units: attraction for elites 9; concept of 76–9

Nelson, A.C. *et al.* 127
Netherlands 2; Creative City concept 222
Neuman, M. 127
New York World's Fair (1939) 52
New Zealand 224, 233; Walking School Bus concept 229, 230
Newman, P. and Kenworthy, J. 127
Ng, Mee Kam 291
Nigeria 49; American planning involvement in 57; British planning influence in 61, 64; planning capacity in 55
Nilsson, Johan 301, 302
Nilsson, K.L. 22n22
'nimbyism,' overcoming trends of 270, 279–82
NIUA (National Institute of Urban Affairs) 81, 82, 86, 87, 90n3
Nomisma Real Estate 248
North, D. 242
Norwegian Development Agency (NORAD) 198
Nourse, H.O. 240
Nowicki, Maciej 56, 88
Nussbaum, M.C. 332
Nye, J.S. 333, 336
Nyerere, Julius 63

O'Donnell, G.A. 334
OECD (Organisation for Economic Cooperation and Development) 124, 125, 128, 224, 257
Ogawa, N. 126
Ohls, J.C. 239
Olds, Kris 306, 307
Olsen, E.O. 239
Olson, C.L. *et al.* 342
*Orientalism* (Said, E.) 191–2
Oryza Sri Lanka Rice Market Report (2005) 144
Ottawa Women's Action Centre Against Violence (WACAV) 224
outside observation 17–18
Owen, Robert 285n3
Owens, S.E. 127

Pacione, M. 253
Packenham, R.A. 333, 335
Padovani, L. 250, 258
Padovani, L. and Vettoretto, L. 250, 258
Pakistan: British planning influence in 62; Doxiadis Foundation in 60; planning capacity in 55
Pal, A. 327n14
Palestine 52; refugees from 55
Palmowski, J. 62
Pandit, Ninad 346n1
*Of Paradise and Power: America and Europe in the New World Order* (Kagan, R.) 336
Park, Robert 75
Parker, E. 31
Parker, J. and Pearce, D. 40
Parpart, J. 194
Parsons Brinckerhoff 57

participation 6, 289–90, 308; American architects in Nationalist China 103–5; civic participation 314; community participation in neighborhood planning, promotion of 303–4; direct participation, Soviet approach 58–9; local participation in development 30, 182; network participation 186–7; *Participation in Post-Socialist Housing* (Abramson, D.B.) 294; participatory planning 19, 128, 219–20, 220, 227, 269–70, 322–3; in Zambian water sector 200, 204, 205, 206, 207, 209, 211, 215
Patricios, Nicholas N. 74
Peattie, L.R. 297, 298, 339
Peel, D. and Lloyd, G. 237
Pempel, T.J. 118, 122
Perera, Nihal 3, 6, 8, 10, 11, 15, 17, 141–69, 326n1, xii–xiii
Perkovic, Jana 3, 4, 8, 10, 17, 20, 85, 219–34, xii
Perry, Clarence 73, 74–9, 85, 86, 87, 90
Perry, M. *et al.* 67
Peru 55, 64
Pfaffenberger, Bryan 151
Philippines 50, 67
Phillips, Asa E. 104
Pieris, G.H. 153
Pinochet, Augusto 318
planning: exchanges in developmentally asymmetrical contexts 289–91; expertise, ethics of 41; field of, characteristics of 1–2; ideas, circulation of 4–5, 7–13; implementation, trans-Pacific planning 307–8; knowledge, politics of 41; knowledge, space of 41–2; microfinance and 41–2; millennial development and 41–2; plan-making process 268–9; plans, developmental intentions in 266–8; problems, differences between MIT and Tsinghua approaches to 296–7; as regulatory tool, failure of 273–8; schools of 55; study in China 300–304; Western planning theories, relevance for China of 291–2; work as real-life drama 8–9
*Planning, Rethinking Ciudad Guayana* (Peattie, L.) 297
planning practices: authoritarianism, effect on 334; business interests, social commons and clash with 343–4; Chile, transforming aid program in 314–18; China, neighborhood planning in 318–24; circuits of knowledge 5–6, 10, 27; cold war, effect on 333; colonialism, moral principles and 343; colonialism, replacement of language of 331–2; communities, identity and framing of planning problems 340–41; compact cities ideas, sustainability and 325–6; cultural differences 16–18; cultural differences, emphasis on 336–7; cultural diversity, universal principles and 332; cultural essentialism, parochial nature of 341;

cultural intermixing, potential for 342; culture and identity, social practice and 341–2; decolonisation and 331; development and democracy, challenges to old paradigm of 333–5; development models, dangers of rigidities in 329; developmental practices, criticisms of 339–40; difference, ideologies of 335–8; differences, emphasis over similarities 329–31; diffusion processes 4–5, 7–13; disciplinary cultures 9; effectiveness in, emphasis for 329–46; Enlightenment, transnational contributions 336, 337–8; ethnic violence, difference and 335–6; exogenous planning ideas 9–10; flows of people and resources 11–13; global community in, development of 19–21; global economy, alternative solutions for 344; global interconnectedness 20–21, 329–30, 345–6; global social commons 343; ideas, global flow of 345–6; identity, immigration and perception of threats to 336–7; identity trap 338–42; independence from colonialism, maturation in 332–3; individuals, multiple identities of 340–41; insider practice 17–18; institutional differences 16–18; international understanding, counter-globalisation and 344; local, preference for emphasis on 339; middle ground of global business 342–4; minority needs, influence on developmental discourse 340; momentum for and channels of diffusion of ideas 11; mono-identities, dangers of 341; moral attitudes 2–3; multicultural history, global history and 338–9; outside observation 17–18; planning cultures, constant flux in 341; planning field, characteristics of 1–2; planning ideas, circulation of 4–5, 7–13; planning schools 55; planning work as real-life drama 8–9; political systems, postcolonial development of 332–3; post-developmentalism 339; post-9/11 events 336; profitability, conflicts in search for 343–4; reflective practice 18; similarities, emphasis over differences 345–6; situating practices 13–16; social justice, importance for future 346; social reform agenda 3; 'Third World,' effect on 334–5; transfer and establishment of 324–5; transfer of, difficulties in 313–14; transfer of, potential for 313–27; translation and adaptation of diffused ideas 10; transnational interaction 1–7; United Nations (UN), creation of 331–2; urbanisation, scale of 6–7; women's safety audits, walking school buses and 221–3
*Planning Theory and Practice* 7, 16, 19
Plesner, Ulrik 159–60, 164, 166
Poland 58, 177, 178; Central Statistical Office 180; National Railways (PKP) 182; PKE (Polish Ecological Club) 182; Polservice

technical agency 59; SIGUS Poland Initiative 294, 297
Polanyi, K. 33, 34
Polenske, Karen 294
policy agendas: agenda setting, prioritisation and 187; commercial centres, policies in support of 131; conservation policies 254, 258–9; development as 'absolute principle' of government policy 291; diffusion of policy, trickiness of 237–8; finance policies 257–8; housing finance policies 257–8; innovation, adoption of 221, 222; policy ideas, institutional structures and 175; policy transfer, endogenously driven 174; rent control policies 254–7; transfer of policy ideas 173–4, 221; urban transport policy change, achievement of 186
Polónyi, Karoly 59
Popper, Karl 238, 241, 242, 245, 254
population density 272–3
Porter, D.R. *et al.* 132
Porter, Michael 330, 331, 342, 343, 344
Portes, A. and Landolt, P. 35
postcolonial transnational planning 47–68; aid-dependence 48–9; American planners in postcolonial world 55–7; British planners in postcolonial world 61–2; colonial planning tradition 49–51; Constantinos Doxiadis, influence of 60–61; control, negotiated imposition and 66–7; deference to 'advanced' economies 66; external imposition, imperial experience of 48, 49–50; financial aid, programmes for 54; French planners in postcolonial world 62; independence, planning in circumstances of 52–5; indigenous professionals 51, 55; inequality, civil checks on state power and 50–51; innovation, test beds for 50; international development agencies 53–4; international exchange, opportunities for 52–3; international flows of ideas and practices 65–6; knowledge networks and flows 67; market practices, ascendence of 67; negotiated imposition 66–7; Otto Koenigsberger, influence of 64–5; planning assistance, neither American nor Soviet 60–62; planning intentions, process of giving form to 51; planning knowledge, distinctiveness of 65–6; planning knowledge, emerging dynamics in postcolonial flows of 62–5, 65–6; power relationships 48–9; Singapore 67–8; Soviet transnational planners 57–60; spatial planning 48; synthesis of international planning community 66; technical assistance, programmes for 54; technical expertise, demand for 54–5
poverty, planning and alleviation of: asset class, microfinance as 31–2; Bangladesh 35–40; democratisation of capital 35; equity and efficiency, concerns with 32; financialisation

of development, Washington consensus and 30–31; global order of development, concern about poverty 28; globalisation of microfinance idea 29; ideas as weapons 27; market failure 33; market fundamentalism 33; market importance 34–5; market societies 34; markets, workings of 33–5; Microcredit Summit 39; microfinance 29; Microfinance Information Exchange (MIX) 32; millennial development 28–9; millennial development, battle of ideas within 34, 36; 'poverty truths' 27; social capital 33–4; social democracy, modernisation of 35; twenty-first-century planning 41–2; Washington consensus 12, 33, 35–6, 37, 38, 40

Prahalad, C.K. 34

Prakash, Gyan 81

Prakash, M.S. and Esteva, G. 156

PriceWaterhouseCoopers 198

*The Protestant Ethic and the Spirit of Capitalism* (Weber, M.) 335

public and social goods, scarcity of 275–6

public intervention, urban planning as tool of 267

public spaces, local initiatives on access to 228–9

Pucher, J. 177

Pucher, J. and Buehler, R. 175, 176–8, 179

Pucher, J. and Kurth, S. 188n6

Pye, L.W. and Verba, S. 335

Qing dynasty in China 112–13

Qizhi, Mao 299

Qotole, M. 192

quality of life in China 321–2

Queensland Transport 229

Rabinow, P. 51

Radaelli, C. 188n3

Rakodi, C. and Simon, D. 193

Randma-Liiv, T. 173, 174

Rankin, K. 33, 40

Ratcliff, Richard 239

rational planning theory 269

Rawls, John 346

real estate development in China 283

*Redistribution and Growth* (Chenery, H. *et al.*) 42n1

reflective practice 18, 168

regional planning 1, 2, 309n6; in developed countries 266–7; identification with geography 323

*Regional Survey of New York and its Environs* (Perry, C.) 76

regulatory control 268; emphasis over developmental planning 269–70; mechanisms, lack of 274

Reinholde, Iveta 8, 10, 173–88, xiii

Ren, G.Y. 327n12

rent control policies 254–7

research resources and freedoms, asymmetry between Chinese and Western partners 304

Residents' Committees in China 320–21, 323

Rhodes, R.A.W. 21n6

Richardson, James 299

Riga: City Council 184–5, 188n7; transport network *(Rigas Satiksme)* 183–4, 185

Rio Earth Summit 118, 120, 128

risk-mitigation rules and WSBs 230–31

Roberts, Bill 57

Robertson, A.F. 334, 339

Robertson, D. 188n4

Robinson, M. 32, 34, 37

Rodgers, D.T. 121

Rodwin, Lloyd 55

Rogers, E.M. 188n3

Rome, Italy 8, 242–4, 245–64, 259; center-periphery division of 242–4; *Espozione Universale di Roma* (EUR) 243; Fair Rent Act (*Equo Canone,* 1978) 255, 257; *Grande Raccordo Annulare* (GRA) 242, 253, 254; historic growth of 243; Instituto Autonomo per le Case Popolari (IACP) 247; population decline (and growth) in 248–9; *Rioni* (historical core) 242, 243, 245, 246, 247, 248, 250–51, 252, 253, 255, 256, 258, 259; *Sistema Direzionale Orientale* (SDO) 243; socio-economic areas and groups 252–4; *suburbi* 242, 243, 246, 247, 249, 252; Urban Renewal Plan (*Piano di Recupero Urbano,* 1978) 258; *Zone Agro Romano* (peripheral agricultural outskirts) 147, 242, 243, 245, 246, 248, 249, 250, 251, 252, 253, 255–6

Roosevelt, Eleanor 332

Rose, R. 173, 174, 188n3, 188n4

Roseland, M. *et al.* 127

Rossant, James 57, 59, 63

Rowe, Peter 300

Rowe, P.G. and Kuan, S. 106

Roy, Ananya 3, 5, 8, 10, 12, 16, 19, 22n31, 27–42, 220, 326n1, xiii

Roy, R. and Srivastava, R.K. 340

Royal Town Planning Institute 12

Ruble, B.A. 59

Russell Sage Foundation, New York 74, 75

Russia 11

Sachs, Jeffrey 33

Sachs, W. 339

Safe Routes to School Program 228–9

safety audits: improvements in built environment, role in 225–6; *see also* women's safety audits, walking school buses and

Safier, M. 64, 65

Said, Edward 146, 191, 192, 346

Sandercock, L. 338

Sands, G. and Bower, L. 240

Santos, M. 335

Sanyal, Bishwapriya 2, 3, 7, 13, 18, 20, 68,
    329–46, xiii
Sarkis, H. 60
Saunders, D. 148
Schall, L. 240
Scholz, Hubert 60
Schön, Donald 18, 168
Schubert, Dirk 74, 86
Schweder, Richard 330
Scott, James C. 89, 148–9, 214
Scudder, Thayer 158
Seers, Dudley 334
Seifert, K. 180
self-development 275–6, 284
Selznick, P, 145
Sen, Amartya 145, 337, 340
Senegal 207
Senior, D. 53, 59
Shanghai 97, 98–9, 100–105, 107, 109, 111,
    113, 114n2, 283; British concession,
    Municipal Council and 99–100; Bureau of
    Public Works 100; construction techniques
    101; foreign concessions in 98–100;
    Greater Shanghai Plan (1930) 103, 104,
    105; Master Plan for Shanghai (1953) 109;
    spatial planning in 99–102, 102–7; Urban
    Planning Exhibition Hall 284; world's largest
    construction site 282
Shanghai Newspaper 102
Sharp, J. and Briggs, J. 67
Shatkin, Gavin 90n1
Shaw, M. and Andrew, C. 224, 226, 227
Shaw, Margaret 234n1
Shen, Y. 103
Shenyang, China 284
Shimaoka, A. et al. 129
Shin, M. 104
Shiqing, Huang 310n11
Shweder, R. and Appiah, A. 342
Shweder, Richard 341, 343
Siberia 59
Sicheng, Liang 299, 302
Silver, Christopher 74, 78, 79
Singapore 15–16, 51, 267; fragmented land
    ownership 279; Land Acquisition Act (1966)
    279–81; land amalgamation, Acquisition
    Act and facilitation of 279–80; Miucheshui
    district, redevelopment of 279; Municipal
    Commissioners 268; public housing in
    280–81
Singer, P. 334, 345
Sino-Japan War 105, 107
Sirivardana, Susil 169n14
Sit, V. 58
Site Planning program (Gary Hack) 298
Sivaramakrishnan, K. and Agrawal, A. 80
Skaburskis, A. 241, 242
Smith, C. 75
social and institutional infrastructure, creation of
    97–102

social aspects of WSBs, positivity in 230
social capital 33–4
social commons 343; clash with business
    interests 343–4
social concerns, spatial planning and 76–8
social democracy, modernisation of 35
social empowerment in Bangladesh 37–8
social inclusion in China 321
social infrastructure, creation of 97–102
social justice, importance for future 346
Social Organization (Cooley, C.) 75
social planning principles, centralised planning
    and 107–10
social practice and planning practices 341–2
social reform agenda, planning practices and 3
social research and urban development 302–3
social welfare, neighborhood institutions and 75
socio-economic data in China, political sensitivity
    and inaccessibility of 304
Sogreah Consultants 153, 155, 156, 157, 160
Sokolov, Sergei Ivanovich 59
Somerville, C.T. and Holmes, C. 240
Sorensen, A. et al. 125
Sorensen, André 3, 4, 7–8, 9–10, 11, 20,
    21n11, 117–36, 220, 222, 291, 325
South Africa, Walking School Bus concept 232
Soviet Union 54, 113; collapse of 330;
    ideological link with China 108–9; Leningrad
    Institute of Urban Research and Planning
    59; planning influence in China 58; planning
    schools in 55
Spain 12, 333
spatial planning 95–114; China 95–114;
    diffusion in China of 96–7; diffusion of
    96–7; discipline of neighborhood units in
    85–6; formal representation in China of
    102–7; postcolonial transnational planning
    48; practice of borrowing in 110–13;
    redistribution of urban growth and 110; in
    Shanghai 99–102, 102–7; social concerns
    and 76–8
Special Interest Group in Urban Settlements
    (SIGUS) 294, 297
specificities 7, 8, 13, 14, 15, 22, 103, 112, 341,
    345
Speelman, Jaap Jan 157
Spencely, Hugh 61–2
Spivak, G.C. 192, 195
Sri Lanka 8, 10, 51, 53; British planning
    influence in 61; Central Engineering
    Consultancy Bureau (CECB) 160, 163;
    Chandrikawewa Project 155–6; Defence
    Ministry 145; Gal-Oya irrigation project 145;
    Institute of Architects 51; mega-projects
    in 149–50; Physical Planners, role of 153,
    155, 156, 157; service centres, hierarchical
    organisation of 153–5; Uda Walawe Project
    157
St Louis Plan (1907) 75
stakeholder competition, regulation of 268–9

Standard & Poor's 32
State Planning Commission, China 108
Stead, Dominic 3, 4, 8, 10, 173–88, 220, 326n1, xiii
Stegman, M.A. 240
Stein, Clarence 76, 88
Stiglitz, Joseph E. 31, 33, 35, 331, 344
Stoer, S.R. and Cortesão, L. 343
Stone, Diane 188n3, 188n4, 221, 222
Strassman, P. 241
Strategic Development Plan (SDP), China 283–4
structural factors: effect on implementation of women's safety audits 221; opposition between structural and agency perspectives 20, 221–2, 342, 347n7; structural change in society 222; structural forces 6, 20, 222
Struyk, R.J. et al. 275
suburbanisation 178–9, 239, 243, 247, 249, 270, 325; private suburban housing estates 276–8
Suchorzewski, W. 177
Sudan, Doxiadis Foundation in 60
Sukarno, President of Indonesia 61, 63
Sun Ke 103
Sun Yat Sen 95, 105
Susith de Alwis, Dharmasiri 144
sustainability: compact cities ideas, sustainability and 126–35; idea in Bangladesh of 38; *Jizoku Kanou na Toshi* ('sustainability and equilibrium in the city') 122; National Land Sustainability Planning Act (Japan, 2005) 117, 127, 134; translation in Japan of sustainability concept 122–3; urban sustainability 117–36
sustainable urbanisation in Asia: challenges for urbanisation in Asia 270–73; China, state-led strategic development plans 283–4; China, unlocking of land resources during transition in 281–2; competition among stakeholders, regulation of 268–9; consensus and planning action 269; development of new towns 283–4; development of old towns 279–82; developmental control, correlation of informal development with non-observance of 275–6; developmental planning 278–84; gated housing estates 277–8; informal development, correlation with non-observance of developmental control 275–6; land scarcity 272–3; local economic development 267; making planning developmental for 265–85; market economics 267–8; 'nimbyism,' overcoming trends of 279–82; plan-making process 268–9; planning as regulatory tool, failure of 273–8; plans, developmental intentions in 266–8; population density 272–3; private suburban housing estates 276–8; public and social goods, scarcity of 275–6; public intervention, urban planning as tool of 267; rapid urbanisation 270–72; rational planning theory 269; regional planning in developed countries 266–7; regulatory control 268; regulatory mechanisms, lack of 274; regulatory urban planning, emphasis over developmental planning 269–70; self-development 275–6; Singapore, Land Acquisition Act (1966) 279–81; suburbanisation 270; urban design ideas, inspiration from 266; urban land development without development control 274–5; urban planning, local economic development and 267; urban planning, nature of 266–70; urban quarters, deterioration in 276–8
Sutcliffe, A. 2, 119, 273
Suzuki, T. 129
Sweden, Kotmale Dam construction in Sri Lanka 145
Sweeney, J.L. 240
Swibel, M. 32
Symes, M. and Pauwels, S. 222
Syria: Doxiadis Foundation in 60; French planning influence in 62

Taiping Rebellion in China 98
Tait, M. and Jensen, O. 8, 21n13, 237
Taiwan 49, 67
Takami, K. 132
Tamagawa, H. and Ehara, N. 126
Tan, B. 67
Tanaka, T. et al. 306
Tanzania 54; American planning involvement in 57; leadership interest in planning matters 63; postcolonial planning in 61; Soviet, East German and Chinese planning involvement in 59–60
Tavits, M. 173
Temkin, K. and Rohe, W. 240
Teng, S.Y. and Fairbank, J.K. 113
Terasawa, M. 132
Teresi, D. 337
Thailand 57, 67, 68n2
Thatcher, Margaret 293
Thijisse, Jacob 52
Third Way ideology 34–5, 40
'Third World' 145; effect on planning practices 334–5
Thomas, C.Y. 339
Thurairajah, A. 151
Tianjin, China 98
Todaro, M.P. 333
Todd, Tom 57
tokenistic consultation 227
Toronto Transit Commission (TTC) 223, 225
*Towards an Eco-City: Calming the Traffic* (Engwicht, D.) 219, 228, 231
Town Planning Institute (TPI) 51, 52, 53, 61
Toye, J.F.J. 333

transfer: and establishment of planning practices 324–5; of planning practices, difficulties in 313–14; of planning practices, potential for 313–27; translation and adaptation of diffused ideas 10
Transit Cooperative Research Program (US, 2003) 178–9
Transjordan 49
transnational interaction in planning practices 1–7
transport policy *see* urban transport
Tranter, P. and Pawson, E. 228
Travers, Kathryn 234n1
Trinh, P.V. and Parenteau, R. 275
Trinidad 49
Troen, S.I. 51
Truman, Harry S. 54, 56, 193, 331
Tucker, D. 49
Tulchin, D. 33
Tunisia, French planning influence in 62
Turner, John 64–5, 67
Turok, I. 267, 285n1
Tyrwhitt, J. 64

Uganda National Water and Sewerage Company 207
UN-Habitat 7, 12, 14, 22n32, 53, 266; Safer Cities Programme 224, 232–3
United Kingdom 2, 125, 133, 163; Ecologically Sustainable Design for Hulme, Manchester 222; imperial possessions 49; Industrial Revolution and emergence of urban planning 273–4; planning capacity in 55; Victoria Dam construction, Sri Lanka 145, 148, 150; Walking School Bus concept 229, 230; Women's Design Service 224, 226
United Nations (UN) 48, 128, 133, 148; creation of 331–2; Development Programme 160; Food and Agriculture Organisation (FAO) 144, 160; Fund for Women (UNIFEM) 225; Housing and Town and Country Planning 52–3; Human Settlements Programme 53; Millennium Development Goals 28, 39; Relief and Rehabilitation Administration 53; Universal Declaration of Human Rights (1948) 330, 332
United States 2, 7, 8, 125, 128; and China, exploitation of Chinese planning study in 304–8; empire of 49–50; Forest Hills Gardens 75, 78–9; funding work of expatriate planners 60; Greenbrook planned community 88; Housing and Urban Development (HUD), Dept. of 324; housing economics 239–40; International Planning Associates (IPA) 57; Marshall Aid Program 54; National Conference of Social Work (1924) 76; National Conference on Home Building and Home Ownership (1931) 78; National Highway Act (1956) 239; neighborhood planning in 318–19; 'Nimby'

(Not In My Back Yard) phenomenon in 270; Peace Corps program in 342; Perry's neighbourhood unit concept 76–9; Point Four Program 54; Regional Plan Association of America (RPAA) 76; Smart Growth 133; St Louis Plan (1907) 75; Tennessee valley development 145; Town Planning Associates 55; USAID 60, 294, 314
universal standards 291
Unwin, Raymond 83
Upham, F. 131, 132
Upton, Robert 20, 21n1, xiii–xiv
Urban Design 293, 297–8; *see also* design
urban planning: land development without development control 274–5; local economic development and 267; nature of 266–70; quarters in urban areas, deterioration of 276–8
urban transport, West–East policy transfer 173–88; agenda setting, prioritisation and 187; analytical framework for studies 175; case studies 179–86; Central and Eastern Europe (CEE), policy context 174, 175–9; change in CEE, rapidity of 186; cultural differences, dealing with 187; differences in national arrangements, dealing with subtilities in 175; domestic champions, need for 175; inspiration from policy examples 175; opportunities for policy change 175; policy change, achievement of 186; policy ideas, institutional structures and 175; policy transfer processes 174; practical goals, emphasis on 187; Riga, Latvia 173, 183–6; site visits, importance of 187; success factors for policy transfer 186–7; transfer of policy ideas 173–4; Wroclaw, Poland 173, 180–83
urbanisation: challenges for urbanisation in Asia 270–73; cities in transition in China 95–114; compact cities ideas, sustainability and 325–6; modernisation in China and 95–114; rapid growth in China 283; rapid growth in China of 283; rapid urbanisation and sustainable urbanisation in Asia 270–72; scale of, planning practices and 6–7; Soviet experience of 109; urban design ideas, inspiration from 266; women's safety audits, walking school buses and 222; *see also* sustainable urbanisation in Asia
Uttar Pradesh Town Planning Organisation 82, 84

Vale, Lawrence J. 150
Van der Heiden, C.N. 50
Van der Top, G.M. 157
Van Hees, I.L.M. 250, 255, 256, 257, 258
Van Roosmalen, P.K.M. 50, 51, 52
Varady, D.P. 240
Venezuela 55; Doxiadis Foundation in 60
Verdeil, E. 15

Verma, Gita Devan 169n12
Verma, Niraj 3, 8, 237–60, xiv
Victorian Health Promotion Foundation
    (VicHealth) 229, 231–2
Vidyarthi, Sanjeev 3, 5–6, 7, 9, 11, 15, 17, 73–
    91, 156, 313, 324, 326n1, xiv
Vietnam 67; Hanoi People's Committee 274;
    Soviet planning influence in 58–9, 63; urban
    development in 274, 275
Vogel, S.K. 123
*Volk ohne Raum* (National Socialist Party) 86

Walking School Buses: concept of 219–20,
    227–32, 233, 234n1, 324; improvements
    in built environment, role in 229–30; vital
    elements of original formulation, loss of
    231–2
Wall Street 32
Wallace, David 57
Wampler, Jan 299, 305, 309n4, 312n10
Wang, B. and Rowe, P.G. 101
Wang, Bing 3, 5, 9–10, 11, 95–114, 326n1, xiv
Wannop, U.A. 3, 266
Ward, Stephen V. 2, 3, 5, 6, 11, 15, 17, 18,
    21n4, 22n15, 22n24, 47–68, 87, 119, 221,
    222, xiv
water management 10, 15; *see also* Zambia
Watson, V. 7
Watts, Kenneth 14, 22n27, 53, 59, 61, 63
Weber, H. 36, 291
Weber, Max 335
Wedaarachchi, Ananda 144
Weerasinghe, Oliver 53
Weissmann, Ernest 53
Wekerle, G. and Whitzman, C. 223, 225
Weldon,P. and Tan, T.H. 281
Wenger, E. 21n6
Weyland, K.G. 237
White, H.C. 239, 240
White, M. and White, L. 74
White, P. 242
Whittlesey, Julian 56
Whitzman, C. and Perkovic, J. 324, 326n1
Whitzman, C. and Pike, L. 220
Whitzman, C. *et al* 226
Whitzman, Carolyn 3, 4, 8, 10, 17, 20, 85,
    219–34, xiv–xv
Widdig, B. 342
Williams, R.H.W. 21n4
Williamson, J. 30
Wilson, T.K. and Bell, M.C. 188n6
Windsor-Liscombe, R. 52
Wirth, Louis 74
Wolfensohn, James 28, 30–31
Wolfowitz, Paul 31
Wolman, H. 188n3, 188n4
Wolman, H. and Page, E. 188n4
Wolputte, Steven Van 192, 214
Women in Cities International (WICI) 219, 223,
    225, 226, 234n1

Women's Safety Audit Guide (1989) 219, 223,
    224, 225, 226–7, 228–9, 232–3, 234n1
women's safety audits, walking school buses
    and 219–34; agency factors, effect on
    implementation 221; Australian Centre
    for the Governance and Management of
    Urban Transportation (GAMUT) 219–20,
    234n1; bureaucratic formalisation of
    WSBs 230–31; Canadian National Crime
    Prevention Council (NCPC) 224; Crime
    Prevention Through Environmental Design
    (CPTED) 223; DisAbled Women's Network
    225; gender focus, loss of 226–7; ideas,
    internationalisation of power of 220;
    improvements in built environment, safety
    audits role in 225–6; improvements in built
    environment, walking school buses and 229–
    30; independent mobility of children 228;
    International Centre for the Prevention of
    Crime, Montreal 224; international planning
    exchanges 221–2; METRAC (metro Toronto
    Women's Action Committee on Public
    Violence Against Women and Children)
    219, 223–4, 225, 226; Montreal Women
    and the City Committee 224–5; Ottawa
    Women's Action Centre Against Violence
    (WACAV) 224; planning practices 221–3;
    policy transfer, levels of 221; public spaces,
    local initiatives on access to 228–9; risk-
    mitigation rules and WSBs 230–31; Safe
    Routes to School Program 228–9; safety
    audits 223–7; social aspects of WSBs,
    positivity in 230; structural factors, effect on
    implementation 221; tokenistic consultation
    227; Toronto Transit Commission (TTC)
    223, 225; *Towards an Eco-City: Calming
    the Traffic* (Engwicht, D.) 219, 228, 231;
    urbanisation 222; Victorian Health Promotion
    Foundation (VicHealth) 229, 231–2; vital
    elements of original formulation of the WSB,
    loss of 231–2; Walking School Bus concept
    219–20, 227–32, 233, 234n1, 324; Women
    in Cities International (WICI) 219, 223, 225,
    226, 234n1; Women's Safety Audit Guide
    (1989) 219, 223, 224, 225, 226–7, 228–9,
    232–3, 234n1
Woodall, B. 123
Woolcock, M. 34
World Bank 10, 12, 28, 30–31, 31, 33–4, 35,
    39, 65, 176–8, 193, 195, 221, 237, 324;
    Comprehensive Development Framework
    30; Structural Adjustment Programme (SAP)
    206; Zambia water project, involvement with
    200, 201, 202, 203, 204, 205, 207, 208,
    209–11, 212, 213–15
World Congress on Environment and
    Development (1987) 126
World Health Organization (WHO) 57
World Social Forum (WSF) 28, 343–4
World Trade Organization (WTO) 36, 344

Wright, G. 49, 290, 291
Wright, Henry 76, 88
Wroclaw, Integrated Plan for Public Transport Development in the City and Agglomeration (2004–2008) 182–3
WRT Design 57
Wu, F. 291
Wu, F. and Yeh, A.G.-O. 305
Wu, L. 295, 299, 302

Xiaoping, Deng 290, 291, 293, 307

Yamamoto, K. 129
Yamamoto, T. 123
Yeang, K. 51
Yeh, A.G.O. and Wu, F.L. 281
Yeoh, B.S.A. 51, 143, 192
Yeung,Y.M. 279
Young, S.C. 22n22
Yugoslavia 53; Polservice in 59
Yunus, Muhammad 29, 36, 39, 40
YWCA (Young Womens' Christian Association) 229

Zachariadis, T. and Kouvaritakas, N. 177, 178
Zambia 10, 49; Asset-Holding Company Mining Municipal Services (AHC-MMS) 200, 201, 202, 203, 204–5, 207–8, 209–10, 212–13, 214; BCHOD and Ernst & Young (2003) 201, 204; Consolidated Copper Mines (ZCCM) 197, 198–9, 200, 201, 205, 206, 208; contesting forms of knowledge 204–11; Copperbelt Province 195, 196, 204, 212, 214, 215; decision-making process, players and platforms 202–3; diffusing and contesting forms of knowledge 211–15; donor-engendered knowledge in water sector, diffusion and contestation of 191–

216; GKW with Grant Thornton Associates (2003) 200; Local Government Act (1991) 196; local *versus* foreign 209–11; Lusaka Water and Sewerage Company 207; mine township services project 199–202; Mining Township Services Project (MTSP) 200, 201, 202–3, 205, 207–8, 209–10, 211, 214; Ministry for Energy and Water Development (MEWD) 196; Ministry for Local Government and Housing (MLGH) 196, 200, 201, 202–3; Movement for Multi-Party Democracy (MMD) 198; National Water Policy (1994) 198; National Water Supply and Sanitation Council (NWASCO) 201, 203; Nkana Water and Sewerage Company (NWSC) 201, 214; organisational loss, fear of 208–9; personal loss, fear of 208–9; privatisation, experience with 206–8; regionalisation of water supply in Copperbelt 197–202; retrenchment, experience with 206–8; single utility formation '1CU' solution 204, 205, 206–7, 208, 209, 211, 213, 214–15; Water Sector Development Group (WSDG) 197, 198, 207; water sector in 195–6; Water Supply and Sanitation Act (1997) 198, 210
Zelinsky, W. 270
Zen Buddhism 117
Zewdou, F. 61
Zhang, F.H. 103
Zhang, Li 143
Zhang, Tingwei 291
Zhang, Y 299
Zhang, Y. and Fang, K. 291, 307
Zhang Zhi-dong 112–13
Zhu, Jieming 3, 15–16, 265–85, 291, xv
Zhu, J.M. 282
Zhu Shenkang 106
Zixuan,Professor Zhu 299, 302
Zoellick, Robert B. 39